BY JON MEACHAM

Songs of America: Patriotism, Protest, and the Music That Made a Nation

The Soul of America: The Battle for Our Better Angels

Destiny and Power: The American Odyssey of George Herbert Walker Bush

Thomas Jefferson: The Art of Power

American Lion: Andrew Jackson in the White House

American Gospel: God, the Founding Fathers, and the Making of a Nation

Franklin and Winston: An Intimate Portrait of an Epic Friendship

Voices in Our Blood: America's Best on the Civil Rights Movement (editor)

BY TIM MCGRAW

STUDIO ALBUMS

Tim McGraw

Not a Moment Too Soon

All I Want

Everywhere

A Place in the Sun

Set This Circus Down

Tim McGraw and the Dancehall Doctors

Live Like You Were Dying

Let It Go

Southern Voice

Emotional Traffic

Two Lanes of Freedom

Sundown Heaven Town

Damn Country Music

The Rest of Our Life (with Faith Hill)

BOOKS

Tim McGraw and the Dancehall Doctors: This Is Ours

My Little Girl (with Tom Douglas)

Love Your Heart (with Tom Douglas)

Humble & Kind

SONGS *of* AMERICA

JON MEACHAM & TIM McGRAW

SONGS *of* AMERICA

Patriotism, Protest, and the Music That Made a Nation

RANDOM HOUSE · NEW YORK

Copyright © 2019 by Merewether LLC and Tim McGraw

All rights reserved.

Published in the United States by Random House, an imprint and division of Penguin Random House LLC, New York.

RANDOM HOUSE and the HOUSE colophon are registered trademarks of Penguin Random House LLC.

Image credits can be found on page 281.
Song lyric credits can be found on page 285.

LIBRARY OF CONGRESS CATALOGING-IN-PUBLICATION DATA
Names: Meacham, Jon, author. | McGraw, Tim, author.
Title: Songs of America: patriotism, protest, and the music that made a nation / Jon Meacham and Tim McGraw.
Description: First edition. | New York: Random House, [2019] | Includes bibliographical references and index.
Identifiers: LCCN 2019014364| ISBN 9780593132951 | ISBN 9780593132968 (ebook)
Subjects: LCSH: Music—Political aspects—United States—History. | Music—Social aspects—United States—History. | Protest songs—United States—History and criticism. | Patriotic music—United States—History and criticism.
Classification: LCC ML3917.U6 M43 2019 | DDC 782.420973—dc23
LC record available at https://lccn.loc.gov/2019014364

Printed in the United States of America on acid-free paper

randomhousebooks.com

9 8 7 6 5 4 3 2 1

FIRST EDITION

Book design by Simon M. Sullivan

FRONT ENDPAPER: On an August 1933 visit to White Top Mountain, Virginia, First Lady Eleanor Roosevelt enjoys a local band's rendition of "Happy Days Are Here Again"—a song that had become synonymous with her husband's presidential campaign the year before.

HALF-TITLE SPREAD: In 1914, the Star-Spangled Banner that inspired Francis Scott Key during the British assault on Baltimore's Fort McHenry a century before was restored.

TITLE PAGE: Nina Simone, whose "Mississippi Goddam" was a classic protest song of the 1960s, in concert at Carnegie Hall in New York City.

SECOND HALF-TITLE SPREAD: On Easter Sunday 1939, Marian Anderson sang before a crowd of 75,000 at the Lincoln Memorial after she was denied permission to perform at Washington's Constitution Hall.

BACK ENDPAPER: An emotional Navy Chief Petty Officer Graham Jackson plays at Warm Springs, Georgia, as the body of President Franklin D. Roosevelt is taken north to Washington and then to Hyde Park, New York, in April 1945.

To Keith and Faith,
Mississippi Women

"A patriotic song is an enchanted key to memory's deepest cells; it touches secret springs, it kindles sacred flames in chambers of the soul unvisited by other agencies. It wakes to life ten thousand slumbering chords and makes them thrill and pulsate—just as if some loving angel's finger touched them—to that grand God-given sentiment of liberty."

—ELIAS NASON,
nineteenth-century American composer

"I, too, sing America."

—LANGSTON HUGHES

CONTENTS

A NOTE TO THE READER   xiii

Overture: The Music of History   2

ONE THE SENSATIONS OF FREEDOM   6

TWO LAND WHERE OUR FATHERS DIED   34

THREE MINE EYES HAVE SEEN THE GLORY   62

FOUR MARCH, MARCH, MANY AS ONE   94

FIVE AS THE STORM CLOUDS GATHER   118

SIX WE SHALL OVERCOME   144

SEVEN ARCHIE BUNKER V. THE AGE OF AQUARIUS   172

EIGHT BORN IN THE U.S.A.   200

Finale: Lift Every Voice   226

ACKNOWLEDGMENTS   231

NOTES   235

BIBLIOGRAPHY   269

IMAGE CREDITS   281

SONG LYRIC CREDITS   285

INDEX   287

A NOTE TO THE READER

I N THE FOLLOWING pages, Jon Meacham wrote the narrative text that takes the American story, with special reference to music that shaped those years, from the period before the Revolutionary War through the attacks of Tuesday, September 11, 2001, and the election of Barack Obama as the forty-fourth president of the United States. As reflected in the source notes at the end of the book, we occasionally drew on Meacham's previous works of history and journalism, including his books about Thomas Jefferson, Andrew Jackson, Franklin Roosevelt, and Winston Churchill, and the more general *The Soul of America,* as well as essays of his first published in *The New York Times, Time, Newsweek*, and *Vanity Fair*.

Writing from his perspective as an artist and performer, Tim McGraw offers his take on selected songs in a series of sidebars. No effort has been made to be encyclopedic; readers will surely argue with us about why one song was included but another wasn't. So be it: We welcome open—and open-hearted—debate.

We also urge readers who are intrigued by the issues raised in the book to engage with the works cited in the source notes and in the bibliography; it's our hope that *The Songs of America* is the opening, not the closing, act in a conversation about the nation's diversity and complexity. For that's among the reasons we undertook the project: to inspire Americans to think more widely and more deeply about the country Abraham Lincoln called "the last best hope of earth."

SONGS *of* AMERICA

THE MUSIC OF HISTORY

"Nothing is more agreeable, and ornamental, than good music; every
officer, for the credit of his corps, should take care to provide it."

—GEORGE WASHINGTON

I N THE BEGINNING were the words—the stately rhythms of the Declaration of
Independence, the passionate eloquence of Thomas Paine's *Common Sense,* the
steady notes of the constitution. All men, Thomas Jefferson asserted, were created
equal, with unalienable rights to life, liberty, and the pursuit of happiness. In building such a nation—a new thing under the sun, founded on an idea, not on brute
strength—we, in Paine's stirring prose, had it in our power to begin the world over
again. And that enterprise, an endless odyssey, would, as the constitution's preamble
put it, have a central, consuming aim: a more perfect union.

History isn't just something we read; it's also something we *hear.* We hear the
musketry on the green at Lexington and Concord and the hoofbeats of Paul Revere's midnight ride. We hear the moans of the wounded and of the dying on the
fields of Antietam and of Gettysburg, the quiet clump of the boots of Grant and Lee
on the porch steps of Wilmer McLean's house at Appomattox—and the crack of a
pistol at Ford's Theatre. We hear the cries of the enslaved, the pleas of suffragists,
the surf at Omaha Beach. We hear a sonorous president, his voice scratchy on the
radio, reassuring us that the only thing we have to fear is fear itself; and we hear
another president, impossibly young and dashing, his breath white in the inaugural
air, telling us to ask not what our country can do for us but what we can do for our
country. And we hear the whoosh of helicopters in the distant jungles of Southeast
Asia and the baritone of a minister, standing before the Lincoln Memorial, telling us
about his dream.

American Revolutionaries on the march in the painting "The Nation Makers," by Howard Pyle.

Such are the sounds of our history, whispers from the American pageant. They are glimpses and glimmers from our common story, a story of promises made and broken, of reform and reaction—a story fundamentally shaped by the perennial struggle between what Abraham Lincoln called "the better angels of our nature" and our worst impulses. That's the stuff of the story of the past, which, as William Faulkner observed, is never dead; it isn't even past. Nor is history a fairy tale or a bedtime lullaby. There was never a once-upon-a-time and there will never be a happily-ever-after. There is, though, the wonderfully American drama of seeking to ensure that hope can overcome fear, that light can triumph over darkness, that we can open our arms rather than clench our fists.

And through it all, through all the years of strife, we've been shaped not only by our words and our deeds but by our music, by the lyrics and the instrumentals that have carried us through dark days and enabled us to celebrate bright ones.

The paramount role of music in life and in the lives of nations has the deepest of roots. Plato and Aristotle wrote of its centrality to the formation of noble human souls and of civilized society; Newton and Shakespeare saw the universe in terms of the harmony—or disharmony—of the spheres; and in the eighteenth-century Age of Enlightenment, the Scottish writer and politician Andrew Fletcher brilliantly linked music and civic life, writing, "I knew a very wise man . . . [who] believed if a man were permitted to make all the ballads, he need not care who should make the laws of a nation." George Washington, for one, understood something of this. In his General Orders to the Continental Army for Wednesday, June 4, 1777—long years of war lay in front of him and of his men—he wrote, "Nothing is more agreeable, and ornamental, than good music; every officer, for the credit of his corps, should take care to provide it."

From Lexington and Concord to Fort Sumter, from Seneca Falls to Selma, from Normandy to Vietnam to 9/11, the American story can seem straightforward. The truth, however, is vastly more complex, and one way to gain a fuller understanding of our confounding nation is to explore the music of patriotism, which is also, inevitably, the music of protest. To us, patriotism celebrates and commemorates; protest critiques and corrects. The two are inextricably intertwined and are as vital to each other as wings to a bird, for the nation cannot soar without both.

A true patriot salutes the flag but always makes sure it's flying over a nation that's not only free but fair, not only strong but just. History and reason summon us to embrace love and loyalty—to a citizenship that seeks a better world, calls on those better angels, and fights for better days. What, really, could be more patriotic than that? What, in the end, could be more *American*?

To Jefferson himself, the author of our Founding prose hymn, music offered a window into human nature. In his literary commonplace book, Jefferson transcribed these lines from a version of Shakespeare's *Merchant of Venice:*

The Man who has not Music in his Soul,
Or is not touch'd with Concord of sweet Sounds,
Is fit for Treasons, Stratagems, & Spoils,
The Motions of his Mind are dull as Night,
And his Affections dark as Erebus:
Let no such Man be trusted.

Henry David Thoreau once wrote, "When I *hear* music, I fear no danger. I am invulnerable. I see no foe. I am related to the earliest times, and to the latest."

That's our mission now: to hear the music that has lifted us from danger, kept us together amid tragedy, united us anew in triumph, and urged us on toward justice. From our earliest times to our latest, we hear not only the spoken but the sung word, and the music of the nation reminds us where we've been, who we are—and what we can become.

CHAPTER ONE

THE SENSATIONS OF FREEDOM

"By uniting we stand, by dividing we fall."

—JOHN DICKINSON, "The Liberty Song," 1768

"Objects of the most stupendous magnitude, measures in which the lives
and liberties of millions, born and unborn, are most essentially
interested, are now before us. We are in the very midst of a Revolution,
the most complete, unexpected, and remarkable of any in the history of
nations."

—JOHN ADAMS, Sunday, June 9, 1776

"Remember the Ladies."

—ABIGAIL ADAMS, to her husband as the Founders debated independence

NIGHT WAS ABOUT to fall. As daylight faded on Friday, June 10, 1768, officials of the British Crown stepped across the wharves of Boston Harbor to seize the *Liberty,* a sloop owned by the merchant John Hancock of Massachusetts. The charge: that Hancock's men had smuggled casks of Madeira wine from the *Liberty*'s hold to avoid paying stiff duties recently imposed under the hated Townshend Acts. Anticipating trouble, the imperial authorities had deployed the heavily armed warship *HMS Romney*—which contemporaries described as a "fine new 50-Gun ship"—for the task. "This conduct provoked the People, who had collected on the Shore," *The Boston Gazette* reported, and the gathering of colonials surged toward the British collector of customs, Joseph Harrison, as he came back off the *Liberty*. On the street adjoining the harbor, Harrison wrote, "we were pursued by the Mob which by this time was increased to a great multitude. The onset was begun by throwing dirt at me, which was presently succeeded by volleys of stones, brickbats,

"We hold these truths": Franklin, Adams, and Jefferson at work on the Declaration of Independence.

sticks, or anything that came to hand. . . . About this time I received a violent blow on the breast which had like to have brought me to the ground, and I verily believe that if I had fallen, I should never have got up again, the People to all appearance being determined on blood and murder."

The royal governor of Massachusetts was flummoxed, denouncing what he called this "Great Riot" in dispatches to London. The colonials, naturally, had a different view. To them, the specter of the *Romney* taking control of Hancock's *Liberty* was an outrage, a veritable act of war. "We will support our liberties," a patriot leader cried after the seizure, "depending upon the strength of our own arms and God."

Hearing the news, John Dickinson of Pennsylvania was moved to pick up his pen to strike a blow in favor of the colonial cause. Born in 1732, raised in Dover, Delaware, and trained as a lawyer in Philadelphia and at the Middle Temple in London, Dickinson had recently published an influential series of essays entitled *Letters from a Farmer in Pennsylvania, to the Inhabitants of the British Colonies.* The Townshend Acts had been the occasion for Dickinson's *Letters;* in Boston, Joseph Harrison had found Dickinson's writings "inflaming and seditious . . . tending to poison and incense the minds of the people and alienate them from all regard and obedience to the Legislature of the Mother Country."

A sustained attempt to argue for the justice of the colonial view that representation was a civil right in the English tradition, the *Letters* would bring Dickinson acclaim, including an honorary degree from the College of New Jersey (later Princeton University). "From infancy," Dickinson had written, "I was taught to love liberty and humanity."

To him and to many of his readers, taxation without representation—including duties on Madeira—was intolerable. "A free people," Dickinson had written, "can never be too quick in observing, nor too firm in opposing, the beginnings of alterations . . . respecting institutions formed for their security." It was essential, he wrote, to guard against the "servitude" that could be "slipped upon us" by new laws and their vigorous enforcement.

His *Letters* had been prose. Now, in the wake of the clash in Boston, he would try poetry, composing a series of verses in honor of the resistance in Massachusetts. "I enclose you a song for American freedom," Dickinson wrote James Otis of Boston. "I have long since renounced poetry, but as indifferent songs are very powerful on certain occasions, I venture to invoke the deserted muses." He told Otis that Arthur

Lee of Virginia, a Dickinson friend, had contributed eight lines of "The Liberty Song." Published in Philadelphia and in *The Boston Gazette* of July 18, 1768, the song was set to William Boyce's "Heart of Oak," a patriotic British number popular with the Royal Navy.

> Come join hand in hand, brave Americans all,
> And rouse your bold hearts at fair Liberty's call;
> No tyrannous acts shall suppress your just claim,
> Or stain with dishonor America's name.
>
> In freedom we're born, and in freedom we'll live;
> Our purses are ready,
> Steady, Friends, steady,
> Not as slaves, but as freemen our money we'll give.
>
> Our worthy forefathers—let's give them a cheer—
> To climates unknown did courageously steer;
> Thro' oceans, to deserts, for freedom they came,
> And, dying, bequeath'd us their freedom and fame.
>
> Their generous bosoms all dangers despis'd,
> So highly, so wisely, their birthrights they priz'd;
> We'll keep what they gave, we will piously keep,
> Nor frustrate their toils on the land and the deep.
>
> The Tree, their own hands had to Liberty rear'd,
> They lived to behold growing strong and rever'd;
> With transport they cry'd, "Now our wishes we gain,
> For our children shall gather the fruits of our pain."
>
> Swarms of placemen and pensioners soon will appear,
> Like locusts deforming the charms of the year;
> Suns vainly will rise, showers vainly descend,
> If we are to drudge for what others shall spend.

Then join hand in hand brave Americans all,
By uniting we stand, by dividing we fall;
In so righteous a cause let us hope to succeed,
For Heaven approves of each generous deed.

All ages shall speak with amaze and applause,
Of the courage we'll show in support of our laws;
To die we can bear—but to serve we disdain,
For shame is to freedom more dreadful than pain.

This bumper I crown for our sovereign's health,
And this for Britannia's glory and wealth;
That wealth and that glory immortal may be,
If she is but just—and if we are but free.

Dickinson had great hopes for his work. Citing the example of Jean-François-Paul de Gondi, Cardinal de Retz, a wily seventeenth-century French cardinal and adventurer, he wrote: "Cardinal de Retz always enforced his political operations by songs. I wish our attempt may be useful."

Dickinson's language was designed to appeal to the emotions of his broad audience. "By uniting we stand, by dividing we fall"; "In so righteous a cause let us hope to succeed"; "To die we can bear, but to serve we disdain"—the song's message was unmistakable. Unity was all; a common cause would carry the day; the stakes could not be higher.

Here, in the middle of the summer of 1768, eight years before the Declaration of Independence, an American patriot was making a popular case for American identity and for American action not in the staid language of the political press but in the more universal and stirring genre of music. "The Liberty Song" quickly spread. "The music began at high noon," *The Boston Evening-Post* reported of a Sunday, August 14, 1768, gathering, "performed on various instruments, joined with voices; and concluding with the universally admired *American* Song of Liberty, the grandeur of its sentiment, and the easy flow of its numbers, together with an exquisite harmony of sound, afforded sublime entertainments to a numerous audience, fraught with a noble ardor in the cause of freedom." To John Adams, Dickinson had done something wondrous. "This," Adams remarked of the song, "is cultivating the sensations of freedom."

THE LIBERTY SONG

I was struck by the melody and structure of this song. We don't really think of the Revolution in terms of music, except maybe "Yankee Doodle Dandy" playing in our heads as we glance over a John Trumbull painting in a textbook. But John Dickinson's words, together with the older British music, create something uplifting and empowering. Having strong rhythm, it would be classified as a march, with around 120 beats per minute. The irony of the choice of the music of the British anthem isn't lost on me—it's shrewd to put new words to an old tune, especially if you're trying to turn the familiar on its head. What really speaks to me is the final verse. Dickinson clearly understands that this is a moment in time that will live on forever (at least he's hoping it will, and hope drives so much of art), and he used this idea to inspire real people to take real steps toward independence—and transformation:

> "All ages shall speak with amaze and applause,
> Of the courage we'll show in support of our laws;
> To die we can bear—but to serve we disdain,
> For shame is to freedom more dreadful than pain."

Dickinson's lyrics provide a moral call to action, putting the political arguments of the hour in a more universal way, which is what music can do. You may not have pored over his *Letters from a Farmer,* but you could hear this song, and see—*hear*—what he was saying. And then you might just believe, with him, that the emerging American cause was worth the fight.   —TIM MCGRAW

Dickinson's composition, Kenneth Silverman, a scholar of American Revolutionary culture, observed, "became not so much useful as indispensable. . . . It enabled people to experience directly the idea of strength in unity, by enacting it in boisterous choral singing. . . . By wedding the current political arguments to music, Dickinson knew, he drew on emotional resources that the words alone could not muster."

YET AMERICA DID not declare its independence in the wake of Dickinson's song, or for eight years afterward. The ensuing period was marked by further taxes and protests, more debate over the nature of representative government, and rising concerns over the role of imperial authority in colonial affairs. How did a group of disparate British North Americans, subjects of the British Empire all their lives, decide to risk everything?

The nation was an experiment—and a risky one at that. Nobody knew if the Revolutionary War would succeed; it has been said that the Founders joked, mordantly, about how they had to hang together or they would surely hang separately.

The decision to declare independence was taken neither lightly nor quickly. The colonists had been long locked in a struggle for power and for control with London. In 1769, the Anglo-Irish statesman Edmund Burke articulated the dynamic developing between Britain and America. "The Americans have made a discovery, or think they have made one, that we mean to oppress them," Burke said. "We have made a discovery, or think we have made one, that they intend to rise in rebellion. . . . We know not how to advance; they know not how to retreat."

The Seven Years' War has only the tiniest of places, if any place at all, in the popular American imagination of the twenty-first century, but the conflict, partly fought in North America as the French and Indian War, was immensely significant in creating the conditions for the Revolution. A British hero of the war, General James Wolfe, who died in arms in Quebec at the Plains of Abraham, gave the colonies what a nineteenth-century scholar of music called the "earliest American soldier-song which became broadly popular." According to legend, on the eve of battle, Wolfe sang:

> The boast of heraldry, the pomp of power,
> And all that beauty, all that wealth ere gave,
> Await alike the inevitable hour;
> The paths of glory lead but to the grave.

The moonlit waters of the St. Lawrence River supposedly inspired a second verse:

> How stands the glass around!
> For shame ye take no care, my boys;
> How stands the glass around!

Parliament's imposition of the Stamp Act—a tax on paper goods—provoked colonial resistance and helped create revolutionary sentiment.

Let wine and mirth abound
The trumpet sounds,
The colors, they are flying, boys.

That was the romantic legacy of the Seven Years' War. The hard reality of it was another matter. In the wake of the British victory, given the expense of maintaining a global empire, London believed the colonies should bear more of the cost for protecting the British dominions—costs that included helping to pay for about ten thousand British troops stationed in North America. Armies that could liberate and protect, the people of British North America knew, could also conquer and subjugate. And, as the British statesman George Grenville, who served as prime minister from 1763 to 1765, reasonably noted, "All men wish not to be taxed."

A pattern took hold. The British Parliament imposed new taxes to raise revenue from British America. Colonists in their sundry capitals (Boston, Annapolis, Philadelphia, Williamsburg, and so on) resisted. The royal governments in the New

World and the establishment in Britain grew impatient with what they saw as a continent populated by the recalcitrant, the unreasonable, and the ungrateful.

In these years Americans played and hummed and sang different versions of "Yankee Doodle Dandy," with its sprightly rhythm; they recited, too, ballads like 1775's "The Pennsylvania Song":

> We'll not give up our birthright,
> Our foes shall find us men;
> As good as they, in any shape,
> The British troops shall ken.
>
> Huzza! Brave boys, we'll beat them
> On any hostile plain;
> For freedom, wives, and children dear,
> The battle we'll maintain.
>
> What! Can those British tyrants think,
> Our fathers cross'd the main,
> And savage foes, and dangers met,
> To be enslav'd by them?
>
> If so, they are mistaken,
> For we will rather die;
> And since they have become our foes,
> Their forces we defy.
>
> And all the world shall know,
> Americans are free,
> Nor slaves nor cowards we will prove,
> Great Britain soon shall see.

The idea of an American "birthright" expressed in these verses was a prevalent one. The American revolutionaries took the positions they did—positions that led to the Declaration of Independence in 1776—partly because they saw themselves as Englishmen who were being denied a full share of the benefits of English life.

Every proposal from London, every thought of a tax, every sign of imperial authority, raised fears of tyranny in America, for as Englishmen they were intuitively on guard against any encroachment on their liberty.

"The Liberty Song," "Yankee Doodle Dandy," and "The Pennsylvania Song" were patriot favorites to sing on the battlefield.

Tauntingly, a British brigade under Lord Percy played "Yankee Doodle" as Tory and rebel forces prepared to clash at Lexington and Concord on Wednesday, April 19, 1775. "In the Spring of 1775," the Boston-born Tory jurist Peter Oliver wrote, "the War began to redden." Delineating between "the King's Troops" and the rebelling "armed Rabble," Oliver described the raw nature of combat at Lexington and Concord. "Many were the instances of the British soldiers' great humanity in protecting the aged, the women & the children from injury; notwithstanding the great provocation they had to a general slaughter." Oliver reported this scene: "There was a remarkable Heroine, who stood at a house door firing at the King's Troops, there being men within who loaded guns for her to fire. She was desired to withdraw, but she answered only by insults from her own mouth, & by balls from the mouths of her muskets. This brought on her own death, & the deaths of those who were within doors."

So it would go for the duration of the war. Scholars now believe about a fifth of white colonists remained loyal to Great Britain—a formidable number that ensured the Revolution would have the feel and the features of a civil war. For loyalists, the Revolution was, in the words of Captain John Ferdinand Dalziel Smyth, an officer of the Queen's Rangers, the "most wicked rebellion against the best of kings, and the most free and mildest of governments." In a song attributed to Smyth, "The Rebels," the loyalists dismissed the "mock-patriot" Americans as "Yankees" who were "all in the wrong":

Ye brave, honest subjects, who dare to be loyal,
And have stood the brunt of every trial,
Of hunting-shirts, and rifle-guns:
Come listen awhile, and I'll sing you a song;
I'll show you, those Yankees are all in the wrong,
Who, with blustering look and most awkward gait,
'Gainst their lawful sovereign dare for to prate,
With their hunting-shirts, and rifle-guns.

The arch-rebels, barefooted tatterdemalions,
In baseness exceed all other rebellions,
With their hunting-shirts, and rifle-guns.
To rend the empire, the most infamous lies,
Their mock-patriot Congress, do always devise;
Independence, like the first rebels, they claim,
But their plots will be damned in the annals of fame,
With their hunting-shirts, and rifle-guns.

Forgetting the mercies of Great Britain's King,
Who saved their forefathers' necks from the string;
With their hunting-shirts, and rifle-guns.
They renounce allegiance and take up their arms,
Assemble together like hornets in swarms,
So dirty their backs, and so wretched their show,
That carrion-crow follows wherever they go,
With their hunting-shirts, and rifle-guns.

These lyrics came from a broader view among loyalists that the patriots fell far below what the Tories saw as the civilized standard of the king's forces. Reporting on the military action at Lexington and Concord, the loyalist Peter Oliver wrote, "Two of the British troops, at fewest, were scalped, & one of them before he was dead. Let Patriots roar as loud as they please about the barbarity of an Indian scalping knife; but let him know that an Indian savage strikes the deadly blow before he takes off the scalp. It was reserved for a *New England* savage, only, to take it off while his brother was alive." After the battle, Jefferson observed, "A frenzy of revenge seems to have seized all ranks of people." In a private letter, the painter John Singleton Copley wrote, "The flame of civil war is now broke out in America, and I have not the least doubt it will rage with a violence equal to what it has ever done in any other country at any time."

Still, the independence-minded colonists were not ready to fight a total war, dispatching an "Olive Branch Petition" to London, addressed directly to George III. The king refused to receive it and had in the meantime issued a hawkish "Proclamation for Suppressing Rebellion and Sedition," asserting that the Americans were in "open and avowed rebellion." This was a serious blow to those seeking reconciliation of some kind with the mother country—hopes further crushed by an October speech of the king's in which he said the rebellion was "manifestly carried on for the purpose of establishing an independent Empire." He also accused the colonists of insincerity and subterfuge, claiming that the Americans "meant only to amuse, by . . . the strongest protestations of loyalty to me, whilst they were preparing for a general revolt."

As 1776 dawned, Thomas Paine published *Common Sense,* a wildly bestselling pamphlet making the case for independence. "The cause of America is," Paine wrote, "in a great measure, the cause of all mankind." His words had remarkable resonance. "Its effects were sudden and extensive upon the American mind," the patriot-physician Benjamin Rush recalled. "It was read by public men, repeated in clubs, spouted in schools, and in one instance, delivered from the pulpit instead of a sermon." In Connecticut, an appreciative reader wrote, "We were blind, but on reading these enlightening words, the scales have fallen from our eyes." George Washington praised Paine's "unanswerable reasoning."

As his subjects absorbed Paine's arguments for a new era in democratic government, George III was brokering treaties with European powers to enlist soldiers for service in the New World—treaties that were leaked to American newspapers, alarming the colonists. There was terrible military news from Canada and fears that the British were about to strike the Atlantic coast from Nova Scotia. For the more forward-leaning Americans, the answer was to declare independence, seek an alliance with France, and risk all in a bold bid for nationhood and for liberty. Hope of a reconciliation with London, perhaps brought on by a change of ministry, had long been pyrrhic and was now more widely seen as irrational.

On Monday, July 1, 1776, Dickinson rose in the Congress to argue that the Americans should wait to see if it was certain that France would enter the war on the side of the new nation before making the final break with Britain. It was an eminently reasonable position, one that in any other month of the crisis might well have prevailed. Yet this time it did not. By Tuesday, July 2, the decision was unanimous: The Declaration of Independence was to be adopted. "Yesterday," John Adams wrote his wife, Abigail, on Wednesday, July 3, 1776, "the greatest question was decided which ever was debated in America; and a greater perhaps never was, nor will be, decided among men." Adams was hearing history's trumpets. "The second day of July, 1776, will be the most memorable epoch in the history of America," he added. "I am apt to believe that it will be celebrated by succeeding generations as the great anniversary festival. It ought to be commemorated as the day of deliverance, by solemn acts of devotion to God Almighty. It ought to be solemnized with pomp and parade, with shows, games, sports, guns, bells, bonfires, and illuminations, from one end of this continent to the other, from this time forward forevermore." The fourth, not the second, would ultimately be the festival date, but Adams's sentiments were exactly right.

The words of the Declaration of Independence are among the most hallowed ever rendered in English. Washington recognized their significance from the first, ordering the Continental Army to muster its brigades to hear the cadences of the declaration as they marched to war. Given that the "Honorable the Continental Congress, impelled by the dictates of duty, policy and necessity, [had] been pleased to dissolve the Connection which subsisted between this Country, and Great Britain, and to declare the United Colonies of North America, free and independent *states*," Washington wrote in his General Orders for Tuesday, July 9, 1776, "the several brigades are to be drawn up this evening on their respective Parades, at six o'clock, when the declaration of Congress, shewing the grounds & reasons of this measure, is to be read with an audible voice." The words would, Washington believed, fuel the men's morale and sense of mission. "The General hopes this important Event will serve as a fresh incentive to every officer, and soldier, to act with

Fidelity and Courage, as knowing that now the peace and safety of his Country depends (under God) solely on the success of our arms," he wrote, "and that he is now in the service of a State, possessed of sufficient power to reward his merit, and advance him to the highest Honors of a free Country."

The preamble met the moment. "We hold these truths to be self-evident," Jefferson wrote, "that all men are created equal; that they are endowed by their creator with certain unalienable rights; that among these are life, liberty & the pursuit of happiness: that to secure these rights, governments are instituted among men, deriving their just powers from the consent of the governed; that whenever any form of government becomes destructive of these ends, it is the right of the people to alter or to abolish it, & to institute new government, laying its foundation on such principles, & organizing its powers in such form, as to them shall seem most likely to effect their safety & happiness."

John Trumbull's rendering of the signing of the Declaration of Independence in Philadelphia on Thursday, July 4, 1776.

"All honor to Jefferson," Lincoln would say of the flawed but brilliant architect of the American promise.

America was founded, then, on an idea—one not fully realized even now, but still an idea worth pondering and, more to the point, pursuing. "Fear is the foundation of most governments," Adams once wrote, "but it is so sordid and brutal a passion, and renders men in whose breasts it predominates so stupid and miserable, that Americans will not be likely to approve of any political institution which is founded on it."

In that spirit, Jefferson's language in the declaration evoked not fear but hope, a fact long recognized by those who followed the Founders in the work of governing the United States. In 1859, Abraham Lincoln wrote: "All honor to Jefferson—to the man who, in the concrete pressure of a struggle for national independence by a single people, had the coolness, forecast, and capacity to introduce into a merely revolutionary document, an abstract truth, applicable to all men and all times, and so to embalm it there, that today, and in all coming days, it shall be a rebuke and a stumbling-block to the very harbingers of re-appearing tyranny and oppression." And in 1963, standing on the steps of the Lincoln Memorial, Martin Luther King, Jr., would call for justice not as a radical break from American thought but simply as the honest recognition that Jefferson's words should self-evidently apply to the many, not to the few—that Jefferson had made, as King put it, "a promise that all men—yes, black men as well as white men—would be guaranteed the unalienable rights of life, liberty, and the pursuit of happiness."

History, it has been said, is an argument without end. What is clear is that something so many people today take for granted—the creation of the American nation—was, as Wellington was to say of Waterloo, the "nearest run thing you ever saw." "I am well aware of the toil and blood and treasure that it will cost us to maintain this Declaration, and support and defend these States," Adams wrote Abigail. "Yet through all the gloom I can see the rays of ravishing light and glory. I can see that the end is more than worth all the Means. And that posterity will triumph in that day's transaction, even although we should rue it, which I trust in God we shall not." Virtually every aspect of human experience and of human aspiration—money, freedom, love, power, fear, and hope—played a role in the drama of American independence, a drama that unfolds still.

Dour but devoted, John Adams believed America was worth all the "toil and blood and treasure" it would cost to build.

THE ODYSSEY BEGUN by the declaration was carried forward by the constitution that was drafted in the summer of 1787—a constitution that took account of ambition and appetite. "If men were angels," James Madison had written in *The Federalist Papers,* "no government would be necessary"—and given that men were so self-evidently unangelic, the American government was designed to check our passions and balance our failings. "The great art of lawgiving consists in balancing the poor against the rich in the legislature, and in constituting the legislative a perfect balance against the executive power, at the same time that no individual or party can become its rival," John Adams wrote. "The essence of a free government consists in an effectual control of rivalries. The executive and the legislative powers are natural rivals; and if each has not an effectual control over the other, the weaker will ever be the lamb in the paws of the wolf. The nation which will not adopt an equilibrium of power must adopt a despotism. There is no other alternative. Rivalries must be controlled, or

The "whole . . . Audience broke forth in the Chorus," Abigail Adams wrote of hearing "Hail Columbia" for the first time.

they will throw all things into confusion; and there is nothing but despotism or a balance of power which can control them."

Americans never fell short in terms of self-regard. "For we must consider that we shall be as a city upon a hill," the Puritan John Winthrop, who crossed the Atlantic aboard the *Arbella,* said in his 1630 sermon "A Model of Christian Charity." "The eyes of all people are upon us, so that if we shall deal falsely with our God in this work we have undertaken, and so cause Him to withdraw His present help from us, we shall be made a story and a byword through the world." More than three centuries later, John F. Kennedy would cite Winthrop in speaking of America's destiny, and Ronald Reagan would add a key modifier to Winthrop's scriptural image and refer, repeatedly and effectively, to the nation as a "shining city upon a hill."

American rhetoric and thought has long been rooted in both religion and in reason. Believing Christians were schooled in a language of liberty shaped by ultimate ideas of life beyond time and space. In a January 1776 sermon, Samuel Sherwood, a Connecticut pastor and kinsman of Aaron Burr, compared the American project to that of Israel. "Liberty has been planted here; and the more it is attacked, the more it grows and flourishes. The time is coming and hastening on, when Babylon the great shall fall to rise no more; when all wicked tyrants and oppressors shall be destroyed forever." A year later, Abraham Keteltas, a former Presbyterian pastor, told a Massachusetts audience that the American cause was "the cause of God," continuing: "We are contending for the rights of mankind, for the welfare of millions now living, and for the happiness of millions yet unborn. . . . [O]ur cause is not only righteous, but most important: it is God's own cause: It is the grand cause of the whole human race, and what can be more interesting and glorious. If the principles on which the present civil war is carried on by the American colonies, against the British arms, were universally adopted and practiced upon by mankind, they would turn a vale of tears, into a paradise of God."

By the time of the Revolutionary War, many Americans were used to hearing the political and the temporal framed in terms of the eternal and the absolute. "We have incontestable evidence that God Almighty, with all the powers of heaven, are on our side," Sherwood said. "Great numbers of angels, no doubt, are encamping round our coast, for our defense and protection. Michael stands ready, with all the artillery of heaven, to encounter the [British] dragon, and to vanquish this black host." Entitled *The Church's Flight into the Wilderness: An Address on the Times,* Sherwood's sermon was preached the same month Paine published *Common Sense.*

As the late Columbia University scholar Robert A. Ferguson argued, many Americans also saw the cause for self-government as one allied with the forces of enlightenment—that revolutionary victories were triumphs of right reason against discredited notions of the immutable authority of princes and prelates. A commonly cited example of the Enlightenment-era nature of the American experience comes from Jefferson: "All eyes are opened, or opening, to the rights of man. The general spread of the light of science has already laid open to every view the palpable truth, that the mass of mankind has not been born with saddles on their backs, nor a favored few booted and spurred, ready to ride them legitimately, by the grace of God."

America was seen as the living embodiment of Enlightenment ideals. "Education, exploration, and invention should unite in the general advance of humanity, but that possibility depends upon prompt action in the more immediate and unpredictable realm of politics," Ferguson wrote. "Progress, in other words, is not a predetermined evolution through fixed stages of history. The moment can yield permanent darkness as easily as additional light. These alternatives, in their starkness, define the fullest meaning of crisis in the eighteenth-century American mind. In the fresh dispensation of the new world, events are freighted with an extraordinary double capacity for either good or ill. The stakes are permanently high. Whatever revolutionary Americans do or do not do, they believe that their actions will change the direction of history—possibly forever." The Revolutionary era thus seemed an existential one, and the new nation believed it had been entrusted with the fate of what George Washington called "the sacred fire of liberty."

The hope was that the United States, with its appreciation of human frailty and its faith in human progress, would keep that flame from flickering out. The enterprise and its stakes were well captured on the occasion of Washington's inauguration as the first president, in 1789, when a writer in the *Gazette of the United States* offered these verses:

. . . see Columbia rise!
Her Empire prop'd by him who arch'd the Skies!
Freedom and Independence—*Arts,* and Peace!
Shall Crown the Scene till Time and Nature cease.

YET THE INSTITUTION of the government framed in 1787 did not signal the dawn of a heavenly kingdom on earth. A country created to liberate chose to subjugate women, enslave African Americans, and persecute indigenous peoples; much of the work of the ensuing centuries would be the difficult fight to apply the words of Jefferson in the declaration not just to *some* but to *all.*

The arguments about inclusion were older than the republic itself. A few months before the Second Continental Congress broke decisively with Great Britain, John Adams was at work in Philadelphia when he received an engaging letter from Abigail. "I long to hear that you have declared an independency—and by the way in the new Code of Laws which I suppose it will be necessary for you to make I desire you would Remember the Ladies, and be more generous and favorable to them than your ancestors," Mrs. Adams wrote. "Do not put such unlimited power into the hands of the Husbands. Remember all Men would be tyrants if they could. If particular care and attention is not paid to the Ladies we are determined to foment a Rebellion, and will not hold ourselves bound by any Laws in which we have no voice, or Representation."

Twenty years on, the *Philadelphia Minerva* of Saturday, October 17, 1795, published a song in line with Mrs. Adams's sentiments. (The verses had first appeared in print in April 1795 in the *Weekly Museum,* a New York magazine.) Set to the tune of "God Save the King," it was called "Rights of Woman":

GOD save each Female's right,
Show to her ravish'd sight
Woman is Free;
Let Freedom's voice prevail . . .

Let Woman have a share,
Nor yield to slavish fear,
Her equal rights declare,
And well maintain.

A voice re-echoing round,
With joyful accents sound,
"Woman is Free;
Assert the noble claim,
All selfish arts disdain;"

Hark how the note proclaim,
"Woman is Free!"

BUT OF COURSE women weren't, and neither were black people. Among the most important literary voices in early America was Phillis Wheatley, an African-born woman who was sold into slavery and arrived in Massachusetts in 1761, when she was about eight. Educated by her owners, John and Susanna Wheatley, Phillis Wheatley was precocious and began writing verse at around age twelve. In 1773, in his *Address to the Inhabitants of the British Settlements in America, upon Slave-Keeping*, Benjamin Rush praised her and her poetry, writing that her "singular genius and accomplishments are such as not only do honor to her sex, but to human nature. Several of her poems have been printed, and read with pleasure by the public." In a 1775 poem titled "To His Excellency George Washington," Wheatley introduced the notion of America as what the scholar Thomas J. Steele called a "fully developed personification" of the goddess Columbia:

Celestial choir! enthron'd in realms of light,
Columbia's scenes of glorious toils I write.
While freedom's cause her anxious breast alarms,
She flashes dreadful in refulgent arms.
See mother earth her offspring's fate bemoan,
And nations gaze at scenes before unknown!
See the bright beams of heaven's revolving light
Involved in sorrows and the veil of night! . . .

Proceed, great chief, with virtue on thy side,
Thy ev'ry action let the Goddess guide.
A crown, a mansion, and a throne that shine,
With gold unfading, *Washington*! Be thine.

She sent the verses to Washington, then in the field, who read them with gratitude. "I thank you most sincerely for your polite notice of me, in the elegant Lines you enclosed; and however undeserving I may be of such encomium and panegyric, the style and manner exhibit a striking proof of your great poetical Talents," Wash-

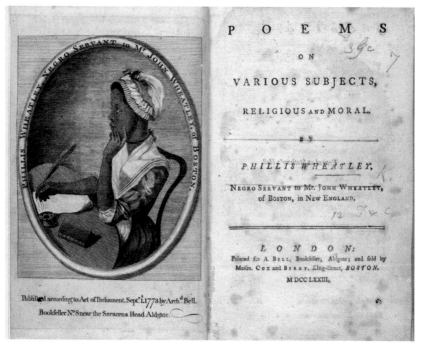

Phillis Wheatley's "Poems on Various Subjects, Religious and Moral," published in 1773; George Washington praised her "genius," and Benjamin Rush wrote that her verses "not only do honor to her sex, but to human nature."

ington wrote Wheatley from Cambridge in February 1776. "In honor of which, and as a tribute justly due to you, I would have published the Poem, had I not been apprehensive, that, while I only meant to give the World this new instance of your genius, I might have incurred the imputation of Vanity. This, and nothing else, determined me not to give it place in the public Prints." (The poem found its way into the *Pennsylvania Magazine* in any event, after Washington sent it to a friend who arranged its publication.) Washington invited Wheatley to call on him, telling her that he would "be happy to see a person so favoured by the Muses, and to whom nature has been so liberal and beneficent in her dispensations."

A devout Christian, Wheatley broached then-verboten notions of equality. In her "On Being Brought from Africa to America," she wrote:

Remember, *Christians, Negros,* black as *Cain,*
May be refin'd, and join th' angelic train.

When she turned her attention to the nation at large, Wheatley wrote of America as a sublime experiment:

> *Lo!* Freedom comes. Th' prescient Muse foretold,
> All Eyes th' accomplish'd Prophecy behold:
> Her Port describ'd, *"She moves divinely fair,*
> *Olive and Laurel bind her golden Hair."*
> She, the bright Progeny of Heaven, descends,
> And every Grace her sovereign Step attends;
> For now kind Heaven, indulgent to our Prayer,
> In smiling *Peace* resolves the Din of *War.*
> Fix'd in *Columbia* her illustrious Line,
> And bids in thee her future Councils shine.
> To every Realm her Portals open'd wide,
> Receives from each the full commercial Tide.
> Each Art and Science now with rising Charms
> Th' expanding Heart with Emulation warms.
> E'en great *Britannia* sees with dread Surprize,
> And from the dazzling Splendor turns her Eyes! . . .
>
> Auspicious Heaven shall fill with fav'ring Gales,
> Where e'er *Columbia* spreads her swelling Sails:
> To every Realm shall *Peace* her Charms display,
> And Heavenly *Freedom* spread her golden Ray.

Voices of reform and of inclusion and of nobility could be heard, then, but were little heeded.

FROM THE MOMENT everything came together, everything seemed to be falling apart. Initially hailed as a hero, the Cincinnatus of the New World, President Washington soon became a figure of partisan strife as the nation divided into two competing factions—the Federalists, led by Washington, Alexander Hamilton, and Adams, and the Republicans, led by Jefferson and Madison.

Naïvely, perhaps, the early leaders of the republic had professed a belief that partisanship could be banished from political life. Washington was to warn the country of what he called "the baneful effects of the spirit of party"—a spirit, he said, that was "unfortunately . . . inseparable from our nature, having its root in the strongest passions of the human mind. It exists under different shapes in all governments, more or less stifled, controlled, or repressed; but, in those of the popular form, it is seen in its greatest rankness, and is truly their worst enemy."

He knew of what he spoke. His eight years as president were riven with partisan warfare as both sides, believing the other possibly fatal to the American experiment, fought openly and covertly to thwart and even destroy the other. Whether the issue was the country's relations with England and with France, finance and the distribution of powers, or simply the ceremonial aspects of the presidency itself, Federalists and Republicans engaged in ferocious fighting. Such party battles, Washington wrote in 1796, served "always to distract the public councils and enfeeble the public administration. It agitates the community with ill-founded jealousies and false alarms, kindles the animosity of one part against another, foments occasionally riot and insurrection. It opens the door to foreign influence and corruption, which finds a facilitated access to the government itself through the channels of party passions."

In 1798, at an hour of war fever that had led to the passage of the Alien and Sedition Acts—designed by Federalists, in part, to enable them to suppress even legitimate political opposition—the kind of party feeling Washington had deplored was pervasive and defining. England and France were at war, and both nations were pressuring the United States to join the fight. Republicans in particular were anxious to support, or at least not actively oppose, the French, who were then in the midst of their own revolution. "The prospect of a rupture with France was exceedingly offensive to the portion of the people who espoused her cause," the Philadelphia lawyer and judge Joseph Hopkinson wrote of the summer of 1798, "and the violence of the spirit of party has never risen higher, I think not so high, in our country, as it did at that time upon that question."

The politics of the moment found expression in song. The Federalist ode "Adams and Liberty," by Robert Treat Paine, Jr., was published in 1798 and was sung to the tune of "To Anacreon in Heaven," an old English club song, as a way for the president's supporters to claim that they, not the Jeffersonian Republicans, were the true Americans:

Ye sons of Columbia, who bravely have fought,
For those rights, which unstained from your Sires had descended,
May you long taste the blessings your valour has brought,
And your sons reap the soil which their fathers defended.
'Mid the reign of mild peace, May your nation increase,
With the glory of Rome, and the wisdom of Greece;
And ne'er may the sons of Columbia be slaves,
While the earth bears a plant, or the sea rolls its waves . . .
Let Fame to the world sound America's voice;
No intrigue can her sons from their government sever;
Her pride is her Adams; His laws are her choice,
And shall flourish, till Liberty slumber for ever.
Then unite, heart and hand,
Like Leonidas' band,
And swear to the God of the ocean and land;
That ne'er shall the sons of Columbia be slaves,
While the earth bears a plant, or the sea rolls its waves.

Nevertheless, Jefferson defeated Adams in the presidential election of 1800, a victory heralded by Jeffersonians as a restoration of the principles of 1776. (Campaigns to make America great again have a long history.) In this partisan view, the heavy Federalist hand was lifted, and what Jefferson had called "the reign of witches" was coming to an end. In his inaugural address on Wednesday, March 4, 1801, the new president spoke of comity amid controversy. "All . . . will bear in mind this sacred principle, that though the will of the majority is in all cases to prevail, that will to be rightful must be reasonable; that the minority possess their equal rights, which equal law must protect, and to violate would be oppression," Jefferson said. "Let us, then, fellow-citizens, unite with one heart and one mind. Let us restore to social intercourse that harmony and affection without which liberty and even life itself are but dreary things." Warm words, but a song sung by his partisans, entitled "Jefferson and Liberty," was sharper in tone:

The gloomy night before us flies,
The reign of Terror now is o'er;

Its Gags, Inquisitors and Spies,
Its herds of harpies are no more
Rejoice! Columbia's Sons, rejoice!
To tyrants never bend the knee,
But join with heart and soul and voice,
For *Jefferson and Liberty*.

So it would go for centuries in American politics—a politics in which freedom of thought and of expression allowed divergent views to contend against one another in what seemed wars without end. That was the price of liberty: The American system was designed for conflict. "Where a constitution, like ours, wears a mixed aspect of monarchy and republicanism," Jefferson wrote, "its citizens will naturally divide into two classes of sentiment, according as their tone of body or mind, their habits, connections, and callings induce them to wish to strengthen either the monarchial or the republican features of the constitution." In 1769, Edmund Burke had seen further than most of his contemporaries, writing, "Party divisions, whether on the whole operating for good or evil, are things inseparable from free government."

Jefferson, too, could be practical about partisanship. "In every free and deliberating society, there must, from the nature of man, be opposite parties, and violent dissensions and discords," he wrote in 1798, "and one of these, for the most part, must prevail over the other for a longer or shorter time." He hated the idea of *reflexive* partisanship, of blind loyalty to one's own side no matter what reason might dictate. "I never submitted the whole system of my opinions to the creed of any party of men whatever, in religion, in philosophy, in politics, or in anything else, where I was capable of thinking for myself," he wrote Francis Hopkinson in 1789. "Such an addiction is the last degradation of a free and moral agent. If I could not go to heaven but with a party, I would not go there at all." Subsequent generations have quoted these lines—especially the last sentence of the observation—as a way of suggesting that partisanship is anathema to the American spirit. That's not quite right and sets an impossible standard for the present. It's more useful to recall that Jefferson also wrote this: "Men have differed in opinion, and been divided into parties by these opinions, from the first origin of societies and in all governments where they have been permitted freely to think and to speak. The same political parties which now agitate the U.S. have existed through all time"; the questions that defined American politics, Jefferson added, were the same kinds of questions "which kept the states of Greece and Rome in eternal convulsions." Jefferson wrote these words in 1813 in a letter to . . . John Adams.

At its best, American public life has moved forward not in moments of total agreement—moments virtually unknown in human experience—but when enough of us have seen that devotion to the ideal of liberty should prevail over our inevitable divisions of opinion. That insight informed one of the most important anthems of the early republic, one written by Joseph Hopkinson, the Philadelphia lawyer and judge, at the height of the 1790s battle between Adams and Jefferson.

At home one Saturday afternoon in April 1798, Hopkinson received an acquaintance—an actor-singer named Gilbert Fox. Fox was starring in a tragedy, *The Italian Monk,* and had advertised a benefit showing. Ticket sales, however, were slow, and Fox was looking for something to revive the box office. "His prospects were very disheartening," Hopkinson recalled, "but he said that if he could get a patriotic song adapted to 'The President's March,' he did not doubt of a full house; that the poets of the theatrical corps had been trying to accomplish it, but had not succeeded." Hopkinson agreed to try his hand at the task and set himself to it without delay.

The next day, a Sunday, Fox returned to Hopkinson's and found that his old friend had composed a four-verse ballad, "Hail Columbia," with a memorable chorus: "Firm, united let us be,/Rallying round our liberty,/As a band of brothers joined,/Peace and safety we shall find."

Hail Columbia! happy land!
Hail, ye heroes! Heav'n-born band!
Who fought and bled in freedom's cause,
Who fought and bled in freedom's cause,
And when the storm of war was gone
Enjoy'd the peace your valor won.
Let independence be our boast,
Ever mindful what it cost;
Ever grateful for the prize,
Let its Altar reach the skies.

Firm, united let us be,
Rallying round our Liberty,

As a band of Brothers joined,
Peace and safety we shall find.

Immortal Patriots, rise once more,
Defend your rights—defend your shore!
Let no rude foe, with impious hand,
Let no rude foe, with impious hand,
Invade the shrine where sacred lies
Of toil and blood, the well-earned prize,
While offering peace, sincere and just,
In heav'n we place a manly trust,
That truth and justice will prevail,
And every scheme of bondage fail.

Sound, sound the trump of fame,
Let Washington's great name
Ring thro the world with loud applause,
Ring thro the world with loud applause,
Let every clime to Freedom dear,
Listen with a joyful ear,
With equal skill, with Godlike pow'r
He governs in the fearful hour
Of horrid war, or guides with ease
The happier times of honest peace. . . .

Joseph Hopkinson of Philadelphia wrote the unifying "Hail Columbia" in part to combat what Washington called "the baneful effects of the spirit of party."

It was a triumph. Abigail Adams, who was in the theater on the night of its debut, told her sister that "the whole . . . Audience broke forth in the Chorus whilst the thunder from their Hands was incessant, and at the close they rose, gave 3 Huzzas, that you might have heard a mile—My head aches in consequence of it."

Hopkinson was pleased. "The object of the author was to get up an American spirit which should be independent of, and above, the interests, passion, and policy of both belligerents [England and France], and look and feel exclusively for our honor and rights . . ." Hopkinson wrote. "Of course the song found favor with both parties, for both were American, [and] at least neither could disown the sentiments and feelings it indicated."

Those sentiments and feelings were supra-partisan. The Revolution was rendered as a righteous undertaking carried through by a "Heav'n-born band"; succeeding generations were called, in an echo of Shakespeare, to be a "band of brothers"; and the work of the ages was the promulgation of liberty—"That truth and justice will prevail,/And every scheme of bondage fail."

"Hail Columbia"—it was initially known as "The Favorite New Federal Song"—grew so popular so fast that Adams and his cabinet, it was reported, attended a later Fox performance "for the express purpose of hearing the new patriotic air." In telling the story of Hopkinson's verses, one writer, C. A. Browne, reported that in December 1860, on the eve of the Civil War, Major Robert Anderson, the commander of the federal Fort Sumter in Charleston Harbor, raised the American flag on the fort as a military band struck up "Hail Columbia." "If South Carolina had, at that moment, attacked the fort," a contemporary of Anderson's wrote, "there would have been no hesitation on the part of any man within it about defending the flag."

"Hail Columbia" was considered by many as *the* national anthem for many years, but a 1931 act of Congress would elevate a different composition to official primacy—a series of lines written about the siege of Fort McHenry, in Maryland, amid a war that's often overlooked but was vital in its day and its way.

CHAPTER TWO

LAND WHERE OUR FATHERS DIED

"Who are we? And for what are we going to fight? Are we the titled slaves of George the Third? The military conscripts of Napoleon the Great? Or the frozen peasants of the Russian czar? No, we are the free born sons of America; the citizens of the only republic now existing in the world; and the only people on Earth who possess rights, liberties, and property which they dare call their own."

—ANDREW JACKSON, calling for militia to fight the British, 1812

"I looked at my hands to see if I was the same person now that I was free. There was such a glory over everything, the sun came like gold through the trees, and over the fields, and I felt like I was in Heaven."

—HARRIET TUBMAN, on crossing into freedom in 1849

MAJOR GEORGE ARMISTEAD knew what he wanted. As the Virginia-born officer took command of Fort McHenry in Baltimore Harbor in the summer of 1813, a year into the War of 1812, he wrote his senior officer: "We, Sir, are ready at Fort McHenry to defend Baltimore against invading by the enemy. That is to say, we are ready except that we have no suitable ensign to display . . . and it is my desire to have a flag so large that the British will have no difficulty in seeing it from a distance." It was a bit of swagger, a touch of bombast, a manifestation of pride—and because it was all those things, it was also very American.

Armistead was in luck, for just such a flag had been recently commissioned. For a fee that came to $405.90, Mary Young Pickersgill of Albemarle Street in Baltimore had agreed to sew a huge (thirty by forty-two feet) Stars and Stripes for Fort McHenry, as well as a storm flag (seventeen by twenty-five feet) for an additional $168.54.

The War of 1812 brought the sacking and burning of Washington, D.C., but ultimately resulted in a greater sense of American identity.

Much of the War of 1812 unfolded on the high seas; this is a depiction of the battle between the USS Constitution *and the British warship* Guerriere.

The flags were for a fort that became the focus of a prolonged British attack, on the tumultuous Tuesday and Wednesday of September 13 and 14, 1814. By chance, a Washington lawyer, Francis Scott Key, was in Baltimore to attempt to secure the release of Dr. William Beanes, an American who had been captured by the British. At the time of the bombardment, Key was aboard a sloop in the harbor, and only by keeping an eye out for the colors could he monitor the battle.

It was a long and terrible day in the middle of a war that was itself long and terrible. The war, which lasted from 1812 to early 1815, was a struggle to ratify the American Revolution. The immediate occasion was resentment over the British impressment of American sailors and concerns over British alliances with Indian tribes who were seen as threats to white American settlers, but, as the historian Gordon S. Wood wrote, "In the end, many Americans came to believe that they had to fight another war with Great Britain in order to reaffirm their national independence and establish their elusive identity." In many ways, the Revolutionary period did not truly conclude until the Treaty of Ghent and the Battle of New Orleans

JACKSON'S VICTORY AT NEW ORLEANS AND DEATH OF GEN⁺ PAKENHAM.

Andrew Jackson's epic victory at New Orleans in the early days of January 1815 propelled "Old Hickory" to national fame, setting the stage for the Age of Jackson.

brought the War of 1812 to a close in 1815. The conflict sometimes known to contemporaries as "Mr. Madison's War," then, can be seen as a climactic chapter in the saga of the Revolutionary War.

Francis Scott Key was a firsthand witness to one of the critical closing hours of that story. Watching the battle for Fort McHenry—the British attack, under the command of Vice Admiral Alexander Cochrane, lasted about twenty-five hours— Key was worried, for Baltimore was at risk of suffering the same fate that had struck Washington a few weeks before: a sacking and burning at the hands of the enemy. The British flotilla in the harbor was extraordinary and included the frigates *Seahorse, Surprise,* and *Severn,* and the "bomb vessels" *Meteor, Devastation, Aetna, Volcano,* and *Terror.* "We were like pigeons tied by the legs to be shot at," Judge Joseph H. Nicholson, who fought under Armistead, wrote. "The men in the fort watched the explosions light up the sky like lightning flashes," Lonn Taylor, Kathleen M. Kendrick, and Jeffrey L. Brodie wrote in a Smithsonian history, *The Star-Spangled Banner.* "Baltimoreans could clearly see the stream of sparks from the bombs' fuses arching

The original "Star-Spangled Banner," made by Mary Young Pickersgill of Baltimore.

through the air. The sounds of a torrential rain, which had worsened during the day, mixed with peals of thunder, which in turn joined the cacophony caused by the mortars, bombs, and rockets."

As Armistead recalled the bombardment, the British fired fifteen to eighteen hundred shells at Fort McHenry. "The only means we had of directing our guns," Armistead wrote in a report to Secretary of War James Monroe, "was by the blaze of their rockets and the flashes of their guns." Reflecting on the attack, Armistead said, "A few of these fell short. A large proportion burst over us, throwing their fragments among us, and threatening destruction. Many passed over, and about four hundred fell within the works." Yet, amazingly, only four Americans were killed, with twenty-four wounded.

Watching from afar—he was on a vessel in Old Roads Bay—Key peered through the mists of dawn and the haze of cannon fire, waiting for enough sunlight to see whether Major Armistead had held his ground.

Then, slowly, the verdict became clear. As Key would write, in verses scribbled on the back of a letter while he was still aboard his sloop, the flag—Mrs. Pickersgill's flag—was there. "As the last vessel spread her canvas to the wind," a British midshipman wrote of the royal forces' withdrawal, "the Americans hoisted a most superb and splendid ensign on their battery, and fired at the same time a gun of defiance."

Key finished his composition at the Indian Queen Hotel in Baltimore, and it was quickly published.

What so proudly we hail'd at the twilight's last gleaming,
Whose broad stripes and bright stars through the perilous fight,
O'er the ramparts we watch'd, were so gallantly streaming?

And the rockets' red glare, the bombs
    bursting in air,
Gave proof through the night that our
    flag was still there;
O say does that star-spangled banner
    yet wave,
O'er the land of the free and the home
    of the brave?

On the shore dimly seen through the
    mists of the deep,
Where the foe's haughty host in dread
    silence reposes,
What is that which the breeze, o'er the
    towering steep,
As it fitfully blows, half conceals, half
    discloses?
Now it catches the gleam of the
    morning's first beam,
In full glory reflected now shines in the
    stream:
'Tis the star-spangled banner, O long
    may it wave
O'er the land of the free and the home
    of the brave.

And where is that band who so
    vauntingly swore
That the havoc of war and the battle's
    confusion,
A home and a country, should leave us
    no more?
Their blood has washed out their foul
    footsteps' pollution.

Francis Scott Key's original lyrics, written after the siege of Fort McHenry (top); the first published sheet-music edition (bottom).

No refuge could save the hireling and slave
From the terror of flight, or the gloom of the grave:
And the star-spangled banner in triumph doth wave,
O'er the land of the free and the home of the brave.

O thus be it ever, when freemen shall stand,
Between their lov'd home and the war's desolation.
Blest with vict'ry and peace, may the Heav'n rescued land,
Praise the Power that hath made and preserved us a nation!
Then conquer we must, when our cause it is just,
And this be our motto: "In God is our trust."
And the star-spangled banner in triumph shall wave,
O'er the land of the free and the home of the brave!

The melody was difficult but relatively well known: "To Anacreon in Heaven," the English song already in circulation as the setting for 1798's "Adams and Liberty." Key's verses were published as handbills and in the Tuesday, September 20, 1814, edition of the *Baltimore Patriot and Evening Advertiser*. Under the headline DEFENSE OF FORT MCHENRY, the newspaper reported that Key had been "compelled to witness the bombardment of Fort McHenry, which the [British] Admiral had boasted that he would carry in a few hours, and that the city must fall. He watched the flag at the fort through the whole day with an anxiety that can be better felt than described, until the night prevented him from seeing it. In the night he watched the Bomb Shells; at early dawn his eye was again greeted by the proudly waving flag of his country."

"The Star-Spangled Banner" is not easy to sing, but even its critics have long acknowledged its power. "It commences on a key so low that all may join in," Elias Nason wrote. "The melodic parts most naturally succeed each other, and, if I may so speak, are logically conjoined and bound together. It consists of solo, duet, and chorus, and thus in unity presents variety. It is bold, warlike, and majestic; stirring the profoundest emotions of the soul, and echoing through its deepest chambers something of the prospective grandeur of a mighty Nation tramping toward the loftiest heights of intellectual dominion."

The War of 1812 gave us, in the fullness of time, a national anthem, but that designation would not come for more than a century, when Congress elevated "The

THE STAR-SPANGLED BANNER

There is a majesty, a pride, and an elevation we feel in our souls when we hear "The Star-Spangled Banner." It may sound expected or even corny, but when I hear the national anthem I feel the honor—and the obligation—of being an American. "The Star-Spangled Banner" unites us as one nation. Written in a rush of inspiration by Francis Scott Key, the lyrics are visual and emotional. When we hear them, we're with him as he watches the bombs in the night and anxiously awaits the sight of the flag still intact. And, with him, we hope that our dreams for the republic will endure. The song leads us to think how far we've come, where we are, and how diligent we must be to continue moving forward. The anthem isn't about martial glory or bombastic nationalism; it's really a song informed by nervous longing.

"The Star-Spangled Banner" is an incredibly challenging song for any singer. Live, say at a major sporting event, you experience a delay from the stadium sound system that can put even the most focused singer in a difficult spot in terms of pitch. And then there is the melody, which covers about an octave and a half range—you need to be able to start low enough to finish those high notes at the end. But, like America, it's worth the trouble.   —T.M.

Star-Spangled Banner" to official status in 1931, in a law signed by President Herbert Hoover.

That Key's anthem focused on the flag rather than on the abstractions of Dickinson's "Liberty Song" or Hopkinson's "Hail Columbia" was telling, for the Stars and Stripes was becoming a more and more prevalent cultural emblem. First commissioned and designed during the Revolution, the flag was commonplace in the War of 1812. "The stars of the new flag represent the constellation of States rising in the West," a Continental Congressman wrote of the colors. "The idea was taken from the constellation Lyra; which, in the hand of Orpheus, signifies harmony. The stars were in a circle, symbolizing the perpetuity of the Union; the ring like the circling serpent of the Egyptians, signifying eternity. The thirteen stripes showed, together with the stars, the number of the United Colonies, and denoted the subordination of the States to the Union, as well as equality among themselves. The red color, which in the Roman day was the signal of defiance, denotes courage, the blue, fidelity, and the white, purity."

The War of 1812 was a milestone in the emergence of a sense of national identity. "Torn from the body to which we are united by religion, liberty, laws, affections, relation, language, and commerce," John Dickinson had worried in 1768, "we must bleed at every vein." An enduring question for Americans was whether the motto adopted by the Continental Congress—"E Pluribus Unum," or "Out of the Many, One"—was a durable and practical vision. And the War of 1812 suggested that the experiment, for all its flaws and derelictions, would go on.

SONG SPOKE TO the unifying impulses of the age. The themes of union and of America's special providential role in the world were part of the air of the time. When Jefferson and Adams died on the same day—the Fourth of July, 1826, the fiftieth anniversary of the Declaration of Independence—eulogists saw the coincidence as evidence, in the words of Daniel Webster, that as "their lives themselves were the gift of Providence," their deaths offered proof "that our country and its benefactors are objects of His care." Speaking at Boston's Faneuil Hall, Webster left his listeners with a celestial image: "Auspicious omens cheer us. Great examples are before us. Our own firmament now shines brightly upon our path. *Washington* is in the clear, upper sky. These other stars have now joined the American Constellation; they circle round their center, and the heavens beam with new light."

In 1831 the Reverend Samuel Francis Smith, then a student at Andover Theological Seminary in Massachusetts, wrote a hymn to the nation that spoke in Websterian terms about the American experiment. A twenty-four-year-old student, Smith had been reading over German patriotic hymns when he got the idea to compose one of his own. "Seizing a scrap of waste paper I began to write, and in half an hour, I think, the words stood upon it, substantially as they are sung today," Smith recalled. The tune for which he wrote was "God Save the King," the British national anthem popular since the mid-eighteenth century. "There is nothing more impudent in the history of plagiarism," the editor of the 1912 *Yale Book of American Verse* wrote, "than our appropriation of 'God Save the King' and dubbing it 'America.'"

The title of Smith's piece was simple but profound: "America," which became known as "My Country 'Tis of Thee":

My country! 'tis of thee,
Sweet land of liberty,
Of thee I sing:
Land where my fathers died,
Land of the pilgrims' pride,
From every mountainside
Let freedom ring!

My native country, thee,
Land of the noble free,
Thy name I love;
I love thy rocks and rills,
Thy woods and templed hills;
My heart with rapture thrills
Like that above.

Let music swell the breeze,
And ring from all the trees
Sweet freedom's song:
Let mortal tongues awake;
Let all that breathe partake;
Let rocks their silence break,
The sound prolong.

Our fathers' God! to Thee,
Author of liberty,
To Thee we sing.
Long may our land be bright
With freedom's holy light;
Protect us by Thy might,
Great God, our King!

A classmate of Smith at Harvard College, Oliver Wendell Holmes, reflecting on his friend's poetic achievement, once wrote, "What is Fame? It is to write a hymn which sixty millions of people [the then population of the country] sing—that is

Samuel Francis Smith wrote "America," popularly known as "My Country 'Tis of Thee," in 1831 as a seminary student in Andover, Massachusetts.

fame." Holmes continued: "Now, there's Smith, his name will be honored by every school child in the land when I have been forgotten for a hundred years. He wrote 'My Country! 'Tis of Thee.' If he had said 'Our Country' the hymn would not have been immortal, but that 'My' was a master stroke. Everyone who sings the song at once feels a personal ownership in his native land. The hymn will last as long as the country."

The "I" v. "We" construction that Smith struck upon is an intriguing one. In the civil rights movement of the mid-twentieth century, Bernice Johnson Reagon would also see a power in the first-person pronoun. A scholar of African American music and culture, curator emeritus at the Smithsonian, and a distinguished professor emeritus at American University, Reagon was also a member of the Student Nonviolent Coordinating Committee's Freedom Singers. Sound, she said, "is a way to extend the territory you can effect. . . . Anybody who comes into that space, as long as you're singing, they cannot change the air in that space. The song will maintain the air as your territory. . . . And in the black community, when you want the communal expression, everybody says 'I.' So if there are five of us here, and all of us say 'I,' then you know that there's a group. A lot of times I've found when people say 'we,' they're giving you cover to not say whether they're going to be there or not." Her example: "This Little Light of Mine," which Reagon said, "means that when a march goes I am going to be there. So it really is a way of saying, the life that I have I will offer to this thing."

The power of Smith's verses in part derives from what Reagon called "the communal expression" of "'I,'" and by the diverse uses to which "My Country, 'Tis of Thee" has been put since its debut on the Fourth of July, 1831, at the Park Street

Church in Boston. There were abolitionist versions like this one, published in 1839 under the pen name "Theta":

My country, 'tis of thee,
Stronghold of slavery—
Of thee I sing:
Land, where my fathers died,
Where men *man's* rights *deride;*
From every mountainside,
Thy deeds shall ring,

My native country! Thee—
Where all men are born free,
If *white* their skin:
I love thy hills and dales,
Thy mounts and pleasant vales;
But hate thy *negro* sales,
As foulest sin.

Let *wailing* swell the breeze,
And ring from all the trees
The *black* man's wrong;
Let every tongue awake,
Let *bond* and free partake.
Let rocks their silence break,
The sound prolong.

Our father's God! To thee—
Author of *Liberty*!
To thee we sing;
Soon may our land be bright,
With *holy Freedom's* light,
Protect us by thy might,
Great God, our King.

MY COUNTRY 'TIS OF THEE

This song spoke to the evolution of our country in that moment, the Age of Jackson, and it's evolved with our country through the years—and that durability and resonance is one hallmark of truly great art.

When you hear it played simply—on a piano, for instance—it feels like a hymn, something I might've sung in church as a boy. With an orchestra, it becomes regal and majestic, a song worthy of presidential inaugurations. We see this throughout so much early music—composers using familiar melodies and rewriting the lyrics for their current political or cultural climate. We still do it. We do it because it works. Listeners, almost unknowingly, recognize an emotion from the past while clinging to the modern message. (In our own time, think about how Kanye West played off a line from Ray Charles's "I Got a Woman" in his "Gold Digger" single.)

John Dickinson did this with "The Liberty Song," but Samuel Francis Smith took things to an even higher level by appropriating "God Save the King" for American hearts and voices. I say "hearts" because "My Country 'Tis of Thee" was—*is*—really about putting not a monarch but the nation itself, and the ideas on which it's founded and with which it endures, at the center of our imaginative lives. And Smith's work has had a kind of power few songs have ever exerted. Whole books have been written about how his language and music have been invoked again and again in the ongoing American struggle.

What we say as a people—and what we sing as a people—matters, for even if we fall short of the ideal, we've got to keep that ideal in front of us, like a beacon through the darkness. "My Country 'Tis of Thee" is one of those beacons.

—T.M.

At the Union's Camp Saxton, in South Carolina, Smith's hymn was the first thing sung by some freed slaves when emancipation came, as 1862 turned into 1863. It was the last thing sung, C.A. Browne noted, by dying men among Colonel Theodore Roosevelt's Rough Riders in Cuba during the Spanish–American War, thus becoming the final words of men fighting for an imperialist vision of Anglo-Saxon civilization. And it gave Martin Luther King, Jr., his peroration at the March on Washington in August 1963.

Whites and blacks, men and women, enslaved and free, the powerful and the powerless: "My Country 'Tis of Thee" was sung by sundry voices for sundry reasons, in calm and in storm. In a way, Oliver Wendell Holmes may have been more right than even he knew when he praised Smith for giving Americans the means to sing not only of *the* country—the task of Dickinson, Hopkinson, and Key—but of one's *own* country, one's own understanding of what the nation, so flawed and yet so noble, so incomplete yet so full of promise, had been, was, and, most important, could be.

THAT, AT LEAST, was the aspiration. In 1837, the English writer Harriet Martineau published a book, *Society in America,* after spending two years in the United States. "I regard the American people as a great embryo poet: now moody, now wild, but bringing out results of absolute good sense: restless and wayward in action, but with deep peace at his heart: exulting that he has caught the true aspect of things past, and at the depth of futurity which lies before him, wherein to create something so magnificent as the world has scarcely begun to dream of," Martineau wrote. "There is the strongest hope of a nation that is capable of being possessed with an idea; and this kind of possession has been the peculiarity of the Americans from their first day of national existence till now."

The idea of liberty was animating, but it was limited. Another English visitor to America in the Age of Jackson, Frances Trollope, was blunt about the inconsistencies of democracy in the United States. "You will see them with one hand hoisting the cap of liberty, and with the other flogging their slaves," Mrs. Trollope, the mother of the novelist Anthony Trollope, wrote in her 1832 book *Domestic Manners of the Americans*. "You will see them one hour lecturing their mob on the indefeasible rights of man, and the next driving from their homes the children of the soil, whom they have bound themselves to protect by the most solemn of treaties."

Her harsh words about the treatment of Native Americans—those whom she called "the children of the soil"—were more than justified. For generations, white Americans had taken the land they wanted to take, driving the native inhabitants ever westward, forever displacing them at will despite treaties and promises. The story is tragic, depressing, and irredeemable. From New England, Jeremiah Evarts attempted to mount a moral case against the removal policies of the first several decades of the nineteenth century, but to no lasting avail. "The questions have forced themselves upon us, as a nation—*What is to become of the Indians? Have they any rights? If they have, What are these rights? And how are they to be secured?*" Evarts wrote in the first of his essays in a series entitled "Present Crisis in the Condition of the American Indians," published in 1829. "Most certainly an indelible stigma will be fixed upon us, if, in the plenitude of our power, and in the pride of our superiority, we shall be guilty of manifest injustice to our weak and defenseless neighbors."

Harriet Beecher Stowe's sister, Catharine, also joined the fight, writing a "Circular Addressed to the Benevolent Ladies of the U. States" in December 1829. Lamenting that "it has become almost a certainty that these people are to have their lands torn from them, and to be driven into western wilds and to final annihilation," Stowe wrote that only "the feelings of a humane and Christian nation" could "prevent the unhallowed sacrifice" of removal.

Nothing, however, would carry the day against the will of the white powers. "I was a stranger in a strange land," John Rollin Ridge, a child of the Cherokee Nation that was driven to the Trail of Tears, wrote from California. The phrase originally comes from Exodus and is echoed in Psalm 137, where the exiled Israelites cry out, "How shall we sing the Lord's song in a strange land?" Such was the fate of the Native Americans, and the music of the tribes spoke of gods and of men, of creation and loss, of joy and of danger.

One song of the Choctaw that dates from at least the 1830s—years in which the tribe was removed from Mississippi to Oklahoma—is entitled "Long Sought Home" and can be translated this way:

Someday when I die
The Great Spirit above will hold me.

Because of the Creator when I die
I am going to be in a good land.

Because of the Creator's mercy
I will be there,
In that distant heavenly land.

*"Someday when I die/The Great Spirit above will hold me," the Choctaw sang on the Trail of Tears—
the forcible removal of Native Americans from their ancestral lands.*

The Navajo sing a "Song of the Earth":

> The Earth is beautiful.
> The Earth is beautiful.
> The Earth is beautiful.
>
> Below the East, the Earth, its face toward the East.
> The top of its head is beautiful.
> The soles of its feet are beautiful.
> Its feet, they are beautiful.
> Its legs, they are beautiful.
> Its body, it is beautiful.
> Its chest, its breast, its head feather,
> they are beautiful. . . .

In his landmark survey of America's music, Richard Crawford cited an 1822 article by Lewis Cass, governor of the Michigan Territory, who quoted a Miami Indian

lyric, "I will go and get my friends—I will go and get my friends—I am anxious to see my enemies. A clear sky is my friend, and it is him I am seeking."

Cass explained that the song was designed to inspire action. "The manner in which these words are sung cannot be described to the reader," Cass wrote. "There is a strong expiration of breath at the commencement of each sentence, and a sudden elevation of the voice at the termination. The Chief, as he passes, looks every person sternly in the face. Those who are disposed to join the expedition exclaim *Yeh, Yeh, Yeh*, with a powerful tone of voice; and this exclamation is continually repeated during the whole ceremony. It is, if I may so speak, the evidence of their enlistment. Those who are silent decline the invitation."

To Crawford, "Cass's account squares with what are now understood as timeless Indian practices. One of the song's traits . . . is that its music has a specific purpose: in this case to recruit volunteers for a mission of war. The text's brevity does not mean that the performance was short. Many commentators of the time reported Indians' tendency to repeat bits of text and music incessantly, and noted the long stretches of time that performances could fill."

The Ojibwa George Copway was an important writer of Native descent, publishing *The Life, History, and Travels of Kah-ge-ga-gah-bowh* in 1847. In it he shared a "dream song" that he said had come to him at age twelve:

It is I who travel in the winds,
It is I who whisper in the breeze,
I shake the trees,
I shake the earth,
I trouble the waters on every land.

"My son," Copway's father told him, "*the god of the winds* is kind to you; the aged tree, I hope, may indicate long life; the wind may indicate that you will travel much; the water which you saw, and the winds, will carry your canoe safely through the waves." It was, in a sense, a father's prayer for a son who would always be in a strange country.

SAMUEL SMITH HAD drafted "My Country 'Tis of Thee" in his quarters in Andover in February 1831; a month before, on New Year's Day, twenty-five miles away in Boston, the abolitionist William Lloyd Garrison began publishing his newspaper, *The Liberator*. "Assenting to the 'self-evident truth' maintained in the American Declaration of Independence, 'that all men are created equal, and endowed by their Creator with certain inalienable rights—among which are life, liberty, and the pursuit of happiness,'" Garrison wrote in the inaugural issue, "I shall strenuously contend for the immediate enfranchisement of our slave population." He continued:

Founded in 1831—the same year Samuel Francis Smith wrote "My Country 'Tis of Thee"— William Lloyd Garrison's Liberator *led the abolitionist cause.*

I am aware that many object to the severity of my language; but is there not cause for severity? I *will* be as harsh as truth, and as uncompromising as justice. On this subject, I do not wish to think, or speak, or write, with moderation. No! no! Tell a man whose house is on fire to give a moderate alarm; tell him to moderately rescue his wife from the hands of the ravisher; tell the mother to gradually extricate her babe from the fire into which it has fallen—but urge me not to use moderation in a cause like the present. I am in earnest—I will not equivocate—I will not excuse—I will not retreat a single inch—*And I Will Be Heard.*

Garrison added these verses in the first *Liberator:*

I swear, while life-blood warms my throbbing veins,
Still to oppose and thwart, with heart and hand,
Thy brutalizing sway—till Afric's chains
Are burst, and Freedom rules the rescued land,—
Trampling Oppression and his iron rod:
Such is the vow I take—So Help Me God!

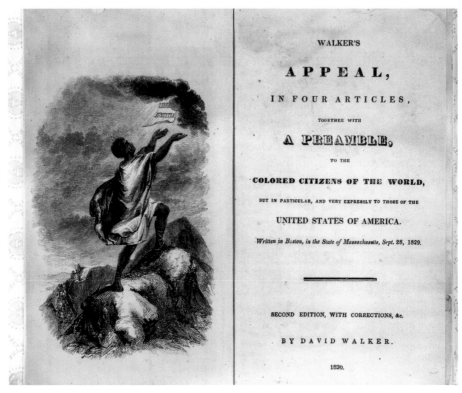

David Walker's "Appeal," published in 1829, closed with a hymn drawn from Psalm 10 that called on the Lord to "Defend the poor from harm."

Two years earlier, in 1829, David Walker, whose father was enslaved, had published his *Appeal to the Colored Citizens of the World,* a pamphlet that worried Southern slaveholders and inspired anti-slavery advocates. The black people of the United States, Walker wrote, were "the most degraded, wretched, and abject set of beings that ever lived since the world began, and I pray God that none like us ever may live again until time shall be no more."

Walker used the language of history and of faith to call on white Americans to consider slavery in light of their own experience and of their own professed religious views. "Now, Americans!" he wrote. "I ask you candidly, [were] your sufferings under Great Britain, one hundredth part as cruel and tyrannical as you have rendered ours under you? . . . Do the whites say, I being a black man, ought to be humble, which I readily admit? I ask them, ought they not be as humble as I? Or do they think that they can measure arms with Jehovah? Will not the Lord yet humble them?" He offered a warning: "The Americans may be as vigilant as they please, but they cannot be vigilant enough for the Lord, neither can they hide themselves, where he will not find them and bring them out." Walker closed by quoting a mid-eighteenth-century hymn drawn from Psalm 10:

Thy presence why withdraw'st, Lord?
Why hid'st thou now thy face,
When dismal times of deep distress
Call for thy wonted grace?

The wicked, swell'd with lawless pride,
Have made the poor their prey:
O let them fall by those designs
Which they for others lay . . .

They fondly think their prosp'rous state
Shall unmolested be;
They think their vain design shall thrive,
From all misfortune free. . . .

Near public roads they lie conceal'd
And all their art employ,
The innocent and poor at once
To rifle and destroy. . . .

But thou, O Lord, at length arise,
Stretch forth thy mighty arm;
And, by the greatness of thy pow'r,
Defend the poor from harm. . . .

LOOKING BACK ON the Age of Jackson and of Walker's *Appeal,* W.E.B. Du Bois recalled that there had been a passing interest in "The Sorrow Songs" of the African American milieu. "Away back in the thirties"—the 1830s—"the melody of these slave songs stirred the nation," Du Bois recalled, "but the songs were soon half forgotten." Such voices, however, could not be forever stilled. Writing in his 1903 book, *The Souls of Black Folk,* Du Bois excerpted an old spiritual:

I walk through the churchyard
To lay this body down;
I know moon-rise, I know star-rise;
I walk in the moonlight, I walk in the starlight;
I'll lie in the grave and stretch out my arms,
I'll go to judgment in the evening of the day,
And my soul and thy soul shall meet that day,
When I lay this body down.

"I know little of music and can say nothing in technical phrase," Du Bois wrote, but he did "know something of men, and knowing them, I know that these songs are the articulate message of the slave to the world. . . . They are the music of an unhappy people, of the children of disappointment; they tell of death and suffering and unvoiced longing toward a truer world, of misty wanderings and hidden ways."

The origins and development of music among African Americans is a saga unto itself, a story of breathtaking creativity and genius flowering amid the most inhumane of circumstances. Drawing on African and Caribbean traditions, inventing their own, and producing a body of work that would ultimately find expression in genres that included gospel, jazz, blues, and, centuries on, hip-hop, black Americans forged a remarkable cultural life and legacy that reaches far beyond any arbitrary racial category. "They that walked in darkness sang songs in the olden days—Sorrow Songs—for they were weary at heart. . . ." Du Bois wrote. "And so by fateful chance the Negro folk-song—the rhythmic cry of the slave—stands today not simply as the sole American music, but as the most beautiful expression of human experience born this side the seas."

The journey had begun, like so much else, with life in slavery. "I have often been utterly astonished, since I came to the north, to find persons who could speak of the singing, among slaves, as evidence of their contentment and happiness," Frederick Douglass wrote in his 1845 *Narrative of the Life of Frederick Douglass, An American Slave.* "It is impossible to conceive of a greater mistake. Slaves sing most when they are most unhappy. The songs of the slave represent the sorrows of his heart; and he is relieved by them, only as an aching heart is relieved by its tears. At least, such is my experience.

I have often sung to drown my sorrow, but seldom to express my happiness. Crying for joy, and singing for joy, were alike uncommon to me while in the jaws of slavery." To Douglass, the songs of the enslaved embodied the tragedy of human chattel.

Recalling life on the Lloyd plantation in eastern Maryland, where he spent part of his youth, Douglass remembered that the enslaved "would make the dense old woods, for miles around, reverberate with their wild songs, revealing at once the highest joy and the deepest sadness. They would compose and sing as they went along, consulting neither time nor tune. The thought that came up, came out—if not in the word, in the sound—and as frequently in one as in the other. . . . I have sometimes thought that the mere hearing of those songs would do more to impress some minds with the horrible character of slavery than the reading of whole volumes of philosophy on the subject could do." The sounds from those forests haunted Douglass. "The mere recurrence to those songs, even now, afflicts me; and while I am writing these lines, an expression of feeling has already found its way down my cheek," he wrote after his escape from bondage. "To those songs I trace my first glimmering conception of the dehumanizing character of slavery."

There were songs like "Sold Off to Georgy [Georgia]":

Farewell, fellow servants! O-ho! O-ho!
I'm going way to leave you; O-ho! O-ho!
I'm going to leave the old county, O-ho! O-ho!
I'm sold off to Georgy, O-ho, O-ho!

The same theme informed another song, about being sold and shipped in chains:

See these poor souls from Africa
Transported to America:
We are stolen and sold to Georgia, will you go along with me?
We are stolen and sold to Georgia, go sound the jubilee.

See wives and husbands sold apart,
The children's screams!—it breaks my heart. . . .

O gracious Lord! When shall it be
That we poor souls shall all be free? . . .

Lord, break them Slavery powers—will you go along with me?
Lord, break them Slavery powers, go sound the jubilee.

Dear Lord! Dear Lord! When Slavery'll cease,
Then we poor souls can have our peace;
There's a better day a-coming, will you go along with me?
There's a better day a-coming, go sound the jubilee.

The expectation of that better day informed much of the music of the enslaved. As Douglass plotted his escape, he and his compatriots, he recalled, sometimes let their hopes get the better of their judgment. Reflecting on the master from whom he broke away, Douglass wrote, "I am the more inclined to think that he suspected us, because, prudent as we were, as I now look back, I can see that we did many silly things, very well calculated to awaken suspicion," continuing:

> We were, at times, remarkably buoyant, singing hymns and making joyous excla-mations, almost as triumphant in their tone as if we had reached a land of free-dom and safety. A keen observer might have detected in our repeated singing of
>
> "O Canaan, sweet Canaan,
> I am bound for the land of Canaan,"
>
> something more than a hope of reaching heaven. We meant to reach the *north*— and the north was our Canaan.
>
> "I thought I heard them say,
> There were lions in the way,
> I don't expect to stay
> Much longer here.
> Run to Jesus—shun the danger—
> I don't expect to stay
> Much longer here,"

It was, Douglass wrote, "a favorite air, and had a double meaning. In the lips of some, it meant the expectation of a speedy summons to the world of spirits; but, in the lips of our company, it simply meant a speedy pilgrimage toward a free state, and deliverance from all the evils and dangers of slavery."

The "double meaning" of which Douglass wrote is also called "masking"—the tradition in African American music of apparently singing about one thing while in fact singing about another. To sing of deliverance from sin, for instance, was also to sing of deliverance from slavery and from discrimination without provoking a white backlash. "Swing Low, Sweet Chariot" is a classic example; the chariot isn't just about going to a heaven beyond the skies, but to a freedom beyond the Mason-Dixon Line. In the mid-twentieth century, the great gospel singer Mahalia Jackson would discuss the device with Studs Terkel, the Chicago writer and radio host. "She explained to me that the spiritual wasn't simply about Heaven [in] 'A City Called Heaven,'" Terkel recalled. "No, the city is here, on Earth. And so, as we know, slave songs were code songs. It was not a question of getting to Heaven, but rather to the free state of Canada or a safe city in the North—liberation here on Earth!"

As a CONDUCTOR on the loose network of escape routes that would come to be known as the Underground Railroad, Harriet Tubman used song as a signal as she led the enslaved north toward freedom through terrifying darkness in the middle years of the nineteenth century. Born circa 1820 into bondage in Maryland, Tubman escaped to Philadelphia in 1849. The story is told that Tubman sang these words as she prepared to flee:

When that old chariot comes,
I'm going to leave you,
I'm bound for the promised land,
Friends, I'm going to leave you.

I'm sorry, friends, to leave you,
Farewell! Oh, farewell!
But I'll meet you in the morning,
Farewell! Oh, farewell!
I'll meet you in the morning,
When you reach the promised land;
On the other side of Jordan,
For I'm bound for the promised land.

It was the most daunting of missions, but Tubman was determined. "For I had reasoned this out in my mind: there were one of two things I had a right to, liberty, or death," she recalled, and "if I could not have one, I would have the other; for no man should take me alive. I should fight for my liberty as long as my strength lasted, and when the time came for me to go, the Lord would let them take me."

On the plantation from which she fled, her "farewell song was long remembered in the cabins." When she crossed into safe territory in the North, she recalled, "I looked at my hands to see I was the same person now [that] I was free. There was such a glory over everything, the sun came like gold through the trees, and over the fields, and I felt like I was in Heaven."

To her credit, her mind was never far from those who remained in the Hell of enslavement. "I was a stranger in a

Harriet Tubman sang spirituals as signals to the enslaved along what came to be known as the Underground Railroad.

strange land," she recalled, and she devoted herself to making freedom possible for others under the most dangerous of conditions. "At one time the pursuit was very close and vigorous," Sarah H. Bradford wrote in *Harriet Tubman: The Moses of Her People*, which was based on interviews with Tubman. Slave-catchers were out in force. "The woods were scoured in all directions, every house was visited, and every person stopped and questioned as to a band of black fugitives, known to be fleeing through that part of the country. Harriet had a large party with her then; the children were sleeping the sound sleep that opium gives; but all the others were on the alert, each one hidden behind his own tree, and silent as death." Tubman left them to secure food, slipping off for a time.

Bradford then recounted the evening from the perspective of the huddled slaves:

"How long she is away! Has she been caught and carried off, and if so what is to become of them? Hark! There is a sound of singing in the distance, coming nearer and nearer. And these are the words of the unseen singer . . ."

> Hail, oh hail, ye happy spirits,
> Death no more shall make you fear,
> Grief nor sorrow, pain nor anguish,
> Shall no more distress you there.
>
> Around Him are ten thousand angels,
> Always ready to obey command;
> They are always hovering round you,
> Till you reach the heavenly land.
>
> Jesus, Jesus will go with you,
> He will lead you to his throne;
> He who died, has gone before you,
> Through the wine-press all alone.
>
> He whose thunders shake creation,
> He who bids the planets roll;
> He who rides upon the tempest,
> And whose scepter sways the whole.
>
> Dark and thorny is the pathway,
> Where the pilgrim makes his ways;
> But beyond this vale of sorrow,
> Lie the fields of endless days.

Tubman sometimes sang another song as well, one drawn from the story of Exodus, the most familiar of images to a people for whom churches, religious gatherings, and spirituals were crucial:

> Oh go down, Moses,
> Way down into Egypt's land;

Tell old Pharaoh
Let my people go.

Oh Pharaoh said he would go cross,
Let my people go,
And don't get lost in the wilderness,
Let my people go.

Oh go down, Moses,
Way down into Egypt's land;
Tell old Pharaoh
Let my people go.

You may hinder me here, but you can't up there,
Let my people go,
He sits in . . . Heaven and answers prayer,
Let my people go!

Oh go down, Moses,
Way down into Egypt's land,
Tell old Pharaoh,
Let my people go."

Sometimes there would be a call-and-response between conductor and passenger. Tubman would sing:

When that old chariot comes,
Who's going with me?

And the reply would come:

When that old chariot comes,
I'm going with you. . . .

Once in freedom, Tubman recalled, now-former slaves would raise their voices in thanksgiving:

Glory to God and Jesus, too,
One more soul got safe;
Oh, go and carry the news,
One more soul got safe. . . .

Glory to God in the highest,
Glory to God and Jesus, too,
For all these souls now safe.

"I HAVE HEARD THEIR groans and sighs," Tubman said of the enslaved, "and seen their tears, and I would give every drop of blood in my veins to free them." One close Tubman ally, Senator William H. Seward of New York, had long articulated a vision of an emancipated America. In opposing the Compromise of 1850—including the Fugitive Slave Act, which required the return of the enslaved to their owners—Seward had said that he foresaw "countless generations . . . rising up and passing in dim and shadowy review before us; and a voice comes forth from their serried ranks, saying: 'Waste your treasures and your armies, if you will; raze your fortifications to the ground; sink your navies into the sea; transmit to us even a dishonored name, if you must; but the soil you hold in trust for us—give it to us free.' "

The Founders and their heirs had sought to live, as Lincoln put it in Springfield in 1858, "half slave and half free." Prevailing racist views of identity and power made this hypocrisy possible and durable, and evolving understandings of equality and liberty led to what Seward would call "the irrepressible conflict"—a war to settle, at last, whether slavery could coexist with American democracy.

CHAPTER THREE

MINE EYES HAVE SEEN THE GLORY

"Sing it again!"

—ABRAHAM LINCOLN, on hearing "The Battle Hymn of the Republic"

"The year of jubilee is come . . . !"

—From "Blow Ye the Trumpet, Blow!," a favorite hymn of Frederick Douglass

FREDERICK DOUGLASS WAS going home. With the successful publication of his *Narrative* in 1845, Douglass had left America for Great Britain to tour and lecture for twenty-one months. In 1847, as he prepared to return to the United States, the abolitionist Julia Griffiths and her brother, T. Powis Griffiths, composed a piece called "Farewell Song of Frederick Douglass: On Quitting England for America—the Land of his Birth." Playing off the promise, though not the reality, of the country evoked by Key's "Star-Spangled Banner," the Griffithses depicted Britain as the true land of liberty, writing:

Farewell to the land of the free! Farewell to the land of the brave.
Alas! That my country should be America! Land of the slave . . .

The song enjoyed a rediscovery in 2018, when the University of Rochester purchased an exceedingly rare copy of its sheet music; as the university noted in announcing the find, the only other known copy is in the British Library. With their verses more than a century and a half ago, the Griffithses had captured a great tragic contradiction at the heart of the American experiment: that a nation conceived in liberty preserved and perpetuated human slavery. "How is it," the eighteenth-century English man of letters Samuel Johnson had wondered, "that we hear the loudest yelps for liberty among the drivers of the negroes?"

Song was an essential element in inspiring Frederick Douglass to plan and execute his escape from slavery.

How, indeed? Few spoke of slavery in America more incisively and eloquently than Douglass, who, on returning to the United States at mid-century, engaged in what the Griffithses had described, in the "Farewell Song," as a war against evil:

Shall I, like a coward, not join the fight?
Shrink from the onslaught when battle is raging
Scared by the enemy's tyrannous might?

The answer was an emphatic *no.* In an Independence Day oration at Rochester, New York, delivered on the fifth of July in 1852, Douglass offered a nuanced yet passionate view of the meaning of America. "Should I seem at ease, my appearance would much misrepresent me," Douglass told his audience at Corinthian Hall. "The little experience I have had in addressing public meetings, in country schoolhouses, avails me nothing on the present occasion."

He was not, he insisted, being falsely or formulaically modest. The tension he felt was real, for his subject was perilous, contradictory, and vast: America itself—American promise and American reality, American greatness and American misery:

> Fellow-citizens, pardon me, allow me to ask, why am I called upon to speak here today? What have I, or those I represent, to do with your national independence? Are the great principles of political freedom and of natural justice, embodied in that Declaration of Independence, extended to us? . . .
>
> I am not included within the pale of this glorious anniversary! Your high independence only reveals the immeasurable distance between us. The blessings in which you, this day, rejoice, are not enjoyed in common.—The rich inheritance of justice, liberty, prosperity and independence, bequeathed by your fathers, is shared by you, not by me. The sunlight that brought life and healing to you, has brought stripes and death to me. This Fourth of July is *yours,* not *mine. You* may rejoice, *I* must mourn.

Douglass slowly, deliberately, *devastatingly,* spoke hard truths:

> What, to the American slave, is your Fourth of July? I answer: a day that reveals to him, more than all other days in the year, the gross injustice and cruelty to which he is the constant victim. To him, your celebration is a sham; your boasted liberty, an unholy license; your national greatness, swelling vanity; your sounds

of rejoicing are empty and heartless; your denunciations of tyrants, brass fronted impudence; your shouts of liberty and equality, hollow mockery; your prayers and hymns, your sermons and thanksgivings, with all your religious parade, and solemnity, are, to him, mere bombast, fraud, deception, impiety, and hypocrisy— a thin veil to cover up crimes which would disgrace a nation of savages.

Douglass closed on a note of hope—realistic hope, to be sure, but hope nonetheless. He painted a portrait of a modern world ever more connected as reason and science led humankind forward:

> I do not despair of this country. There are forces in operation, which must inevitably work the downfall of slavery. . . . Nations do not now stand in the same relation to each other that they did ages ago. No nation can now shut itself up from the surrounding world, and trot round in the same old path of its fathers without interference. The time was when such could be done. Long established customs of hurtful character could formerly fence themselves in, and do their evil work with social impunity. Knowledge was then confined and enjoyed by the privileged few, and the multitude walked on in mental darkness. But a change has now come over the affairs of mankind. Walled cities and empires have become unfashionable. The arm of commerce has borne away the gates of the strong city. Intelligence is penetrating the darkest corners of the globe. It makes its pathway over and under the sea, as well as on the earth. Wind, steam, and lightning are its chartered agents. Oceans no longer divide, but link nations together. . . . The fiat of the Almighty, "Let there be Light," has not yet spent its force.

Here was an American making a cogent case for the justice of abolition. Douglass was part of a chorus of voices seeking to end slavery, but there were also voices rising to defend enslavement. In March 1861, Alexander H. Stephens, the vice president of the newly formed Confederate States of America, spoke about the white Southern cause in an address at Savannah, Georgia. Where Douglass had spoken of reason and the global spread of Enlightenment ideals as grounds to hope for abolition, Stephens seemed to dwell in another realm of reality altogether, insisting that the world, far from moving toward broader equality, was primed to embrace the Confederate view of innate—and immutable—black inferiority.

"The new [Confederate] constitution has put at rest, forever, all the agitating questions relating to our peculiar institution, African slavery, as it exists amongst us [and] the proper status of the negro in our form of civilization," Stephens said. "This was the immediate cause of the late rupture and present revolution."

He then drew on history. "Jefferson in his forecast, had anticipated this, as the 'rock upon which the old Union would split,'" Stephens said, continuing:

> He was right. . . . It was an evil they knew not well how to deal with, but the general opinion of the men of that day was that, somehow or other in the order of Providence, the institution would be evanescent and pass away. This idea . . . rested upon the assumption of the equality of races. This was an error. . . .
>
> Our new government is founded upon exactly the opposite idea; its foundations are laid, its cornerstone rests, upon the great truth that the negro is not equal to the white man; that slavery subordination to the superior race is his natural and normal condition. This, our new government, is the first, in the history of the world, based upon this great physical, philosophical, and moral truth.

Stephens linked the Confederate view of perpetual racial inequality to great scientific insights, suggesting that black inferiority was a principle as well established as the orbit of the earth around the sun or the circulation of blood in the human body. "With us," he said of the newly seceded government, "all of the white race, however high or low, rich or poor, are equal in the eye of the law. Not so with the negro. Subordination is his place. He, by nature, or by the curse against Canaan, is fitted for that condition which he occupies in our system," adding: "I cannot permit myself to doubt the ultimate success of a full recognition of this principle throughout the civilized and enlightened world." It might take time, he acknowledged, but he claimed to be confident of eventual victory, saying:

> As I have stated, the truth of this principle may be slow in development, as all truths are and ever have been, in the various branches of science. It was so with the principles announced by Galileo. It was so with Adam Smith and his principles of political economy. It was so with Harvey, and his theory of the circulation of the blood. It is stated that not a single one of the medical profession, living at the time of the announcement of the truths made by him, admitted them. Now, they are universally acknowledged. May we not, therefore, look with confidence to the ultimate universal acknowledgment of the truths upon which our system rests? . . .

The substratum of our society is made of the material fitted by nature for it, and by experience we know that it is best, not only for the superior, but for the inferior race, that it should be so. It is, indeed, in conformity with the ordinance of the Creator. It is not for us to inquire into the wisdom of His ordinances, or to question them. For His own purposes, He has made one race to differ from another, as He has made "one star to differ from another star in glory." The great objects of humanity are best attained when there is conformity to His laws and decrees, in the formation of governments as well as in all things else. Our confederacy is founded upon principles in strict conformity with these laws. This stone which was rejected by the first builders "is become the chief of the corner," the real "cornerstone" in our new edifice.

THERE, THEN, WERE two starkly divergent views of humankind that fed the flames of what Lincoln called the "fiery trial" of the Civil War. We know that Douglass was right and Stephens was wrong, but the adjudication of the argument would claim three quarters of a million lives and very nearly end the American Union. "I am, like many others," Harriet Martineau observed, "almost in despair for the great Republic"—a reasonable and widespread fear. A question raised by the Griffithses' "Farewell Song" for Douglass required a definitive answer—could America remain the "land of the Slave," or would it, in Francis Scott Key's language, genuinely become the "land of the free"? And so two songs, written three and a half decades and an ocean apart, framed a conundrum that only combat would resolve.

The prose of the war could be splendid and often had its own quasi-musical rhythms. Like Douglass's, Abraham Lincoln's words echo through the ages. Consider the president's Second Annual Message to Congress, in late 1862:

Fellow-citizens, *we* cannot escape history. We of this Congress and this administration, will be remembered in spite of ourselves. No personal significance, or insignificance, can spare one or another of us. The fiery trial through which we pass, will light us down, in honor or dishonor, to the latest generation. We *say* we are for the Union. The world will not forget that we say this. We know how to save the Union. The world knows we do know how to save it. We—even *we here*—hold the power and bear the responsibility. In *giving* freedom to the *slave,* we *assure* freedom to the *free*—honorable alike in what we give, and what we preserve. We shall nobly save, or meanly lose, the last best hope of earth.

Prose doesn't get much better than that, yet song was as much a part of Civil War America as speech. The music of the war "rang out from parlor pianos in homes across the country; it thundered from crowds of civilians at political rallies; it beat the steady rhythms of soldier life; and it declared the newfound freedom of African-Americans," as the scholar Christian McWhirter wrote. "Although it was certainly a prominent part of northern and southern culture before 1861, the war catapulted music to a new level of cultural significance. More than mere entertainment, it provided a valuable way for Americans to express their thoughts and feelings about the conflict. Conversely, songs influenced the thoughts and feelings of civilians, soldiers, and slaves—shaping how they viewed the war."

From Chicago, George F. Root composed perhaps the earliest song of the war after Fort Sumter, "The First Gun Is Fired," which he had ready within three days of the Confederate attack on the federal installation in Charleston Harbor:

The first gun is fired!
"May God protect the right!"
Let the freeborn sons of the North arise
In power's avenging might;
Shall the glorious Union our fathers have made,
By ruthless hands be sunder'd?
And we of freedom's sacred rights
By trait'rous foes be plunder'd?
Arise! arise! arise!
And gird ye for the fight!
And let our watchword ever be,
"May God protect the right!"

He later put Henry S. Washburn's poem "The Vacant Chair," about a family's grief at the death of a soldier, to music:

We shall meet but we shall miss him,
There will be one vacant chair;

We shall linger to caress him,
While we breathe our evening prayer. . . .

True, they tell us wreaths of glory
Evermore will deck his brow,
But this soothes the anguish only,
Sweeping o'er our heartstrings now.
Sleep today, O early fallen,
In thy green and narrow bed.
Dirges from the pine and cypress
Mingle with the tears we shed.

Why were the men of the Union fighting? Why were so many chairs to be forever vacant? In 1861, Oliver Wendell Holmes tried to explain by writing a new verse for "The Star-Spangled Banner":

When our land is illumined with Liberty's smile,
If a foe from within strike a blow at her glory,
Down, down with the traitor who dares to defile
The Flag of her stars and the page of her story!

By the millions unchained
Who their birthright have gained
We will keep her bright blazon forever unstained.
And the Star-spangled Banner in triumph shall wave
While the land of the Free is the home of the brave.

A transporting vision of a truly free America, one that disposes of the "traitor who dares to defile/The Flag of her stars and the page of her story!" The problem was that this vision was fanciful, not factual, and, as Frederick Douglass had said, exclusive, not inclusive. The words Holmes wrote were aspirational, and the music of the Union cause—"John Brown's Body," "The Battle Hymn of the Republic," "The Battle Cry of Freedom," "We Are Coming, Father Abraham," "Marching Through Georgia," and the songs of the enslaved—was to fill the air, and to fire the imagination, with images of righteous struggle. The Hutchinson Family Singers, who hailed from New Hampshire, had prepared the ground in the antebellum years, singing songs about emancipation and liberty to broad audiences. During the war, the Hutchinsons put John Greenleaf Whittier's abolitionist poem "We Wait beneath the Furnace Blast" to music:

What breaks the oath
Of the men o' the South?
What whets the knife
For the Union's life?—
Hark to the answer: *Slavery*!

To listen to the music of the Union cause, there could be no higher calling, no more divine mission, than the abolition of slavery and the salvation of the constitutional order conceived at Philadelphia in 1787. In "The Battle Cry of Freedom," Root wrote:

The Union forever, Hurrah, boys, hurrah!
Down with the traitor, Up with the star;
While we rally round the flag, boys, rally once again,
Shouting the battle cry of freedom . . .

We will welcome to our numbers the loyal, true and brave,
Shouting the battle cry of freedom,
And although they may be poor, not a man shall be a slave,
Shouting the battle cry of freedom.

So we're springing to the call from the East and from the West,
Shouting the battle cry of freedom,
And we'll hurl the rebel crew from the land we love the best,
Shouting the battle cry of freedom.

In the fullness of time, Lincoln would purportedly tell Root that the composer had "done more than a hundred generals and a thousand orators" by framing the conflict so powerfully. Music, however, could mask some of the war's complexities.

Lincoln's history, and America's, would be nobler if he had always been a fearless soldier in the cause of abolition.

But he was not. In his anguish over slavery and Union, Lincoln was in some senses a representative white American—a man whose journey to a more perfect Union was complicated by the prevailing white prejudices and economic realities of the time. "I am naturally anti-slavery," Lincoln wrote in April 1864. "If slavery is not wrong, nothing is wrong. I cannot remember when I did not so think, and feel." As early as 1854, speaking in Peoria, Illinois, Lincoln had called slavery a "monstrous injustice," saying: "Let us re-adopt the Declaration of Independence, and with it, the practices, and policy, which harmonize with it. . . . If we do this, we shall not only have saved the Union; but we shall have so saved it, as to make, and to keep it, forever worthy of the saving."

He was less certain, though, about exactly how to design and implement this plan of salvation. "If all earthly power were given me, I should not know what to do, as to the existing institution," he said at Peoria, continuing:

> My first impulse would be to free all the slaves, and send them to Liberia, to their own native land. But a moment's reflection would convince me, that whatever of high hope, (as I think there is) there may be in this, in the long run, its sudden execution is impossible. . . . What then? Free them all, and keep them among us as underlings? Is it quite certain that this betters their condition? . . . Free them, and make them politically and socially, our equals? My own feelings will not admit of this; and if mine would, we well know that those of the great mass of white people will not. . . . A universal feeling, whether well or ill-founded, cannot be safely disregarded. We cannot, then, make them equals. It does seem to me that systems of gradual emancipation might be adopted; but for their tardiness in this, I will not undertake to judge our brethren of the south.

His consuming concern on coming to the presidency was the rescue of the Union so long as slavery remained an exclusively Southern institution. In 1858, Lincoln had said, "I will say then that I am not, nor ever have been, in favor of bringing about in any way the social and political equality of the white and black races." At his first inauguration, in 1861, Lincoln tried to allay slaveholders' anxieties, saying, "Apprehension seems to exist among the people of the Southern States that by the accession

"The fiery trial": President Lincoln in conference with General George B. McClellan at Antietam. The Union victory there helped convince the president to issue the Emancipation Proclamation.

of a Republican Administration their property and their peace and personal security are to be endangered. There has never been any reasonable cause for such apprehension. Indeed, the most ample evidence to the contrary has all the while existed and been open to their inspection. It is found in nearly all the published speeches of him who now addresses you. I do but quote from one of those speeches when I declare that—'I have no purpose, directly or indirectly, to interfere with the institution of slavery in the States where it exists. I believe I have no lawful right to do so, and I have no inclination to do so.'"

By the summer of 1862, however, it had become evident to him that emancipation, even in a limited way, would be militarily wise while having the virtue of being morally right. After the Confederate defeat at Antietam in September, Lincoln told his cabinet that he had struck a bargain with God: If the Union forces could prevail in Maryland, he, the president, would move on emancipation. Now that that victory had come, Lincoln said, he was ready to act—and with the Emancipation Proclamations of September 1862 and New Year's Day 1863, he imbued the Union cause with ultimate moral meaning.

Music greeted the order that the

"Forever free": The text of Lincoln's Emancipation Proclamation, which liberated the enslaved in the states in rebellion against the United States of America.

enslaved in states in rebellion would be "forever free." As Eileen Southern, the historian of African American music, wrote, "Black men assembled in 'rejoicing meetings' all over the land on the last night of December in 1862, waiting for the stroke of midnight to bring freedom to those slaves in the secessionist states." In Washington, a gathering of African Americans sang Harriet Tubman's old favorite:

Go down, Moses,
Way down in Egypt land;
Tell old Pharaoh,
Let my people go.

According to Southern, a woman in the crowd offered a new verse, to the delight of what was described as "the vast assembly":

GO DOWN, MOSES and
SWING LOW, SWEET CHARIOT

Haunting and compelling, "Go Down, Moses" moves me deeply. I am pulled into the struggle for freedom with the minor chords and the major sentiment of this spiritual tune. Whatever your color, whatever your background, you can feel the African rhythm down in your soul. As a well-known African American spiritual, it lends itself to great artistic interpretation. (One of the most popular is by the incomparable Louis Armstrong, whose distinct voice could take any song to a new place.)

"Swing Low, Sweet Chariot" is another favorite spiritual of mine. Joan Baez sang this at the Woodstock festival. There's power in the intersection of spiritual and folk music. And it's great—and very American—that one of the most famous songs of all time was written by an Oklahoma slave, Wallace Willis. I envision that moment when the unimaginable demands of his life in enslavement were overwhelming and he felt this deep-down longing for freedom—then realized that the only freedom he may know lay in death.　　　　　—T.M.

Go down, Abraham,
Away down in Dixie's land;
Tell Jeff Davis
To let my people go.

LINCOLN'S DECISION ON emancipation came in the same months that Julia Ward Howe's "The Battle Hymn of the Republic" was becoming popular. A poet and activist from Boston, Howe had joined her husband and a few others in coming south to watch the Grand Review of the Army of the Potomac at Bailey's Cross-roads in northern Virginia. Inspired by what she'd seen, Howe rose in the night in her room at Willard's Hotel near the White House and, in the gloom, wrote new verses to a familiar piece. The tune for which she was composing was well known in abolitionist circles and among Union soldiers as "John Brown's Body," an anthem commemorating the anti-slavery martyr who had been executed after leading a raid on Harpers Ferry:

John Brown's body lies a-mouldering in the grave,
John Brown's body lies a-mouldering in the grave,
John Brown's body lies a-mouldering in the grave,
But his soul goes marching on.

Glory, glory, hallelujah,
Glory, glory, hallelujah,
Glory, glory, hallelujah,
His soul goes marching on.

He's gone to be a soldier in the Army of the Lord,
He's gone to be a soldier in the Army of the Lord,
He's gone to be a soldier in the
    Army of the Lord,
His soul goes marching on. . . .

John Brown died that the slaves
    might be free,
John Brown died that the slaves
    might be free,
John Brown died that the slaves
    might be free,
His soul goes marching on.

The immediate occasion for Howe's own verses came from her own singing of "John Brown's Body" with the soldiers she had encountered earlier that day. One of her party, the Reverend James Freeman Clarke, had challenged her to improve on the existing song. "Mrs. Howe, why do you not write

In 1861, Julia Ward Howe awoke in the night at Willard's Hotel in Washington, D.C., to scribble down the verses to what became "The Battle Hymn of the Republic."

some good words for that stirring tune?" Howe rose to the challenge. "And so, to pacify the dear old man, I promised to try."

The poem she scribbled in the darkness elevated the fight for the Union to the noblest of planes:

Mine eyes have seen the glory of the coming of the Lord:
He is trampling out the vintage where the grapes of wrath are stored;
He hath loosed the fateful lightning of His terrible swift sword:
His truth is marching on.

I have seen Him in the watch fires of a hundred circling camps,
They have builded Him an altar in the evening dews and damps;
I can read His righteous sentence by the dim and flaring lamps:
His day is marching on.

I have read a fiery gospel writ in burnished rows of steel:
"As ye deal with My contemners, so with you My grace shall deal;
Let the Hero, born of woman, crush the serpent with his heel,
Since God is marching on."

He has sounded forth the trumpet that shall never call retreat;
He is sifting out the hearts of men before His judgment-seat:
Oh, be swift, my soul, to answer Him! Be jubilant, my feet!
Our God is marching on.

In the beauty of the lilies Christ was born across the sea,
With a glory in his bosom that transfigures you and me:
As he died to make men holy, let us die to make men free,
While God is marching on.

The vision of the armies of the Lord on the march in the cause of true justice was compelling, and the verses were first published in *The Atlantic Monthly* in February 1862. "Do you want this, and do you like it, and have you any room for it in the January number?" Howe had written *Atlantic* editor James Fields, who paid her five dollars for the poem, which he printed on the cover of the magazine with a title of his devising: "The Battle Hymn of the Republic" was fully born.

Lincoln loved it, calling out, "Sing it again!" after hearing Charles McCabe, a Methodist minister and a chaplain in the 122nd Ohio Volunteer Infantry, perform it in the hall of the House of Representatives on Tuesday, February 2, 1864. "Take it all in all," Lincoln later told McCabe, "the song and the singing, that was the best I ever heard."

According to Eileen Southern, though, "Black soldiers seemed to prefer their own texts...and used the tune for marching songs, camp songs, social songs, and even religious songs." She cited one such version:

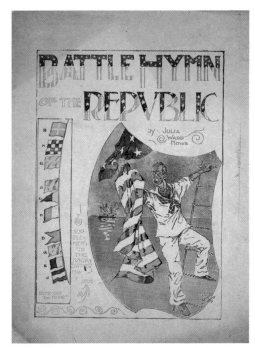

Sheet music for "The Battle Hymn of the Republic," the title "Atlantic Monthly" editor James Fields gave to Howe's poem.

> We are done with hoeing cotton, we
>   are done with hoeing corn,
> We are colored Yankee soldiers, as
>   sure as you are born;
> When Massa hears us shouting, he will think 'tis Gabriel's horn,
> As we go marching on.

By mid-1862 the Union needed more soldiers willing, as Howe had put it, to "die to make men free." President Lincoln called for three hundred thousand additional soldiers, inspiring this Biblical poem from a Quaker, James Sloan Gibbons, which was first published in the New York *Evening Post* of Wednesday, July 16, 1862, and set to music:

> We are coming, Father Abraham, three hundred thousand more,
> From Mississippi's winding stream and from New England's shore.
> We leave our plows and workshops, our wives and children dear,
> With hearts too full for utterance, with but a silent tear.

THE BATTLE HYMN OF THE REPUBLIC, THE BATTLE CRY OF FREEDOM, and WE ARE COMING, FATHER ABRAHAM

"The Battle Hymn" is one of my first musical memories. As a young child, I went to audition for a part in a play. Instead of giving me a song to sing, they asked if I knew anything, and I knew Julia Ward Howe's majestic song (or at least the first verse). A big part of its power is how it links the human and the divine, the small and the large, the particular and the universal. Told from the perspective of a soldier for justice—and it could be a traditional soldier under arms or anyone who fights to right wrongs—"The Battle Hymn" is about pilgrims on earth taking on the Lord's work. This can be tricky—humility means we can't confuse our will with God's—but history tells us that we make our greatest advances in America when religious conviction informs political action. From abolition to civil rights, ministers of the Lord have led us to higher ground.

The "Battle Hymn" lyrics point to Christ's salvation of man as the ultimate guide to how we should act here on earth. Fighting for the Union was a Christian responsibility, a mission from God that required action and came with God's blessing. It was the ultimate religious motivation: Christ saved you, now you must go save freedom.

In "The Battle Cry of Freedom" we have a great example of music's incredible ability to unify words, beat, and melody into a form that can motivate us in times of war and struggle. I can picture Union soldiers marching off with a righteous cause in their heart and this drumbeat driving them onward.

With "Father Abraham," I'm struck by the first line: "We are coming, Father Abraham, three hundred thousand more." That's a lot of lives unified and willing to die for the Union cause. I love that this song feels like an upbeat march musically, even though lyrically it's clear that these troops left their families for bloody rivers and death alongside their brothers. But you can hear the belief in their cause in the upbeat tempo. It's a song for the beginning of a war, when spirits and righteousness are high.

—T.M.

We dare not look behind us but steadfastly before.
We are coming, Father Abraham, three hundred thousand more!
We are coming, coming, our Union to restore,
We are coming, Father Abraham, three hundred thousand more!

America's music could be as racially complicated as the country itself, a fact well illustrated by the man known as "America's Troubadour," Stephen C. Foster. Widely considered the most successful songwriter of the mid-nineteenth century, he wrote for the blackface minstrel stage, a popular genre in the middle decades of the 1800s. "Essentially it consisted of an exploitation of the slave's style of music and dancing by white men, who blackened their faces with burnt cork and went on the stage to sing 'Negro songs' (also called 'Ethiopian songs'), to perform dances derived from those of the slaves, and to tell jokes based on slave life," Eileen Southern wrote. Two archetypes drove the shows: the enslaved plantation hand "Jim Crow" and the enslaved urban "dandy dressed in the latest fashion, who boasted of his exploits among the ladies," known as "Zip Coon."

Foster, who drank himself to death in 1864, at age 37, was famous for "Old Uncle Ned," "Oh! Susanna," "My Old Kentucky Home," and "Old Folks at Home" ("Swanee River"), among others. During the war he wrote a few conventional songs that drew on the emotions of the time. One was 1862's "Was My Brother in the Battle?":

Tell me, tell me, weary soldier From the rude and stirring wars,
Was my brother in the battle where you gained those noble scars?
He was ever brave and valiant, and I know he never fled.
Was his name among the wounded or numbered with the dead?
Was my brother in the battle when the tide of war ran high?
You would know him in a thousand by his dark and flashing eye.

Tell me, tell me weary soldier, will he never come again,
Did he suffer 'mid the wounded or die among the slain?

A year later, in 1863, Foster published "For the Dear Old Flag I Die!" with lyrics by George Cooper. Like "Was My Brother in the Battle?" it was a meditation on the

WAS MY BROTHER IN THE BATTLE?

With this song, we find ourselves face-to-face with one of the greatest songwriters ever, Stephen Foster. Who doesn't know "Oh! Susanna"?

He is acknowledged by many as the first professional songwriter—certainly one of the first songwriters in the sense of how we think of songwriters today. His ability to find a melody and lyric that touched the American public was unmatched, and his songs would travel around the world painting a picture of this still-young country. This particular song is so incredibly sad—sung from the point of view of a sibling who's wondering what has become of his brother in harm's way.

Strikingly, this timeless question of war is never answered. We are left to wonder and share in Foster's words of belief—whatever the brother's fate, "He was ever brave and valiant." Foster knew that there was incredible power in leaving the question unresolved, for the song leaves us longing to know, and engaged long after the music stops. —T.M.

tragedy of war. As "Death's cold hand" grips the "wounded drummer boy," the lad finds comfort in thoughts of his mother, and of home:

For the dear old Flag I die,
Said the wounded drummer boy;
Mother, press your lips to mine;
O, they bring me peace and joy!
'Tis the last time on earth
I shall ever see your face
Mother take me to your heart,
Let me die in your embrace . . .

Farewell, mother, Death's cold hand
Weighs upon my spirit now,
And I feel his blighting breath

Fan my pallid cheek and brow.
Closer! closer! to your heart,
Let me feel that you are by,
While my sight is growing dim,
For the dear old Flag I die.

IN THE CONFEDERATE States of America, the essential Southern anthem—
"I Wish I Was in Dixie's Land"—was conceived, written, and first performed in
New York, as part of a minstrel revue. And as so often happens with lasting pieces of
music, it was composed hurriedly. In March 1859, Daniel Decatur Emmett, who was
writing and performing for Bryant's Minstrels, was asked to produce a new number
for a show. Emmett, a native of Ohio, complied, and "Dixie" was born. Verses and
versions abound, but these words were, and are, fairly common to the song:

I wish I was in the land of cotton,
Old times there are not forgotten;
Look away! Look away! Look away! Dixie Land.
In Dixie's Land where I was born in,
Early on one frosty mornin',
Look away! Look away! Look away! Dixie Land.

Then I wish I was in Dixie, Hooray! Hooray!
In Dixie's Land I'll take my stand
to live and die in Dixie.
Away, away, away down south in Dixie.
Away, away, away down south in Dixie.

That the song was written to be performed by blackface performers is a little-
noted but vital fact. "Dixie" was composed by a white man and sung by whites who
were pretending to be blacks who were supposed to be pining nostalgically for the
South. Context is all: minstrel singers on a New York stage suggesting that the "land
of cotton" was preferable to the free North. The tune was popular in the North and
in the South; Lincoln himself admired it.

The imperative to give the Confederacy a common sense of identity as it marched

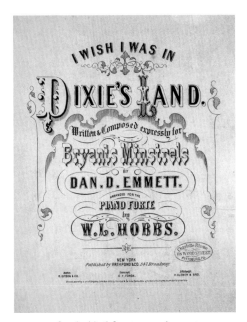 

Written for the blackface minstrel stage in New York by Daniel Decatur Emmett (right), "I Wish I Was in Dixie's Land" became the anthem of the Confederate States of America.

into war was evident even before Jefferson Davis's inauguration. In the Secession Winter, as Southern state after Southern state left the Union, Mississippi flew what became known as the "Bonnie Blue Flag," a blue banner with a single five-point star, as a replacement for the Stars and Stripes. Written by Harry Macarthy, a performer who was known as the "Arkansas Comedian," "The Bonnie Blue Flag" offered the Confederacy a kind of instant history (though, as Steven H. Cornelius pointed out in his history of the music of the war, they got the order of secession wrong). Macarthy also borrowed the Shakespearean image of a "band of brothers" from "Hail Columbia," writing:

> We are a band of brothers and native to the soil,
> Fighting for the property we gained by honest toil;
> And when our rights were threatened, the cry rose near and far,
> Hurrah for the Bonnie Blue Flag that bears a single star!
>
> Hurrah! Hurrah!
> For Southern rights, hurrah!

I WISH I WAS IN DIXIE'S LAND

What a challenging song to dissect. The history of "Dixie" is one of the reasons history is so important: I promise that there are precious few folks, North or South, who have much (or any) idea that the anthem of the Confederacy was written for blackface performers in New York City—or that Abraham Lincoln said it was one of his favorite tunes. In just those two details, you get a sense of the tangled complexity of America's story. For a lot of white Southerners, the song evokes warm memories of home; for a lot of African Americans, it's one more tragic reminder of the horrors of slavery and the all-too-persistent realities of racism.

Structurally, the music would lend itself to performers dancing, although today we are more familiar with a slower-tempo version. But "Dixie" is a song that requires us to think about it fully, not partially. It's not just any other song but a part of a past that's troubling, tragic, and not even *past*.

And so I have to reconcile my memory of this song with its history and its purpose. I grew up in Northeast Louisiana, surrounded by cotton fields, on a street beside a cotton gin in the one-stoplight town of Start. My stepdad, Horace, was a truck driver who hauled cotton seed all over the Southeast, and I spent a lot of time as a kid riding along with him, listening to 8-track tapes of country-music icons Merle Haggard and George Jones. Those are some of my favorite childhood memories. Cotton and country music were how I grew up, so when I hear the refrain "I wish I was in the land of cotton . . ." I sing along and think about my little postage stamp of earth, with a reflexive emotional longing to go back to the simplicity of being a kid in Louisiana.

Then, though, my brain kicks in, and I remember all that the song represents to so many others, and what history, not my heart, tells me it means. "Dixie" is an inescapable part of Southern and of American history, and I have no doubt that it portrays a pro-slavery point of view and relegates African Americans to the most un-American of places: a place where human beings are considered inferior because of the color of their skin and the circumstances of their birth. That may have been who we were, but it can't be who we are.   —T.M.

Hurrah for the Bonnie Blue Flag that
bears a single star.

As long as the Union was faithful to
her trust,
Like friends and like brethren, kind
were we, and just;
But now, when Northern treachery
attempts our rights to mar,
We hoist on high the Bonnie Blue
Flag that bears a single star.

First gallant South Carolina nobly
made the stand;
Then came Alabama and took her by
the hand;
Next, quickly Mississippi, Georgia,
and Florida,
All raised on high the Bonnie Blue
Flag that bears a single star.

*"The Bonnie Blue Flag," by the "Arkansas
Comedian" Harry Macarthy, was an early attempt
to find a unifying song for the states that were
seceding from the Union.*

Ye men of valor gather round the banner of the right,
Texas and fair Louisiana join us in the fight;
Davis, our loved President, and Stephens statesmen rare,
Now rally round the Bonnie Blue Flag that bears a single star.

And here's to brave Virginia! the Old Dominion State,
With the young Confederacy at length has linked her fate;
Impelled by her example, now other states prepare
To hoist on high the Bonnie Blue Flag that bears a single star.

Then here's to our Confederacy, strong we are and brave,
Like patriots of old we'll fight, our heritage to save;
And rather than submit to shame, to die we would prefer,
So cheer for the Bonnie Blue Flag that bears a single star.

Then cheer, boys, cheer, raise a joyous shout,
For Arkansas and North Carolina now have both gone out;
And let another rousing cheer for Tennessee be given
The single star of the Bonnie Blue Flag has grown to be eleven.

"Like patriots of old": Such was a central claim of the Confederacy, that it, not the
Union, represented the true principles of '76. As time went on, Macarthy replaced
the word "property" in the song's opening verse with "liberty" in order to minimize
that the war was about slavery. By singing of "liberty," the rebels were better able to
sustain the idea that they were at war to create a nation that was the real heir of the
Founders—work that had fallen to men such as Thomas "Stonewall" Jackson, the
Confederate hero, who was celebrated in "Stonewall Jackson's Way":

He's in the saddle now! Fall in!
Steady! The whole brigade!
Hill's at the ford, cut off—we'll win
His way out, ball and blade!
What matter if our shoes are worn?
What matter if our feet are torn?
"Quick-step! We're with him before dawn!"
That's "Stonewall Jackson's way." . . .

Ah, maiden, wait, and watch, and yearn
For news of Stonewall's band!
Ah, widow, read, with eyes that burn,
That ring upon thy hand!
Ah, wife, sew on, pray on, hope on!
Thy life shall not be all forlorn.
The foe had better ne'er been born
That gets in Stonewall's way.

On the other side of enemy lines, William T. Sherman's march through Georgia
and the Carolinas inspired at least one enslaved community to sing a song that had
been written as a Northern minstrel number by a white abolitionist, Henry Clay
Work. Frightened by the coming of Union troops, a South Carolina master fled. His

enslaved population was more than a little amused. "My old master run off and stay in the woods a whole week when Sherman's men [came] through," Lorenza Ezell told a Works Progress Administration writer during the New Deal. He remembered their then singing a "funny song"—Henry Clay Work's:

> White folks, have you seen old master
> Up the road, with his moustache on?
> He pick up his hat and he leave real sudden
> And I believe he's up and gone.
>
> Old master run away
> And us darkies stay at home.
> It must be now that Kingdom's comin'
> And the year of Jubilee.
>
> He look up the river and he seen that smoke
> Where Lincoln's gunboats lay.
> He big enough and he old enough and he ought to know better,
> But he gone and run away.
>
> Now that overseer want to give trouble
> And trot us 'round a spell,
> But we lock him up in the smokehouse cellar,
> With the key done throwed in the well.

IN A RECOLLECTION of Friday, July 19, 1861, just before the Battle of Bull Run, Elias Nason wrote of an evening he spent with Michigan's Fourth Regiment at Fairfax Court House in northern Virginia. "The stillness of the nightfall was broken only by the report of an occasional rifle from the surrounding forest," Nason wrote. "The lights of the camp were gradually extinguished and the weary soldiers were about to spread themselves upon the broad and verdant campus of the Court House for repose." Then a colonel called out, "Come, boys, let's have a song!"

After the Civil War, the cause of white supremacy replaced the defense of slavery as a consuming concern, and "Dixie" was seen in many quarters as a "patriotic song," despite its origins.

The troops were delighted for the chance to relieve the tension. In the darkness they sang "Hail Columbia," "The Star-Spangled Banner," and "Old Hundred," a familiar doxology. "These great songs sung," Nason wrote, "the weary men, though in the front of death, sank into slumbers so profound, that the rain which soon came pattering down through the foliage of the oak trees (I remember the first drop that struck my cheek) did not awaken them."

The capacity of music to reassure and to remind is one of its cardinal virtues. That was true for the men of the Michigan Fourth, and it was true of their commander in chief. "Mr. Lincoln's love of music was something passionate, but his tastes were simple and uncultivated, his choice being old airs, songs, and ballads, among which the plaintive Scotch songs were liked best," the journalist Noah Brooks recalled. The president had a fondness for "songs which had for their theme the rapid flight of time, decay, [and] the recollection of early days." Lincoln's favorite song was not about politics but about life—"Twenty Years Ago," a meditation on the narrator's lost youth as he returns home after two decades:

> I've wandered by the village, Tom—I've sat beneath the tree,
> Upon the school-house playing-ground which sheltered you and me;
> But none are left to greet me, Tom, and few are left to know,
> That played with us upon the green just twenty years ago . . .
>
> My lids have long been dry, dear Tom, but tears came in my eyes,
> I thought of her I loved so well—those early-broken ties;
> I visited the old church-yard, and took some flowers to strew,
> Upon the graves of those we loved, some twenty years ago.
>
> Some are in the church-yard laid, some sleep beneath the sea,
> But few are left of our old class, excepting you and me;
> But when our time shall come, dear Tom, and we are called to go,
> I hope they'll lay us where we played just Twenty Years Ago.

To FREDERICK DOUGLASS, there had never been "a nobler and grander war than that which the loyal people of this country are now waging against the slaveholding rebels." In the end, the clash of arms and of ideas was the redemptive test of the American Revolution—the republic itself was on trial. At Gettysburg in 1863, President Lincoln spoke, as Douglass had, in the vernacular of the Declaration of Independence:

> Four score and seven years ago our fathers brought forth on this continent, a new nation, conceived in Liberty, and dedicated to the proposition that all men are created equal.
>
> Now we are engaged in a great civil war, testing whether that nation, or any

nation so conceived and so dedicated, can long endure. We are met on a great battle-field of that war. We have come to dedicate a portion of that field, as a final resting place for those who here gave their lives that that nation might live. It is altogether fitting and proper that we should do this.

But, in a larger sense, we cannot dedicate—we cannot consecrate—we cannot hallow—this ground. The brave men, living and dead, who struggled here, have consecrated it, far above our poor power to add or detract. The world will little note, nor long remember what we say here, but it can never forget what they did here. It is for us the living, rather, to be dedicated here to the unfinished work which they who fought here have thus far so nobly advanced. It is rather for us to be here dedicated to the great task remaining before us—that from these honored dead we take increased devotion to that cause for which they gave the last full measure of devotion—that we here highly resolve that these dead shall not have died in vain—that this nation, under God, shall have a new birth of freedom—and that government of the people, by the people, for the people, shall not perish from the earth.

The notion of redemption—that the bloodshed of the war could, mysteriously yet unmistakably, expiate the sins of slavery and lead to a "new birth of freedom"—was on Lincoln's mind and in his heart. A Union victory and the liberation of the enslaved would mean that America had, at least for a time, been delivered from evil in a day of "jubilee." The prospect of salvation—from sin in general and from slavery in particular—was the message of a favorite hymn of Frederick Douglass, "Blow Ye the Trumpet, Blow!":

Blow ye the trumpet, blow,
The gladly solemn sound,
Let all the nations know
To earth's remotest bound,
The year of jubilee is come:
Return, ye ransom'd sinners, home!

Jesus, our great High-Priest,
Hath full atonement made;
Ye weary spirits rest,
Ye mournful souls be glad,

The year of jubilee is come:
Return, ye ransom'd sinners, home! . . .

Ye slaves of sin and hell,
Your liberty receive,
And safe in Jesus dwell,
And bless'd in Jesus live:
The year of jubilee is come:
Return, ye ransom'd sinners, home!

WITH THE UNION'S advantages and victories in the field, jubilee was at hand in the late winter and early spring of 1865. In his second inaugural, delivered on Saturday, March 4, 1865, however, Lincoln spoke more of tragedy than of triumph. He wanted victory—which would come thirty-six days later, with Lee's surrender to Grant at Appomattox—but he also longed for postbellum reunion and reconciliation. Speaking of both Northerners and Southerners, Lincoln mused: "Both read the same Bible and pray to the same God, and each invokes His aid against the other." Of slavery, the president noted: "It may seem strange that any men should dare to ask a just God's assistance in wringing their bread from the sweat of other men's faces, but let us judge not, that we be not judged." It was a conciliatory address, one that sought to acknowledge the ambiguity of history and the cosmic nature of the conflict. "Fondly do we hope, fervently do we pray, that this mighty scourge of war may speedily pass away," Lincoln said. "Yet, if God wills that it continue until all the wealth piled by the bondsman's two hundred and fifty years of unrequited toil shall be sunk, and until every drop of blood drawn with the lash shall be paid by another drawn with the sword, as was said three thousand years ago, so still it must be said 'the judgments of the Lord are true and righteous altogether.'"

The Biblical allusion was to Psalm 19—a kind of musical moment, given that the psalms were the songbook of the Hebrew Bible—and Lincoln's point was stark. If the war went on, if more men had to die, then so be it, for such was the will of the Almighty. Lincoln believed the war was an inevitability in the Jeffersonian course of human events. "I claim not to have controlled events, but confess plainly that events have controlled me. . . ." Lincoln had written to a correspondent in Kentucky in April 1864. "If God now wills the removal of a great wrong, and wills also that we of the North as well as you of the South, shall pay fairly for our complicity in that wrong, impartial history will find therein new cause to attest and revere the justice and goodness of God."

A year later, the second inaugural looked ahead, not backward, in the hope that the events of the future would prove the sacrifices of war worthwhile: "With malice toward none, with charity for all, with firmness in the right as God gives us to see the right, let us strive on to finish the work we are in, to bind up the nation's wounds, to care for him who shall have borne the battle and for his widow and his orphan, to do all which may achieve and cherish a just and lasting peace among ourselves and with all nations."

In his "Song, On the Death of President Abraham Lincoln," published after Lincoln's assassination at Ford's Theater, Silas S. Steele imagined an enduring role for Lincoln in the American story. Sung to the tune of "Annie Laurie," Steele's song said that Lincoln had been "Our Pilot and our Guide," and had "For Freedom lived and died." Going forward, Steele prayed:

> Let his Counsel still be nigh,
> And the Savior of our Union,
> Is with Washington on high.

DOUGLASS DESERVES THE last word on the war and on Lincoln, the man who often seems to loom largest over the history not only of the American presidency but of the nation. In 1876, Douglass said this as he dedicated a monument to the martyred president in Washington:

> It must be admitted, truth compels me to admit, even here in the presence of the monument we have erected to his memory, Abraham Lincoln was not, in the fullest sense of the word, either our man or our model. In his interests, in his associations, in his habits of thought and in his prejudices, he was a white man.
>
> He was preeminently the white man's President, entirely devoted to the welfare of white men. . . . To protect, defend, and perpetuate slavery in the States where it existed Abraham Lincoln was not less ready than any other President to draw the sword of the nation. . . . We are at best only his step-children; children by adoption, children by force of circumstances and necessity. . . . Our faith in him was often taxed and strained to the uttermost, but it never failed.

Douglass insisted that Lincoln must be considered wholly, not partially.

> Had he put the abolition of slavery before the salvation of the Union, he would have inevitably driven from him a powerful class of the American people and rendered resistance to rebellion impossible. Viewed from the genuine abolition ground, Mr. Lincoln seemed tardy, cold, dull, and indifferent; but measuring him by the sentiment of his country, a sentiment he was bound as a statesman to consult, he was swift, zealous, radical, and determined.

America would endure. "According to the popular English view," Edward Dicey of the London *Daily Telegraph* had written in 1863, "the whole country is in a state of revolution, trade is bankrupt, and the entire progress of the nation stopped for years to come, yet here, in the West, in the very heat of the war, there was a great country growing into existence by rapid strides. The great march of civilization was still, as ever, tending westward, building railroads, clearing forests, reclaiming wild lands, raising cities, and making the wilderness into a fertile country. This progress westward across the prairie is the great fact of American history; and those who want to understand the real character of the present civil war, must remember that this progress is still going on without ceasing."

Progress was indeed an American reality. The country would march on, uncertainly and imperfectly and inconsistently. But at least it would march as one.

T HE POSSIBILITIES OF progress were evident in the postbellum experience of the Jubilee Singers of Nashville's Fisk University. In the autumn of 1871, with the school for African Americans facing financial ruin, the singers undertook a series of concert tours to raise money for the university. They would perform for Ulysses S. Grant and for Queen Victoria; by bringing the songs of the enslaved to a wide audience, the Jubilee Singers are credited with helping to give the broad American public an appreciation of the talent—and, in a larger sense, of the *humanity*—of the formerly enslaved. "For months, they journeyed through Ohio and Pennsylvania and into New York, singing the secret soul music of their ancestors," Andrew Ward wrote in his *Dark Midnight When I Rise: The Story of the Fisk Jubilee Singers*. "Expelled from hotels, their clothes running to rags, they struggled in obscurity, performing at small-town churches, halls, street corners, and train stations. But as word of their extraordinary artistry spread, they began one of the most remarkable trajectories in American history: from whipping post and auction block to concert hall and throne room."

The group's reach was enormous. A cousin of William Seward's, Thomas Freling-huysen Seward of New York, published a collection of spirituals, *Jubilee Songs: As Sung by the Jubilee Singers of Fisk University,* and their music moved even the occasionally acerbic Mark Twain. "I am expecting to hear the Jubilee Singers to-night, for the fifth time (the reason it is not the fiftieth is because I have not had fifty opportunities)," Twain wrote in 1875 in a request for a rendition of "John Brown's Body," which he had heard them sing before.

Frederick Douglass understood the Jubilee Singers' power. "You are doing more to remove the prejudice against our race than ten thousand platforms could do," Douglass told the Jubilee Singers in a visit at his home in Washington, D.C., in 1875. In his meeting with them, Douglass thought back to the old days of his enslavement. "I can remember songs that I heard fifty years ago, when a slave," Douglass said, and then began to sing:

Run to Jesus—shun the danger—
I don't expect to stay much longer here:
He will be our dearest friend,
And will help us to the end—
I don't expect to stay much longer here. . . .

The singers in the room, it was recalled, "soon caught the melody and joined him in the refrain": "Run to Jesus—shun the danger—/I don't expect to stay much longer here." As the song ended, Douglass remarked, "It was while singing this song that the idea of escaping from slavery was first suggested to my mind. As the thought grew upon me, the song became more and more a favorite, and I used to sing it about the plantation continually. My master was very well pleased, for he thought I was thinking about heaven, but I was thinking all the time about that other country up North." Impressed, the Jubilee Singers added Douglass's old favorite to their repertoire. Douglass had sung of running to Jesus, and he had run to freedom. As the nineteenth century would begin to wane, the country would find itself running ahead, too, to a new time that was beset by old problems.

CHAPTER FOUR

MARCH, MARCH, MANY AS ONE

"Daughters of freedom arise in your might!"

—Suffrage anthem, 1871

"And we won't come back till it's over, over there."

—"Over There," by George M. Cohan, 1917

N THE AUTUMN of 1915, on a beautiful October day, more than twenty-five thousand marchers walked up Fifth Avenue in New York to the cheers, *The New York Times* reported, of a quarter of a million spectators. Thirty bands took part, playing different marching tunes, and there were fifteen thousand yellow banners on display. "The noise of traffic," *The Washington Post* wrote, gave "way to music mingled with the cheers of women." At dusk, fifteen bands joined together to play "The Star-Spangled Banner" at the 59th Street fountain at the entrance to Central Park. "As darkness fell," the *Post* reported, "the lights of shops still disclosed the seemingly endless lines of marchers, eight and sixteen abreast." The passage of the Nineteenth Amendment would finally come in time for the 1920 presidential election—a new day of jubilee.

The roots of the march could be said to stretch back to Abigail Adams and her admonition that the Founders "Remember the Ladies." As with the cause of independence in the Revolutionary War era and with abolition and secession in the years before and during the Civil War, songs offered a window on the feelings of the time. "Daughters of Freedom, the Ballot Be Yours" was published in 1871 and became a standard of the movement:

Daughters of freedom arise in your might!
March to the watchwords Justice and Right!

The suffrage leaders Susan B. Anthony and Elizabeth Cady Stanton together in 1895.

From Seneca Falls to the Progressive era, the cause of women's suffrage was long, anguishing—but finally successful.

Why will ye slumber? wake, O wake!
Lo! on your legions light doth break!
Sunder the fetters "custom" hath made!
Come from the valley, hill and glade!
Daughters of freedom, the truth marches on,
Yield not the battle till ye have won!
Heed not the "scorner," day by day
Clouds of oppression roll away!

A watershed moment along the journey had come in the autumn of 1872, when the suffrage leader Susan B. Anthony opened her morning newspaper in Rochester, New York—and arose in her might.

The editorial, as she chose to read it, couldn't have been clearer. Perusing the

Friday, November 1, 1872, edition of the *Rochester Democrat and Chronicle,* Susan B. Anthony took the words of the lead piece literally. "Now register!" the newspaper said. The presidential election was the next week, and the editors called on their readers to exercise the right to vote. "Today and tomorrow are the only remaining opportunities," the paper said. "If you were not permitted to vote, you would fight for the right, undergo all privations for it, face death for it. You have it now at the cost of five minutes' time to be spent in seeking your place of registration and having your name entered. . . . Register now!"

Anthony thought that a wonderful idea. The Eighth Ward's registry office doubled as a barbershop, and she gathered her three sisters and set out to follow the *Democrat and Chronicle*'s civic exhortation. "There was nothing," Anthony biographer Ida Husted Harper wrote, "to indicate that this appeal was made to men only." Presenting herself to the ward's three registrars—two Republicans and one Democrat—Anthony saw their reluctance and then read them both the Fourteenth Amendment and the relevant article in the New York State Constitution—neither of which said anything about the franchise being limited to men only. Flummoxed, the officials "at length" accepted the Anthonys' registrations. (The Democrat dissented but was outvoted.)

The following Tuesday, Election Day, Anthony turned out early to cast her vote for Ulysses S. Grant in his contest against Horace Greeley. "Well I have been & gone & done it!!" she wrote to her friend and ally Elizabeth Cady Stanton. "Positively voted the Republican ticket—straight—this AM at 7 o'clock and *swore my vote in at that.* . . . So we are in for a fine agitation in Rochester." Anthony was a key figure in a movement that in many ways had its origins in the July 1848 Seneca Falls Convention for women's rights. "We hold these truths to be self-evident: that all men and women are created equal," the convention had put forth in its "Declaration of Sentiments and Resolutions." Anthony echoed the point: "It was we, the people; not we, the white male citizens; nor yet we, the male citizens; but we, the whole people, who formed this Union," she said after her 1872 vote. "And we formed it, not to give the blessings of liberty, but to secure them; not to the half of ourselves and the half of our posterity, but to the whole people—women as well as men."

For daring to vote in Rochester in the 1872 election, Anthony was arrested, charged, and tried. When the marshal came to apprehend her, he was respectful, even bashful; with her sense of the dramatic, Anthony asked him to handcuff her.

(He declined.) At her trial for illegally voting in a federal election, before Judge Ward Hunt in the United States Circuit Court for the Northern District of New York, Anthony was asked, after being convicted by an all-male jury, whether she had "anything to say." Anthony rose and addressed the court.

"Yes, your honor, I have many things to say; for in your ordered verdict of guilty, you have trampled under foot every vital principle of our government," Anthony said. "My natural rights, my civil rights, my political rights, my judicial rights, are all alike ignored. Robbed of the fundamental privilege of citizenship, I am degraded from the status of a citizen to that of a subject; and not only myself individually, but all of my sex, are, by your honor's verdict, doomed to political subjection under this, so-called, form of government."

Interrupting, the judge said: "The Court cannot listen to a rehearsal of arguments the prisoner's counsel has already consumed three hours in presenting."

Anthony pressed on. "May it please your honor," she replied, "I am not arguing the question, but simply stating the reasons why sentence cannot, in justice, be pronounced against me. Your denial of my citizen's right to vote, is the denial of my right of consent as one of the governed, the denial of my right of representation as one of the taxed, the denial of my right to a trial by a jury of my peers as an offender against law, therefore, the denial of my sacred rights to life, liberty, property and—"

Judge Hunt cut her off. "The Court," he said, "cannot allow the prisoner to go on." In the end, Anthony was fined one hundred dollars and court costs, but she refused to pay, and the government never collected. "If it is a mere question of who has got the best of it," one newspaper wrote, "Miss Anthony is still ahead; she has voted and the American constitution has survived the shock. . . . [T]he world jogged on as before."

MANY OF THE women who'd fought for abolition—Harriet Tubman and Julia Ward Howe among them—now turned to suffrage. "During the first two thirds of my life, I looked to the masculine ideal of character as the only true one," Howe wrote in 1899, reminiscing about 1869. "I sought its inspiration, and referred my merits and demerits to its judicial verdict. In an unexpected hour a new light came to me, showing me a world of thought and of character quite beyond the limits within which I had hitherto been content to abide. The new domain now made clear to me was that of true womanhood—woman no longer in her ancillary relation to her opposite, man, but in her direct relation to the divine plan and purpose, as a free agent, fully sharing with man every human right and every human responsibility. This discovery was like the addition of a new continent to the map of the world, or of a new testament to the old ordinances."

That new continent had its own music. The suffragist Rebecca Naylor Hazard wrote the lyrics for "Give the Ballot to the Mothers," sung to the tune of "Marching Through Georgia." It echoed the Civil War's theme of deliverance in the language of "jubilee," with women's suffrage, not abolition, as the current goal:

Hurrah! hurrah! we bring the jubilee!
Hurrah! hurrah! the homes they shall be free!
So we'll sing the chorus from the mountains to the sea—
Giving the ballot to the mothers.

Bring the dear old banner, boys, and fling it to the wind;
Mother, wife and daughter, let it shelter and defend.

Marchers heading up Fifth Avenue in New York City in a huge suffrage demonstration on Saturday, October 23, 1915.

"Equal Rights" our motto is, we're loyal to the end—
Giving the ballot to the mothers.

I T WAS A big, bold, contradictory time. As the twentieth century dawned, the nation had been growing both in scale and in ambition. In addition to suffrage, the
Progressive movements addressed the excesses of the Gilded Age, and by 1917, the
nation would be at war in Europe in a convulsive struggle with far-ranging implications at home and abroad. The America that had gone to war was undergoing seis-
mic changes as the country became more urban, more diverse, and more engaged in
the broader world. And there was, inevitably, fierce reaction to rising immigration,
a foreign war, agitation for women's suffrage, and persistent pleas for an end to Jim
Crow. The century's first decades gave us the NAACP and the American Civil Liberties Union—and, not coincidentally, a revived Ku Klux Klan, which began a reign
of terror at its refounding at Stone Mountain, Georgia, in the autumn of 1915.

The Klan was the most dramatic manifestation of white anxiety about the shifting nature of the nation. While women marched, African Americans fought, too, for
a rightful portion of the American promise. "The principle of racial and class equality is at the basis of American political life," Jane Addams said of the battle for civil
rights, "and to wantonly destroy it is one of the gravest outrages against the Republic."

A ND YET HERE was a great truth: Appomattox had been a beginning, not an
ending, as white Southerners, often abetted, explicitly and implicitly, by whites
in the North, secured legalized segregation after the Union victory. In the wake of
the war, the Virginia Confederate and journalist Edward Alfred Pollard argued for
the defense of the "Lost Cause" of white supremacy. The issue was no longer slavery
but white dominance, which Pollard described as the "true cause of the war" and the
"true hope of the South." The focus: the reassertion of states' rights and the rejec-
tion of federal rule.

In the summer of 1867, the former Virginia governor and Confederate general
Henry A. Wise traveled to Hanover, Virginia, for a fundraising appeal to construct
an Episcopal church. "There is now a bold and avowed attempt," Wise said, "going

"The battle we wage," W.E.B. Du Bois said of civil rights, "is not for ourselves alone but for all true Americans."

far beyond the emancipation of the blacks and the guardianship of freedmen to subject the white to the domination of the black race in the South and to make slaves of free men as well as freedmen of slaves . . . in order to create a balance of power to perpetuate the amalgamated and consolidated despotism of a new and mongrel republicanism." Turning his eyes northward, Wise appealed to feelings of racial, not sectional, solidarity. "If negro equality and domination can be forced on us," he said, "it can and must be forced upon the whites of the Northern states." Wise's agenda was clear: an alliance among defeated Southerners and other whites open to preserving white supremacy.

Many white Americans had feared a post-slavery society in which emancipation might lead to equality, and they ensured that no such thing should come to pass, North or South. Against terrible odds and through gloomy years, reformers continued to wage their long war to overcome racial injustice as the twentieth century began. In 1905, a group led by Du Bois met at Niagara, New York, to issue a declaration of principles. "We will not be satisfied to take one jot or tittle less than our full manhood rights," Du Bois said at the movement's second annual meeting at Harpers Ferry the next year. "The battle we wage is not for ourselves alone but for all true Americans. It is a fight for ideals, lest this, our common fatherland, false to its

*Founded in 1905, the Niagara Movement for racial equality helped lead
to the creation of the NAACP.*

founding, become in truth the land of the thief and the home of the Slave—a byword and a hissing among the nations for its sounding pretensions and pitiful ac-
complishment."

Note the allusion to the language of Francis Scott Key: "land of the thief" (not
"the free") and the "home of the Slave" (not "the brave"). "The Star-Spangled Banner," like the Declaration of Independence, was seen as a promissory American text,
and, like the women suffragists, the Niagara Movement, as the effort became known,
was calling on the nation to live up to its sacred founding document. "The morning
breaks over blood-stained hills," Du Bois said at Harpers Ferry. "We must not falter,
we may not shrink. Above are the everlasting stars."

Poetic words, but more-lasting poetry, written by James Weldon Johnson, was in

*The composers Bob Cole, James Weldon Johnson, and J. Rosamond
Johnson; the Johnsons created "Lift Every Voice and Sing," which
became known as the "Negro National Hymn."*

circulation in African American circles. Johnson was the author of the lyrics to "Lift Every Voice and Sing"; his brother, J. Rosamond Johnson, composed the music. The Johnsons had produced the piece for a Lincoln's Birthday celebration in Jacksonville, Florida, in 1900, where five hundred schoolchildren sang the song. "Shortly afterwards my brother and I moved away from Jacksonville to New York, and the song passed out of our minds," James Weldon Johnson recalled. "But the school children of Jacksonville kept singing it; they went off to other schools and sang it; they became teachers and taught it to other children. Within twenty years it was being sung over the South and in some other parts of the country. Today the song, popularly known as the Negro National Hymn, is quite generally used":

> Lift every voice and sing
> Till earth and heaven ring,
> Ring with the harmonies of Liberty;
> Let our rejoicing rise
> High as the listening skies,
> Let it resound loud as the rolling sea.
> Sing a song full of the faith that the dark past has taught us,

An image from the twentieth annual meeting of the NAACP, held in 1929; Du Bois and James Weldon Johnson are pictured on the bottom row, fifth and sixth from the left.

Sing a song full of the hope that the present has brought us.
Facing the rising sun of our new day begun,
Let us march on till victory is won.

Stony the road we trod,
Bitter the chastening rod,
Felt in the days when hope unborn had died;
Yet with a steady beat,
Have not our weary feet
Come to the place for which our fathers sighed?
We have come over a way that with tears has been watered,

We have come, treading our path through the blood of the slaughtered,
Out from the gloomy past,
Till now we stand at last
Where the white gleam of our bright star is cast.

God of our weary years,
God of our silent tears,
Thou who hast brought us thus far on the way;
Thou who hast by Thy might
Led us into the light,
Keep us forever in the path, we pray.

Lest our feet stray from the places, our God, where we met Thee,
Lest our hearts drunk with the wine of the world, we forget Thee;
Shadowed beneath Thy hand,
May we forever stand.
True to our God,
True to our native land.

The song's success was organic. "I have commonly found printed or typewritten copies of the words pasted in the back of hymnals and the song books used in Sunday schools, Y.M.C.A.s and similar institutions and I think that is the manner by which it gets its widest circulation," Johnson recalled. "Nothing I have done has paid me back so fully as being part creator of this song." Du Bois, who had helped found the NAACP in 1909, met Johnson in 1916, and by 1919 the organization had made Johnson's song its official hymn.

It is a song of tempered hope. It assumes that the present is better than the past

LIFT EVERY VOICE AND SING

This song's been cherished by the civil rights movement in its several incarnations. Written early in the twentieth century to commemorate Abraham Lincoln's birthday, it became known as the "Negro National Hymn." Sixty years after its composition, it was still cherished and sung in the movement of the 1950s and 1960s. After so much misrepresentation and exploitation of black people with minstrelsy and the pain of so many spirituals and hymns, I can see how this song finally felt like a proud representation of African American art, culture, and history.

Music makes us feel *seen,* and this song allowed a new image of African Americans to be seen within and without black culture. The lyrics acknowledge the past but sketch a hopeful picture of the future. Modern performers—from Beyoncé at the Coachella festival (where she was the first black woman to headline the event) to Aloe Blacc at Super Bowl 53—continue to keep the song and its message alive.   —T.M.

and prays that the future may be better yet. Johnson's verses express, too, a faith in America itself—a "native land" to which we owe allegiance. "There is nothing in 'Lift Every Voice and Sing' to conflict in the slightest degree with use of 'Star-Spangled Banner' or 'America' ['My Country 'Tis of Thee'] or other patriotic songs," Johnson observed in 1926. "It is fully as patriotic, among possibilities are that it may grow in general use among white as well as colored Americans."

Johnson's other poetry bore the same witness. In his "Father, Father Abraham," published in Du Bois's magazine, *The Crisis,* in 1913, Johnson wrote of Lincoln's martyrdom:

To-day we consecrate ourselves
Anew in hand and heart and brain,
To send this judgment down the years:
The ransom was not paid in vain.

At the March on Washington in August 1963, Benjamin Mays, the president of Morehouse College, quoted "Lift Every Voice" in his benediction. And a century after the founding of the NAACP, the Reverend Joseph Lowery recited the final verse of Johnson's song while offering the closing prayer at the 2009 inauguration of Barack Obama.

"God of our weary years," Lowery said, standing on the West Front of the Capitol, "God of our silent tears, thou who has brought us thus far along the way, thou, who has by thy might led us into the light, keep us forever in the path, we pray, lest our feet stray from the places, our God, where we met thee, lest our hearts, drunk with the wine of the world, we forget thee. Shadowed beneath thy hand may we forever stand—true to thee, O God, and true to our native land." Lowery then turned from past to present: "We truly give thanks for the glorious experience we've shared this day. We pray now, O Lord, for your blessing upon thy servant, Barack Obama, the forty-fourth president of these United States, his family and his administration."

In our own time, problems of race remain persistent. In her history of the song, *May We Forever Stand,* published in 2018, the Princeton scholar Imani Perry wrote, "There is no song that touches me so deeply, but while the Black National Anthem (or Negro National Hymn), 'Lift Every Voice and Sing,' is powerful, we should not be sentimentally attached to it or any other composition just for tradition's sake."

Yet the Johnsons' hymn speaks still. "I, like many other people," Perry wrote, "find singing 'Lift Every Voice and Sing' alongside other people of conscience to be one bulwark against a pessimism that threatens to descend at every turn." Not a bad legacy for a song that's been sung for more than a century.

I T WAS A busy day. On Wednesday, May 1, 1940, President Franklin D. Roosevelt drafted a letter to King George VI, stopped off for a visit with the White House doctor, and looked forward to lunch with Sumner Welles, the under secretary of state. There was much to think about, and to discuss. Adolf Hitler's Wehrmacht had struck Norway and was on the verge of its blitzkrieg through Western Europe. The invasion of France and of the Low Countries had been secretly scheduled for the next week. London was in chaos. "These have indeed been most crowded days & I have had to do my utmost to keep pace with the ceaseless flow of telegrams," Win-

"Over There": American soldiers along the Western Front, the scene of terrible trench warfare in the Great War.

ston Churchill, then the First Lord of the Admiralty, wrote during the assault on Norway. Churchill had held the same office during the Great War, two decades before, in the same years in which the young Roosevelt had served as assistant secretary of the Navy. The two were both transported back to the old cataclysm in the midst of the new.

"It is because you and I occupied similar positions in the World War that I want you to know how glad I am that you are back again in the Admiralty," FDR had written Churchill on Monday, September 11, 1939, on the occasion of Churchill's return to the cabinet. "Your problems are, I realize, complicated by new factors, but the essential is not very different." Roosevelt's message, Churchill said, "takes me back to 1914 and it is certainly a most unusual experience to occupy the same post fighting the same enemy 25 years later."

The Great War was very much on the president's mind on this springtime Wednesday in Washington. At 11:30 A.M., FDR presented the Congressional Gold Medal to George M. Cohan, the vaudevillian, performer, composer, and author of several songs that had played a role in the war effort in World War I under Roosevelt's old chief, Woodrow Wilson. Cohan had starred as Roosevelt on Broadway in a production called *I'd Rather Be Right,* and the cheerful president called out, "Well, how's my double?" as Cohan came into the Oval Office.

The medal had been authorized, as *The New York Times* headline put it, in recognition of Cohan's "old war songs"—songs that had brought the always-fractious country together in 1917–18 and that were resonant again in 1940. Cohan's "I'm a Yankee Doodle Boy," for instance, had been popular during the Great War.

I'm a Yankee Doodle Dandy,
A Yankee Doodle, do or die;
A real live nephew of my Uncle Sam's,
Born on the Fourth of July.

Like Francis Scott Key a century or so before, Cohan had also drawn inspiration from the Stars and Stripes.

You're a grand old flag
You're a high-flying flag
And forever in peace may you wave

You're the emblem of the land I love
The home of the free and the brave
Every heart beats true under Red, White,
    and Blue
Where there's never a boast or brag
"But should old acquaintance be
    forgot"
Keep your eye on the grand old flag.

In awarding the gold medal, Congress singled out Cohan's "Over There," an anthem
that played on the existing language of patriotism. It evoked the American Revolution's
"Yankee Doodle," employed the Revolutionary
phrase "Son of Liberty," and added the imagery
of global mission for a country long defined by
its distance from the Old World:

Johnny, get your gun, get your gun, get your
    gun.
Take it on the run, on the run, on the run.
Hear them calling you and me,
Every son of liberty.
Hurry right away, no delay, go today.
Make your daddy glad to have had such a
    lad.
Tell your sweetheart not to pine
To be proud her boy's in line.

Johnny, get your gun, get your gun, get your
    gun.
Johnny, show the "Hun" you're a son-of-a-
    gun.
Hoist the flag and let her fly
Yankee Doodle do or die.

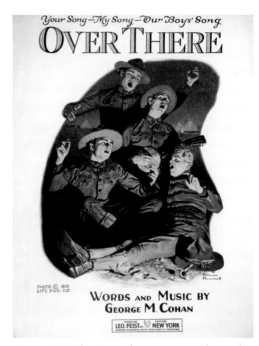

George M. Cohan's songs became immensely popular in wartime.

Pack your little kit, show your grit, do your bit.
Yankee to the ranks from the towns and the tanks.
Make your mother proud of you
And the old red-white-and-blue

Over there, over there,
Send the word, send the word over there
That the Yanks are coming, the Yanks are coming
The drums rum-tumming everywhere
So prepare, say a prayer,
Send the word, send the word to beware—
We'll be over, we're coming over,
And we won't come back till it's over, over there.

Cohan had written most of it in a burst in New York City and at his house at Great Neck, Long Island, after reading the headlines about Woodrow Wilson's declaration of war. Calling his family together, Cohan announced that he had a new song. "So we all sat down and waited expectantly because we always loved to hear him sing," Cohan's daughter, Mary, recalled. "He put a big tin pan from the kitchen on his head, used a broom for a gun on his shoulder, and he started to mark time like a soldier," as he broke into the words of "Over There."

Musing about his audience with FDR years later, Cohan recalled, "Funny about them giving me a medal. All I wrote was a bugle call. I read those war headlines and I got to thinking and to humming to myself. . . ." But, of course, "Over There" was more than a bugle call. It was an inspired, and inspiring, song of resolve and of duty—"show your grit, do your bit"; "Make your Mother proud of you."

The lyrics spoke, too, to an American sense of identity that could be traced as far back as John Winthrop—a vision of the nation's role as a universal force for good. "'Over There' became not only the most popular song of World War I but the manifestation of a perdurable American theme as well," Cohan biographer John McCabe wrote. "As Cohan often said, he had simply dramatized a bugle call, but in its incisive notes and words he had also delineated something elemental in the American character—the euphoric confidence that the coming of the Yanks was the march of the good guys to effect infamy's overthrow."

This sense of destiny had been evident as President Wilson delivered the April

1917 war speech that would so capture Cohan's attention. "The world must be made safe for democracy . . . ," Wilson said. "Its peace must be planted upon the tested foundations of political liberty. We have no selfish ends to serve. We desire no conquest, no dominion. . . . We are but one of the champions of the rights of mankind. We shall be satisfied when those rights have been made as secure as the faith and the freedom of nations can make them."

The Great War was an era of turmoil, dissent, and passion. In the name of national security, Wilson and the Congress restricted freedom of expression, passing legislation to protect the military draft from interference or protest; the Espionage Act of 1917 and the Sedition Act of 1918 criminalized dissent. As many as four hundred publications were censored, and Attorney General A. Mitchell Palmer was the architect, with J. Edgar Hoover, of controversial raids on suspected radicals. The federal trespasses on basic constitutional norms during this "Red Scare"—so called because of fears that Soviet Bolshevism was a threat to the United States—led to the formation, in 1920, of the American Civil Liberties Union.

The war itself gave rise to protest, a strain of sentiment embodied in 1915's "I Didn't Raise My Boy to Be a Soldier," a song written by Alfred Bryan and marketed, in sheet music, as "A Mother's Plea for Peace":

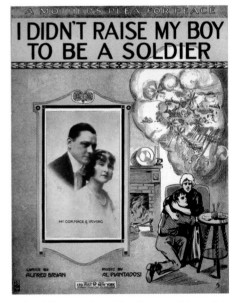

Subtitled "A Mother's Plea for Peace," "I Didn't Raise My Boy to Be a Soldier" was an early piece of protest music.

> I didn't raise my boy to be a soldier,
> I brought him up to be my pride and joy,
> Who dares to place a musket on his shoulder,
> To shoot some other mother's darling boy?
> Let nations arbitrate their future troubles,
> It's time to lay the sword and gun away,
> There'd be no war today,
> If mothers all would say,
> "I didn't raise my boy to be a soldier."

Another song, by George Graff, Jr., picked up the title of an old Civil War number, "Let Us Have Peace":

Lord God of love, let us have peace,
From war's vain sacrifice give us release,
Grant peace that victories war cannot know,
God of the Ages,
Thy mercy show.
Hast Thou not seen
Thy fields and meadows green
Red with the blood of men where war hath been?

OVER THERE and
I DIDN'T RAISE MY BOY TO BE A SOLDIER

In my mind, "Over There" is a classic patriotic song from the great world wars. I was intrigued by the lyric reference to every "Son of Liberty," which harkens back to John Dickinson's "Liberty Song" in the Revolutionary era. So much of music builds on prior ideas and themes, and it's something I've recognized in a lot of patriotic songs. It's as though we're all in an ongoing conversation about the country, about its greatness and its faults, and music is a vital part of that conversation. Listening to the original version of "Over There" by Billy Murray, I found it to be incredibly positive and uplifting—which, of course, was George M. Cohan's goal. War, as General Sherman said, is hell, and music is often one of the few tools that commanders and soldiers can deploy to remind them of why they're out there—or "over there"—risking everything.

Speaking of which: I simply can't imagine the pain a mother must feel at losing a son (or daughter) in war. "I Didn't Raise My Boy to Be a Soldier" is a forerunner to all the iconic anti-war music of the 1960s. This song brings home the real impact of the decision to go to war. It's not all about parades and glory; at heart, combat is brutal, and every soldier who falls lives on in the hearts of those who loved him (or, in the twenty-first century, her). Musically, it's intriguing that the song has the feel of a march juxtaposed against the message of peace in the lyrics. While melodically I'm called to battle, lyrically I'm called to contemplate the price that's to be paid for waging war.   —T.M.

FOR ALL THE difficulties of the age, there was always hope. After World War I, the poet Katharine Lee Bates, the author of "America the Beautiful," was told that American soldiers at Verdun, the scene of unspeakably bloody trench warfare, had marked the Armistice by singing her verses. The news brought tears to her eyes.

Composed after an excursion to Pikes Peak outside Colorado Springs in the Rocky Mountains in 1895, "America the Beautiful" had been set to the music of "Materna," by Samuel A. Ward. "The hymn has gone far afield, with the Young Men's Christian Association, the Young Women's Christian Association, the Society of Christian Endeavor, and the obser-

Katharine Lee Bates believed her poem "America the Beautiful," set to "Materna" by Samuel A. Ward, endured because "Americans are at heart idealists."

vance of the Sunday School Centennial," Bates recalled. "The Australian Christian Endeavorers have adopted it, setting it to music of their own and substituting the word, Australia, for America. It is sung in Canada with the refrain, 'O Canada,' and in Mexico with the refrain, 'Mi Mejico.' It has even gone into reform schools and prisons . . . and has been translated, for the benefit of our immigrants, into Italian and German."

O beautiful for spacious skies,
For amber waves of grain,
For purple mountain majesties,
Above the fruited plain!
America! America!
God shed His grace on thee
And crown thy good with brotherhood
From sea to shining sea!

O beautiful for pilgrim feet,
Whose stern, impassioned stress
A thoroughfare for freedom beat
Across the wilderness!
America! America!
God mend thine every flaw,
Confirm thy soul in self-control,
Thy liberty in law!

O beautiful for heroes proved
In liberating strife,
Who more than self their country loved,
And mercy more than life!
America! America!
May God thy gold refine

AMERICA THE BEAUTIFUL

The poetry of the lyrics is so visual: amber, purple, alabaster. This is one of those songs that can take you from the dark to the light in an instant, not least because of the colors Katharine Lee Bates evokes in her writing. Multiple melodies have been placed over the words through time, and it lends itself to so many interpretations on a musical level.

Bates was a poet, and you can tell: Her aesthetic sensibility clearly informed her verses. And she was a tough woman. In a tiny red notebook she kept as a girl, she wrote, "Girls are a very necessary portion of creation. They are full as necessary as boys. . . . Sewing is always expected of girls. Why not of boys. Boys don't do much but outdore [sic] work. Girls work is all in doors. It isn't fair."

It wasn't, and it began to change because of the suffrage movement led by women like Elizabeth Cady Stanton and Susan B. Anthony, among so many others. It's a movement that's still going, part of the unfinished work of the country.

—T.M.

Till all success be nobleness,
And every gain divine!

O beautiful for patriot dream
That sees beyond the years
Thine alabaster cities gleam
Undimmed by human tears!
America! America!
God shed His grace on thee
And crown thy good with brotherhood
From sea to shining sea!

In 2016, Barack Obama would tell *The New Yorker*'s David Remnick that Ray Charles's version of "America the Beautiful" would, for him, "always be . . . the most patriotic piece of music ever performed—because it captures the fullness of the American experience, the view from the bottom as well as the top, the good and the bad, and the possibility of synthesis, reconciliation, transcendence."

Charles himself had a similarly complex understanding of the piece. "Remember, I got to first feel the music, do somethin' with the song," Charles told *Rolling Stone* in an interview published in 1973. "And that's why in that album you have a song like 'America.' . . . I love this country, man. And I wouldn't live in no place else. You understand. My family was born here. My great-grandparents were born here. I think I got as much roots in this country as anybody else. So I think when somethin's wrong, it's up to me to try to change it. I was sayin' that America is a beautiful country. It's just some of our policies that people don't dig."

Bates would have likely agreed. "That the hymn has gained . . . such a hold as it has upon our people," Bates remarked, "is clearly due to the fact that Americans are at heart idealists, with a fundamental faith in human brotherhood." That idealism was under constant challenge, but Professor Bates was on to something: Only by staying on freedom's thoroughfare can our patriot dreams ever move from the ideal to the real.

*Marian Anderson sings from the steps of the Lincoln Memorial on Easter Sunday 1939;
seventy-five thousand people flocked to the National Mall to hear her.*

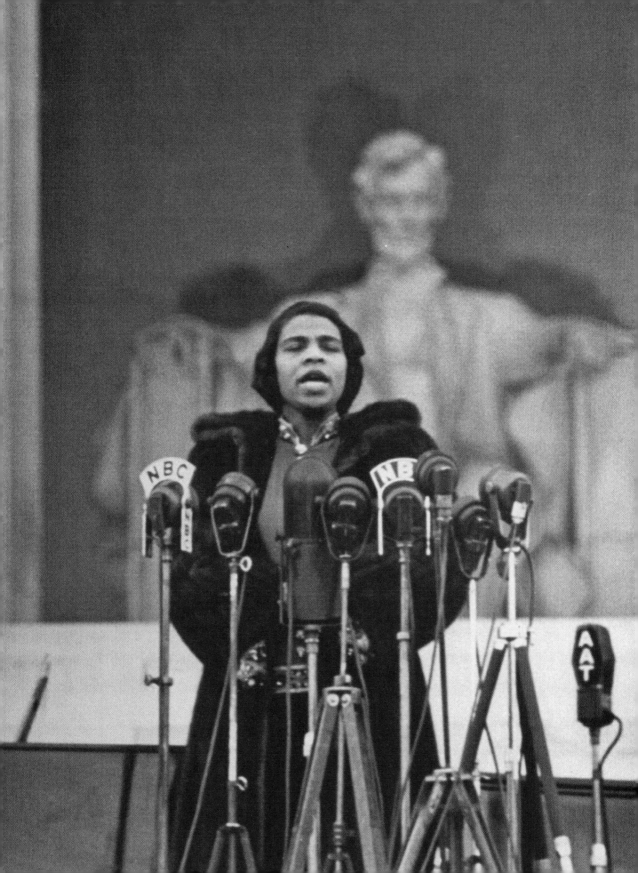

CHAPTER FIVE

AS THE STORM CLOUDS GATHER

"I've seen the dust so black I couldn't see a thing."

—WOODY GUTHRIE, on the Dust Bowl and the
Great Depression in the song "Dust Bowl Blues"

"Songs make history and history makes songs."

—IRVING BERLIN, on the coming of World War II

"A voice one hears once in a hundred years."

—ARTURO TOSCANINI, on Marian Anderson

THE CITY WAS thronged. On Thursday, September 3, 1936, tens of thousands of people lined the streets of Des Moines, Iowa, to catch a glimpse of President Franklin D. Roosevelt, who arrived by train at the Rock Island station at noon. Troops from the Fourteenth Cavalry stood at attention as uniformed buglers greeted the commander in chief, who emerged from *Pioneer,* his private carriage, balanced on the arm of his youngest son, John Roosevelt. Smiling broadly and waving to a cheering crowd, Roosevelt was transferred to an open car, where he sat next to the governor of Iowa and the mayor of Des Moines. Their destination: a meeting of Midwestern and Plains governors at the state capitol to discuss drought relief—a summit that included Roosevelt's opponent in the coming presidential election, Alf M. Landon of Kansas. The presence of the two major-party candidates in Des Moines, which was already unusually full because of the late-summer Iowa State Fair, created an electric atmosphere. 100,000 JAM CITY TO CHEER NOMINEES, *The Washington Post* reported. Police sirens blared as the president's motorcade inched its way through the city's business district. As the president rode along, he

The author of "God Bless America," Irving Berlin was a vital composer in both world wars, seen here playing for American soldiers.

waved his Panama hat to acknowledge the spectators, some of whom, *The New York Times* wrote, were standing six deep. Ticker tape came down in bursts, and the crowds were in what the *Times* called a "holiday spirit."

It was a classic, and common, scene from the annals of the Roosevelt presidency, a reign in which the aristocratic FDR managed to create an intimate bond with great swaths of the people—so much so that when he died, in April 1945, ordinary Americans would tell journalists: "I never met him, but I feel as if I lost my greatest friend." Such was Roosevelt's magnetism and power—a magnetism and a power on vivid display on that September Thursday in Des Moines, roughly seven years into the Great Depression.

Nearly half a century later, at least one admirer could recall FDR's parade from the train station to the capitol in great detail. A young sportscaster at Des Moines's WHO radio station had been visibly thrilled as he hurried to the window of his offices on Walnut Street to take in the motorcade. "Franklin Roosevelt was the first president I ever saw," Ronald Reagan told a gathering of Roosevelt family and New Dealers at a 1982 centennial celebration of the thirty-second president's birth. "What a wave of affection and pride swept through that crowd as he passed by in an open car . . . a familiar smile on his lips, jaunty and confident, drawing from us reservoirs of confidence and enthusiasm some of us had forgotten we had during those hard years. Maybe that was FDR's greatest gift to us. He really did convince us that the only thing we had to fear was fear itself."

Speaking in the East Room, Reagan, now the fortieth president, paid tribute to the Democrat for whom he had voted four times—in 1932, 1936, 1940, and 1944. "FDR was denounced by some as a traitor to his class," Reagan said. "But people who said that missed the whole point of what he believed in and what this country's all about. There's only one class and that's 'We, the People.'" The sight of Roosevelt in Des Moines, Reagan recalled, was when he had "first felt the awe and majesty of this office."

The kind words were more than a little surprising to some in the audience, not a few of whom had been skeptical of their host as they sat down to their lunch of lobster bisque and chicken Veronique. A former New Dealer himself, a self-described "near-hopeless hemophiliac liberal" from mid-century, Reagan had grown more conservative in the 1950s and early '60s and had changed parties. Since then Reagan had been seen in many quarters, as he put it during the 1980 presidential campaign, as a "combination of Ebenezer Scrooge and the mad bomber," bent on dismantling Roosevelt's legacy. At his inauguration in January 1981, amid high inflation and interest rates, Reagan had denounced the growth of the federal establishment—growth that had begun under FDR—and said: "In this present crisis, government is not the solution to our problem; government is the problem."

Yet there was no such talk in the East Room as Reagan warmly remembered FDR. "This great nation of ours is a caring, loving land," Reagan said. "Its people have a zest for life and laughter, and Franklin Roosevelt shared those qualities. But we're also a practical people with an inborn sense of proportion. We sense when things have gone too far, when the time has come to make fundamental changes. Franklin Roosevelt was that kind of a person, too." FDR, in other

Affirming his faith in the future, FDR addressed the Democratic National Convention in Chicago in 1932—the gathering that gave the party its theme song "Happy Days Are Here Again."

words, belonged not to the past but to the present and to the future. "Every generation of Americans has faced problems and every generation has overcome them," Reagan said. "Like Franklin Roosevelt we know that for free men hope will always be a stronger force than fear, that we only fail when we allow ourselves to be boxed in by the limitations and errors of the past." The president then offered a toast: to "Happy days—now, again, and always."

The reference was unmistakable, for Franklin Roosevelt and the song "Happy Days Are Here Again" were inseparable in the political imaginations of Americans conversant with the years of what the historian Arthur M. Schlesinger, Jr., called

"The Age of Roosevelt." Written by Jack Yellin, with music by Milton Ager, the song had been created before the October 1929 stock-market crash, for an MGM movie called *Chasing Rainbows,* which was released in early 1930.

The public heard it in the context of hard economic times and, as historians have noted, the song's "seemingly upbeat lyrics laughed off the Depression; better days had to be coming."

The song entered the nation's political consciousness at the Democratic National Convention at the Chicago Stadium in 1932, which had also been the site of the Republican convention. The venue's organist, Al Melgard, had prepared and played "Happy Days Are Here Again" for both conventions, but, as Donald A. Ritchie pointed out in an account of the 1932 campaign, "The song's bouncy rhythm seemed out of sync with the somber Republican proceedings and went unnoticed." Roosevelt, who was seeking the presidential nomination, had planned to have "Anchors Aweigh" as his theme song, reminding delegates and listeners on the radio of his tenure as assistant secretary of the Navy during the Great War. From his command post at the Congress Hotel, Roosevelt adviser Louis Howe listened to his secretary, a fan of "Happy Days Are Here Again," sing it out for him. Impressed, the wizened politico sent word to the hall to change course: "Happy Days Are Here Again" was now the FDR standard.

A fitting choice, for insistent optimism was one of Roosevelt's great gifts to the country. By 1932, the Great Depression had consumed the United States, and the nation was at risk of a violent break from democratic capitalism. In accepting the presidential nomination at the Democratic National Convention in Chicago that July, FDR addressed himself to the future. "Wild radicalism has made few converts, and the greatest tribute that I can pay to my countrymen is that in these days of crushing want there persists an orderly and hopeful spirit on the part of the millions of our people who have suffered so much," Roosevelt said. "To fail to offer them a new chance is not only to betray their hopes but to misunderstand their patience." Progress, Roosevelt believed, would come with thoughtful, straightforward engagement with the problems of the age. "I pledge you, I pledge myself," FDR said, "to a New Deal for the American people."

Roosevelt refused to concede that America's day was past. "This great Nation will endure as it has endured, will revive and will prosper," he told the country after taking the oath of office on Saturday, March 4, 1933. "So, first of all, let me assert my firm belief that the only thing we have to fear is fear itself—nameless, unreasoning, unjustified terror which paralyzes needed efforts to convert retreat into advance."

No less astute an observer than Winston Churchill, watching Roosevelt from London in 1934, understood the task FDR faced. "Many doubt if he will succeed," Churchill wrote in *Collier's* magazine. "Some hope he will fail. . . . But succeed or fail, his impulse is one which makes towards the fuller life of the masses of the people in every land, and which as it glows the brighter may well eclipse both the lurid flames of German Nordic self-assertion and the baleful unnatural lights which are diffused from Soviet Russia."

Privately, Roosevelt wondered if all would come out right—if he could, in the end, rescue capitalism and democracy from the existential threats of fascism and communism. A friend told him he might well be remembered as the greatest of presidents if he succeeded in resolving the Great Depression but that he would go down as the worst if he failed. "If I fail," Roosevelt replied, "I shall be the last one." Publicly, though, he never wavered in his belief that happy days would return.

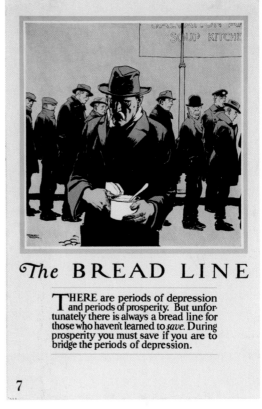

The Great Depression was of such scope that "Brother, Can You Spare a Dime?" had a tragically wide resonance.

ROOSEVELT'S SHOW OF confidence required immense effort, for no one—including the president himself—truly knew if the skies above would be blue again. In the popular "Brother, Can You Spare a Dime?" (Bing Crosby sang a successful version, released in 1932; the music was by Jay Gorney with lyrics by E.Y. "Yip" Harburg) the narrator is an unemployed veteran of the Great War—a man who has done his bit, played by the rules, kept his end of the bargain, and yet is now in a bread line, begging for the money he used to earn but, through no fault of his own, now can't. Plaintive and sad, the song was grimly applicable to innumerable shattered lives. The task that fell to Roosevelt: to rescue a nation torn between the hope of "Happy Days Are Here Again" and the soul-crushing reality of "Brother, Can You Spare a Dime?"

Woody Guthrie spoke to that "Can You Spare a Dime?" sphere of discontent in America. Born in Oklahoma in 1912, Guthrie was a wanderer, a folk philosopher, and one of the great American songwriter-musicians. "A song," he once said, "ain't nothing but a conversation fixed up to where you can talk it over and over without getting tired of it." In his songs (and in columns in the late 1930s for a communist publication, *People's World*) Guthrie was, in a way, scoring John Steinbeck's *The Grapes of Wrath* and Dorothea Lange and Walker Evans's Dust Bowl photographs. "A folk song," Guthrie wrote, "is what's wrong and how to fix it or it could be who's hungry and where their mouth is or who's out of work and where the job is or who's broke and where the money is or who's carrying a gun and where the peace is." He sang of

BROTHER, CAN YOU SPARE A DIME?

So melancholy—this one always hits me hard, especially the Bing Crosby version. It's about powerlessness and broken promises, which is what so many enduring songs are about. The narrator did everything he was supposed to do but the world failed him anyway, and that's where politics so often comes in, because if We the People can't help out individual people in trouble, then the fabric of the country frays.

I've always heard stories about the Great Depression, and I can only imagine how hard that was for people. I never considered myself poor growing up, but we definitely had to stretch to make ends meet. This song makes me think of all the times my mother fought to keep food on the table and how difficult it must have been to keep her spirits up. The thought of anyone who wants to work and provide for their family but can't absolutely tears me up. And it should tear all of us up.

—T.M.

During the Great Depression, the Dust Bowl devastated many lives amid drought, economic hardship, and lost hope.

the Dust Bowl and of broken lives, of fear and of endurance, depicting the Depression as an event on a scale with Armageddon. "I've seen the dust so black," Guthrie sang in "Dust Bowl Blues," "that I couldn't see a thing."

In 1938, the drift toward chaos and bloodshed in Europe prompted the composer Irving Berlin to excavate a song he'd written in 1918, "God Bless America." He arranged for the singer Kate Smith to perform it on her CBS radio show on Armistice Day 1938, and Smith would record the number in early 1939. (In 2019, news of her having sung "That's Why Darkies Were Born" and "Pickaninny Heaven" led the New York Yankees and the Philadelphia Flyers to ban her rendition of "God Bless America.") In the late 1930s, fearing Hitler, listeners did not have to think hard about what she meant when she spoke of "the storm clouds" gathering "far across the sea" or "the night" that required "a light from above."

Guthrie, though, heard something else in Berlin's verses: a triumphalism that portrayed America simplistically and sentimentally. And so Guthrie wrote a reply. Initially entitled "God Blessed America," it became "This Land Is Your Land," a song that grew in popularity during and after World War II. (By 1968, Robert Kennedy was suggesting that "This Land Is Your Land" ought to be the national anthem.) The language of the song was fluid, but one verse said:

> In the shadow of the steeple I saw
>   my people,
> By the relief office I seen my people;
> As they stood there hungry, I stood
>   there asking
> Is this land made for you and me?

It was a query that subsequent generations would repeatedly pose. The verse, however, has often been omitted from widely published and frequently sung versions of the song. Another pointed lyric about a "big high wall" with a "Private Property" sign—an image of capital-

Woody Guthrie's "This Land Is Your Land" was written in response to "God Bless America"—an example of the perennial American debate about the country's promise and reality.

istic coldness—also slipped into the mists. Why is a bit of a mystery, but the lyrics were perhaps thought too provocative for the broad public. Pete Seeger, an artistic heir to the Guthrie tradition, was praised for singing what are sometimes called the "forbidden verses" during a concert celebrating Barack Obama's inauguration in 2009.

T HE WAR TO bring the country closer to fulfilling the promise of the declaration was a longtime concern of Eleanor Roosevelt. The niece of one president and the wife of another, Mrs. Roosevelt was a tireless reformer, often pressing her husband to go further, faster, on issues of social justice, including civil rights.

One of her causes was anti-lynching legislation to address the brutality of extra-legal white murders of African Americans. Despite her pressure, Congress, dominated by white Southern Democrats, never enacted measures to curb the mob

THIS LAND IS YOUR LAND

Woody Guthrie was to rock and roll what Hank Williams, Sr., was to country music. He was a singer-songwriter in the way we think of it today, especially in country music, with a guitar in hand, scribbling lyrics on a notepad. It sounds simple, but lyrically he's singing with a cause and a message—a rebellion that would fuel those who came after, like Bob Dylan and Bruce Springsteen.

Guthrie was born in Oklahoma, and he was part of the great Dust Bowl Migration west, locating in California. He would ultimately move east to New York and begin to build his legacy as one of the greatest folk artists and writers. During World War II, he supported the cause by performing his songs, often on an acoustic guitar with a sticker that said THIS MACHINE KILLS FASCISTS.

The Dust Bowl Migration greatly influenced Guthrie's outlook on the world and his songwriting. In "This Land Is Your Land," he's survived that mighty struggle, and he's come to realize its vast beauty and bounty.

But he knows, too, that all is not perfect and may never be. His music is testament to the work that we all have to do, whether it's with a guitar or with the ballot.

—T.M.

violence that killed an estimated 3,500 African Americans between 1882 and 1968. Moved by reports of these murders, a New York City schoolteacher, Abel Meeropol, crafted a poem, "Strange Fruit," which Billie Holiday recorded in 1939. "I wrote 'Strange Fruit,'" Meeropol recalled, "because I hate lynching and I hate injustice and I hate the people who perpetuate it." It was an explicit, moving depiction of the horrors of lynching in the South.

Holiday's song offered no redemption, and the pain in her voice is moving even now. "Nobody could *say the words* even as Miss Holiday did," Lena Horne told the writer David Margolick, who wrote a book about the song. "It wasn't about singing. It was about feeling things artfully in your soul."

In early 1939, around the time Holiday was first singing "Strange Fruit" in the Café Society nightclub in Greenwich Village, the Daughters of the American Revolution refused to allow the singer Marian Anderson to perform at the organization's

Eleanor Roosevelt resigned from the Daughters of the American Revolution after the organization refused to allow Marian Anderson (right) to perform at Washington's Constitution Hall.

Constitution Hall, not far from the White House. The DAR's venue, the group said, was for "white artists" only. Mrs. Roosevelt, a member of the organization, resigned from the DAR in protest, writing in her "My Day" newspaper column: "They have taken an action which has been widely talked on in the press. To remain as a member implies approval of that action, therefore I am resigning." When Anderson was told of the First Lady's resignation, the singer said, "I am not surprised at Mrs. Roosevelt's action, because she seems to me to be one who really comprehends the true meaning of democracy."

An alternative plan took shape: The Interior Department, under Secretary Harold Ickes, would invite Anderson to sing at the Lincoln Memorial. "I don't care if she sings from the top of the Washington Monument," FDR said, "as long as she sings."

An African American who had won global acclaim, Anderson had "a voice one hears once in a hundred years," remarked the great conductor Arturo Toscanini. Born in Philadelphia in 1897, Anderson was dignity itself. Asked in later years about the controversy, she declined to attack the DAR for its discriminatory decision. "Music to me means so much, such beautiful things," she said, "and it seemed impossible that you could find people who would curb you, stop you, from doing a thing which is beautiful."

The concert was planned for 5:00 P.M. on Easter Sunday, April 9, 1939. Anderson's management and civil rights advocates joined forces, and much of official Washington lent its support to the effort. "In this great auditorium under the sky, all of us are free," Harold Ickes said in introducing Anderson to a national radio audience. "When God gave us this wonderful outdoors and the sun, the moon and the stars, He made no distinction of race, or creed, or color."

Alluding to the construction, at the Tidal Basin, of a memorial to Thomas Jefferson (it was to be dedicated in 1943), Ickes linked past and present. "Genius, like justice, is blind," he said. "For genius, with the tip of her wing, has touched this woman, who, if it had not been for the great mind of Jefferson, if it had not been for the great heart of Lincoln, would not be able to stand among us today a free individual in a free land. Genius draws no color line." He held the DAR to account, saying, "There are those, even in this great capital of our democratic Republic, who are either too timid or too indifferent to lift up the light that Jefferson and Lincoln carried aloft."

The sun broke through the clouds as Anderson sang. In a remarkable tableau, seventy-five thousand people had come to hear the concert, and the image of an African American standing in the same frame with Lincoln to sing of the "sweet land of liberty" was historic, stirring, *hopeful*. It was, *The Washington Post* reported, "one of the largest assemblages Washington had seen since Lindbergh came back from Paris in '27, a gaily-dressed Easter throng that stretched from the Lincoln Memorial to the Washington Monument Hill, and sent its northern flank as far as Constitution Avenue." Among their number were Supreme Court Justice Hugo L. Black, Secretary of the Treasury Henry Morgenthau, Walter White of the NAACP, and a number of senators.

A consummate professional, Anderson was nevertheless overwhelmed by the crowd and the setting. "There seemed to be people as far as the eye could see," she recalled. "It was a tremendous thing and my heart beat like mad—it's never beat like that before—loud and strong and as though it wanted to say something." Her selections for this Easter concert included "Ave Maria," "Gospel Train," and "Nobody Knows the Trouble I've Seen."

"It was another kind of communication," Todd Duncan, a Washington singer and voice teacher, told the *Post* when Anderson died, at age ninety-six, in 1993. "It was not a communication of mind, the heart or the flesh. It was a communication of the soul of man, which never dies and will never die. The feeling that I got that day is something that I had never, never experienced before . . . 75,000 to 85,000 people standing there . . . and the sight of Abraham Lincoln with this black woman standing in a beautiful fur coat in front of a big Steinway piano singing, 'My Country 'Tis of Thee,' is a thing you don't see or hear or feel every day. I know my soul has it and it will never, ever leave."

Toward the end of the program, Anderson sang a favorite spiritual, "My Soul's Been Anchored in the Lord":

I'm going to pray and never stop,
My soul's been anchored in the Lord.
Until I've reached the mountain top,
My soul's been anchored in the Lord.

The New Deal arts administrator, Edward Bruce, remarked that the concert was "the most civilized thing that has happened in this country for a long time." Writing in the *Post,* the journalist Ernest K. Lindley thought that Anderson had sung "My Country 'Tis of Thee" as it was never sung before. She had taken a different tack from Samuel Smith and from Oliver Wendell Holmes, who had praised the hymn's first-person formulation. Instead, Anderson sang, ". . . to thee *we* sing."

Listening, Lindley was struck by the concert's power. "The wet eyes all around me were not especially surprising, since there are a lot of sentimental folk in the world," Lindley wrote. "I retained just enough of my reportorial faculties to scan several United States Senators from Northern states who had wangled seats along the front of the upper platform where the photographers couldn't miss them. All of those particular senators can smile, shake hands, and be thoroughly agreeable quite mechanically. But I don't believe one of them could send the tears trickling down the sides of his nose just to please some of his constituents. When they began to quiver around the mouth and sniffle discreetly I was sure that something pretty big was happening."

The impressions of that Easter afternoon were borne out through the years. "It was a tour de force that stirred and sensitized the national psyche to the reality of

MY SOUL'S BEEN ANCHORED IN THE LORD and HE'S GOT THE WHOLE WORLD IN HIS HANDS

Marian Anderson was one of the finest singers—male or female—in American history. She was a thread between her Easter Sunday 1939 concert and the 1963 March on Washington; she sang "My Soul's Been Anchored in the Lord" at the first and "He's Got the Whole World in His Hands" at the second. I connect with the anchor theme in "My Soul's Been Anchored in the Lord." Here African American music has gone from the spiritual, which was more about getting through, to the political, with music as an instrument of social change. Their struggle may be mighty, but so is their anchor: "Until I reach the mountaintop . . . my soul is anchored." Anchored in the mountaintop. Glorious.

I imagine a lot of folks' first encounter with these songs was in the church. Both African American spirituals, they moved from the pews and the choirs to the people and the capital. And as a parent, the thing that really stands out for me with "He's Got the Whole World in His Hands" is how this song has become a song for our children. Its sing-along verses with a single hook line repeated over and over make it easy for everyone to join together, lifting voices in praise.   —T.M.

racial discrimination, even as it symbolized bedrock American values," the *Washington Post*'s Bart Barnes wrote in a 1993 obituary of Anderson. And the afternoon came to loom large in the history of the fight for racial equality. "Tactically, the modern civil rights movement came of age on Easter Sunday 1939," the historian Scott A. Sandage wrote. "The concert . . . was, significantly, the first black mass action to evoke laudatory national publicity and earn a positive place in American public memory (our sometimes collective, always political sense of our past)."

A successful precedent had been set. "We are on the right track," the civil rights activist Mary McLeod Bethune wrote on Monday, April 10, 1939. "Through the Marian Anderson protest concert we made our triumphant entry into the democratic spirit of American life." This much, at least, was clear: "Since the concert I have heard a good many comments to the effect that it served to improve race relations," Ernest Lindley wrote in the days after the concert. "Perhaps it did, although for all I know it may have the opposite effect, and certainly nothing seems to go very far toward solving one of the toughest problems our forebears have bequeathed to us. I think, though, that the contralto voice of this colored girl out of the slums of Philadelphia, singing from the steps of the Lincoln Memorial, made everyone who heard her feel a little nobler."

Anderson made another kind of history, too, when, in 1955, she became the first African American soloist to sing at the Metropolitan Opera in New York, as Ulrica in Verdi's *Un Ballo in Maschera*. Of her Met debut, Anderson recalled, "The curtain rose on the second scene and I was there onstage, mixing the witch's brew. I trembled, and when the audience applauded and applauded and applauded before I could sing a note, I felt myself tightening into a knot." The episode was recounted in her *New York Times* obituary, which added: "It did not matter that at 57 she was past her vocal prime. As Howard Taubman noted in his review in the *Times,* 'men as well as women were dabbing at their eyes' during the tumultuous ovation.'" They were cheering whatever her voice could do—and what her courage had already done.

T HE WEEK BEFORE the Anderson concert at the Lincoln Memorial, Adolf Hitler had delivered a bellicose speech at Wilhelmshaven in Germany. "We are so sure of ourselves because we are strong, and we are strong because we are united, and also because we keep our eyes open!" Hitler told his people. "He who does not possess power loses the right to live! . . . We thus realize that the 'Volksgenossen,' more than two million in number, who died in the Great War, did not die in vain. From their sacrifice a new Great German Reich has arisen. From their sacrifice this strong young German Reich of the 'Volk' has been called to life and has now stood its test in life. And in the face of this sacrifice, we would not fear any sacrifice if it should ever become necessary. This the world should take note of!" Then, on Thursday, April 6, 1939, Britain agreed to come to the defense of Poland in the event of attack.

These kinds of reports were as familiar as they were frightening. Hitler had come to power in Germany in January 1933, in the same season in which Roosevelt was sworn in as president. The führer's rise and reign unfolded as isolationist sentiment in America deepened. To many in the United States, foreign affairs were seen as depleting distractions. Roosevelt, however, believed, as he put it, that it was "a very small world," and that the rise and spread of airpower made America more vulnerable to foreign attacks. He did not win the argument in the thirties, when Congress enacted neutrality legislation designed to keep Americans from openly supporting any belligerent nation.

Hitler's ambitions and intentions were hardly mysterious. Germany had been driven by imperial desire in the Great War, and defeat had only made the nation hungrier to seize land to extend its borders and influence. Austria and the Sudetenland region of Czechoslovakia fell in 1938; Jews were targeted, terrorized, and killed in the Kristallnacht pogrom of November 9 and 10 that fall.

After Kristallnacht, and as war came in 1939, the English composer Michael Tippett wrote an oratorio about the systemic Nazi assaults on the Jewish people, *A Child of Our Time.* Tippett used the music of African Americans—the songs of Tubman and of Douglass, of enslavement and of jubilee—to evoke the themes of persecution and, possibly, of deliverance. "I sent to America for a collection of spirituals," Tippett recalled. "I opened the collection, and found that it contained words and tunes for every dramatic or religious situation that could be imagined." The volume he'd ordered: *The Book of American Negro Spirituals,* edited by James Weldon Johnson, with music arranged by J. Rosamond Johnson and with additional songs by Lawrence Brown. Tippett incorporated "Steal Away," "Nobody Knows the Trouble I See, Lord," "Go Down, Moses," "Oh, By and By," and "Deep River" into *A Child of Our Time.* So it was that the songs of the chained in the New World spoke to the crisis of the Old.

B Y THE LAST day of January 1939, just over two months before the Anderson concert, FDR had become convinced that, as he put it, there was "a policy of world domination between Germany, Italy, and Japan." That August, Hitler and Joseph Stalin concluded a mutual nonaggression pact, thus freeing Hitler to strike Poland and westward, which he did beginning on the first day of September 1939. Roosevelt was awoken at three o'clock in the morning by a call from the American ambassador to France, William Bullitt, who reported the news of the invasion of Poland. "Well, Bill, it's come at last," the president said. "God help us all."

May 1940 was a critical month. On Friday, May 10, Winston Churchill became prime minister at the grimmest of moments. "I felt as if I were walking with Destiny," Churchill recalled of his arrival at the pinnacle, "and that all my past life had been but a preparation for this hour and for this trial." In Washington, Roosevelt was less certain. Churchill was seen as a drinker, as an adventurer, as a sentimental-ist. Harold Ickes recalled that in a cabinet meeting that momentous Friday, the president said that he "supposed Churchill was the best man that England had, even if he was drunk half of his time."

On Thursday, May 23, 1940, Arthur Schlesinger, Jr., wrote in his journal, "Hitler is not a mere imperialist conqueror, somewhat nastier and gaudier than the Kaiser, but moved essentially by economic needs and governed by considerations of expediency. His war is not a war for markets and colonies. It is a revolution and a crusade. . . . [Hitler] is the prophet of a new religion, and like all prophets is out to convert or destroy. It is democracy or Nazism."

Roosevelt, however, did not believe America was ready to do much of anything for Britain. A poll in this period, William L. Langer and S. Everett Gleason wrote in their 1952 study, *The Challenge to Isolation,* "indicated that only 7.7 percent of the population was in favor of entering the war at once and only 19 percent believed that the country should intervene if the defeat of the Allies appeared certain, as against 40 percent that *opposed American participation under any circumstances*" [emphasis added]. These were thought to be the quarrels of other people, far away.

The aviator Charles Lindbergh was a leading voice of isolation. "It is not difficult to understand why Jewish people desire the overthrow of Nazi Germany," Lindbergh said. "The persecution they suffered in Germany would be sufficient to make bitter enemies of any race. No person with a sense of the dignity of mankind can condone the persecution of the Jewish race in Germany. But no person of honesty and vision can look on their pro-war policy here today without seeing the dangers involved in such a policy, both for us and for them. . . . Their greatest danger to this country lies in their large ownership and influence in our motion pictures, our press, our radio, and our Government."

In 1940, the president had told Henry Morgenthau, "If I should die tomorrow, I want you to know this. I am absolutely convinced that Lindbergh is a Nazi."

WHILE ROOSEVELT WAS constrained by the times, Churchill faced the exigencies of circumstance in a much more immediate way. Confronted with the collapse of France and the prospect of an invasion of England itself, the prime minister rallied the nation on Tuesday, June 4, 1940:

Even though large tracts of Europe and many old and famous States have fallen or may fall into the grip of the Gestapo and all the odious apparatus of Nazi rule, we shall not flag or fail. We shall go on to the end, we shall fight in France, we shall fight on the seas and oceans, we shall fight with growing confidence and growing strength in the air, we shall defend our island, whatever the cost may be. We shall fight on the beaches, we shall fight on the landing grounds, we shall fight in the fields and in the streets, we shall fight in the hills; we shall never surrender, and even if, which I do not for a moment believe, this island or a large part of it were subjugated and starving, then our Empire beyond the seas, armed and guarded by the British fleet, would carry on the struggle, until, in God's good time, the new world, with all its power and might, steps forth to the rescue and the liberation of the old.

The Battle of Britain in 1940 was, in Churchill's phrase, his nation's "finest hour."

After the Battle of Britain, the American Walter Kent composed a song, with lyrics by Nat Burton, to commemorate the defense of liberty in the skies over the English Channel. "(There'll Be Bluebirds Over) The White Cliffs of Dover" spoke of combat and captured the human longing for freedom and for peace.

SACRED MUSIC BROUGHT Churchill and Roosevelt together. In August 1941, at Placentia Bay off Newfoundland, Roosevelt and Churchill rendezvoused in secret to talk over the war—a war that the United States had not yet entered. At a Sunday morning service aboard the HMS *Prince of Wales,* the British prime minister did all he could to create a shared sense of mission with the president by drawing on their common Anglican vernacular. "I have," Churchill remarked beforehand, "chosen some grand hymns." Together with the assembled sailors, the president and the prime minister sat in the sea air and sang:

> O God, our help in ages past,
> Our hope for years to come,
> Our shelter from the stormy blast,
> And our eternal home . . .

There was the General Confession, the Lord's Prayer, and then the second hymn:

> Onward, Christian soldiers,
> Marching as to war,
> With the cross of Jesus
> Going on before!
> Christ, the Royal Master,
> Leads against the foe;
> Forward into battle,
> See, his banners go . . .

There was a reading from the Book of Joshua: "Be not afraid: for the Lord thy God is with thee whithersoever thou goest." More prayers followed, then a final hymn:

> Eternal Father, strong to save,
> Whose arm hath bound the restless wave,
> Who bidd'st the mighty ocean deep
> Its own appointed limits keep:
> O hear us when we cry to Thee
> For those in peril on the sea . . .

Vera Lynn's sentimental performance of "White Cliffs of Dover" captured the emotional currents of war.

Music had made the moment. "It was a great hour to live," Churchill recalled. To Elliott Roosevelt, his son, the president said, "If nothing else had happened while we were here, that would have cemented us. 'Onward, Christian soldiers.' We *are,* and we *will* go on, with God's help."

Matters were settled four months later with the Japanese attack on Pearl Harbor. At about five o'clock on the seemingly endless afternoon of Sunday, December 7, 1941—word of the Japanese strike had come a few hours earlier—President Roosevelt was preparing the war speech he was to deliver to Congress the next day. Summoning his secretary, Grace Tully, into his study, where he was seated at his desk, Roosevelt lit a cigarette, inhaled deeply, and went to work.

"Sit down, Grace," the president said. "I'm going before Congress tomorrow. I'd like to dictate my message. It will be short."

Roosevelt began, Tully recalled, with "the same calm tone in which he dictated his mail. Only his diction was a little different as he spoke each word incisively and slowly, carefully specifying each punctuation mark and paragraph. 'Yesterday comma December 7 comma 1941 dash a day which will live in world history dash the United States of America was suddenly and deliberately attacked by naval and air forces of the Empire of Japan period paragraph.'"

Roosevelt and Churchill met secretly at sea off Newfoundland in August 1941. At a shipboard church service, they sang hymns and prayed together. "It was," Churchill recalled, "a great hour to live."

The address, as promised, was brief. "I ask," FDR dictated, "that the Congress declare that since the unprovoked and dastardly attack by Japan on Sunday comma December 7 comma a state of war has existed between the United States and the Japanese Empire period end." The president made a final edit, changing his initial phrase "world history" into the more memorable "infamy."

Far from Washington, a Navy chaplain at Pearl Harbor was inspiring a fighting man's anthem. Under attack that Sunday morning aboard the USS *New Orleans,* Lieutenant Howell M. Forgy exhorted the crew to "Praise the Lord and pass the ammunition"—a phrase that led to a Frank Loesser song.

After Pearl Harbor, Irving Berlin returned to the Army's Camp Upton, on Long Island, to do his own bit for the war. "Songs make history and history makes songs," Berlin said. "It needed a French Revolution to make a 'Marseillaise' and the bombardment of Fort McHenry to give voice to 'The Star-Spangled Banner.'" Now it needed Irving Berlin.

He was born Israel Baline in Tyumen, Russia, in 1888. Berlin's parents fled anti-Semitic Cossack pogroms, coming to America in 1893. Young Berlin made his fortune as a Tin Pan Alley songwriter—he had started out as a singing waiter in New York City on Pell Street and at Union Square—and during the Great War he wrote *Yip, Yip, Yaphank,* an all-Army revue to raise money for the war effort. A favorite song from the show was the witty "Oh, How I Hate to Get Up in the Morning."

With America back in a second world war, Berlin reprised his work from two decades before, creating *This Is the Army,* a Broadway show that became a movie starring George Murphy, Alan Hale, Ronald Reagan, and Joan Leslie. (A turn by heavyweight champion Joe Louis, however, could not rescue the movie from trafficking in racial stereotypes, including what Berlin biographer Laurence Bergreen described as

THE WHITE CLIFFS OF DOVER and YOU'LL NEVER KNOW

"The White Cliffs of Dover" is incredibly pensive. Listening to Vera Lynn's version of this classic song, I am transported into her dream of what the future will bring. So wistful, it leaves any listener longing for the dark days to be over. And while I'm not sure Dover really *had* bluebirds, I can see how the song would capture the sentiment and imagination of the citizens of Britain and those who fought so valiantly in their skies.

"You'll Never Know" also resonated with the troops during World War II, and it's easy to see why. It was a hit in America with one of my idols, Frank Sinatra. Vera Lynn made it a hit in Britain, and many entertainers have recorded it through the years. Vera Lynn's version really embodies that feeling of separation for a soldier gone off to war—the longing, almost desperate tone in her delivery hits you straight in the heart. The track is sparse, letting the vocal stand out. She is so connected with this lyric and has placed herself within this song in a way that makes the listener not only believe everything she's saying but think that she's saying it straight to them. Performances like this are rare and should be treasured. It's an art to match songs with artists—and when it's done right, the result can be timeless.   —T.M.

"a transvestite blackface number.") There was a cameo of Kate Smith singing, of course, "God Bless America," and the climactic song, "This Time," was a pledge of America's determination "to win the war that wasn't won" in Europe after the Treaty of Versailles.

In wartime, the simpler the song, the more powerful it was, not least because life under fire was so emotionally complicated. Writing from Normandy after the launch of Operation Overlord in June 1944, Ernie Pyle, the *Stars and Stripes* correspondent, reported on the stark realities of war. "Now that it is over it seems to me a pure miracle that we ever took the beach at all," Pyle wrote. "For some of our units it was easy, but in this special sector where I am now our troops faced such odds that our getting ashore was like my whipping Joe Louis down to a pulp. In this column I want to tell you what the opening of the second front in this one sector entailed, so that you can know and appreciate and forever be humbly grateful to those both dead and alive who did it for you." He went on:

> Ashore, facing us, were more enemy troops than we had in our assault waves. The advantages were all theirs, the disadvantages all ours. The Germans were dug into positions that they had been working on for months, although these were not yet all complete. A one-hundred-foot bluff a couple of hundred yards back from the beach had great concrete gun emplacements built right into the hilltop. These opened to the sides instead of to the front, thus making it very hard for naval fire from the sea to reach them. They could shoot parallel with the beach and cover every foot of it for miles with artillery fire. . . .
>
> Medical corpsmen attended the wounded as best they could. Men were killed as they stepped out of landing craft. An officer whom I knew got a bullet through the head just as the door of his landing craft was let down. Some men were drowned. . . .
>
> Our men were pinned down for a while, but finally they stood up and went through, and so we took that beach and accomplished our landing. We did it with every advantage on the enemy's side and every disadvantage on ours. In the light of a couple of days of retrospection, we sit and talk and call it a miracle that our men ever got on at all or were able to stay on.

THE MOST MOVING music of the war was the music that moved the troops themselves—songs of longing and loss, of love and hope. There was "We'll Meet

Again," "You'll Never Know," and Big Band numbers by Glenn Miller, Benny Goodman, and others. It was the age of songs such as "Boogie Woogie Bugle Boy," and Miller and the Andrews Sisters each had a hit with "Don't Sit Under the Apple Tree (with Anyone Else But Me)." Miller, whose "Moonlight Serenade" was a signature song, lobbied to join the military once America entered the war. (Born in 1904, he was in his late thirties.) Bing Crosby wrote the government a letter of recommendation, saying that Miller was "a very high type young man, full of resourcefulness, adequately intelligent and a suitable type to command men or assist in organization." Commissioned in the Army Air Force, Miller set out, he said, to "put a little more spring into the

Sung from the perspective of a soldier at war, "We'll Meet Again" offered hope amid the gloom of separation.

feet of our marching men and a little more joy into their hearts." Regular military bands resisted Miller's attempts to bring the music forward from the Great War to the 1940s. "Look, Captain Miller," one is said to have complained, "we played those Sousa marches straight in the last war and we did all right, didn't we?"

"You certainly did, Major," Miller replied, according to the story. "But tell me one thing: Are you still flying the same planes you flew in the last war, too?"

Miller's mission to update military music beyond John Philip Sousa, author of such standards as "Stars and Stripes Forever," "Semper Fidelis" (the official Marine march), and "The Washington Post March," provoked a wartime controversy after *Time* quoted Miller saying, "There hasn't been a successful Army band in the country. . . . We've got to keep pace with the soldiers. . . . Why, there's no question about it—anybody can improve on Sousa." Miller denied making the remark, but the damage was done. As George T. Simon, an early drummer in Miller's band, wrote, "Deprecating Sousa in those war years was like insisting your local Boy Scout troop smoked pot."

Yet Miller pressed on, playing for the troops, for war bond drives, and over the radio. On a broadcast on Saturday, June 10, 1944, a few days after D-Day, he announced, "It's been a big week for our side. Over on the beaches of Normandy our boys have fired the opening guns of the long awaited drive to liberate the world." The band's opener that day was "Flying Home," a jazz number by Lionel Hampton (Ella Fitzgerald would later sing a powerful version) that, for African American GIs, signified a journey toward the kind of freedom at home they'd been fighting for abroad.

FRANKLIN ROOSEVELT DIED of a cerebral hemorrhage on the afternoon of Thursday, April 12, 1945, in his cottage at Warm Springs, Georgia. As the president's body was being moved to the train for the trip to Washington, a naval chief petty officer, Graham Jackson, tears streaming down his face, played "Going Home" on his accordion.

With that, Franklin Delano Roosevelt was taken north toward home—first to Washington and then to Hyde Park, New York, where he was buried in the rose garden at Springwood, his ancestral home on the banks of the Hudson. At Warm Springs, after "Going Home," Graham Jackson had played one of Roosevelt's favorite hymns, "Nearer, My God, to Thee." Its final verse:

> There in my Father's home, safe and at rest,
> There in my Savior's love, perfectly blest;
> Age after age to be nearer, my God, to Thee.

IN THE EDITIONS of The New York Times announcing the death of the president, the newspaper lamented the loss not only of FDR's mind but of his heart. "Gone," the Times wrote, "is the fresh and spontaneous interest which this man took, as naturally as he breathed air, in the troubles and the hardships and the disappointments and the hopes of little men and humble people." A grand piece of prose, composed on deadline for the paper that hit the streets on Friday, April 13, 1945, and surely true. And when President Reagan, in 1982, spoke of FDR's centennial, the language was equally eloquent: "Historians still debate the details of his intentions, his policies and their impact," Reagan said of Roosevelt. "But all agree that, like the Founding Fathers before him, FDR was an American giant, a leader who shaped, inspired, and led our people through perilous times. He meant many different things to many different people. He could reach out to men and women of diverse races and backgrounds and inspire them with new hope and new confidence in war and peace."

In the song "Tell Me Why You Like Roosevelt," Otis Jackson sang the same sentiments:

In the year of nineteen and forty-five,
A good president laid down and died.
I knew how all the poor people felt,
When they received the message "We've lost Roosevelt."

Woody Guthrie may have offered the most timeless memorial to the fallen Roosevelt. In a song addressed to Eleanor, Guthrie remembered FDR as a providential figure:

Dear Mrs. Roosevelt, don't hang your head and cry;
His mortal clay is laid away, but his good work fills the sky;
This world was lucky to see him born.

There is, really, nothing more to say on the matter. The world *was* lucky to see him born.

CHAPTER SIX

WE SHALL OVERCOME

"Bobby Dylan says what a lot of people my age feel, but cannot say."

—JOAN BAEZ

"Lord have mercy on this land of mine."

—NINA SIMONE, in "Mississippi Goddam," written after the bombing
of Birmingham's 16th Street Baptist Church, 1963

"In a sense, songs are the *soul* of a movement."

—MARTIN LUTHER KING, JR.

I N THE EARLY evening hours of Monday, October 22, 1962—the speech was
broadcast on television and on radio at 7:00 P.M. in the East—President John F.
Kennedy solemnly warned the nation of an existential crisis: The Soviet Union was
deploying missiles in Communist Cuba, an act that put enemy nuclear weapons less
than fifteen minutes away from Washington, D.C. When he'd first learned the news
on the morning of Tuesday, October 16, Kennedy was stunned. "He can't do this to
me," the president said as he was briefed, in bed, about Soviet leader Nikita Khrushchev's decision. In those first moments of one of the most perilous periods in
human history, Kennedy called his brother Robert Kennedy, the attorney general, to
give him the word. "Oh shit. Shit! Shit!" RFK said when he saw the photos of the
missiles.

The end of everything seemed all too possible. A year earlier, Robert Shelton of
The New York Times had reviewed a Greenwich Village performance by a young folk
singer, Bob Dylan. "His clothes may need a bit of tailoring," Shelton wrote of Dylan,
"but when he works his guitar, harmonica or piano, and composes new songs faster

*A commemorative portfolio of the Wednesday, August 28, 1963, March on Washington, published by the
National Urban League.*

than he can remember them, there is no doubt that he is bursting at the seams with talent." In the fall of 1962, Dylan had sat down at a typewriter and written the apocalyptic "A Hard Rain's A-Gonna Fall." It was, Dylan said, a "song of desperation . . . a song of terror." A biographer, Howard Sounes, wrote, "As the missile crisis reached its apogee in October, musicians all over the Village were playing the new song, including Richie Havens and Pete Seeger."

Born Robert Zimmerman in 1941 in Duluth, Minnesota, Dylan grew up in Hibbing—which he later described as a "town that was dying"—and legally changed his name in tribute to Dylan Thomas in 1962. Dylan liked to say that he'd wandered the country as a young man, once writing, "I was making my own [D]epression / I rode freight trains for kicks / An' got beat up for laughs / Cut grass for quarters / An' sang for dimes." In Greenwich Village and on the folk circuit, Dylan broke out, and his canon includes "The Death of Emmett Till," about the 1955 lynching of a black teenager in Money, Mississippi; "The Times They Are A-Changin'"; "With God on Our Side"; and many others. "Bobby Dylan says what a lot of people my age feel, but cannot say," Joan Baez remarked in the first half of the decade. In the second half, the *Village Voice* critic Richard Goldstein wrote, "Today, he is Shakespeare and Judy Garland to my generation. We trust what he tells us."

Should total nuclear war come in the fall of 1962, though, there would be nothing left to tell: Singer and audience would be annihilated. It was just possible, then, that "A Hard Rain's A-Gonna Fall" would be the last song Dylan would ever write.

But in Washington, the president delivered. Eighteen months earlier, JFK had authorized an ill-conceived invasion of Cuba at the Bay of Pigs. He was horrified by his failure to see the flaws in the planning. "How could I have been so stupid?" he asked in the aftermath. To make sense of the botched incursion, he turned to his predecessor, Dwight Eisenhower, a man whom he'd derided during the 1960 campaign but who suddenly proved to be a source of insight.

Eisenhower asked a crucial question: "Mr. President, before you approved this plan [for the invasion], did you have everybody in front of you debating the thing so you got the pros and cons yourself and then made the decision, or did you see these people one at a time?"

Kennedy's answer was not reassuring. "Well, I did have a meeting. . . . I just approved a plan that had been recommended by the CIA and by the Joint Chiefs of Staff. I just took their advice." He would never do that again. The haphazard planning of the 1961 Bay of Pigs would give way, in October 1962, to a crisis-management apparatus known as ExComm, or the Executive Committee of the National Security Council. As the missile crisis unfolded, Kennedy resisted being seduced by any one faction of advisers.

The author of two books—*Why England Slept,* about appeasement, and *Profiles in Courage,* about political valor—he was a man of the urgent present, intrigued by the past. History guided him hour by hour. In September 1960, Kennedy had written a review of a book by the British historian and strategist B. H. Liddell Hart, *Deterrent or Defense,* and highlighted this observation of Hart's: "Keep strong, if possible. In any case, keep cool. Have unlimited patience. Never corner an opponent, and always assist him to save face. Put yourself in his shoes—so as to see things through his eyes. Avoid self-righteousness like the devil—nothing is so self-blinding."

During those thirteen days, Kennedy considered things from Khrushchev's point of view and resisted rushing to judgment. A book he had read was very much on his mind: Barbara W. Tuchman's *The Guns of August,* which argued that the European powers had blundered into World War I. "The great danger and risk in all of this," Kennedy told his aides, "is a miscalculation—a mistake in judgment."

To JFK, history taught that pride, emotion, and hurry were the enemies of the good. "If anybody is around to write after this, they are going to understand that we made every effort to find peace and every effort to give our adversary room to move," JFK said at the time. "I am not going to push the Russians an inch beyond what is necessary." Reason trumped passion, and a deal—the removal of missiles in Cuba in exchange for the removal of missiles in Turkey—ended the crisis peaceably.

Kennedy was so elated that he joked that it was a good night to go to the theater. He might as well get himself shot, he was implying, for he would never again achieve such heights. Jacqueline Kennedy remembered, "when it all turned so fantastically," that her husband had said, "'Well, if anyone's ever going to shoot me, this would be the day they should do it.' . . . Because he saw then that he would be—you know, he said, it will never top this."

It was a glorious hour for diplomacy, for Dylan's "hard rain" had not fallen. "Even so," Howard Sounes wrote in his biography of Dylan, *Down the Highway,* "there was still a crackling energy in the air. Bob was the artist who had captured the zeitgeist in song, and he would do so again and again as the decade unraveled."

AND UNRAVEL IT did. In June 1963 in Tuscaloosa, Alabama, Governor George C. Wallace—who'd promised in his January inaugural to defend "segregation now . . . segregation tomorrow . . . segregation forever"—would fight the integration of the University of Alabama. In Mississippi, meanwhile, Medgar Evers, field secretary for the NAACP, would walk from his car to the door of his house in Jackson, when a shot rang out. *The New York Times*'s Claude Sitton described the assassination: "The sniper's bullet struck him just below the right shoulder blade. The slug crashed through a front window of the home, penetrated an interior wall, ricocheted off a refrigerator and struck a coffee pot. . . . Evers staggered to the doorway, his keys in his hand, and collapsed near the steps. His wife, Myrlie, and their three children rushed to the door. . . ." The assassin was a Klansman, Byron De La Beckwith, and in response Bob Dylan wrote "Only a Pawn in Their Game," a reflection on how white Southern politicians used race to keep poor whites consumed with hating blacks— "to hang and to lynch." And in September four little girls would die in a Klan bombing of the 16th Street Baptist Church in Birmingham.

The civil rights movement was powered by song. "The fear down here is tremendous," Phyllis Martin, field secretary for the Student Nonviolent Coordinating Committee, said. "I didn't know whether I'd be shot at, or stoned, or what. But when the singing started, I forgot all that. I felt good within myself. We sang 'Oh Freedom' and 'We Shall Not Be Moved,' and after that you just don't want to sit around anymore. You want the world to hear you, to know what you're fighting for!" To John Lewis, music was everything. "If it hadn't been for music, the civil rights movement would have been like a bird without wings," Lewis recalled. "I really believe that."

In Albany, Georgia, in December 1961, in the midst of a concerted campaign to integrate the city, police under Chief Laurie Pritchett were booking some 260 civil rights protesters. In the movement's spirit of nonviolence, the soon-to-be-imprisoned activists were singing songs such as "We Shall Overcome." There, deep in the segregated South, the jail guards found themselves "singing and humming songs along with the prisoners," *The New York Times* reported. There was a similar moment in Charlotte, North Carolina, at a sit-in, where an officer was seen singing "before he caught himself"; in Americus, Georgia, a guard was reported to have "requested a song" from his prisoners.

These examples were offered up in a front-page *Times* piece in the summer of 1962. "The songs, old and new, are used at mass meetings, demonstrations, prayer vigils, on Freedom Rides, in jails and before sit-ins," the critic Robert Shelton wrote. "The music rings with the bombast of election songs, the sanctity of marching tunes for a holy crusade and the spirit-building of fraternity anthems." Shelton had an eye for the important trend.

In chronicling the civil rights movement, Shelton noted that a "new tributary of 'freedom songs,' bold words set to old melodies, is making the deep river of Negro protest in song run faster." To the tune of "Go Down, Moses," for example, activists who were resisting Chief Pritchett in Albany sang:

Go down, Kennedy,
Way down in Georgia land,
Tell old Pritchett
To let my people go.

Such topical verses played their role, but the foundational music of faith remained central. "We all share the same songs," Martin Luther King, Jr., told the *Times*. "They give the people new courage and a sense of unity. I think they keep alive a faith, a radiant hope, in the future, particularly in our most trying hours." In one of those trying hours in Georgia, a state NAACP official recalled, it was religious music that reassured and pointed the way forward at an organizing meeting. "The people were cold with fear," the official said. "Music did what prayer and speeches could not do in breaking the ice."

And songs could put the white forces of oppression on notice. Bernice Johnson Reagon recalled a moment in Dawson, Georgia, where the police did not seem disposed to join in the music. "I sat in a church and felt the chill that ran through a small gathering of Blacks when the sheriff and his deputies walked in," Reagon said. "They stood at the door, making sure everyone knew they were there. Then a song began. And the song made sure that the sheriff and his deputies knew we were there. We became visible, our image was enlarged, when the sound of the freedom songs fill all the space in that church."

Music, then, could be a tool of justice. "In a sense, songs are the *soul* of a movement," King had observed in a *Playboy* interview published in January 1965. "Consider, in World War II, '*Praise the Lord and Pass the Ammunition*,' and in World War I, '*Over There*' . . . and during the Civil War, '*Battle Hymn of the Republic*' and '*John Brown's Body*.' A Negro song anthology would include sorrow songs, shouts for joy, battle hymns, anthems. Since slavery, the Negro has sung throughout his struggle in America. 'Steal Away' and 'Go Down, Moses' were the songs of faith and inspiration which were sung on the plantations. For the same reasons the slaves sang, Negroes today sing freedom songs, for we, too, are in bondage. We sing out our determination that 'We shall overcome, black and white together, we shall overcome someday.'"

The lyrics King chose to underscore—"We Shall Overcome"—were from the anthem of the movement:

We shall overcome, we shall overcome,
We shall overcome someday;
Oh, deep in my heart, I do believe,
We shall overcome someday.

The history of "We Shall Overcome" is complicated and circuitous. Scholars can identify at least seven antecedents or, to shift the metaphor, seven tributaries that formed the river of the song that we know now. As traced by Victor V. Bobetsky, a professor of music at Hunter College who edited a collection of essays on the question, there was the eighteenth-century Italian hymn tune "O Sanctissima"; "No More Auction Block" (closely related to "Many Thousands Gone," a Fisk Jubilee number, and which also helped inspire "Blowin' in the Wind"); Charles Albert Tindley's 1900 hymn "I'll Overcome Someday"; Roberta Evelyn Martin's 1945 "I'll Be Like Him Someday"; Kenneth Morris and Atron Twigg's "I'll Overcome Someday"; the hymn "I'll Be All Right"; and the labor movement's "I Will Overcome." And finally, in the 1950s, "We Shall Overcome" emerged.

In the middle of the twentieth century a version was sung during union protests, and the musician Pete Seeger heard a form of the song from Zilphia Horton of the Highlander Folk School in Tennessee. "I Will Overcome"—the original lyric—became "We Shall Overcome." Like the song itself, the shift from "will" to "shall" is shrouded in folk mystery. "It could have been me," Seeger recalled, "but it might have been Septima Clark, the director of education at Highlander. She always preferred 'shall,' since it opens up the voice and sings better." After he heard Seeger sing it at Highlander in 1957, Martin Luther King, Jr., remarked, "The song really sticks with you, doesn't it?"

As much hymn as ballad, "We Shall Overcome" has a kind of stateliness, a certain

WE SHALL OVERCOME and I HAVE A DREAM

When I hear "We Shall Overcome," I think of Dr. Martin Luther King, Jr. I think most of us do. We hear it and we see the photographs of those brave souls who marched and who died in the towns and cities that so many of us love but that, not too long ago, were battlefields.

I also hear passages from Dr. King's speeches—which were really sermons, calling on America to repent and make amends, to be who we said we were—intermingled with the simple but powerful words that came out of the labor and civil rights protest movements.

And in it I sense the power of music to move people. The brilliance of "We Shall Overcome" lies in its capacity for many different voices to join in—a fitting metaphor if ever there was one. A folk song, it has all the hallmarks of great folk music in that it summons the listeners to become singers—it's music as action.

With Dr. King's "I Have a Dream"—not a song, but a kind of prose poetry—I hear the passion from *all* of Dr. King's sermons. I have recollections of seeing clips of Dr. King's speech at the March in Washington from very early on in my life. Indeed, this speech deeply touched me and made me realize for the first time the strength in words delivered masterfully. Politicians, preachers, and singers are really in the same business—using sound to move hearts and change minds. More than half a century after his assassination in Memphis, Dr. King sings still.

—T.M.

dignity. "It made us feel we could face almost anything—the storms of the movement, the storms of life itself," John Lewis recalled. "Nobody could turn us around." Lewis's memories of the movement are set to music. When he thinks of Mississippi, he remembers sitting in a field in Greenwood with "Bobby Dylan—he was singing, quietly, for us." And when he thinks of Alabama, he recalls the lyrics he and his fellow SNCC volunteers would make up on the spot:

Oh, Wallace, you can never jail us all
Segregation's gonna fall.

They'd sing these improvised words with conviction, for they knew that no matter how tortuous the path to justice, justice was in fact on their side.

The Freedom Singers, whose roots lay in the Albany Movement, exemplified the theme of hope, taking the harsh realities on the ground and seeking to see the terrors of the day as surmountable challenges. They sang "Ain't Gonna Let Nobody Turn Me Around," listing injunctions, hatred, racism, injustice, and jail cells as obstacles that would be overcome on the march to "freedom land." In 2010, they performed the song in the East Room of the White House for President Barack Obama, a world away and a half century on from the early 1960s. Bernice Johnson Reagon (who was onstage with Rutha Harris, Charles Neblett, and Toshi Reagon) stopped early in the number to tell the audience that they had to sing along—because, she said, "you can never tell when you might need it!"

The movement had its national aspects, and popular music had long at least softened the harsher edges of racial division. As a teenager, the singer-songwriter Carole King first encountered genuine diversity through music. The New York radio personality Alan Freed would hold live shows, and King remembered an Easter Jubilee production at the Brooklyn Paramount Theater. Boarding the train at Sheepshead Bay, King was struck by the size of the crowds headed to the show. "Other than a friend of my dad's from the firehouse," King wrote in her memoir *A Natural Woman*, "I had rarely seen people of color in my neighborhood unless they were there to deliver furniture, clean houses, or perform other menial tasks. In April 1955, not only was Alan Freed's stage integrated, the audience was polychromatic." After the performance, King and her date were by the stage door and glimpsed LaVern Baker, B. B. King, the Moonglows, Mickey Baker, and the Penguins. She was hooked. "At that moment I knew I wanted to mean something to these people," King recalled. "I didn't want to *be* one of them. I just wanted them to know who I was and consider me worthy of respect." At Freed's 1957 Labor Day revue, King was electrified when Little Richard lit up the stage. "He began to sing and play the piano with an eruption of energy that continued unabated for decades," King recalled. "Though I knew little about the gospel music that had informed him, Little Richard's powerful presence that night was *suffuuuuused* with the spirit. It was a remarkable experience for this Jewish teenager to hear him sing nonsense syllables with the full capability of an astonishing vocal range that complemented the blazing rhythm coming out of his fingers."

Now, in the early 1960s, northern voices like Bob Dylan's offered consolation and support to those in the South. "Blowin' in the Wind," "This Little Light of Mine," "Oh Freedom," and "Woke Up This Morning with My Mind Stayed on Freedom" joined "We Shall Overcome" as part of the Northern folk branch of the music of the movement. "I love my country, but I am ashamed of it," the folk singer and composer Tom Paxton, whose songs included "The Dogs of Alabama," said in midsummer 1963. "I feel we have let our brothers and our countrymen down and only by righting this wrong can we hold our heads high again. However little this song may help, at least it's one more nail in the coffin of Jim Crow."

DYLAN'S WORK IN particular helped spark other artists. After "Blowin' in the Wind," for example, Sam Cooke wrote "A Change Is Gonna Come." A son of the Mississippi Delta, Cooke was a gospel singer—he first came to prominence with the group The Soul Stirrers—who made a pioneering professional shift into popular music and was a successful music-business entrepreneur. His hits included "You Send Me," "Chain Gang," and "Twisting the Night Away"; the Rock & Roll Hall of Fame—Cooke was inducted, posthumously, in 1986—describes him as "the definitive soul man . . . seductive, devoted, elegant, and moving. These qualities, combined with his dazzling, pure voice, made him irresistible to audiences regardless of race or religion."

"A Change Is Gonna Come," released in late 1964, is Cooke's most political song. Reflecting on the song's fiftieth anniversary, the music writer David Cantwell argued in a *New Yorker* essay that Cooke and Dylan "were wading up different streams of the American song for inspiration. Dylan found much of his melody in the nineteeth-century black spiritual 'No More Auction Block for Me' . . . , while his voice and phrasing, and his austere and static strum, are indebted to the Depression-era folk style of Woody Guthrie. By contrast, the melody to 'A Change Is Gonna Come,' with

The Rock & Roll Hall of Fame calls Sam Cooke "the definitive soul man."

its long dynamic lines that trek the peaks and valleys of arranger Rene Hall's lush orchestral landscape, shows Cooke working off of Tin Pan Alley standards, film music, and show tunes." Cantwell believed that Cooke was drawing in part on "Ol'

Man River," the number from Jerome Kern and Oscar Hammerstein's 1927 musical "Show Boat," a song generally associated with Paul Robeson. "A Change Is Gonna Come," Cantwell wrote, was a formidable thing: "brooding but bright."

Ray Charles had recently (in 1963) recorded his own cover of "Ol' Man River," and Chuck Berry had released "Promised Land" in 1964, a rock-and-roll number describing a cross-country journey from Norfolk, Virginia, through the segregated South to a new day in California. Berry wasn't known to be political, which makes "Promised Land" a sign of how pervasive the civil rights movement had become and how the convention of "masking" (the conveyance of political meaning in religious or, sometimes, in seemingly innocuous terms) continued to be essential. Berry was singing about the route of the Freedom Rides but never said so directly, thus making the song playable on the radio.

Curtis Mayfield of the Impressions was a master of masking. Reflecting on his "Keep on Pushing," a song about the determination to press on against all odds and

A CHANGE IS GONNA COME

Two things strike me about Sam Cooke and this song. First is his nature as a true artist. At the top of his game, he took a huge creative risk with "A Change Is Gonna Come." Born in Mississippi but raised in Chicago, Sam experienced the horrors of the Jim Crow South firsthand while touring. He saw folk artists like Dylan writing clever protest songs and knew that he had an even larger platform through his success in pop music. (He was ahead of his time in business, too, having started his own publishing company and record label.) Sam could be heard by both black and white audiences at once and deliver an individual message to both. There's a pain in his voice as he addresses the issue of segregation, and yet a strength that he's certain things will get better ("I *know* a change is gonna come") at a time when he couldn't really be so certain.

Second was his artistic bravery. As a musician with hits, there's always pressure to keep doing what you've done. I am grateful—and inspired—that Sam Cooke didn't do that. He was brave. He wrote a song of truth and hope at a time when being careful and putting out another "Twist" would have been easier and far less risky.

—T.M.

"If they ask you who you are," Odetta said at the march, "tell them you're a child of God."

all obstacles, Mayfield observed, "Gospel was your foundation and there's been many a song coming from the black church. All you had to do was change some few lyrics. 'Keep on Pushing' was intended, written[,] as a gospel song. But all I needed to do to lock it in with the Impressions was say 'I've got my strength' instead of 'God gave me strength.'" Other examples of songs heard very differently by white and black audiences include Ray Charles's "Georgia On My Mind," which he recorded in 1960; Stevie Wonder's "I Was Made to Love Her"; Martha Reeves's "Dancing in the Street"; and Ruby and the Romantics' "Our Day Will Come."

Chuck Berry's apparently apolitical hit "Johnny B. Goode" fell into this category, too. In his autobiography, Berry expressed pride that the song is the story of talent, perseverance, and success. "I imagine most black people naturally realize but I feel safe in stating that NO white person can conceive of the feeling of obtaining Caucasian respect in the wake of a world of dark denial, simply because it is impossible to view the dark side when faced with brilliance," Berry wrote. "'Johnny B. Goode' was created as all other things and brought out of a modern dark age. With encouragement he chose to practice, shading himself along the roadside but seen by the brilliance of his guitar playing. Chances are you have talent. But will the name and the light come to you? No! You have to 'Go!'"

AT THE MARCH on Washington for Jobs and Freedom on Wednesday, August 28, 1963, Joan Baez sang "We Shall Overcome" (as well as "Oh Freedom") to the crowd on the National Mall; she was one of fourteen performers who were an official part of the day of speeches and solemnities. The songs of the March on

Joan Baez, Bob Dylan, and Peter, Paul, and Mary performed at the March on Washington.

Washington offer a microcosm of the political panoply of life in these years as gospel and folk, and black and white, came together to acknowledge the difficulty of the struggle and the justice of the claims of those seeking equality.

The marchers themselves sang en route to and on the mall. From the microphone, Odetta cried out, "If they ask you who you are, tell them you're a child of God," and sang "I'm On My Way." Dylan sang "Only a Pawn in Their Game" (unimpressed, Russell Baker of the *Times* called it "a lugubrious mountain song") and, with Baez, "When the Ship Comes In," which struck a deliverance theme.

Peter, Paul, and Mary performed "If I Had a Hammer" ("The Hammer Song") and Dylan's "Blowin' in the Wind," which they'd already recorded and released on Tuesday, June 18, 1963. A huge hit, their rendition of "Blowin' in the Wind" was reported to be "the fastest-selling single in the history of Warner Records," and it was resonating culturally and politically. "Radio stations in Cleveland, Washington, Philadelphia, and Worcester, Mass., have played 'Blowin in the Wind' every hour on the hour," *The New York Times* reported, "some as a pop tune and others as a broadcast 'editorial.'" The Freedom Singers were there, and Mahalia Jackson sang two gospel songs—"I Been 'Buked and I Been Scorned" and "How I Got Over."

Jackson did more than sing. When Martin Luther King stepped to the microphones for his remarks, he did not begin as well as he'd hoped. His sermon had been

Mahalia Jackson sang "I Been 'Buked and I Been Scorned" and "How I Got Over"; she also prompted King, as she put it, to "Tell 'em about the dream."

drafted by too many hands late the previous night at the Willard Hotel, and one sentence he was about to deliver was particularly awkward: "And so today, let us go back to our communities as members of the international association for the advancement of creative dissatisfaction."

He'd begun to extemporize, searching for the right words to stir the crowd, when Jackson, who was standing nearby, spoke up. "Tell 'em about the dream, Martin," Jackson said. King left his text altogether at this point. "I have a dream," King continued, "that one day this nation will rise up, live out the true meaning of its creed: 'We hold these truths to be self-evident, that all men are created equal.'"

Drawing on "My Country 'Tis of Thee," King projected an ideal vision of an exceptional nation:

> I have a dream today. . . .
>   I have a dream that one day every valley shall be exalted, every hill and mountain shall be made low, the rough places will be made plain, and the crooked

BLOWIN' IN THE WIND

If there ever was an answer that's hard to understand, it would be "the answer" that Bob Dylan tells us is "blowin' in the wind."

Maybe that's a huge piece of this masterpiece—the ambiguity. He leaves it up to us to figure out what it all means. Lord knows this can be frustrating, but sometimes poetry is just that: confounding and confusing at first, then, if it's truly great art, the confusion gives way to illumination. Maybe not a five-point program for progress, or a clearly delineated yes-or-no answer, but a new angle of vision.

Some of the most powerful songs let you fill in the gaps, leaving intentional space in words or thoughts or unusual phrases that challenge the listener to think and reflect. There is huge power in that.   —T.M.

places will be made straight, and the glory of the Lord shall be revealed, and all flesh shall see it together.

This is our hope. This is the faith that I go back to the South with. With this faith we will be able to hew out of the mountain of despair a stone of hope. With this faith we will be able to transform the jangling discords of our nation into a beautiful symphony of brotherhood. With this faith we will be able to work together, to pray together, to struggle together, to go to jail together, to stand up for freedom together, knowing that we will be free one day.

This will be the day when all of God's children will be able to sing with new meaning: "My country, 'tis of thee, sweet land of liberty, of thee I sing. Land where my fathers died, land of the pilgrims' pride, from every mountainside, let freedom ring!'"

By closing with the words of Samuel Francis Smith, words composed 132 years before in Andover and once sung from these steps by Marian Anderson, words lifted countless times by countless Americans, words of freedom and of aspiration, King framed the civil rights cause as a fundamentally *American* cause.

Marian Anderson sang that day, thus linking her 1939 breakthrough moment with that of the present. She was offering, she told the crowd, a "Negro spiritual,"

By summoning the words of Samuel Francis Smith in "My Country 'Tis of Thee" in his peroration, King framed the civil rights cause as a fundamentally American one.

"He's Got the Whole World in His Hands"—old words now being sung to bring about a new world.

THE GLOW DID not last. On Sunday morning, September 15, 1963, in Birmingham, Alabama—the third Sunday after the March on Washington—fourteen-year-old William Bell was getting ready for church when he heard the explosion. It was 10:22 A.M., and the sound of the dynamite going off at the 16th Street Baptist Church roared across the city. The noise startled the Bells, who lived nearly three miles away on Fifth Avenue Southwest, in the city's Titusville neighborhood. Young Bell's father rushed him and the rest of the family into the car and drove to the church, where they found chaos and tragedy. Four young girls, Bell's contemporaries, had been massacred by a white supremacist's bomb: Denise McNair, age eleven, and Carole Robertson, Cynthia Wesley, and Addie Mae Collins, all fourteen. "Every individual in this town knew at least one of the girls or knew their families," Bell, who grew up to serve as Birmingham's mayor, recalled. "Carole Robertson is a cousin of mine. Denise McNair went to school with my brother. Her mother taught my brother. You felt it, the pain of it."

September 15 was the annual "Youth Day" at the 16th Street church. The girls were gathering before the 11:00 A.M. service—a service they were to lead in the sanctuary. They had finished the day's Sunday school lesson in Mrs. Ella C. Demand's class (its title: "The Love That Forgives") when the dynamite hidden by a group of Ku Klux Klansmen went off. "Short of a mass holocaust," *The Washington Post* wrote from Birmingham, "the bombing of the Negro church last Sunday must be considered a maximum tragic failure in race relations."

Denise McNair, 11; Carole Robertson, 14; Addie Mae Collins, 14; and Cynthia Wesley, 14, were murdered in the Klan bombing of Birmingham's 16th Street Baptist Church on Sunday, September 15, 1963.

News of the attack reached a young musician, Nina Simone, as she sat on that Sunday morning in her garage-apartment hideaway in Mount Vernon, New York. Descended from enslaved black Southerners, Simone had been born in Tryon, North Carolina, in 1933 and was making her mark in the New York world of soul music as the movement gathered momentum. She was friends with Langston Hughes and James Baldwin, but she acknowledged that her focus was largely on her career and her young family, not on civil rights. "I was always aware of what the vanguard of black artists and thinkers were concerned with," Simone recalled, "but I wasn't an activist in any sense; I heard the conversations flow around me at Langston's or in the Blue Note with Jimmy Baldwin . . . and a political awareness seeped

"It was more than I could take," Nina Simone said of the news of the attack on the 16th Street Baptist Church, "and I sat struck dumb in my den like St. Paul on the road to Damascus."

into me without my having even to think about it. But I wasn't taking the trouble to educate myself in an organized way—where would I find the time?"

Then came the Evers assassination and the 16th Street church bombing. "It was more than I could take, and I sat struck dumb in my den like St. Paul on the road to Damascus," Simone recalled. "I suddenly realized what it was to be black in America in 1963, but it wasn't an intellectual connection . . . it came as a rush of fury, hatred, and determination."

In the confusion and the rage of the moment, Simone collected a bunch of tools and tried, incoherently, to assemble a homemade gun. "I had it in my mind to go out and kill someone, I didn't know who, but someone I could identify as being in the way of my people getting some justice for the first time in three hundred years," she recalled. Her husband found her and spoke wise words. "Nina," he said, "you don't know anything about killing. The only thing you've got is music."

He was right, and she knew it. Within an hour, Simone, sitting at her piano, had composed what she called her "first civil rights song, and it erupted out of me quicker than I could write it down." It was called "Mississippi Goddam." In performance, she would say, "The name of this tune is 'Mississippi Goddam,' and I mean every word of it":

Alabama's gotten me so upset
Tennessee made me lose my rest
And everybody knows about Mississippi goddam
Alabama's gotten me so upset
Tennessee made me lose my rest
And everybody knows about Mississippi goddam
Can't you see it
Can't you feel it
It's all in the air
I can't stand the pressure much longer
Somebody say a prayer
Alabama's gotten me so upset
Tennessee made me lose my rest
And everybody knows about Mississippi
    goddam . . .
Hound dogs on my trail
School children sitting in jail
Black cat cross my path
I think every day's gonna be my last
Lord have mercy on this land of mine
We all gonna get it in due time
I don't belong here
I don't belong there
I've even stopped believing in prayer

The resulting song, "Mississippi Goddam," was recorded live at Carnegie Hall and released in 1964.

So much was happening so fast; so much blood was being shed. Hearing the news of the Birmingham church bombing on the radio, John Lewis, a young activist with the Student Nonviolent Coordinating Committee, traveled to Birmingham from his parents' home in Pike County, Alabama. Late in the afternoon of the day of the attack, he was there, outside the sanctuary, wondering. "It was unreal to stand there and try to absorb what had happened," Lewis recalled. "I looked at the people stand-

MISSISSIPPI GODDAM

This song was actually banned by certain radio stations, and it's a hard song to listen to. But we have to listen to it, because art is about truth—and Nina Simone was speaking the rawest kind of truth.

She wrote it in a dark moment. Medgar Evers, the NAACP field secretary in Mississippi, had been shot down outside his house; four little girls had been murdered inside Birmingham's 16th Street Baptist Church in a terrorist attack planned and executed by Ku Klux Klansmen.

Simone used to say that her art was a reflection of her times. Often, we don't like the reflection we see in a mirror, but we can't responsibly turn away, however brutal the reflection.

That's what hits me here. This song practically requires you to look within, regardless of how painful that might be, and acknowledge the truth so that you can find the path forward. —T.M.

ing on that sidewalk across the street, these black men and women of Birmingham, who had lived through so much, and I knew that they had to be asking themselves, How much *more*? What *else*? What's *next*? . . . Four children killed on a Sunday morning in church, in God's house. What *could* be next?" The face of Jesus was blown out of one of the 16th Street Baptist Church's windows during the attack, an eerie symbol of a world where hate, in the moment of the bombing, had overshadowed love.

A memorial window—a gift from the people of Wales—depicts a crucified Jesus and a quotation from the Gospel of Matthew, Chapter 25: "Inasmuch as ye have done it unto the least of these my brethren, ye have done it unto me." The Jesus in the window is a black man, arms outstretched, reaching, it seems, to a future beyond the blood and the bombs—a future that appeared far distant. A *Washington Post* reporter asked a "white housewife" in a Birmingham supermarket what she made of the bombing. "Terrible," she replied. "But—well, that's what they get for trying to force their way where they're not wanted."

King preached the funeral for three of the four victims. "God still has a way of wringing good out of evil," he said. "And history has proven over and over again that unmerited suffering is redemptive. The innocent blood of these little girls may well serve as a redemptive force that will bring new light to this dark city."

John Coltrane's jazz composition "Alabama" took its cadences from King's eulogy. In this Coltrane was working in a tradition of "socially aware jazz" that included Art Blakey's "Freedom Rider," Max Roach's "Freedom Now Suite," and Charles Mingus's "Fables for Faubus."

In the streets outside the funeral services, mourners sang improvised verses to the tune of "We Shall Overcome":

They did not die in vain.
They did not die in vain,
We shall overcome
Someday.

IN October 1963, President Kennedy contemplated the connection between the artistic and political worlds on a trip to Amherst College. The invitation had come from an alumnus, John J. McCloy, the diplomat and banker who was a former assistant secretary of war, high commissioner for Germany, and president of the World Bank. The small liberal-arts college in Massachusetts was breaking ground for a library that would be named for the late Robert Frost. An admirer of Frost's who had arranged for the poet to read at his inauguration in 1961, President Kennedy was happy to speak at the ceremony.

At Amherst, Kennedy talked of the place he had come to. "Many years ago, Woodrow Wilson said, what good is a political party unless it's serving a great national purpose?" the president asked. "And what good is a private college or university unless it's serving a great national purpose?" He reminded his listeners that their luck in life came at a price: service to others. JFK paraphrased Winston Churchill, who had said, at Harvard University in 1943, "The price of greatness is responsibility." Kennedy made the point this way: "Privilege is here, and with privilege goes responsibility."

To JFK, protest was part and parcel of the project of America. "If sometimes our great artists have been the most critical of our society, it is because their sensitivity and their concern for justice, which must motivate any true artist, makes him aware that our Nation falls short of its highest potential," the president said. "I see little of more importance to the future of our country and our civilization than full recognition of the place of the artist. If art is to nourish the roots of our culture, society must set the artist free to follow his vision wherever it takes him. We must never forget that art is not a form of propaganda; it is a form of truth." To Kennedy, "the highest duty of the writer, the composer, the artist is to remain true to himself and to let the chips fall where they may. In serving his vision of the truth, the artist best serves his nation."

He closed with a quotation from Frost, one of hope:

Take human nature altogether since time began . . .
And it must be a little more in favor of man,
Say a fraction of one percent at the very least . . .

"The heart of the Presidency," Kennedy remarked elsewhere, is "informed, prudent, and resolute choice." That he chose to spend a portion of his time musing aloud about poetry and power was his way of giving that heart the fullest expression he could. He led practically, and he led spiritually. We can ask for no more than that.

Then came Dallas. Assassinated on Friday, November 22, 1963, Kennedy was buried at Arlington National Cemetery after rites at the Capitol and a funeral mass at St. Matthew's Cathedral. Mourners recalled the four days from the motorcade at Dealey Plaza in Texas to the lighting of the eternal flame at Kennedy's grave at Arlington as a blur of grief and shock. Washington, it was said, was filled with the sounds of sobs and with the music of the Navy hymn, "Eternal Father, Strong to Save," played in honor of Kennedy's service in the Pacific in World War II. Its final verse:

O Trinity of love and power!
Our brethren shield in danger's hour;
From rock and tempest, fire and foe.
Protect them wheresoever they go. . . .

ON SUNDAY, MARCH 7, 1965, a voting-rights march from Selma to Montgomery had barely begun when Alabama state troopers charged a line of nonviolent demonstrators led by the twenty-five-year-old John Lewis. Inhaling tear gas and reeling from two billy-club blows to his head, Lewis felt everything dimming. He could hear screams and slurs and the clop-clop-clop of the troopers' horses. His skull fractured, his vision blurred, Lewis believed the end had come. "People are going to die here," he said to himself. "*I'm* going to die here."

Television cameras recorded the Alabama troopers' attack on Lewis and his fellow marchers. That evening, ABC interrupted a Sunday night broadcast of the film *Judgment at Nuremberg* to show the footage. The day would come to be known as "Bloody Sunday," and the scene at the bridge proved a turning point in the life of the nation.

The day's violence inspired music such as Grant Green's "The Selma March," from the album *His Majesty King Funk,* but the larger legacy came in a more traditional setting: that of a presidential address.

At two minutes past nine o'clock on the evening of Monday, March 15, Lyndon Johnson addressed the Congress and seventy million Americans. "At times history and fate meet at a single time in a single place to shape a turning point in man's unending search for freedom. So it was at Lexington and Concord. So it was a century ago at Appomattox. So it was last week in Selma, Alabama." Johnson continued:

"People are going to die here," said John Lewis, shown here under attack on Bloody Sunday in Selma. "I'm going to die here."

King and Lewis wept as they watched President Johnson invoke the mantra of the movement: "And we shall overcome."

This was the first nation in the history of the world to be founded with a purpose. The great phrases of that purpose still sound in every American heart, North and South: "All men are created equal"—"government by consent of the governed"—"give me liberty or give me death." Well, those are not just clever words, or those are not just empty theories. In their name Americans have fought and died for two centuries, and tonight around the world they stand there as guardians of our liberty, risking their lives. . . . Many of the issues of civil rights are very complex and most difficult. But about this there can and should be no argument. Every American citizen must have an equal right to vote. There is no reason which can excuse the denial of that right. There is no duty which weighs more heavily on us than the duty we have to ensure that right.

Yet the harsh fact is that in many places in this country men and women are kept from voting simply because they are Negroes. . . .

There is no moral issue. It is wrong—deadly wrong—to deny any of your fellow Americans the right to vote in this country.

There is no issue of States rights or national rights. There is only the struggle for human rights. . . .

What happened in Selma is part of a far larger movement which reaches into

every section and State of America. It is the effort of American Negroes to secure for themselves the full blessings of American life.

Their cause must be our cause too. Because it is not just Negroes, but really
it is all of us, who must overcome the crippling legacy of bigotry and injustice.

And we shall overcome.

And we shall overcome. As he listened to Johnson repeat the civil rights refrain, King,
watching in Selma, wept. The song of a movement had become the mantra of a
president.

KING'S AND LEWIS'S nonviolent strategy was hardly the only vision on offer in
the war to change the calculus of race and power in America. Malcolm X and
the Black Power Movement wanted to move further, faster—"by any means necessary," in Malcolm's words. In a January 1965 telegram he sent to George Lincoln
Rockwell, the head of the American Nazi Party, Malcolm warned that if Rockwell's
"present racist agitation against our people there in Alabama causes physical harm
to Reverend King or any other black Americans who are only attempting to enjoy
their rights as free human beings . . . you and your Ku Klux Klan friends will be met
with maximum physical retaliation from those of us who are not handcuffed by the
disarming philosophy of nonviolence, and who believe in asserting our right of self-
defense—by any means necessary."

Malcolm loved music and understood its innate power. "Music, Brother, is
ours—it is us—and like us it is always here—surrounding us—like the infinite par-
ticles that make up Life, it cannot be seen—but can only be felt—Like Life!!!" Malcolm wrote in a 1950 letter. "No, it is not created—but like the never-dying
Soul—eternally permeates the atmosphere with its Presence—ever-waiting for its
Master—the Lordly Musician—the Wielder of Souls—to come and give it a
Temple—mould it into a Song."

In 1967, Aretha Franklin took a song of Otis Redding's and made it her own forever: "Respect," which was heard as a feminist anthem and as an assertion of black
pride. "For the Black Panthers and their supporters, 'Respect' sent an unambiguous
message to white America: From now on, black folk would take care of business in
their own way," Craig Werner wrote in his *A Change Is Gonna Come: Music, Race, and the
Soul of America.* "The day of the Tom had come to an end. As much as any speech or

manifesto, 'Respect' defined the energy of the freedom movement as its center of gravity shifted from Martin Luther King's interracial coalition to the unapologetically black organizations headed by, to use James Brown's term, a 'new breed' of photogenic firebrands, including H. Rap Brown, Stokely Carmichael, Eldridge Cleaver, and Huey Newton."

"Respect," in Franklin's hands, was about not only race but gender. "There is no one who can touch her," Mary J. Blige wrote of Franklin in *Rolling Stone*. "She is the reason why women want to sing." Franklin's rendition of Gerry Goffin and Carole King's "(You Make Me Feel Like) a Natural Woman" was another song that put a woman's experience at the center of the narrative. Of Franklin, Barack Obama told *The New Yorker*'s David Remnick in 2016, "Nobody embodies more fully the connection between the African-American spiritual, the blues, R&B, rock and roll—the way that hardship and sorrow were transformed into something full of beauty and vitality and hope. American history wells up when Aretha sings. That's why, when she sits down at a piano and sings 'A Natural Woman,' she can move me to tears."

T HE HOUR WAS late, about half past nine on the evening of Wednesday, April 3, 1968. At the Mason Temple in Memphis, the seat of the Pentecostal Church of God in Christ, Martin Luther King began to speak. A heavy storm had blown through at dusk, keeping turnout light at the rally for the city's striking sanitation workers. King hadn't wanted to leave the Lorraine Motel, where he was staying, but had conceded when his friend Ralph Abernathy called him and said he needed to brave the rain.

It had already been a long day. In Atlanta, King's commercial Eastern Air Lines flight to Memphis had been held up for fear of a bomb in the baggage hold. "Ladies and gentlemen," the pilot had told the passengers, "I want to apologize for the delay. But today we have on board Dr. Martin Luther King, Jr., and we have to be very careful—we had the plane guarded all night—and we have been checking people's luggage. Now that everything's clear, we are preparing for takeoff."

Now King struck elegiac notes in the Memphis night. "Well, I don't *know* what will happen now," King told the crowd. "We've got some difficult days ahead. But it really doesn't matter with me now. Because I've been to the mountaintop. And I don't mind." He went on:

Like anybody, I would like to live—a long life—longevity has its place. But I'm not concerned about that now. I just want to do God's will. And He's allowed me to go up to the mountain. And I've looked over. And I have seen the promised land. I may not get there with you. But I want you to *know, tonight,* that we, as a people, will get to the promised land!

So I'm happy tonight.
I'm not worried about *anything.*
I'm not fearing *any* man.

Above the cries of his followers, many of whom were transported by the emotion of his presentation, King uttered his final public words: "Mine eyes have seen the glory of the coming of the Lord!"

And so there is a line, however jagged, between Julia Ward Howe, who hastily composed her hymn of liberty in the dark of night more than a century before, and the last earthly evening of Martin Luther King.

The next day—Thursday, April 4—King retreated to Room 306 at the Lorraine, worrying about the strike and working on his sermon for Sunday. Its title: "Why America May Go to Hell." By 5:00 P.M., he was hungry and looked forward to supper. Always fastidious—a prince of the church—King shaved, put on cologne, and stepped onto the balcony. He paused; a .30-06 rifle shot slammed him back against the wall.

Among his last words at the Lorraine before the assassination was a request for a song. The musician Ben Branch was scheduled to perform at a mass meeting that night after dinner. "Ben, make sure you play 'Precious Lord, Take My Hand,' in the meeting tonight," King said. "Play it real pretty."

He never heard the hymn—or anything else—again. At King's funeral services in Atlanta, "My Heavenly Father, Watch Over Me" and "If I Can Help Somebody" were sung, and his old friend Mahalia Jackson took the stage at a public memorial at Morehouse College. She was, *The Washington Post* reported, "crying with anguish into the microphone" as she honored his last request. "Precious Lord," she sang, "take my hand / Lead me on, let me stand."

King's mortal pilgrimage was done. A distraught Nina Simone's "Why (The King of Love Is Dead)" paid tribute; in Atlanta, a mule-drawn cart carried his body through the city's streets. An estimated one hundred twenty million Americans watched the funeral. Mourners in the April heat included Jacqueline Kennedy, Richard Nixon, Robert F. Kennedy, Hubert H. Humphrey, Harry Belafonte, Mar-

Coretta Scott King led the march of mourners behind the mule-drawn cart bearing her husband's body from Ebenezer Baptist Church. The silence was interrupted by choruses of "The Battle Hymn of the Republic" and "We Shall Overcome," among other songs of the movement.

lon Brando, Sammy Davis, Jr., Aretha Franklin, Eartha Kitt, Jackie Robinson, Diana Ross and the Supremes, and Stevie Wonder. The segregationist governor of Georgia, Lester Maddox, declined to attend, spending the day in the gold-domed state capitol under an increased guard. He was, *Newsweek* wrote, worried about "the expected onset of Armageddon." "If they come in here," Maddox told his troopers, "we're gonna stack 'em up." Yet there was no violence from the surging mourners in Atlanta—only grief.

The march to the cemetery was long—more than three and a half miles—and the silence was interrupted from time to time by choruses of "The Battle Hymn of the Republic," "We Shall Overcome," "This Little Light of Mine," and "Dr. King Comes Marching In," sung to the tune of "When the Saints Go Marching In."

At journey's end, King's epitaph was drawn not from scripture but from the canon of African American spirituals: "Free at last; free at last; thank God Almighty I'm free at last."

CHAPTER SEVEN

ARCHIE BUNKER V.
THE AGE OF AQUARIUS

"I want to thank you, Mr. President, not for any one thing, just for everything."

—JOHN WAYNE, in remarks to Richard Nixon, 1973

"We gotta get out of this place."

—THE ANIMALS, in a song popular with American troops in Southeast Asia

RICHARD NIXON WAS desperate for friendly faces. In the late winter of 1974, as the Watergate scandal enveloped him and talk of impeachment grew more insistent, the besieged president chose a warm audience for a by-then-unusual venture outside the safe havens of the White House, Camp David, and his getaways at San Clemente, California, and Key Biscayne, Florida. On Saturday, March 16, Nixon flew from Washington to Nashville, the capital of a state, Tennessee, that he'd carried with 67.7 percent of the vote against George McGovern in 1972.

The occasion was the opening of a new fifteen-million-dollar performance venue for the Grand Ole Opry, the country-music institution that was moving from its home at the downtown Ryman Auditorium out to a new theme-park-and-hotel complex known as Opryland. Purists were unhappy. "By God, this is one old boy that ain't setting foot inside that place," a country fan sitting at Tootsies Orchid Lounge, a favorite bar near the Ryman, remarked. "Hell, you can't even buy a beer out there."

Nixon had bigger problems to worry about. His aim was straightforward: to rally support for a troubled presidency. On the Saturday Nixon was in Tennessee, *Newsweek* closed a cover with a stark headline: ALL ABOUT IMPEACHMENT. *Time*, meanwhile, wrote: "Richard Nixon is rapidly running out of options in his struggle to

In a surreal White House meeting, Elvis Presley called on President Nixon on Monday, December 21, 1970.

survive Watergate. Last week he exercised a fresh one.... Nixon embarked on a drive to save himself by appealing directly to the public."

Arriving in Nashville, Nixon held a rally at a Tennessee Air National Guard hangar, and the cheers of the crowd overwhelmed protesters who were chanting for impeachment. Leaving nothing to chance, the White House had sent technicians to town five days earlier to make sure the sound system was optimal for the president's remarks. One 1969 country song, by Merle Haggard, had become a kind of Middle American anthem, "Okie from Muskogee."

Seeking a friendly venue as Watergate engulfed him, Nixon spent an evening at the Grand Ole Opry in March 1974.

Through the years Haggard could be ambivalent about "Okie." "We wrote it to be satirical originally," Haggard recalled. "But then people latched on to it, and it really turned into this song that looked into the mindset of people [the hippies] so opposite of who and where we were." A Reuters piece in 1970 observed that "Haggard has tapped, perhaps for the first time in popular music, a vast reservoir of resentment among Americans against the long-haired young and their 'underground' society." In a 1970 *Rolling Stone* interview, Haggard was blunt about the counterculture protestors: "I don't like their views on life, their filth, their visible self-disrespect." In later years he said that he'd been "dumb as a rock" when he wrote the song, but at other times he could also stand by it. "That's how I got into it with the hippies," he said on another occasion. "I thought they were unqualified to judge America, and I thought about them lookin' down their noses at something that I cherished very much, and it pissed me off."

Whatever Haggard's views about the song—then or later—it was popular in Nixon's America (as was Haggard's "The Fightin' Side of Me," another hit from 1969). In Nashville, supporters of the president passed out song sheets entitled "Stand Up and Cheer for Richard Nixon," sung to the tune of "Okie from Muskogee":

> I'm sick of what I'm reading in the papers,
> I'm tired of all that trash on TV,
> Stand up and cheer for Richard Nixon . . .
> I've been hearing talk about impeaching
> The man we chose to lead us through these times.
> But talk like this could weaken and defeat us,
> Let's show the world we're not the quitting kind.

In "Okie from Muskogee," Merle Haggard gave the "silent majority" a song to sing.

Onstage with Roy Acuff later in the evening, Nixon turned to the business at hand. Returning POWs from Vietnam, the president said, thrilled to country music more than to any other genre—"it touched them and touched them deeply after that long time away from America." He went on:

> What country music is, is that first it comes from the heart of America, because this is the heart of America, out here in Middle America. Second, it relates to those experiences that mean so much to America. It talks about family, it talks about religion, the faith in God that is so important to our country and particularly to our family life. And as we all know, country music radiates a love of this Nation, [of] patriotism.
>
> Country music, therefore, has those combinations which are so essential to America's character at a time that America needs character, because today—one serious note—let me tell you, the peace of the world for generations, maybe centuries to come, will depend not just on America's military might, which is the greatest in the world, or our wealth, which is the greatest in the world, but it is going to depend on our character, our belief in ourselves, our love of country, our willingness to not only wear the flag but to stand up for the flag. And country music does that.

The president closed by leading, from the piano, a rendition of "God Bless America." Buoyed by the cheers, Nixon had done the best he could to turn "Nashville's love of country music to his current political theme: That what is important is patriotism and national defense, not Watergate," as John Herbers of *The New York Times* described the president's mission.

Nixon knew his audience. The South was both hospitable and hawkish, an unusual combination in the years of LBJ and of Nixon. As the war in Vietnam unfolded, claiming about fifty-eight thousand American lives, followed by Watergate and Nixon's fall, America was at once in conflict and in conversation with itself. The country was riven by region, class, party, and religion; America seemed best understood as a struggle at home between the musical *Hair*'s Age of Aquarius and Archie Bunker, the fictional protagonist of Norman Lear's television series *All in the Family*.

We can hear the sounds of that battle in the music of the era. Social customs and values largely taken for granted were under assault. The country seemed powerless in Vietnam and unmoored at home. By late 1967, columnist Joseph Kraft had put the phrase "Middle Americans" in political circulation. Nixon called them "the great silent majority." In 1970, the editors of *Time* named "the Middle Americans" as the Man and Woman of the Year. With the exceptions of Daniel Patrick Moynihan and Henry Kissinger, the magazine wrote, Nixon's administration was "like the reunion photograph of a Depression class that rose to the top by Horatio Alger virtues."

From Woodstock to the marches for peace in Washington, the great anti-war music and the countercultural touchstones loom large even now. John Lennon's call to "Give Peace a Chance" has a more dominant place in the popular memory than, say, Loretta Lynn's "Dear Uncle Sam" or John Wayne's recording of John Mitchum's prose poem to the nation of Richard Nixon, "America, Why I Love Her." Yet an understanding of the America of that tumultuous time—and an understanding of the first decades of the twenty-first century—requires an appreciation of the tensions and divergent views of the United States in the Vietnam era.

AT FIRST, THE war in Southeast Asia seemed a sequential chapter in the story of what Time-Life founder Henry Luce had called the American Century. One generation had met Wilson's challenge from 1917 to 1918; another, the call to arms issued by FDR; now, in the middle of the 1960s, the sons of those who fought World War II (and the Korean War) were suiting up for their own hour upon the stage.

OKIE FROM MUSKOGEE and
THE AGE OF AQUARIUS

Pivoting off the counterculture, Merle Haggard composed and recorded the country music standard "Okie from Muskogee." In just six weeks, "Okie" would top the country singles chart and go on to win single of the year from the Country Music Association.

Anything Haggard moves me. It's practically in my DNA. You could say I graduated from the college of Merle. Probably no other individual country artist was a bigger influence on me. His stark lyrics, delivered with the ultimate country voice, move the listener. In a way, he was a voice for the so-called "Silent Majority."

Preceding "Okie from Muskogee" by six months is "The Age of Aquarius." "Aquarius/Let the Sunshine In" was a big hit single for the 5th Dimension, who had broken through with a Jimmy Webb hit, "Up, Up and Away." Things really exploded for the group when they released "Aquarius" together with the title "Let the Sunshine In" as a medley from the musical *Hair*. Billboard magazine ranked it as the number two single for the year 1969. Although it came at the end of the decade, this song from the play *Hair* came to define the end of the sixties and the hippie movement.

I would come to discover the medley years later. Are they songs of protest? To me, they are songs of change—they are among those songs that bridge the gap of generational change.

—T.M.

Or at least it felt that way early on. On Sunday, January 30, 1966, Ed Sullivan went on the air with a typical program. Dinah Shore was there, singing "Chim Chim Cher-ee," "Something Wonderful," and a blues medley, as was José Feliciano, who did "Flight of the Bumble Bee." The Four Tops performed a medley of four hit songs: "The Whole World Swings with You," "It's the Same Old Song," "Something About You," and "I Can't Help Myself" ("Sugar Pie, Honey Bunch"). There were three comedy acts—Dick Capri, Jackie Vernon (now best known for being the voice of Frosty the Snowman in the late-sixties and seventies Christmas specials), and

The war in Vietnam starkly divided the nation along political and cultural lines—chasms reflected in the music of the era.

Topo Gigio, the Italian puppet. A wooden clog dance and precision archery rounded out the show. But the most resonant performance of the evening came when Staff Sergeant Barry Sadler, a member of the Army's elite special forces, sang "The Ballad of the Green Berets," written by Sadler and Robin Moore. (John Wayne would star in a 1969 movie, *The Green Berets,* that also helped popularize the song.) Standing ramrod straight, in uniform, before an image of the Green Beret insignia bearing the Latin motto *De Oppresso Liber* (To free the oppressed), Sadler, who'd been wounded in Vietnam, painted a portrait of valor and strength.

In 1966, a song like "The Ballad of the Green Berets" could find a big audience. It was, in fact, "*the* most popular song of 1966," Doug Bradley and Craig Werner wrote in *We Gotta Get Out of This Place: The Soundtrack of the Vietnam War,* "surpassing 'We Can Work It Out,' 'Paint It Black,' the Association's 'Cherish,' and a host of Motown classics, including the Four Tops' 'Reach Out, I'll Be There' and the Supremes' 'You Can't Hurry Love.'"

By 1968, however, with the draft, increasing troop deployments, the miseries of combat, and no clear path to victory, voices of protest rose in a crescendo. Sixty-eight was the nadir of virtually everything. "It was a year which dealt badly with everyone whom it touched," Ward Just wrote in *The Washington Post* toward the end of 1968. "It struck down the good and the bad indiscriminately, and at the end of it, by November, the country seemed no closer to healing the sickness—whatever it was. Querulous, dissatisfied, mad, the public looked for explanations; the public looked for leaders." The essay quoted Paul Simon and Art Garfunkel, and their quiet cri de coeur, "Mrs. Robinson," which longed for heroes, as representative of the angst of the age.

R ESTORATION AND REDEMPTION would take more than Joe DiMaggio, who was name-checked in Simon and Garfunkel's hit. "I look over this campus, and I don't see many black faces," Robert Kennedy told students in Omaha during the intense RFK presidential campaign that ended when Kennedy was gunned down in the kitchen of the Ambassador Hotel in Los Angeles. "What you want is for the poor boy to fight this war, the boy whose parents haven't the money to send him to college . . . I don't think that's acceptable."

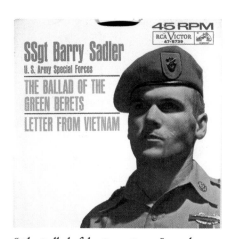

"The Ballad of the Green Berets" was the No. 1 song in America in 1966.

Creedence Clearwater Revival wrote a song, "Fortunate Son," which lamented what Kennedy had been talking about: the ability of the rich and the well connected to elude military service. The song was "a confrontation between me and Richard Nixon," CCR's John Fogerty recalled. "The haves, the people who have it all . . . During the Vietnam War, these were the people who didn't have to go to war. I was thinking about David Eisenhower, the grandson of Dwight, who married Julie Nixon."

THE BALLAD OF THE GREEN BERETS
and FORTUNATE SON

"The Ballad of the Green Berets" is a great patriotic song, and it was very nearly dated even when it was released. That Barry Sadler's straight-ahead march—the music lets the message of the lyric stand out—was so successful in 1966 tells us a lot about how the Vietnam War was viewed in the earlier days of our involvement, because it's hard to imagine the song doing as well two years later.

Still, it's hard not to feel pride when you listen to this song. Maybe it's not cool to say that, but it's true: Sadler's anthem is traditional in tone and in theme, and tradition works musically here.

Three years later brought a very different song. In 1969, Creedence Clearwater Revival released "Fortunate Son," a rock number incorporating the timeless motif of poor men fighting rich men's wars. (John Fogerty himself served in the Army Reserve.)

What I feel is the intensity of Fogerty's vocal delivery. Whereas Barry Sadler was matter-of-fact, angst and anger are the dominant emotions in CCR's song. Placed over a rock track—bass, drums, and electric guitars—there's no escaping the point of the powerful words, which are allowed to stand out.

"Fortunate Son" comes in at just over two minutes long. That was all CCR needed to create something that would be added to the National Recording Registry by the Library of Congress for its significance to the time.   —T.M.

Pete Seeger was even more direct in "Bring Them Home," and, in 1967, he'd released the anti-war "Waist Deep in the Big Muddy," which implicitly took on President Johnson's leadership. In the lyrics, Seeger evoked 1942 and a "big fool" of a commanding officer who insists, stupidly, that a platoon cross an uncrossable river—and the commander refuses to recognize reality no matter how bad things get. "It got the most explosive approval of any song I have ever sung," Seeger recalled, and CBS cut it from a taped appearance of Seeger on *The Smothers Brothers Comedy Hour* in 1967. (The network later caved and allowed the song to be broadcast; only the CBS affiliate in Detroit refused to air it altogether.)

Edwin Starr recorded the anti-war "War" in 1970, but other songs were more subtle. Jimmy Webb wrote "Galveston," sung by Glen Campbell, from the perspective of a soldier afraid and far from home.

That was the view from the U.S. troops in Vietnam; Martha and the Vandellas reversed the perspective with their 1966 "Jimmy Mack." It's a complicated piece because it's as much about temptation as it is about steadfast loyalty in love—the last thing a soldier would want to hear from his girl.

In Vietnam itself, perhaps the most popular song among the troops had an unmistakable message. Sung by the Animals, the refrain was powerful:

> We gotta get out of this place
> If it's the last thing we ever do
> We gotta get out of this place
> Girl, there's a better life for me and
>   you

Pete Seeger's "Waist Deep in the Big Muddy" and "Bring Them Home" were powerful anti-war anthems.

There was another resonant song in-country: "Green, Green Grass of Home," a haunting, fatalistic ballad told, it's revealed in the final verse, by a death-row inmate facing execution. Porter Wagoner sang one version, Tom Jones another. For soldiers who themselves felt under a kind of death sentence, the song spoke volumes.

"MUSIC DOESN'T CREATE movements," the scholar and historian Craig Werner says, "but if a movement exists, it can power and drive that movement." In the case of the Vietnam War, music powered and drove not only anti-war sentiment but also the cause of civil rights and issues of race. In 1968, James Brown released "Say It Loud—I'm Black and I'm Proud," which resonated at home and in Southeast Asia, and his "Papa's Got a Brand New Bag" was part of the soundtrack of Black Power.

GREEN, GREEN GRASS OF HOME
and GALVESTON

I love classic country music, and it gets no better than "Green, Green Grass of Home." Curly Putman's lyrics paint a detailed picture of life, before revealing it's just a dream. At the end the narrator looks back and wonders if he focused on what really mattered. It speaks to many of us, I think, because we all have some of that kind of regret. Like "We Gotta Get Out of This Place," "Green, Green Grass" was adopted by soldiers because the lyrics resonated with their plight in the field—examples of how great songs can be applied to different situations and contexts.

Written by Jimmy Webb and popularized by Glen Campbell, whom I revere, "Galveston" was, like "Fortunate Son," explicitly about the war ("I clean my gun and dream of Galveston").

Later, Campbell would do a different, but more emotional, live version, accompanied by an orchestra, and with a dramatically slowed-down tempo. I find this version haunting, and it allows you to pull out the meaning of each word with Campbell's flawless and raw emotional vocal.   —T.M.

Brown had the most notable of careers. In his Rock & Roll Hall of Fame biography, Brown is lauded for his versatility and durability: "He was variously tagged 'Soul Brother Number One,' 'the Godfather of Soul,' 'the Hardest Working Man in Show Business,' 'Mr. Dynamite,' and even 'the Original Disco Man.' This much is certain: what became known as soul music in the sixties, funk music in the seventies and rap music in the eighties is directly attributable to James Brown. His transformation of gospel fervor into the taut, explosive intensity of rhythm & blues, combined with precision choreography and dynamic showmanship, served to define the directions black music would take from the release of his first R&B hit ('Please Please Please') in 1956 to the present day." Politically, he'd made his mark early. "By the late Sixties," the Hall of Fame says, "Brown had attained the status of a musical and cultural revolutionary, owing to his message of black pride and self-sufficiency."

In an interview with Craig Werner and Doug Bradley for their study *We Gotta Get*

The Animals sang "We Gotta Get Out of This Place," which Vietnam veterans recalled as the defining song of the war.

WE GOTTA GET OUT OF THIS PLACE

This song was written by one of the most successful songwriting teams of all time, husband and wife Barry Mann and Cynthia Weil. They have been inducted into the Rock & Roll Hall of Fame, and the breadth of their songwriting is astonishing. From "You've Lost That Lovin' Feelin'" by the Righteous Brothers to the Drifters' "On Broadway," Mann and Weil melded rock, pop, and R&B influences throughout their songs.

"We Gotta Get Out of This Place" was an anthem for Vietnam soldiers and anti-war protesters. As the story goes, the writers intended to pitch it to the Righteous Brothers, and then Mann considered recording it himself. But before he could, the Animals' producer, Mickie Most, recorded it. The lyrics were tweaked and the sound incorporated the working-class roots of the band members.

Bruce Springsteen credits this song as one of his biggest influences. The bass line hits you immediately. Sparse, the track begins to build over the gritty vocal of Eric Burdon. The tension increases until the chorus takes hold and the music moves into the background and closes with the line: "Girl, there's a better life for me and you," wrapping up the sentiment of the song perfectly.   —T.M.

James Brown (shown performing in Vietnam in 1968) and Aretha Franklin were central figures in the changing America of the sixties and beyond.

Out of This Place, John Martinez, a musician who served as a machine gunner in Vietnam, recalled the cacophony of Qui Nhon. "[A] lot of times at night," Martinez said, "the white guys would hang out in one area, the blacks in another. The southerners listening to country and playing poker. The black guys were listening to Aretha and James Brown."

Aretha: That's all he had to call her. Everybody knew—and knows—who he meant. In her "Chain of Fools," she sang a kind of R&B version of Seeger's "Waist Deep in the Big Muddy," a song that its audience in Vietnam interpreted as an indictment of failed leadership. There was, though, a note of hope in "Chain of Fools": Franklin predicted that one day the chain would break and the captives would go free—or, in terms of the war, go home. "I've had a lot of servicemen—Vietnam vets—come up to me and tell me how much my music meant to them over there," Franklin recalled. "I'm sure all those guys were in a lot of pain, something you or I can't imagine." To assuage—or to try to assuage—that pain, GIs listened to Otis Redding, who'd written "Respect," and his and Steve Cropper's "(Sittin' on) The Dock of the Bay," and to Simon and Garfunkel's "Bridge Over Troubled Water" and "Homeward Bound," which was all they wanted to be.

THE WAR OVER the war at home could turn deadly, too. On Monday, May 4, 1970, not long after President Nixon expanded the American combat effort into Cambodia, National Guardsmen opened fire on anti-war protesters at Kent State University in Ohio, killing four and wounding nine. In California, Neil Young quickly wrote "Ohio" and recorded it with David Crosby, Stephen Stills, and Graham Nash.

On the Fourth of July on the National Mall, the two Americas clashed again. The planned spectacle of the Independence Day program—including a sermon by the Reverend Billy Graham, a rendition of "God Bless America" by Kate Smith, fireworks, comedy by Bob Hope, a recital of the Pledge of Allegiance by Red Skelton, and the singing of "The Star-Spangled Banner," led by Pat Boone—was interrupted by counterculture protesters, some of whom had gathered for a July Fourth marijuana "smoke-in."

In front of the Lincoln Memorial stage, the "Honor America" crowd carried patriotic signs. (One boy's read PATRICK HENRY, PAUL REVERE, AND SPIRO T. AGNEW) and listened to Graham preach the virtues of a more traditional understanding of the country and its conventions. "Let the world know that the vast majority of us still proudly sing: 'My Country 'tis of thee, sweet land of liberty,' " Graham said. "America needs to sing again! America needs to celebrate again! America needs to wave the flag again!"

Protesters near the Washington Monument, meanwhile, yelled obscenities, threw several rocks at police, set off firecrackers to spook police horses, were tear-gassed, pushed a truck that was part of the official fireworks display into the reflecting pool and smashed its windows, paraded naked, and carried Vietcong flags right side up and American flags upside down, a traditional signal of distress.

As Kate Smith sang Irving Berlin's familiar words, the protesters yelled back, "He, Ho, Ho Chi Minh"; "One, two, three, four, we don't want to fight your fucking war." One buttoned-down Fourth of July celebrant said, "Don't argue with the traitors, they're yellow," and a dissenter replied, "It's your war, not mine." One woman from Norwalk, Connecticut, in a red, white, and blue dress and carrying an HONOR

A young female protester takes her stand in front of armed police at an anti-war rally at the 1968 Democratic National Convention in Chicago.

AMERICA—UNITED WE STAND placard—the latter phrase of John Dickinson's echoing 202 years on—told a *Washington Post* reporter that she "wanted her children to 'be aware of our traditions. I want them to know that there's room for dissent but that we support our country.'" Of the protesters splashing in the reflecting pool— some nude—she added, "I don't even necessarily disagree with them," but "Do they have to use obscenities?"

Jack Benny played the violin, Dinah Shore sang "America the Beautiful," and the whole cast of the show closed with "The Battle Hymn of the Republic"—while police ringed the stage, after a gas bomb sent a huge part of the crowd surging for safety. Amid the chaos, Bob Hope tried a joke: "It looks like Vietnam, doesn't it?"

IN 1973, HOPE was back in town to host a White House dinner for prisoners of war returning from Vietnam. The program included John Wayne, Sammy Davis, Jr. (who'd suggested the idea of the dinner to Nixon), Vic Damone, Ricardo Montalbán, and an aged Irving Berlin, who led the gathering in "God Bless America." Berlin's voice, Nixon recalled, "came out loud and strong. Many now wept openly as we repeated the stirring and simple verse over and over until, at the end, some of the men almost seemed to be shouting so that the words could be heard all the way to Hanoi: 'God bless America, my home sweet home.'"

A chorus of former prisoners sang "The POW Hymn," which had been written in captivity by Air Force Colonel J. Quincy Collins. The swaggering Wayne drew cheers when he told the crowd, "I'll ride into the sunset with you anytime." Nixon was delighted when "the Duke" paid tribute to the commander in chief. "I want to thank you, Mr. President, not for any one thing, just for everything."

JOHNNY CASH WAS a unique figure, but his views on the war were fairly rep- resentative. Neither a ferocious hawk nor a reflexive dove, Cash toured the Far East for the USO and left us an intriguing canon about the era. "Cash was greatly troubled by the Vietnam War," the biographer Robert Hilburn wrote in *Johnny Cash: The Life*. "His natural instinct was to support his country at all costs, but his visits to hospitals and talks with soldiers hit him hard, and he admitted his doubts to his brother Tommy. 'Maybe,' he said, 'they may be dying for a cause that isn't just.'" In "What Is Truth?" he meditated on the generation gap, and his "Singin' in Vietnam Talkin' Blues" gave Cash the chance to talk about his time in the war zone—his "little trip into a living hell."

In 1974, the year Nixon was forced from office, Cash wrote a more traditionally patriotic song, "Ragged Old Flag":

You see, we got a little hole in that flag there
When Washington took it across the Delaware.
And it got powder-burned the night Francis Scott Key
Sat watching it writing *Say Can You See.*
And it got a bad rip in New Orleans
With Pakenham and Jackson tuggin' at its seams.
And it almost fell at the Alamo
Beside the Texas flag, but she waved on though
She got cut with a sword at Chancellorsville
And she got cut again at Shiloh Hill.

SINGIN' IN VIETNAM TALKIN' BLUES

Johnny Cash. The Man in Black. Truly an iconic artist and totally underrated as a songwriter. His writing credits include hits from the 1950s ("Cry, Cry, Cry" and "Folsom Prison Blues") well into the 1960s ("I Walk the Line"). His music was a reflection of how he felt, and we can hear him questioning his government, as well as his own feelings, in songs he wrote about the Vietnam War.

"Singin' in Vietnam Talkin' Blues" is intriguing because it's the only recitation song we have highlighted. From his *Man in Black* album, this song was inspired by a trip he and his wife, June Carter Cash, took to Vietnam to entertain the troops. The choice of a recitation (and incorporating that very idea into the title) tells me he wanted the lyrics to dramatically rise above the musical side of the record. It's as if he's having a conversation with us about what he saw and felt. This isn't a studio track; it's from the heart. He tells us in the song they were scared when they heard bombs exploding at night, which isn't exactly what you'd expect from Johnny Cash. And yet with that booming voice, it's impossible not to feel the pain he felt for the troops, and the fear that anybody under fire would experience.

—T.M.

There was Robert E. Lee, Beauregard, and Bragg
And the south wind blew hard on that *Ragged Old Flag.*
On Flanders field in World War One
She got a big hole from a Bertha Gun.
She turned blood red in World War Two,
She hung limp, and low, by the time it was through.
She was in Korea and Vietnam,
She went where she was sent by Uncle Sam.
Native Americans, brown, yellow and white
All shed blood for the Stars and Stripes.
In her own good land here she's been abused,
She's been burned, dishonored, denied, and refused.
And the government for which she stands
Has been scandalized throughout the land.

And she's getting threadbare, and wearing thin,
But she's in good shape, for the shape she's in.
'Cause she's been through the fire before,
And I believe she can take a whole lot more.

"Ragged Old Flag" is a complex piece—a defense of the flag at a time when it's "been abused/She's been burned, dishonored, denied, and refused," while also calling Nixon's lies to account: "And the government for which she stands / Has been scandalized throughout the land." That Cash sung of the flag's being "ragged" is key to the song's power—in Cash's take, the Stars and Stripes wasn't a window decal but an emblem of an ethos of liberty that had to be fought for. Taken all in all, the song

Johnny Cash's "Ragged Old Flag" album cover.

captures Cash's ambivalence about American glory and American sin: "But she's in good shape, for the shape she's in."

Late in his life, in 1993, Cash recorded an elegiac song about Vietnam, "Drive On," which was laced with the same sense of tragedy. Life will never be what we want it to be, and the best we can do, in the end, is to endure, seeking love in a fallen world that's destined to disappoint us.

CONSIDERING THE SOURCE, it was a startling claim. A longtime lieutenant of Henry Luce, journalist Richard Clurman found himself chatting one day in the late 1960s with Leonard Bernstein, the legendary composer and conductor of the New York Philharmonic.

"Elvis Presley," Bernstein said, "is the greatest cultural force in the twentieth century."

Taken aback, Clurman, who recounted the exchange to the writer David Halberstam, offered an alternative.

"What about Picasso?"

"No, it's Elvis," Bernstein replied. "He introduced the beat to everything and he changed everything—music, language, clothes, it's a whole new social revolution— the Sixties comes from it."

The Presley legend has proven durable and intriguing not least because it mirrors much of American culture in his lifetime and beyond. His fantastic rise and his long sad slide, in his later years, into an overweight, gun-toting, prescription-drug-abusing conspiracy theorist about communism and the counterculture (he hated the Beatles, once telling President Nixon that the British band threatened American values) tap into fundamental questions about race, mass culture, sexuality, and working-class anxiety in postwar America. A poor boy made good in the prosperous fifties, Presley experienced tension and feared disorder in the sixties before breaking down totally in the hectic seventies. In his music and in his movies, in his private worlds at Graceland and in Las Vegas, Presley was a forerunner of the reality-TV era, in which celebrities play an outsize role in the imaginative lives of their fans.

He was born in 1935 in Tupelo, Mississippi, in the hilly upcountry region of the state the writer Julia Reed has described as the "Balkans of the South." (The other two distinct Mississippi worlds are the Delta and the Gulf Coast.) His father struggled to eke out a living, working different jobs and signing up for FDR's

Works Progress Administration after doing time at Mississippi's Parchman Farm prison for forging a check. His mother was devoted to her son, all the more so because Presley had a twin brother who was stillborn. Elvis grew up as a member of the Assembly of God, a denomination that emphasized personal religious experiences. Music and singing were essential means of creating ecstatic moments of transcendence; it was a vibrant, emotional, very public form of faith. The individual was the vessel of the Holy Spirit—a performer, if only for the congregation, and Presley absorbed both white and black gospel in Mississippi.

Eventually the family moved to Memphis, which was perfect for Presley. A longtime cotton hub, the city, like Presley himself, sat between the blues-soaked Delta and the virtually all-white country world of Nashville.

"Elvis Presley," Leonard Bernstein said, "is the greatest cultural force in the twentieth century."

In the summer of 1954, after a brief, not-quite-successful visit the year before, Presley cut a record with the producer Sam Phillips, who ran Sun Records on Union Avenue.

A few days later, at an open-air performance at the Overton Shell in Memphis, Presley played the two songs from that recording. As Joel Williamson, the scholar of Southern history, observed, Presley took "That's All Right" (written by an African American blues musician, Arthur Crudup) and the flip side, "Blue Moon of Kentucky" (written by a white bluegrass man, Bill Monroe), and made them his own. "Elvis, using his God-given rich and versatile voice, perfected by practice, gave [the songs] a different turn," Williamson wrote. "Just as 'That's All Right' was not black anymore, 'Blue Moon' was no longer hillbilly; it was joyous, country-come-to-town and damn glad to be there." The audience, led by the ecstatic young women in the crowd, went wild. "I was scared stiff," Presley recalled. "Everyone was hollering, and I didn't know what they were hollering at."

They were, of course, hollering at *him*, transported by his electric physicality and his extraordinary voice, which ranged comfortably from baritone to tenor and above. He did not simply sing. He became the music, as though possessed by a spirit of joy and release back at the Assembly of God. It was sexual, yes, and thus disturbing to the more placid and puritanical of observers, but it was inescapably religious, too, in the sense that religion evokes realities ordinarily hidden from the human eye. Here, on a stage in a park near the banks of the Mississippi in western Tennessee, was something new in American popular culture: a white man drawing on the deep tradition of African American blues and making it his own. In the popular mind, a fresh genre—a different epoch—was coming into being. "Hearing him for the first time," Bob Dylan said, "was like busting out of jail."

Presley was a vehicle—cultural critics would say he was a mimic and even a thief—for the black musical and spiritual experiences of his native Mississippi. Sam Phillips, who recorded artists such as B. B. King and Ike Turner in a still-segregated South, understood the underlying realities of a Jim Crow America. Chuck Berry and Little Richard would be early breakout stars across the color line, but Phillips believed more had to be done to integrate the cultural and commercial markets. "I knew that for black music to come to its rightful place in this country," Phillips said, "we had to have some white singers come over and do black music—not copy it, not change, not sweeten it. Just do it." With Presley (as well as Carl Perkins, Bill Haley, and Jerry Lee Lewis, among others), Phillips's prophecy came true, but not without understandable resentment from the architects of the tradition Presley was drawing on. "I was making everybody rich, and I was poor," Arthur Crudup said. "I was born poor, I live poor, and I'm going to die poor."

In the white mainstream, the Elvis story was quintessentially American—the poor boy rising to riches from largely impoverished obscurity (his family lived in a federal housing project in Memphis after moving to Tennessee) on the strength of his talent, not on the circumstances of his birth. "I don't know what it is," Presley told *The Saturday Evening Post* in 1956. "I just fell into it, really. My daddy and I were laughing about it the other day. He looked at me and said, 'What happened, E? The last thing I can remember is I was working in a can factory and you were drivin' a truck' . . . It just caught us up."

Presley emerged at the moment the machinery of post–World War II mass culture was beginning to hum. The world was on the move. Old barriers were under siege. New possibilities were opening up. It was the age of the GI Bill and *Brown v. Board of Education,* of suburbs and television, of interstate highways and fast food. Material prosperity in Eisenhower's America was startling. Families whose forebears had struggled on the fringes of farming and of debilitating manufacturing work suddenly had more money (and more things, ranging from TVs to washing machines to cars) than they could have imagined even two decades before, in the depths of an economic crash that seemed to go on forever. One unexpected boon from the post–World War II boom: Disposable income—especially for teenagers—was rising, which meant kids were able to consume the product that Presley was offering.

A key element of that product: sexuality. This wasn't Bing Crosby up there; it wasn't even Frank Sinatra, who sang so intimately and so searchingly. Presley was different. Beyond his husky, unique voice, Presley, with his gyrating hips and hooded eyes, seemed to embody human desire more than any other popular male performer of his time. One report in Presley's FBI file—created and maintained under the decades-long reign of J. Edgar Hoover—described a La Crosse, Wisconsin, show in lurid terms. It was, the informant said, "the filthiest and most harmful production that ever came to La Crosse for exhibition to teenagers"; the live Elvis was projecting nothing less than "sexual gratification on stage."

A white man singing traditionally black music; a young performer producing sexual heat; a Southern kid going national: little wonder Presley struck so many as so refreshing in the mid-1950s. On September 9, 1956, Presley made his first appearance on *The Ed Sullivan Show,* producing an 82.6 percent television rating. His second turn on the show was also a blockbuster, and by the time Presley sang for Sullivan on a third occasion—the one where CBS directed that the cameras show Presley only from the waist up—the buttoned-down host had been won over. "I wanted to say to Elvis Presley and the country," Sullivan intoned, "that this is a real decent, fine boy."

His evident religious commitment also helped Presley win broader acceptance. As with so many Southern men, he could seem equally at home in church on Sunday mornings as in the juke joints on Saturday nights (even if he didn't actually turn up in church much as he grew older). Americans are familiar with the type. We had one for president for two terms at the close of the twentieth century: Bill Clinton, whose mother, Virginia, positively worshipped Elvis. "I loved Elvis," Bill Clinton recalled in his presidential memoir. "I could sing all his songs. . . . Beyond his music, I identi-fied with his small-town southern roots." And like Clinton, Presley was a model compartmentalizer. In Presley's case, he created music that celebrated a freer, more open attitude toward sex, while simultaneously releasing popular gospel tracks. As has often been remarked of charismatic figures such as the fictional James Bond and the real-life Presley, women wanted to be with him; men just wanted to be him.

His descent in the seventies was marked by an obsession with collecting police badges and firearms; it was as though, perhaps, he was seeking the emblems and means of control as he himself grew more erratic. In 1970, en route to Washington, Presley wrote President Nixon a letter on American Airlines notepaper, claiming that he had new insights into the youth unrest around the country as well as into communist "brainwashing" techniques. Would the president be interested in Pres-ley becoming a secret agent of the federal government? The request led to an im-promptu meeting in the Oval Office, where a puzzled Nixon listened to Presley's ramblings about the moral degeneration of the country.

Though the session was bizarre—Presley had presented himself at the White House without an appointment, only to be admitted to see Nixon—the gist of the conversation was not that different from what many white Americans of Presley's background might've said to the president at the time. Presley had been born into the demographic that helped elect Nixon—the ones who didn't protest, who didn't grow their hair long, who didn't burn their draft cards or run the country down (ba-sically the Okies from Muskogee).

Like the nation itself in the years of Vietnam and of Watergate, Presley was torn between patriotism and self-indulgence, clinging sentimentally to an older, warmer vision of America as he fed his own appetites for opioids and for fried peanut butter and banana sandwiches. Presley's own contradictions were like the country's as it hurtled—even stumbled—through a difficult and self-involved era.

I F PRESLEY AND Nixon represented one pole of American life, their antithesis could be found at the Woodstock Music and Art Fair in upstate New York in 1969. The three-day festival featured Richie Havens, Sweetwater, Bert Sommer, Ravi Shankar, Tim Hardin, Melanie Safka, Arlo Guthrie, Joan Baez (who sang "Swing Low, Sweet Chariot" and "We Shall Overcome"), Quill, Country Joe McDonald, Santana, John Sebastian, the Keef Hartley Band, The Incredible String Band,

Canned Heat, Mountain, the Grateful Dead, Creedence Clearwater Revival, The Who, Jefferson Airplane, Joe Cocker, Country Joe and the Fish, Janis Joplin, Ten Years After, The Band, Johnny Winter, Sly & the Family Stone, Blood, Sweat & Tears, Crosby, Stills, Nash, & Young, Paul Butterfield Blues Band, and Sha Na Na. Joni Mitchell wasn't there—she had stayed in New York City, at the Sherry-Netherland hotel, in order to be certain of making a scheduled appearance on *The Dick Cavett Show*—but afterward wrote a song, "Woodstock," that portrayed the festival in terms of a generation's mythic (but doomed) effort to return to a garden of innocence. "Her version of the song is a modal dirge," David Yaffe wrote in his *Reckless Daughter: A Portrait of Joni Mitchell*. "It can be played on nothing but the black keys on the piano—a minor chord, a suspended chord, and moving down to the ninth chord. . . . It is a purgation. It is an omen that something very, very bad will happen when the mud dries and the hippies go home. That garden they had to get back to—it was an illusion."

In the last performance of the event, Jimi Hendrix made a bit of history with an electric instrumental rendition of "The Star-Spangled Banner" on his guitar. "You can leave if you want to," Hendrix had told the crowd. "We're just jamming, that's all. Okay? You can leave, or you can clap." He was playing in the early-morning hours of the last day of the festival—it had run over schedule so badly that Hendrix, who'd been slated to appear at 11:00 P.M. the evening before, did not go onstage until 8:00 A.M. Hendrix's "Star-Spangled Banner" was a showstopper. "The song had long been a showcase for Jimi to display his innovative use of feedback, with his guitar mimicking the

"We play it the way the air is in America today," Jimi Hendrix said of "The Star-Spangled Banner." "The air is slightly static, see."

sounds of rocket explosions and ambulance wails," Charles R. Cross wrote in his Hendrix biography, *Room Full of Mirrors*. "Jimi's version was the rare example of a musical performance that challenged the listener to hear the song any other way in the future. Through feedback and sustain, he had taken one of the best-known tunes in America and made it his own." A fellow artist, Curtis Mayfield, said, "Jimi's approach to music transcends racial barriers. His imagination spoke to people on a deeper level than that."

The impact was immediate. "I was working in the 'bad trip tent' as a nurse when he started to play it," Roz Payne, the activist and independent filmmaker, recalled, according to Cross. "Everything seemed to stop. Before that, if someone would have played 'The Star-Spangled Banner,' we would have booed; after that, it became *our* song." Talking about the performance later, Hendrix said, "We play it the way the air is in America today. The air is slightly static, see."

Indeed it was. In "What's Going On," Marvin Gaye sang of weeping mothers and dying boys in a call for comity amid war abroad and riots at home.

As the civil rights movement seemed to crescendo with the legislative achievements of 1964 and 1965, the ongoing battles to ensure equality for women continued. At the 1976 Democratic National Convention in New York City, Barbara Jordan, a congresswoman from Texas, made history as the party's keynote speaker at Madison Square Garden. "It was one hundred and forty-four years ago that members of the Democratic Party first met in convention to select a Presidential candidate," Jordan told the delegates who had gathered to nominate Jimmy Carter for president. "Since that time, Democrats have continued to convene once every four years and draft a party platform and nominate a Presidential candidate. And our meeting this week is a continuation of that tradition. But there is something different about tonight. There is something special about tonight. What is different? What is special?" She paused, then said:

> I, Barbara Jordan, am a keynote speaker.
> A lot of years passed since 1832, and during that time it would have been most unusual for any national political party to ask a Barbara Jordan to deliver a keynote address. But tonight, here I am. And I feel that notwithstanding the past that my presence here is one additional bit of evidence that the American Dream need not forever be deferred.

Jordan's keynote was emblematic of a changing country. An African American woman at center stage, the voice of authority at the quadrennial meeting of the party of the slaveholding Jefferson and Jackson: The image was something that would have been unimaginable in previous generations.

Issues concerning the empowerment of women took on a much larger role in national life in the 1960s and 1970s. Lesley Gore's "You Don't Own Me," Janis Joplin's "Me and Bobby McGee," Helen Reddy's "I Am Woman," Loretta Lynn's "The Pill," The Staple Singers' "When Will We Be Paid," and Dolly Parton's "Just Because I'm a Woman" and "9 to 5" reflected an era of slow revolution as ossified gender roles gave way.

Understandings of sexual identity underwent a similar redefinition in the decades since the 1960s. Diana Ross's "I'm Coming Out," Elton John's "Elton's Song," Melissa Etheridge's "Come to My Window," and Lady Gaga's "Born This Way" were a few of the markers along the route from the Stonewall riots in 1969 through the landmark U.S. Supreme Court decision on marriage equality in 2015. "The Constitution promises liberty to all within its reach," the court's majority opinion declared, "a liberty that includes certain specific rights that allow persons, within a lawful realm, to define and express their identity." The journey toward more general acceptance of the equality of LGBTQ people continues in the music of singers such as Brandi Carlile, who won a Grammy in 2019 for an album that included "The Joke," a song that explores, among other things, the struggle of growing up gay.

ELVIS PRESLEY WOULDN'T see the seventies through. In the middle of August 1977, preparing for a tour, Presley was found dead at Graceland, officially of heart failure. There was much controversy about the cause of death, but what's clear is that he died an opioid addict. Journalists and biographers discovered that from January 1977 until Presley's death, his doctor, the flashy George "Nick" Nichopoulos, prescribed the singer at least 8,805 pills and sundry forms of drugs, including Dilaudid, Quaaludes, Percodan, Demerol, and cocaine hydrochloride. (To reconstruct the prescription record, investigators had to contact 153 pharmacies in the aftermath of Presley's death.) He was forty-two years old.

Was Leonard Bernstein right? Did the "whole sixties" come from Presley? Surely much of it did, and the seventies, too, and the eighties, and down to our own day.

Presley's life is an American tragedy—a talent of epic proportions cut short by in-
dulgence and appetite—and it's a story that's not yet over. Shawn Klush, an Elvis
tribute artist, put it well: "People love him, not only for his talent, but because he was
a great, humble, kind man. He loved God. He loved his parents. He loved his country." His country loved him back—for his voice, for his spirit, and because it saw in
him, for better and for worse, what it was, and what it hoped to be.

In concert in the 1970s, Presley popularized "An American Trilogy," which
opened with a bit of "Dixie," shifted to a section of "The Battle Hymn of the Republic," moved on to a verse of "All My Trials," and then climaxed with a return to
"Glory, glory, hallelujah." The inclusion of "All My Trials," about the deathbed words
of a parent to a child, is perhaps the composition's most intriguing element: "Hush,

AN AMERICAN TRILOGY

This is one of my favorites medleys of all time. It combines three disparate songs
with roots in the Civil War—"Dixie," "The Battle Hymn of the Republic," and "All
My Trials." "The Battle Hymn" drew its melody from "John Brown's Body." The
concept for this marriage belongs to Mickey Newbury. He was from a time of
great Nashville storytellers like Kris Kristofferson, Wayne Carson, Tom T. Hall,
and Bobby Braddock, among others.

There's a genius element to combining these songs. "Dixie" is slowed down
considerably. But when the messages of these songs are combined, it becomes
a moving anthem with a huge spiritual component. The grief and sorrow pour
from both Newbury's and Presley's performances. Elvis's longtime friends the
Jordanaires sang background and added a great gospel element to the medley,
which he featured on his *Aloha from Hawaii* television special. What strikes me
most about Elvis's version is how in so many ways it's more in the line of early
songs of America and builds to several crescendo moments. Newbury stayed
more acoustic.

And I personally connect with "All My Trials," with its roots in a Bahamian
lullaby. Its spiritual message that it will all soon be over is an eternal one.   —T.M.

little baby / Don't you cry . . . But all my trials will soon be over." The hope of the trilogy, it seems, is that the clash of visions between "Dixie" and "The Battle Hymn of the Republic"—of, really, the clash between the blackface lyrics of Daniel Emmett and the ennobling verses of Julia Ward Howe—may one day end in the coming of the Lord, whose truth will be marching on.

CHAPTER EIGHT

BORN IN THE U.S.A.

"She's still a beacon, still a magnet for all who must have freedom, for all the pilgrims from all the lost places who are hurtling through the darkness, toward home."

—RONALD REAGAN, Farewell Address to the Nation, 1989

"Of the many tragic images of that day, the picture I couldn't let go of was of the emergency workers going *up* the stairs as others rushed down to safety. . . . If you love life or any part of it, the depth of their sacrifice is unthinkable and incomprehensible."

—BRUCE SPRINGSTEEN on the terrorist attacks of September 11, 2001

I T WAS AN unlikely pairing of author and subject. In the summer of 1984, the conservative columnist George F. Will attended—and, even more remarkably, enjoyed—a Bruce Springsteen concert in suburban Washington. With his bow ties, dry wit, and scholarly disposition—he favored allusions to the Founding Fathers and Anthony Trollope, among others—Will, educated at Trinity College in Connecticut, at Oxford, and at Princeton, had won a Pulitzer Prize for commentary and was a mainstay of televised political commentary in the Carter and Reagan years. "There is not a smidgen of androgyny in Springsteen, who, rocketing around the stage in a T-shirt and headband, resembles Robert De Niro in the combat scenes of *The Deer Hunter*," Will wrote of a late-August "Born in the U.S.A." show. "This is rock for the United Steelworkers, accompanied by the opening barrage of the battle of the Somme." Will's host brought along cotton for his ears. Briefly insulted, Will recalled, he "made it three beats into the first number before packing my ears."

In his concertgoing costume of a bow tie and double-breasted blazer, Will was

Nearly 3,000 people died in the attacks of Tuesday, September 11, 2001—what President Bush would call a "day of fire."

Bruce Springsteen in a performance of "Born in the U.S.A.," Los Angeles, 1985.

playing to type and acknowledged that Springsteen's fans "regarded me as exotic fauna . . . and undertook to instruct me." He reported a "typical tutorial":

"What do you like about him?"
Male fan: "He sings about faith and traditional values."
Male fan's female friend, dryly: "And cars and girls."
Male fan: "No, no, it's about community and roots and perseverance and family."
She: "And cars and girls."

Will took Springsteen's work ethic—the columnist remarked on the smell of Ben-Gay backstage—as a manifestation of the virtues of the free market. "In an age of lackadaisical effort and slipshod products, anyone who does anything—anything legal—conspicuously well and with zest is a national asset," Will wrote. "Springsteen's tour is hard, honest work and evidence of the astonishing vitality of America's regions and generations. They produce distinctive tones of voice that other regions and generations embrace. There still is nothing quite like being born in the U.S.A."

True, but Will's conservative take on Springsteen's oeuvre elided the complexities of the lyrics themselves. A son of blue-collar New Jersey, Springsteen had long sung of working-class anxiety and the shadowy precincts of what President Reagan, in a riff on John Winthrop, thought of as the "shining city on a hill."

To Springsteen, "Born in the U.S.A." was, he recalled in his memoir, "a protest song, and when I heard it thundering back at me through the Hit Factory's gargantuan studio speakers, I knew it was one of the best things I'd ever done. It was a GI blues, the verses an accounting, the choruses a declaration of the one sure thing that could not be denied . . . birthplace. Birthplace, and the right to all of the blood, confusion, blessings and grace that come with it. Having paid body and soul, you have earned, many times over, the right to claim and shape your piece of home ground."

In the aftermath of George Will's encounter with the "Born in the U.S.A." tour, the reelection campaign of Reagan and George H. W. Bush, which was then under way against the Democratic ticket of Walter Mondale and Geraldine Ferraro, sought to adopt Springsteen, and his song, as its own. In a speech at Hammonton, New Jersey, on Wednesday, September 19, 1984, Reagan said, "America's future rests in a thousand dreams inside your hearts; it rests in the message of hope in songs so many young Americans admire: New Jersey's own Bruce Springsteen. And helping you make those dreams come true is what this job of mine is all about."

The sunny but conservative president appropriating the work of a self-styled blue-collar poet laureate: It was a perfect campaign story. "The president's press office," *The New York Times* reported dryly, "could not immediately say what Springsteen tune might be Mr. Reagan's favorite." (The White House later offered up "Born to Run," but no one really believed it.)

Springsteen in particular was having none of it. He responded inside of a week, obliquely but unmistakably. "There's really something dangerous happening to us out there," Springsteen said at a show in Pittsburgh. "We're slowly getting split up into two different Americas. Things are gettin' taken away from people that need them and given to people that don't need them, and there's a promise getting broken. In the beginning the idea was that we all live here a little bit like a family, where the strong can help the weak ones, the rich can help the poor ones. I don't think the American dream was that everybody was going to make it or that everybody was going to make a billion dollars, but it was that everybody was going to have an opportunity and the chance to live a life with some decency and some dignity and a chance for some self-respect."

The Reagan–Springsteen divide was a microcosm of the larger political and cultural divides of post–World War II America. In a *Rolling Stone* interview, Springsteen put the matter as well as anyone could. "I think what's happening now is people want to forget," he told the magazine. "There was Vietnam, there was Watergate, there was Iran—we were beaten, we were hustled, and then we were humiliated. And I think people have a need to feel good about the country they live in. But what's happening, I think, is that the need—which is a good thing—is gettin' manipulated and exploited. And you see the Reagan reelection ads on TV—you know, 'It's morning in America.' And you say, well, it's not morning in Pittsburgh. It's not morning above 125th Street in New York. It's midnight, and, like, there's a bad moon risin'. And that's why when Reagan mentioned my name in New Jersey, I felt it was another manipulation, and I had to disassociate myself from the president's kind words."

There was, of course, another view of the enigmatic and magnetic Reagan, a complicated figure and a consequential president. He battled Alzheimer's disease after he left the White House, and, in the late 1990s, with his brain ravaged, he could remember only his beginnings. As Reagan's memory faded, the years seemed to fall away: the presidency, the governorship, Hollywood, sportscasting. In chats with guests in his Los Angeles office and in bits of conversation with his family at home in Bel Air, he'd talk about his early days in Illinois on the Rock River. "You know, that's where I used to be a lifeguard," Reagan would say, gazing at a picture of the river that hung in his Century City office. "I saved seventy-seven lives." There had been a log, he'd go on, where he carved a notch for every swimmer he rescued. "It was obviously an important part of his life, something he cherished," an aide recalled. "Being a lifeguard was ever-present in his memory." The image lingered when everything else was disappearing.

A man given to thinking in visual terms, Reagan could be moved as much by music as by movies. On the Saturday before his inauguration, in January 1981, Reagan was dazzled by a concert at the Lincoln Memorial. On a night of fireworks and cheers, the Mormon Tabernacle Choir had sung "God Bless America" and "The

Battle Hymn of the Republic"; according to *Washington Post* reporter and Reagan biographer Lou Cannon, the president-elect, watching and listening, had become quietly emotional.

"Ken, did you have a chance to get to that ceremony at the Lincoln Memorial last night?" Reagan asked his speechwriter Ken Khachigian the next day.

"No, sir, I was at the office," he said.

"I don't think I've been to anything quite like it," Reagan said. "That Lincoln Memorial . . . it's such a beautiful place. I've never been filled with such a surge of patriotism. It was so hard not to cry during the whole thing. That choir, the Mormon Tabernacle Choir, singing 'God Bless America.' Well, it was cold, but it was so moving, I was crying frozen tears."

The country Reagan was to lead was suffering from what his predecessor, Jimmy Carter, had described, in July 1979, as a "crisis of confidence." As the 1970s ended, inflation spiked, interest rates soared, the Soviets invaded Afghanistan, and Islamic militants took U.S. diplomats hostage in Iran. Carter would be the fifth American president in twenty years. "The erosion of our confidence in the future," he told the country in mid-1979, "is threatening to destroy the social and the political fabric of America."

A former movie actor, television host ("General Electric Theater" and "Death Valley Days"), corporate spokesman, and governor of California, Reagan was in many ways a conservative reply to Roosevelt's New Deal, Harry Truman's Fair Deal, and Lyndon Johnson's Great Society. "No government ever voluntarily reduces itself in size," Reagan said in a televised speech on behalf of Barry Goldwater's presidential campaign in late October 1964. "Government programs, once launched, never disappear. Actually, a government bureau is the nearest thing to eternal life we'll ever see on this earth."

His critique was couched in the language of American optimism. "You and I are told increasingly that we have to choose between a left or right, but I would like to suggest that there is no such thing as a left or right," Reagan said. "There is only an up or down—up to a man's age-old dream, the ultimate in individual freedom consistent with law and order—or down to the antheap of totalitarianism, and regardless of their sincerity, their humanitarian motives, those who would trade our freedom for security have embarked on this downward course."

His words could be stark. "You and I know and do not believe that life is so dear and peace so sweet as to be purchased at the price of chains and slavery," Reagan said in his broadcast for Goldwater—a conservative manifesto so powerful that Reagan's legions still simply refer to it as "The Speech," and everyone knows what they're talking about. "If nothing in life is worth dying for," Reagan asked of the Cold War, "when did this begin—just in the face of this enemy? Or should Moses have told the children of Israel to live in slavery under the pharaohs? Should Christ have refused the cross? Should the patriots at Concord Bridge have thrown down their guns and refused to fire the shot heard 'round the world? The martyrs of history were not fools, and our honored dead who gave their lives to stop the advance of the Nazis didn't die in vain." He paraphrased Churchill: "'The destiny of man is not measured by material computation. When great forces are on the move in the world, we learn we are spirits—not animals.'" In closing, Reagan borrowed a phrase from FDR's 1936 acceptance speech to the Democratic National Convention, saying, "You and I have a rendezvous with destiny. We will preserve for our children this, the last best hope of man on earth, or we will sentence them to take the last step into a thousand years of darkness."

Reagan, then, should have been a divisive politician—a man about whom the nation was closely and bitterly split. In the White House, he'd prove a contradictory figure. He mangled facts; caricatured welfare recipients; presided over a dark recession in 1981–82; seemed uncaring about the emerging HIV/AIDS crisis; and plunged the country into the Iran-Contra scandal. And yet while many people were consistently critical of him, he left office with a 63 percent approval rating. The man himself seemed to dwell just above the arena, escaping widespread political enmity.

His personal gifts were enormous and helped smooth the rough edges of his rhetoric and of his policies. "Some of the N.S.C. [National Security Council] staff are too hard line & don't think any approach should be made to the Soviets," the president wrote in his diary in April 1983. "I think I'm hard line & will never appease but I do want to try & let them see there is a better world if they'll show *by deed* they want to get along with the free world."

He'd begun his presidency with a darker tone about the Soviets. At Reagan's first White House press conference, on Thursday, January 29, 1981, Sam Donaldson of ABC News had asked, "Mr. President, what do you see as the long-range intentions of the Soviet Union? Do you think, for instance, the Kremlin is bent on world domination that might lead to a continuation of the Cold War, or do you think that under other circumstances détente is possible?"

Reagan's reply was pointed. "I know of no leader of the Soviet Union since the revolution, and including the present leadership," the president said, "that has not more than once repeated in the various Communist congresses they hold their determination that their goal must be the promotion of world revolution and a one-world Socialist or Communist state, whichever word you want to use. Now, as long as they do that and as long as they, at the same time, have openly and publicly declared that the only morality they recognize is what will further their cause, meaning they reserve unto themselves the right to commit any crime, to lie, to cheat, in order to attain that, and that is moral, not immoral, and we operate on a different set of standards, I think when you do business with them, even at a détente, you keep that in mind."

By the time he was leaving office, however, the world was very different—and he had helped make it so. "In this Moscow spring," he told students at Moscow State University in May 1988, "we may be allowed [this] hope: that freedom, like the fresh green sapling planted over Tolstoy's grave, will blossom forth at last in the rich fertile soil of your people and culture. We may be allowed to hope that the marvelous sound of a new openness will keep rising through, ringing through, leading to a new world of reconciliation, friendship, and peace." The old lifeguard could put another notch on the log.

For many Americans, Reagan at once embodied and evoked the nation as they would like it to be. His was in part a leadership of imagination, of projecting a vision of the world that was more Norman Rockwell than Norman Lear. He was, in other words, an artist of America, a musician whose voice and melodies enabled a goodly number of his followers to transcend the limitations and disappointments and anxieties of their workaday worlds and cast themselves as players on a larger stage, one on which Americans did good and great things.

THE SONG MOST associated with the Reagan vision can be seen as a conservative "Born in the U.S.A."—Lee Greenwood's "God Bless the U.S.A." Greenwood had toiled for nearly two decades as a Las Vegas lounge singer (and occasional card dealer) before finding success in Nashville and winning the 1983 Country Music Association Male Vocalist of the Year award.

"The song was a response to the hurt and anger I felt after the [Soviet] downing of a Korean jet on a flight from New York to Seoul in 1983, with 269 passengers aboard, including 63 Americans," Greenwood recalled. "I could not forget the scenes of weeping men, women, and children who had just been told the grim news that their loved ones would never return." Looking back on "God Bless the U.S.A.," Greenwood mused, "Did I know the song was special, a hit from the beginning? Well, every time you go into the studio to record a song, you think it is going to be a hit. But, yes, I knew this song was special because of the response we received whenever we sang it live."

As the 1984 presidential race took shape, Reagan ad maestro Sig Rogich was with BBDO's Phil Dusenberry one afternoon and happened to hear Greenwood's "God Bless the U.S.A." Rogich knew it would be a fantastic score for the Reagan "It's Morning in America" campaign, and he called Greenwood the next day to see if he could use the song in commercials for the president. Thrilled, the singer licensed it to the campaign for a dollar. (The deal enraged Lew Wasserman, the head of MCA, Greenwood's record company, but by the time Wasserman got involved, Reagan had heard the song, loved it, and Wasserman, who'd represented Reagan in Hollywood, reluctantly gave in.)

In Greenwood's telling, the song came to the president's attention through Merv Griffin, a pal of Mrs. Reagan's. Greenwood had sung it on Griffin's show and the host sent a videotape of the performance to the First Lady, who loved it.

However the song reached the Reagan high command, it quickly became the Reagan-Bush reelection anthem and is now a conservative standard. Greenwood's song was as unapologetically upbeat about America in the Age of Reagan as George Cohan had been in World War I and Irving Berlin had been in World War II and Barry Sadler had been in the Vietnam era. Though there's no ambivalence in "God Bless the U.S.A." about the national enterprise, the song's optimism isn't entirely schmaltzy. In the opening lyrics, the narrator muses about what he'd do if he lost everything and had to begin again. The song's solution to the hypothetical problem is one that could resonate with liberals as well as conservatives, Democrats as well as Republicans, for the answer to the doomsday scenario is one with deep roots in the American experience: He'd take advantage of the America of second chances and hurl himself back into the arena.

The imagined nation of "God Bless the U.S.A." is one of opportunity, a place where Americans, to borrow a phrase of Lincoln's, have a "fair chance" to rise and thrive. There's no impenetrable darkness in Greenwood's song, only crises to be

BORN IN THE U.S.A. and GOD BLESS THE U.S.A.

The parallels here pretty much stop with the titles. Greenwood's "God Bless the U.S.A." is an extremely patriotic, borderline over-the-top anthem that still ensures a standing ovation when performed today. It was a huge hit and has become a Red State favorite. Springsteen's "Born in the U.S.A." was a working-class song, a blue-collar anthem detailing the mistreatment of returning Vietnam War veterans.

Years ago, trying to defend my band in a bar fight, I said something like, "No one calls my guys assholes but me." "Born in the U.S.A." works that way for me. It points out some ugly truths about how vets were received and about how the country doesn't work for everybody, but Springsteen's music reminds us that for all of that it's still our country. Bruce has that uncanny ability in his songwriting to make you feel that we're in this together, however painful it may be. You're in it together.

—T.M.

overcome in a land secured by sacrifice and open to all. Where Springsteen sang of broken promises and unfulfilled dreams, Greenwood insisted on perpetual promise and enduring dreams. Neither was wholly right nor wholly wrong; the country works for some and doesn't work for others, which is in the nature of things. Like America, the songs are a matter of emphasis and of perspective.

AS ARE POLITICS. In what was perhaps the most brilliant critique of Reagan in real time, the then New York governor Mario Cuomo turned Reagan's favorite image of the shining city against the president. "The hard truth is that not everyone is sharing in this city's splendor and glory," Cuomo said in his keynote address to the 1984 Democratic National Convention. "A shining city is perhaps all the president sees from the portico of the White House and the veranda of his ranch, where everyone seems to be doing well. But there's another city; there's another part to the shining city; the part where some people can't pay their mortgages, and most young people can't afford one, where students can't afford the education they need, and middle-class parents watch the dreams they hold for their children evaporate." For many, Cuomo argued, the Gipper's America was a movie in which they had no part.

And yet, in forty-nine of fifty American states, a majority of those who voted on Tuesday, November 6, 1984, chose to entrust their fates to Ronald Reagan for another four years. In our era of closely divided presidential elections—the winner in four out of the eight contests since Reagan's reelection hasn't broken the 50 percent mark in the popular vote—the magnitude of the verdict of 1984 is striking. In the way we measure such things, the Reagan victory was really the last time Americans were anything close to unified in the choice of a president.

Does that mean more of us preferred Lee Greenwood to Bruce Springsteen? No. But it does mean that Reagan's leadership repays attention, for his success tells us that optimism and large-heartedness—as opposed to pessimism and narrow definitions of who can be an American—are presidential virtues. Reagan did not glower, he smiled. Reagan did not build walls, he opened his arms. And he hoped the nation would always follow his example.

"And so, goodbye": President Reagan prepares to deliver his farewell address, Wednesday, January 11, 1989.

At 9:00 P.M. Eastern Time on the winter Wednesday of January 11, 1989, the president, one month shy of his seventy-eighth birthday, delivered his thirty-fourth and final Oval Office speech to the American people.

Reagan was honest about what it's really like to sit behind that desk. "One of the things about the presidency is that you're always somewhat apart," Reagan told the country. "You spend a lot of time going by too fast in a car someone else is driving, and seeing the people through tinted glass—the parents holding up a child, and the wave you saw too late and couldn't return. And so many times I wanted to stop, and reach out from behind the glass, and connect. Well, maybe I can do a little of that tonight."

By acknowledging the distance between the people and the powerful, he closed it, bringing his listeners into his orbit in rather the way his old hero Franklin Roosevelt used to do with his fireside chats. Neither Reagan nor Roosevelt turned red in the face or bullied or blustered; they spoke to us neighbor-to-neighbor, affirming the nature of self-government.

Invoking John Winthrop, Reagan said, "I've spoken of the shining city all my political life, but I don't know if I ever quite communicated what I saw when I said it." It was a free, proud city, built on a strong foundation, full of commerce and creativity, he said, adding, "If there had to be city walls, the walls had doors, and the doors were open to anyone with the will and the heart to get here."

Whatever his faults, Ronald Reagan believed in the possibilities of a country that was forever reinventing itself. "And how stands the city on this winter night?" Reagan asked. "More prosperous, more secure, and happier than it was eight years ago. . . . And she's still a beacon, still a magnet for all who must have freedom, for all the pilgrims from all the lost places who are hurtling through the darkness, toward home."

They hurtle through that darkness even now. Reagan would have us light the lamp.

GREENWOOD'S PERSPECTIVE ON the country was Reagan's. There were, as always, other perspectives—many others—and one of the most influential was that of Run-DMC, a pioneering rap group that played a critical role in the rise of hip-hop. In 1983, in a kind of rap version of Mario Cuomo's argument at the Democratic convention the next year, Run-DMC indicted "the way it is" in "It's Like

Lee Greenwood performs his signature "God Bless the U.S.A." at a Reagan centennial celebration at the fortieth president's Simi Valley, California, library in 2011.

That." (Grandmaster Flash and the Furious Five's "The Message" was a similar number.)

Hip-hop's initial commercial and cultural success was roughly concurrent with the Reagan presidency. "The sharp contrast between a White House that is announcing 'Morning in America' and a black culture that is mourning the racial divides in this country was clear from the beginning," the professor and scholar Michael Eric Dyson says. "You get the politicization from the start. When Chuck D said rap music is the CNN of black America, he understood that hip-hop is both the reality of the streets and, for white America, a window on that reality. It is a sonic fiction being generated to tell the truth about black folk in America, and therefore about America itself."

There were, to be sure, sundry truths. Artists such as Jay Z, Snoop Dogg, Lauryn Hill, and Queen Latifah built cultural bridges once thought fanciful. "They taught black America an important lesson: You don't have to cross over to white America; you can get white America to cross over to you," Dyson says. "Rappers were talking about these enclaves of civic horror called ghettoes and slums and, by owning the story, were restoring the humanity and agency of a black culture." And there were

Tupac Shakur's incandescent poetry exemplified the fury and the fire of the emerging world of hip-hop in the post-Reagan years.

gangsta songs like N.W.A.'s "Fuck tha Police" on their album *Straight Outta Compton* and Ice-T's "Squeeze the Trigger."

The power of hip-hop has shaped each post-Reagan generation. Urgent and energetic, rap music is protest itself. Tupac Shakur's 1991 "Words of Wisdom," for instance, is fiery poetry. "What's more a part of the American Dream than these guys from nothing, seeking everything and not letting anything get in their way?" Dyson says. "'My community, my street, my hood'—there's a path from Run DMC to Obama running for president. What hip-hop did was create an image in the minds of young white people that a smart black guy could talk intelligently. There would have been no Obama without Jay Z."

TUESDAY, SEPTEMBER 11, 2001, dawned bright and blue, and it promised to be a beautiful late-summer day. American Airlines Flight 11, nonstop from Boston to LAX, took off at 7:59 A.M. Eastern time. A passenger named Mohammed

Atta was in business class, in seat 8D. Within fifteen minutes, the jet had reached 26,000 feet. About sixteen seconds later, air-traffic control in Boston issued a routine directive to the pilots to head up to 35,000 feet.

No one replied. Flight 11 had gone dark.

Reports of what happened between 8:14 and 8:46, reconstructed by the 9/11 Commission, come from flight attendants who called the ground as the hijacking unfolded. There were stabbings and the spraying of Mace; the taking of the cockpit; and Atta's assumption of the controls. As the plane headed toward New York, officials on the ground thought the hijackers might be bound for Kennedy Airport. The rest of the story is in the words of Madeline "Amy" Sweeney, one of the flight attendants still on a phone line. "Something is wrong. We are in a rapid descent . . . we are all over the place." It was about 8:44. "We are flying low. We are flying very, very low. We are flying way too low." A pause, then: "Oh my God, we are way too low." American Flight 11 struck the North Tower of the World Trade Center at 8:46:40, and the world changed.

Oh my God, we are way too low: Amy Sweeney's words marked the opening chapter of a new era in American life, one in which innocents found themselves transformed into combatants by the fiat of a faraway fanatic and his followers. That fanatic—the elusive embodiment of ancient evil in a new century, the man who made a living hell of Sweeney's final moments—met his own end on Monday, May 2, 2011, when American military forces, in a nighttime raid, killed him in a walled compound along a dirt road in Pakistan. Osama bin Laden, the terrorist leader in his early fifties who seemed somehow ageless, was shot in the chest and head and buried at sea. Amy Sweeney and the roughly three thousand other victims of 9/11—as well as the victims of bin Laden's other attacks, from East Africa to Yemen—were avenged.

Bin Laden had declared war on the West, especially on America. He claimed he was doing so in the name of Allah. The extreme reading of Islam that provided him his rhetoric and his ethos, however, was secondary to the more elemental force that drove him: the will to power. The failure to capture or kill him sooner flummoxed three presidential administrations, from Bill Clinton to Barack Obama. In retrospect (that wondrous thing), we can see how bin Laden moved from smaller-scale bombings, especially the 1998 attacks on American embassies in Africa, to what Al Qaeda called the "spectacular" misery of 9/11. From Langley to Tora Bora to a thousand unknown points in between, men and women acting for our collective security

The second tower of the World Trade Center explodes. "Where were you," Alan Jackson would ask in song, "when the world stopped turnin'?"

have lived and fought and died to disrupt Al Qaeda, struggling in a common cause that was all too easy to put out of mind.

Americans like to look to tomorrow. It's the frontier spirit in us, the restlessness that brought so many to the New World from the Old. But without remembering yesterday, we may fail to learn from even the very recent past. For Americans in the nineteenth century, slavery and the Civil War were shaping events; in middle of the twentieth century, there were Munich and Pearl Harbor and then Vietnam; now there is 9/11 and its fallout, not least the Iraq War.

Our central yesterday remains that now-distant Tuesday in 2001. It is the day that has affected every subsequent day, from Manhattan to Kabul to Baghdad to Islamabad. At the heart of the story of that day are people like Peter Hanson, a passenger on United Airlines Flight 175, the plane that hit the South Tower nearly

"I can hear you," President Bush cried through the bullhorn at Ground Zero. *"The rest of the world hears you, and the people who knocked these buildings down will hear all of us soon."*

twenty minutes after Amy Sweeney's American Airlines jet struck the North Tower. In a call to his father, Lee, seconds before the end, Peter said: "It's getting bad, Dad—a stewardess was stabbed . . . It's getting very bad on the plane . . . I think we are going down . . . Don't worry, Dad—if it happens, it'll be very fast—my God my God."

It did happen. On the Friday after the attacks, George W. Bush stepped up into the lectern of Washington National Cathedral to address a nation in shock. The memorial service for the victims of Tuesday's horrors alternated between mourning and resolve. The congregation sang "O God, Our Help in Ages Past" and "A Mighty Fortress Is Our God"; it listened to solo renditions of Katharine Lee Bates's "America the Beautiful," Albert Malotte's setting of "The Lord's Prayer," and a U.S. Army Orchestra performance of Berlin's "God Bless America."

"We come before God to pray for the missing and the dead, and for those who loved them," Bush said. "On Tuesday, our country was attacked with deliberate and massive cruelty. We have seen the images of fire and ashes and bent steel. . . . War has been waged against us by stealth and deceit and murder. This nation is peaceful, but fierce when stirred to anger. This conflict was begun on the timing and terms of others. It will end in a way and at an hour of our choosing."

Grief, the president said, must lead to determination. "In every generation, the world has produced enemies of human freedom," Bush told the nation. "They have attacked America because we are freedom's home and defender. And the commitment of our Fathers is now the calling of our time." As the service came to a close, the congregation sang the hymn that had been composed by Julia Ward Howe in a distant Washington night at Willard's Hotel: "Mine eyes have seen the glory of the coming of the Lord. . . ."

There had been some behind-the-scenes debate about the hymn's verses. Some White House staffers and Cathedral officials had quietly objected to the martial nature of Ward's poem. Its "words and images were unabashedly militant," as John Stauffer and Benjamin Soskis wrote in a study of "The Battle Hymn," and Karen Hughes, a senior adviser to President Bush, "felt the need to run the selection by the president. She let him know that some churches considered the song excessively bellicose and had removed it from their hymnals." Bush was unfazed. "Defiance," he told Hughes, "is good." The hymn would be sung—including the unflinching "As He died to make men holy / Let us die to make men free."

In his homily at the service, Billy Graham had acknowledged the unfathomable mystery of evil and the limitations of earthly reassurance. "No matter how hard we try," Graham said, "words simply cannot express the horror, the shock and the revulsion we all feel."

Music came closer. From "The Lord's Prayer" to "The Battle Hymn of the Republic," the music of the day reflected the hour's complex emotions. "The music that filled Washington National Cathedral on Friday—and wafted across airwaves and out of countless televisions nationwide—struck a delicate balance between inspirational religious repertoire and patriotic songs bound to touch a chord with most Americans," the *Chicago Tribune* wrote. "That was precisely the point, according to those who selected the music, which played a central role in this service and in the public consciousness, as it traditionally has done in times of national crisis or war."

Beyond the cathedral, many Americans turned to music to make sense of the deadliest single-day attack on America since Pearl Harbor. On a Friday, September 21, 2001, broadcast entitled "America: A Tribute to Heroes," musicians sought to console and to inspire. Performers included Springsteen ("My City of Ruins"), Stevie Wonder and Take 6 ("Love's in Need of Love Today"), U2 ("Peace on Earth";

"Walk On"), Faith Hill ("There Will Come a Day"), Tom Petty and the Heartbreak-ers ("I Won't Back Down"), Enrique Iglesias ("Hero"), Neil Young ("Imagine"), Alicia Keys ("Someday We'll All Be Free"), Limp Bizkit and John Rzeznik ("Wish You Were Here"), Billy Joel ("New York State of Mind"), the Dixie Chicks ("I Be-lieve in Love"), Dave Matthews ("Everyday"), Wyclef Jean ("Redemption Song"), Mariah Carey ("Hero"), Bon Jovi ("Livin' on a Prayer"), Sheryl Crow ("Safe and Sound"), Sting ("Fragile"), Eddie Vedder ("Long Road"), Paul Simon ("Bridge Over Troubled Water"), Celine Dion ("God Bless America"), and Willie Nelson with the company ("America the Beautiful").

The details of what President Bush would call a "day of fire" found expression in new music. When reports came of Todd Beamer's final words—"Let's roll"—as he and passengers aboard United Airlines Flight 93 stormed the cockpit in the skies above Pennsylvania, Neil Young, who had been similarly moved by the Kent State shootings thirty years before, wrote "Let's Roll," an anthem about the courage of Beamer and his compatriots.

Young was telling the story of Flight 93's martyred heroes; in "Where Were You (When the World Stopped Turning)?" Alan Jackson sang about the impact of the day on the rest of us. By asking the question of his audience—Where were *you?*—Jackson brought the whole country into the story of the day and affirmed the cen-trality of things we tend to take for granted. Part of Jackson's chorus was from St. Paul's First Letter to the Corinthians: "And now these three remain: faith, hope, and love. But the greatest of these is love."

Where Jackson was warm, his fellow country artist Toby Keith was warlike. In "Courtesy of the Red, White and Blue (The Angry American)" Keith was martial, plain-spoken, and provocative. His was an anthem not of anguish but of anger. The essayist Verlyn Klinkenborg wrote of catching Keith's singing the song on Country Music Television in the summer of 2002. "Mr. Keith is a solid slab of a man, a for-mer football player and Oklahoma oilhand," Klinkenborg wrote. "On CMT he wore a flat-crowned, pure-white cowboy hat and a long goatee that was half Buffalo Bill, half buffalo. He struck out into the song, and the audience sang along with him. The music was solemn, almost dirge-like. Imagine, if you can, a cross between the slow part of 'American Pie' and 'Ballad of the Green Berets.'"

THESE WERE VOICES from Nashville; in New Jersey, Bruce Springsteen meditated on the firemen and the cops who had laid down their lives for others. "Of the many tragic images of that day, the picture I couldn't let go of was of the emergency workers going *up* the stairs as others rushed down to safety," Springsteen recalled. "The sense of duty, the courage, ascending into . . . what? The religious image of ascension, the crossing of the line between this world, the world of blood, work, family, your children, the breath in your lungs, the ground beneath your feet, all that is life, and . . . the next, flooded my imagination. If you love life or any part of it, the depth of their sacrifice is unthinkable and incomprehensible. Yet what they left behind was tangible. Death, along with all its anger, pain and loss, opens a window of possibility for the living. It removes the veil that the 'ordinary' gently drapes over our eyes. Renewed sight is the hero's last loving gift to those left behind." His "Into the Fire," on the 2002 album *The Rising,* was an ode to those heroes. In addition to

THE RISING

In the Grammy Award–winning album *The Rising,* released about ten months after 9/11, Springsteen offers us a mirror to see what we are feeling, and a salve for healing in every word. They say that great songwriting tells you how you feel about something in a way you didn't even know how to express. On *The Rising,* Bruce shows us what we were feeling but *couldn't* express.

He gives us a modern-day hymnal with this body of work, with words and music to grieve 9/11, along with a sense of community that we're going to get through it, together. The chorus of "Into the Fire," an ode to the more than 300 firefighters lost that awful day, transforms the pain of losing these brave heroes into a mantra of hope.

"My City of Ruins" is another favorite from this album. Written before 9/11, it takes on a broader impact from its original purpose (to draw attention to the revitalization of Asbury Park). The city is the people, with words to come back stronger than ever. It's understandable how these songs have come to be anthems for the brave men and women of the New York fire and police departments. Rise up.

—T.M.

the title track, *The Rising* also featured "My City of Ruins" and "Lonesome Day," songs that were heard in the context of the opening years of the war on terror, a struggle that brought its own ambiguities and uncertainties. Neither as unified as in World War II nor as overwhelmingly divided as in Vietnam, the post-9/11 nation was the kind of place Springsteen had sung about so long: searching and wondering, nostalgic and nervous.

T HERE WERE FLASHES of controversy that were reminiscent of the 1960s and early '70s. In 2003, as U.S. troops prepared to invade Saddam Hussein's Iraq, the Dixie Chicks protested President Bush's leadership. "Just so you know, we're on the good side with y'all," Natalie Maines said from the stage during a performance in London. "We do not want this war, this violence, and we're ashamed that the president of the United States is from Texas." Facing a fan backlash and boycotts—including being pulled from many radio playlists—Maines said, "We are currently in Europe and witnessing a huge anti-American sentiment as a result of the perceived rush to war. While war may remain a viable option, as a mother, I just want to see every possible alternative exhausted before children and American soldiers' lives are lost. I love my country. I am a proud American."

It wasn't enough. "As a concerned American citizen, I apologize to President Bush because my remark was disrespectful," Maines said in a subsequent statement. "I feel that whoever holds that office should be treated with the utmost respect." Three years later, she would un-apologize, saying, "I don't feel he is owed any re-spect whatsoever."

"I mean, the Dixie Chicks are free to speak their mind," Bush replied when asked about Maines's London comment. "They can say what they want to say. . . . they shouldn't have their feelings hurt just because some people don't want to buy their records when they speak out. You know, freedom is a two-way street. But I . . . don't really care what the Dixie Chicks said. I want to do what I think is right for the American people, and if some singers or Hollywood stars feel like speaking out, that's fine. That's the great thing about America. It stands in stark contrast to Iraq, by the way."

Toby Keith was a bit less nuanced in his reaction. In 2002, Maines had dismissed Keith's "Courtesy of the Red, White and Blue" as "ignorant," adding, "It targets an entire culture—and not just the bad people who did bad things. You've got to have some tact. Anybody can write, 'We'll put a boot in your ass.'" Now, after London, Keith fired back by flashing a manufactured image of Maines with Saddam Hussein on huge screens as he sang "Courtesy" in concert.

The episode—the Dixie Chicks call it "the Incident" (with a capital "I")—raised profound questions about free speech and its implications. There were death threats and slurs, angry call-ins and widespread censorship. Attacked as "hillbilly Jane Fondas," the Chicks were photographed nude for the May 2, 2003, cover of *Entertainment Weekly* with terms like "Saddam's Angels," "Traitors," "Hero," "Dixie Sluts," and "Proud Americans" written on their bodies.

The controversy was a perfect storm. The anti-war, anti-Bush sentiments were expressed not in song, where they might have been less incideniary, but as a remark from the stage in a foreign country, which was off-putting to people in-

The iconic Entertainment Weekly *cover shot, photographed by James White, after Natalie Maines of the Dixie Chicks said they were "ashamed" of George W. Bush and the march to war in Iraq in 2003.*

clined to be outraged in the first place. And they came as the cultural divides between what we now call Red and Blue America were growing, with country fans predominately tending to be red state folks. (The dichotomy comes from the color the networks use on their election-night maps to show which candidate has won which state. In 2000, George W. Bush's red territory and Al Gore's blue were so ubiquitious during the recount phase that the contrasting palette became a common political terminology.)

In a column published on the Country Music Television website, the writer Chet Flippo gave Maines a tutorial on the dynamics of protest. "What do you expect country fans to say when a country star dumps on the president?" Flippo wrote. "That audience is tolerant of artists' mistakes and foibles: drunkenness, drug use, adultery, no-shows and any amount of indulgent behavior. What that audience will not tolerate is an artist turning on that audience. And Maines's attack on Bush was in effect a direct attack on the country audience. And its values. And its patriotism . . . Memo to Natalie Maines: You're an artist? And you have a message? Hey, put it in a song. We'll listen to that. But, otherwise—shut up and sing."

The Chicks had red-state roots but now needed blue-state support to stay alive professionally. "I'd rather have a smaller following of really cool people who get it, who will grow with us as we grow and are fans for life," the Chicks' Martie Maguire said, "than people that have us in their five-disc changer with Reba McEntire and Toby Keith." It worked, to an extent. In 2006 they released an album and a defiant single, "Not Ready to Make Nice," and did well at the Grammys the following year. Country music, however, never welcomed them back, and the break between one of the most commercially successful female groups in history and the prevailing culture of red-state America is a case study in a polarization that endures nearly two decades on.

T HE TWO MEN could hardly have been more different. One the fatherless son of a single mother, the other a scion of the most important American political family since the Adamses; one a cool, intellectual analyst, the other an instinctive gut player who didn't look back once a decision was made. Yet there they were, together in the East Room of the White House on a May day in 2012, inexorably linked by history: Barack Hussein Obama and George Walker Bush.

The occasion was the unveiling of George and Laura Bush's White House portraits. "It's been said," Obama told the audience, "that no one can ever truly understand what it's like being president until they sit behind that desk and feel the weight and responsibility for the first time. And that is true. After three and a half years in office—and much more gray hair—I have a deeper understanding of the challenges faced by the presidents who came before me, including my immediate predecessor, President Bush. In this job, no decision that reaches your desk is easy. No choice you make is without costs. No matter how hard you try, you're not going to make everybody happy. I think that's something President Bush and I both learned pretty quickly."

With an ironic twinkle, Bush marked the moment with a bit of self-deprecation, or at least self-awareness: "I am also pleased, Mr. President," Bush said to Obama,

The Obamas at the Democratic National Convention 2008. "Yes We Can" by will.i.am
was a viral sensation; the campaign had also used Brooks & Dunn's "Only in America."

"that when you are wandering these halls as you wrestle with tough decisions, you will now be able to gaze at this portrait and ask, 'What would George do?' "

History is full of examples of presidents thinking and talking about their predecessors, seeking inspiration or warning from the successes and the failures of those who came before. The enormity of that shared experience—of the feeling of holding ultimate power and ultimate responsibility—can create strange connections and alliances once the heat of battle has faded.

Bush and Obama shared something else: a song. In the fall of 1999, Kix Brooks and a few songwriting pals were on Brooks's farm in Tennessee, killing time. "After a good long day in the woods, we were sitting back at one of my cabins going on about how amazing it was that we could live a life like we live, just making words rhyme, and making up stories that people might care about," Brooks recalled. "At some point, I realized we were a couple of grown men just sitting around talking about how much we loved America. Sounds corny maybe, but we were feeling it, and I said, 'Man, we've got to write this thing.' " The result was "Only in America," which Brooks and his partner, Ronnie Dunn, soon recorded.

Brooks & Dunn performed the song at the pre-inaugural celebration for George W. Bush in 2001, and the forty-third president played "Only in America" as an anthem in the 2004 campaign. When Bush's team asked for the OK to use it at rallies, Brooks replied, "Well, of course; I'm always excited when someone likes my work." Reflecting on the song, Brooks said, "It was never meant to be political; it was patriotic, not partisan."

That was clear in 2008, when Brooks and his wife, Barbara, were watching Barack Obama accept the Democratic nomination for president in Denver. The Black Eyed Peas' will.i.am had recorded "Yes We Can," a song punctuated with quotations from a memorable speech of Obama's in New Hampshire early in 2008; it was a viral success. But now, in Colorado, at the end of the evening, as the young Obama family stood on the stage, "Only in America" was suddenly reverberating through the stadium:

Sun comin' up over New York City
School bus driver in a traffic jam

ONLY IN AMERICA

This Brooks & Dunn song was written by my fellow Louisiana native Kix Brooks, along with Don Cook and Ronnie Rogers. It came out before 9/11 but was definitely caught in the wave of songs that rolled in after the tragedy. Its universal message, contrasted with the themes of other songs that came out post-9/11, has allowed it to have an ongoing life and involvement in our political discourse through conventions and rallies. It is a fairly straightforward country track, building off major rock-guitar licks. It's musically uplifting.

Broken down lyrically, it is obvious in its messages of hopes and dreams— a common theme of many of the songs we've considered.

As a country founded on hopes and dreams and a better life, it seems fitting we close there. The universal message of "Only in America" contrasted with the themes of other songs that came out post-9/11. It's of the moment but not limited by it, and it will be sung for a long time coming.   —T.M.

Staring out at the faces in a rearview mirror
Lookin' at the promise of the Promised Land
One kid dreams of fame and fortune
One kid helps pay the rent
One could end up going to prison
One just might be president
Only in America
Dreamin' in red white and blue
Only in America
Where we dream as big as we want to
We all get a chance
Everybody gets to dance
Only in America

There, briefly, in a time of warring camps, was a bit of common ground as two parties—two Americas, really—celebrated their competing visions of the future to the sound of the same song. A small thing, but in a dissonant world, every moment of harmony counts—and if we share music, we might just shout in anger a little less and sing in unity a bit more. Or so we can hope.

LIFT EVERY VOICE

"Let America be the dream the dreamers dreamed."

—LANGSTON HUGHES

T HE ART COULD not have been more glorious. For thirteen hours at the White House on Monday, June 14, 1965, Lady Bird and Lyndon Johnson hosted several hundred guests at an elaborate Festival of the Arts. "Our paint- ing and music, architecture and writing, have profoundly shaped the course of mod- ern art," President Johnson told the gathering. "From jazz and folk song to the most complex abstractions of word and image, few parts of the world are free from the spreading influence of American culture. I do not pretend to judge the lasting values of these works. But if art is important to man, then American art is deeply impor- tant to mankind."

By any measure, the art and artists on hand were spectacular: paintings by Jackson Pollock, Jasper Johns, Mark Rothko, Willem de Kooning, Grace Hartigan, Edward Hopper, and Andrew Wyeth; photographs by Walker Evans, Richard Avedon, and Robert Capa; sculpture by Alexander Calder, Louise Nevelson, and Isamu Noguchi; film clips honoring Alfred Hitchcock (for *North by Northwest*), Elia Kazan (for *On the Waterfront*), Fred Zinnemann (for *High Noon*), and George Stevens, Sr. (for *Shane*); theatrical scenes from Tennessee Williams's *The Glass Menagerie* and Arthur Miller's *Death of a Salesman;* and a lunchtime keynote from George F. Kennan, the diplomat and intellectual author of Cold War containment.

America being America, and artists being artists, the day was not without contro- versy. The poet Robert Lowell had declined the Johnsons' invitation and then pub- licly denounced the administration for its policy in Vietnam, among other foreign-policy issues; the critic Dwight Macdonald tried to have it both ways, show- ing up for the festival but seeking signatures for an anti-Johnson statement. Ralph

Duke Ellington at the White House Festival of the Arts, Monday, June 14, 1965.

Ellison was underwhelmed by the petition drive, such as it was, dismissing it with a single word: *adolescent.* The Kennedy-Johnson adviser and speechwriter Richard Goodwin told Macdonald that the on-site agitation was "the height of rudeness." Charlton Heston, the star of *Ben-Hur* and *The Ten Commandments,* may have put it most vividly, remarking, "He belts me in his movie reviews. Why should I sign his lousy petition?" Macdonald collected fewer than ten names. "The others," *Time* noted, "were either embarrassed or outraged."

The writer John Hersey, the author of *Hiroshima,* offered a statement before reading a section of his account of the 1945 atomic attack on Japan. "Let these words be a reminder," Hersey said. "The step from one degree of violence to the next is imperceptibly taken, and cannot easily be taken back. The end point of these little steps is horror and oblivion. We cannot for a moment forget the truly terminal dangers, in these times, of miscalculation, of arrogance, of accident, of reliance not on moral strength but on mere military power. Wars have a way of getting out of hand."

Johnson was unhappy about the dissonant voices, but he sought to make the best of things by staking out the high ground. "Your art is not a political weapon," the president said. "Yet much of what you do is profoundly political. For you seek out the common pleasures and visions, the terrors and the cruelties, of man's day on this planet. And I would hope that you would help dissolve the barriers of hatred and ignorance which are the source of so much of our pain and danger. In this way you work toward peace—not only the peace which is simply the absence of war but the peace which liberates man to reach for the finest fulfillment of his spirit." It was, really, the best—and only—thing the president could say in a moment of dissent.

Toward the end of the festival, as evening came, a turbaned Marian Anderson introduced a musical program in the state dining room, noting that "strong, firm, young American voices" were now being heard across Europe. The audience then listened to Roberta Peters of the Metropolitan Opera sing "Glitter and Be Gay" from Leonard Bernstein's *Candide* and "Summertime" from George Gershwin's *Porgy and Bess.* The Joffrey Ballet performed after remarks by Gene Kelly.

Then Duke Ellington and his orchestra took the stage, and the tension of the day dissipated somewhat. He opened with "Take the 'A' Train." "Ties were loosened, shoes and jackets came off," the conductor Maurice Peress recalled. "I remember smiles and dancing. We were caught in the delicious, delirious embrace of Duke's music." Ellington played the "Black" movement of his symphony about the African

American experience, *Black, Brown and Beige.* The composition included "Come Sunday," a spiritual. "God of love," the lyrics read, "please look down and see my people through."

In 1941, Ellington had delivered a speech that took as its text Langston Hughes's poem "I, Too." "I contend that the Negro is the creative voice of America, is creative America," Ellington had said then. "We stirred in our shackles and our unrest awakened Justice in the hearts of a courageous few, and we re-created in America the desire for true democracy, freedom for all, the brotherhood of man, principles on which the country had been founded." Those principles are eternal, but so is the war to make them concrete in the life of the nation.

It's a war without end. In the first decades of the twenty-first century, we find ourselves in a dispiriting moment in which what Ellington called "the brotherhood of man" is at best elusive and at worst out of reach. Many, if not most, Americans say they think the country is on the wrong track, and their faith in the future is tenuous. A common theme—*the* common theme, really, of the public conversation about America at the moment—is succinct and sad: We are divided as rarely, if ever, before, and the ferocious partisanship of the age lies at the heart of our discontent.

Many of the forces in evidence in our time, though, are not new. Nativism, xenophobia, cultural populism, and broad political fear have shaped the republic from the beginning and likely always will. Anxiety and its manifestations in the public square ebb and flow—and, truth be told, they mostly flow.

The military historian Sir Michael Howard, who served as the Regius Professor of Modern History at Oxford in the 1980s, once described a lecture he delivered as a young academic to a group of Army officers. The subject: the World War II battles in Italy in 1943–45. "I sketched as best I could its rationale, its course and its consequences, with some deeply felt comments on the quality of leadership on both sides," Howard recalled. "At the end there was a silence which I correctly gauged to be disapproving. It was broken by a young man in the front row asking impatiently, 'But what were its *Lessons*?'"

All of us sometimes share the young officer's anxious curiosity: What are the *lessons* we can draw from this brief survey of history and music? Given the current state of the nation, can music play any role in smoothing out the sharp edges of our disagreements and easing the tensions of tribalism?

History suggests it can. There's something about the transporting capacity of music, something about its odd but undeniable ability to create a collective experience by firing our individual imaginations, that's more likely to open our minds and our hearts to competing points of view. Of course, it's neither a narcotic nor a panacea, but music can recast the most charged and complicated of issues in ways that may lead to actual conversation rather than reflexive confrontation.

America is about debate, dissent, and dispute. We're always arguing, always fighting, always restless—and our music is a mirror and a maker of that once and future truth. "The Liberty Song" v. "The Rebels"; "The Battle Hymn of the Republic" v. "I Wish I Was in Dixie's Land"; "Happy Days Are Here Again" v. "Brother, Can You Spare a Dime?"; "The Ballad of the Green Berets" v. "Fortunate Son"; "Born in the U.S.A." v. "God Bless the U.S.A.": The whole panoply of America can be traced—and, more important, *heard* and *felt*—in the songs that echo through our public squares. And if we can *hear* and *feel* how the other guys hear and feel, we're better equipped to press on toward a more perfect union.

On that June day in 1965, when he hosted the Festival of the Arts, President Johnson touched on the significance of the artistic enterprise in his remarks to the painters, writers, sculptors, photographers, and musicians who gathered together at the White House, however uneasily, under the roof of the most vivid symbol of temporal political power in the land. "You are still reaching for the understanding beyond capture," Johnson said. "But in that effort you not only explain a nation. The search itself enlarges America in heart, in spirit, in purpose, and in grandeur."

Artists and audience, activists and observers, we're all still reaching for an understanding of how we might make our union a bit more perfect. For the song of America is not finished; the last notes have not yet been played. In that spirit, in that cause, now and always, let us lift every voice, and sing.

ACKNOWLEDGMENTS

JON MEACHAM

This project began, really, in my yard in Nashville. On an unseasonably warm winter afternoon, my friend and neighbor Tim McGraw suggested that we team up to tell the story of the nation not only through words (my part) but through music (his, which I probably don't need to point out). I had just published a book, *The Soul of America: The Battle for Our Better Angels,* about how the nation often gets big stuff wrong but can, at times, rise above its baser instincts. Why not explore that national soul, Tim asked, through music?

I was in. The result is the book you're reading and, we hope, the performances of the "Songs of America" events that you'll be able to come to. Because—let's be honest—you'd probably rather hear McGraw sing than me type. I know *I* would.

We are grateful to several members of the academic community for their kindness and assistance; each graciously read all or parts of the manuscript amid busy lives and demanding schedules. (They bear no responsibility for the final product, of course; that's on us.) Craig Werner, professor of Afro-American Studies at the University of Wisconsin and the author of several essential books (among them *A Change Is Gonna Come: Music, Race, and the Soul of America* and *We Gotta Get Out of This Place: The Soundtrack of the Vietnam War*, written with Doug Bradley), was a judicious and invaluable reader. Michael Eric Dyson, University Professor of Sociology at Georgetown University and Renaissance man, guided us on the question of hip-hop. Imani Perry, the Hughes-Rogers Professor of African-American Studies at Princeton University, is a scholar of many things, and we drew on her wisdom about James Weldon Johnson's "Lift Every Voice and Sing," the subject of her book *May We Forever Stand: A History of the Black National Anthem*. David Blight, Class of 1954 Professor of American History and Director of the Gilder Lehrman Center for the Study of Slavery, Resistance, and Abolition at Yale University, was generous on Frederick Douglass, the subject of David's recent (and marvelous) biography, *Frederick Douglass: Prophet of Freedom*. Christian McWhirter, Lincoln Historian at the Abraham Lincoln Presidential Library and Museum in Springfield, Illinois, and the author of the terrific *Battle Hymns: The Power and Popularity of Music in the Civil War*, read and commented on the Civil War sections. And as ever, Michael Beschloss is a devoted and selfless friend.

Will Byrd was invaluable in keeping the authors in good order; he is a steadfast friend and counselor. CAA's Rachel Adler, Cait Hoyt, and Kate Childs are a superb team. At Random House—my publishing home for just about two decades—I am, as always, grateful to the marvelous Kate Medina, Erica Gonzalez, Dennis Ambrose, Avideh Bashirrad, Benjamin Dreyer, Rebecca Berlant, Porscha Burke, Simon Sullivan (for the beautiful design of the book), Paolo Pepe (for the wonderful jacket), Karen Fink, Mary Moates, Maria Braeckel, Susan Corcoran, Leigh Marchant, Barbara Fillon, Andrea DeWerd, Katie Tull, Carol Poticny (for splendid photo research), and Kathy Lord (for her copyedit of the manuscript). And Gina Centrello remains the best of publishers and of friends—a tough combination, but she pulls it off with remarkable grace and skill.

John Lewis, Michael Eric Dyson, Sig Rogich, and Kix Brooks took time to share thoughts and recollections with us; we are hugely grateful. Doris Kearns Goodwin, Quincy Jones, and Ken Burns were generous with their time and their formidable talents. As noted, I drew on several existing essays of mine for sections of the book, and I am grateful to my editors at *The New York Times*, particularly Clay Risen; at *Time*; and at *Newsweek*. *Time*'s Anna Rumer in Washington contributed reporting to the essay on the fortieth anniversary of the death of Elvis Presley, and I fondly remember working with Vern E. Smith and Veronica Chambers on a *Newsweek* project commemorating the thirtieth anniversary of Martin Luther King, Jr.'s death. And Maynard Parker, Mark Whitaker, Evan Thomas, Howard Fineman, Ann McDaniel, Mark Miller, and Tom Watson each played roles in allowing me to write the 2004 remembrance of Ronald Reagan that we drew on to discuss the 1980s. My thanks to them all.

This book would not have been possible without the tireless, insightful, and cheerful assistance of Mike Hill. This is our seventh project together, and my debt to Mike is incalculable. Merrill Fabry checked the manuscript with care and intelligence; our thanks to her. Charles Robinson and Brad Joe of the Choctaw Nation of Oklahoma kindly provided us with a Choctaw song and its translation. In Nashville, Bill Lloyd offered the benefit of years of experience in the music business. Roxanne Oldham was essential in the tricky work of obtaining permissions for the quoted song lyrics, as was Evan Rosenblum. Margaret Shannon, longtime historian at Washington National Cathedral, was always on call. And Jack Bales is secure in his standing as the nation's finest bibliographer.

For courtesies small and large, thanks to Amanda Urban, Oscie and Evan Thomas, Nick Zeppos, Beth and John Geer, Julia Reed, Callie Khouri, Beth Laski, James Ring Adams, Sean Wilentz, Karl Rove, Katie Hill, and Eddie Glaude, Jr.

This book is dedicated to two daughters of Mississippi, Keith Meacham and Faith Hill. For me, as always, Mary, Maggie, and Sam are the *de facto* dedicatees. They are the center of everything, even if they have been particularly merciless in their opinions about their father's musical abilities (or lack thereof). They call 'em as they see 'em—or, in keeping with the spirit of this book, *hear* 'em.

TIM MCGRAW

How can we know where we are going without some perspective on where we have been? That's why history fascinates me—it's the *story* of what made us a people and a nation. And telling stories is at the heart of what I'm always trying to do on stage or in a studio. The "Songs of America" project, then, is a piece of what I've spent so much of my life doing: taking the raw material of life and weaving it together into what I hope is something that not only entertains but illuminates.

My life as an artist has allowed me to meet some of the most amazing people in the world. It has given me a chance to look into their lives through meaningful conversation, gaining perspective and understanding. Sometimes these encounters are with a hope of taking away something that I will incorporate into a performance of some kind but always with the desire to learn and be better in my life.

One of those people is Jon Meacham. Out of our conversations together over the past few years the idea for this book was born. We were both enchanted by the fact that interwoven into the fabric of our national story were songwriters and performers creating lyrics and melodies at times of great challenge. From forming the country itself to overcoming the economic hardship of the Great Depression to fighting for rights, civil and otherwise, songs have told us much, and still do.

Music can give you a respite from the grind of life, to find an escape so that you can unwind from the pressures of life. But it can also shape and transform people and countries. When America was being founded and developed, artists—writers and performers—were in the moment. They were either leading with their writings or reflecting the sentiment of the population. Think of this: As our country was being formed, the writers of the day were as close in time to the era of Shakespeare as they were to our own age. We as songwriters are always trying to put into words what someone else is thinking. Empowering them.

Partnering with Jon has allowed me to voice some of my thoughts and ideas in the context of our American history. In these pages, I hope you can feel my passion for this country and my belief that we can continue to evolve and change and be better. I hope you can feel that in my music as well. And if my celebrity can be of any influence, I'd use it to encourage you to dig in and read and explore more about our incredible nation and its music. If you have interest in an era or a song, go further: read more books, listen to every version of the song, ask your friends or family. There are more songs and historical moments we just couldn't get to, and we certainly don't want to imply that this is a comprehensive effort. I encourage all of you to do your own research and learn more about the crossroads of history and music in our country. Find other songs. When you are digging into history, keep music and its role and influence in mind. Mine down into the different musical versions of the songs we've highlighted and discover how they have been adapted musically, but also see how they have been adapted in terms of patriotism or protest or politics.

I want to thank the readers for going on this journey of history and music with us. I hope you've enjoyed a deeper look into the intersection of the sounds and sagas of America. Knowledge is power and we hope to empower you to want to learn more.

Thanks to my team, especially Scott Siman and Kelly Clague, for being sounding boards and helping me flesh out my ideas for the song critiques. I am grateful to Random House for believing in this project and to everyone there for all your hard work to bring it to life. And a special thanks to Will Byrd for helping to keep us on the right track at the right time.

NOTES

OVERTURE: THE MUSIC OF HISTORY

3 "Nothing is more agreeable" George
Washington, "General Orders, June 4, 1777,"
Papers of George Washington: Revolutionary War Series,
vol. 9, ed. Philander D. Chase (Charlottesville,
Va., 1999), 603.

4 Plato and Aristotle See, for instance, Elias
Nason, *A Monogram on Our National Song* (Albany,
N.Y., 1869), 2–3. For the philosophy of music
more generally, see, for instance, Mary B.
Schoen-Nazzaro, "Plato and Aristotle on the
Ends of Music," *Laval théologique et philosophique,* 34
(3), 1978, 261–273; Andrew Kania, "The
Philosophy of Music," *The Stanford Encyclopedia of
Philosophy,* Fall 2017 Edition, ed. Edward N.
Zalta, https://plato.stanford.edu/archives
/fall2017/entries/music/.

4 Newton and Shakespeare Nason, *A
Monogram on Our National Song,* 2–3. See also, more
generally, James Gleick, *Isaac Newton* (New York,
2004); Harold Bloom, *Shakespeare: The Invention of
the Human* (New York, 1998); Jacques Barzun,
*From Dawn to Decadence: 1500 to the Present: 500 Years of
Western Cultural Life* (New York, 2001).

4 Andrew Fletcher brilliantly Andrew
Fletcher, *The Political Works of Andrew Fletcher*
(London, 1737), 372. The observation comes in
the course of Fletcher's "Account of a Conversa-
tion Concerning a Right Regulation of
Governments for the Common Good of
Mankind: In a Letter to the Marquess of
Montrose, December 1, 1703."

4 "Nothing is more agreeable" George
Washington, "General Orders, June 4, 1777,"
Papers of George Washington: Revolutionary War Series,
vol. 9, ed. Philander D. Chase (Charlottesville,
Va., 1999), 603.

5 To Jefferson himself Jon Meacham, *Thomas
Jefferson: The Art of Power (AOP)* (New York,
2012), 56.

5 In his literary commonplace book
Thomas Jefferson, *The Papers of Thomas Jefferson,*
ed. Douglas L. Wilson (Princeton, N.J., 1989),
115. See also *AOP,* 56.

5 "When I *hear* music" Henry David Thoreau,
Journals, Vol. 2, eds. Bradford Torrey and Francis
H. Allen (New York, 1962), 1107.

5 the music of the nation We have often
drawn on Jon Meacham's previous works for the
context of the times we examine in these pages.
Other essential works include: Robert James
Branham and Stephen J. Hartnett, *Sweet Freedom's
Song: "My Country 'Tis of Thee" and Democracy in
America* (New York, 2002); C. A. Browne, *The
Story of Our National Ballads* (New York, 1919);
James H. Cone, *The Spirituals and the Blues: An
Interpretation* (Maryknoll, N.Y., 1991); Danny O.
Crew, *Suffragist Sheet Music: An Illustrated Catalogue of
Published Music Associated with the Women's Rights and
Suffrage Movement in America, 1795–1921, with Complete
Lyrics* (Jefferson, N.C., 2002); Louis Charles
Elson, *The National Music of America and Its Sources*
(Boston, 1899); David Ewen, *Great Men of
American Popular Song* (Englewood Cliffs, N.J.,
1970); Robert A. Ferguson, *The American
Enlightenment, 1750–1820* (Cambridge, Mass.,
1997); W. T. Lhamon, Jr., *Jump Jim Crow: Lost Plays,
Lyrics, and Street Prose of the First Atlantic Popular
Culture* (Cambridge, Mass., 2003); Vera Brodsky
Lawrence, *Music for Patriots, Politicians, and Presidents:
Harmonies and Discords of the First Hundred Years*
(New York, 1975); Jill Lepore, *These Truths: A
History of the United States* (New York, 2018);
William Manchester, *The Glory and the Dream: A
Narrative History of America, 1932–1972* (Boston,
1974); Greil Marcus, *Mystery Train: Images of
America in Rock 'n' Roll Music,* 6th Edition (New
York, 2015); Christian McWhirter, *Battle Hymns:
The Power and Popularity of Music in the Civil War*
(Chapel Hill, N.C., 2012); Elias Nason, *A

Monogram on Our National Song (Albany, N.Y., 1869); John Stauffer and Benjamin Soskis, *The Battle Hymn of the Republic: A Biography of a Song That Marches On* (New York, 2013); Eileen Southern, *The Music of Black Americans: A History,* Third Edition (New York, 1997), and Southern, ed., *Readings in Black American Music* (New York, 1983); Craig Werner, *A Change Is Gonna Come: Music, Race & the Soul of America* (Ann Arbor, Mich., 2006); Doug Bradley and Craig Werner, *We Gotta Get Out of This Place: The Soundtrack of the Vietnam War* (Amherst, Mass., 2015).

CHAPTER ONE: THE SENSATIONS OF FREEDOM

7   "BY UNITING WE STAND" *The Boston Gazette,* July 18, 1768. See also http://www.masshist.org /database/viewer.php?item_id=257&pid=2.

7   "OBJECTS OF THE MOST STUPENDOUS" John Adams to William Cushing, June 9, 1776, http://www.masshist.org/publications/adams -papers/index.php/view/PJA04d124.

7   "REMEMBER THE LADIES" Abigail Adams to John Adams, Massachusetts Historical Society, March 31–April 5, 1776, https://www.masshist .org/digitaladams/archive/doc?id=L17760331aa.

7   NIGHT WAS ABOUT TO FALL *The Boston Gazette,* June 20, 1768, reported that the episode took place "towards Evening"; Robert Middlekauff, *The Glorious Cause: The American Revolution, 1763–1789* (New York, 2005), 166–171, places the event "at sunset." See also "The Seizure of John Hancock's Sloop 'Liberty,'" *Proceedings of the Massachusetts Historical Society,* Third Series, Vol. 55, October 1921–June 1922, 239–284; Kenneth Silverman, *A Cultural History of the American Revolution* (New York, 1976), 112–115.

7   THE CHARGE *Proceedings of the Massachusetts Historical Society,* 239–261; Middlekauff, *Glorious Cause,* 166–167.

7   ANTICIPATING TROUBLE *Proceedings of the Massachusetts Historical Society,* 249–253.

7   A "FINE NEW" Ibid., 249.

7   "THIS CONDUCT PROVOKED" *The Boston Gazette,* June 20, 1768.

7   THE BRITISH COLLECTOR OF CUSTOMS D. H. Watson, "Joseph Harrison and the *Liberty* Incident," *William and Mary Quarterly,* Vol. 20, No. 4, October 1963, 585–595.

7   "WE WERE PURSUED" Ibid., 590. See also *The Boston Gazette,* June 20, 1768.

8   THIS "GREAT RIOT" *Proceedings of the Massachusetts Historical Society,* 254.

8   "WE WILL SUPPORT" Ibid., 255.

8   JOHN DICKINSON OF PENNSYLVANIA Allen Johnson and Dumas Malone, eds., *Dictionary of American Biography* (New York, 1959), 299. See also William Murchison, *The Cost of Liberty: The Life of John Dickinson* (Wilmington, Del., 2013), and Milton E. Flower, *John Dickinson: Conservative Revolutionary* (Charlottesville, Va., 1983).

8   AN INFLUENTIAL SERIES OF ESSAYS John Dickinson, *Letters from a Farmer in Pennsylvania,* https://history.delaware.gov/museums/jdp /events/dickinsonletters/pennsylvania-farmer -letters.html.

8   "INFLAMING AND SEDITIOUS" Watson, "Joseph Harrison and the *Liberty* Incident," *William and Mary Quarterly,* 588.

8   AN HONORARY DEGREE *Dictionary of American Biography,* 299.

8   "FROM INFANCY" Dickinson, *Letters from a Farmer in Pennsylvania,* https://history.delaware.gov /museums/jdp/events/dickinsonletters /pennsylvania-farmer-letters.html.

8   "A FREE PEOPLE" Silverman, *A Cultural History of the American Revolution,* 111.

8   TO GUARD AGAINST Ibid.

8   "I ENCLOSE YOU" Justin Winsor, ed., *The Memorial History of Boston, Including Suffolk County, Massachusetts, 1630–1880,* III (Boston, 1882), 131.

8   HE TOLD OTIS Ibid.

9   PUBLISHED IN PHILADELPHIA Flower, *John Dickinson: Conservative Revolutionary,* 71. See also Lawrence, *Music for Patriots, Politicians, and Presidents,* 26–27, and Oscar Brand, *Songs of '76: A Folksinger's History of the Revolution* (New York, 1972), 7–9.

9   IN *THE BOSTON GAZETTE* Murchison, *The Cost of Liberty,* 71–72; Winsor, ed., *The Memorial History of Boston,* 131.

9   "COME JOIN" *The Boston Gazette,* July 18, 1768. See also http://www.masshist.org/database /viewer.php?item_id=257&pid=2.

10   CITING THE EXAMPLE John Dickinson, *The Political Writings of John Dickinson,* ed. Paul Leicester Ford (New York, 1970), 421. The letter to Otis was dated July 4, 1768.

10   "THE LIBERTY SONG" Silverman, *A Cultural*

History of the American Revolution, 113. "The song," Silverman wrote, "became a favorite in little more than a month." Ibid.

10 "THE MUSIC BEGAN" Ibid.

10 "THIS," ADAMS REMARKED Ibid.

11 "BECAME NOT SO MUCH" Ibid., 112–113.

12 THE ENSUING PERIOD *AOP,* 28–31; 68–71; 535–537; Middlekauff, *Glorious Cause,* 3–311. See, more generally, Bernard Bailyn, *The Origins of American Politics* (New York, 1968), and *The Ideological Origins of the American Revolution* (Cambridge, Mass., 1992); Gordon S. Wood, *The Creation of the American Republic, 1776–1787* (Chapel Hill, N.C., 1998), *The Radicalism of the American Revolution* (New York, 1993), *The American Revolution: A History* (New York, 2003), *The Idea of America: Reflections on the Birth of the United States* (New York, 2011), *Revolutionary Characters: What Made the Founders Different* (New York, 2006); Lawrence Henry Gipson, *The British Empire Before the American Revolution,* Vol. XIII, *The Triumphant Empire: The Empire Beyond the Storm, 1770–1776* (New York, 1967); Alan Taylor, *American Colonies* (New York, 2002); Edmund S. Morgan and Helen M. Morgan, *The Stamp Act Crisis: Prologue to Revolution* (Chapel Hill, N.C., 1995); Trevor Colbourn, *The Lamp of Experience: Whig History and the Intellectual Origins of the American Revolution* (Indianapolis, 1998), 3–47; Francis D. Cogliano, *Thomas Jefferson: Reputation and Legacy* (Charlottesville, Va., 2006), 21–24; Alfred F. Young, "English Plebeian Culture and Eighteenth-Century American Radicalism," in *The Origins of Anglo-American Radicalism,* ed. Margaret Jacob and James Jacob (London, 1984), 187–212; Mary Beth Norton, "John Randolph's 'Plan of Accommodations,'" *William and Mary Quarterly,* Third Ser., 28, No. 1, January 1971, 103–120.

12 IT HAS BEEN SAID THAT THE FOUNDERS The remark is often attributed to Benjamin Franklin, probably wrongly; https://founders.archives.gov/documents/Franklin/01-22-02-0284. See Carl Van Doren, *Benjamin Franklin* (New York, 1938), 551–552.

12 "THE AMERICANS HAVE MADE" "Speech on Townshend Duties, 19 April 1769," *The Writings and Speeches of Edmund Burke,* Vol. II, ed. Paul Langford (Oxford, 1980), 231. See also Virginia History, Government, and Geography Service,

Road to Independence: Virginia 1763–1783 (Memphis, Tenn., 2010), 33.

12 THE SEVEN YEARS' WAR *AOP,* 30–31. Fred Anderson, *Crucible of War: The Seven Years' War and the Fate of Empire in British North America, 1754–1766* (New York, 2001), is essential. See also Middlekauff, *Glorious Cause,* 17–73, and Norman K. Risjord, *Jefferson's America, 1760–1815* (Lanham, Md., 2010), 71–96.

12 THE "EARLIEST AMERICAN SOLDIER-SONG" Nason, *A Monogram on Our National Song,* 15–16.

13 THE HARD REALITY *AOP,* 30; 540–541.

13 "ALL MEN WISH" Barbara W. Tuchman, *The March of Folly: From Troy to Vietnam* (New York, 1984), 142.

14 "YANKEE DOODLE DANDY" Browne, *The Story of Our National Ballads,* 2–28; Elson, *The National Music of America,* 127–154; Nason, *A Monogram on Our National Song,* 18–29; O. G. Sonneck, *Report on "The Star-Spangled Banner," "Hail Columbia," "America," "Yankee Doodle,"* (New York, 1972), 79–156.

14 1775'S "THE PENNSYLVANIA SONG" Frank Moore, *Songs and Ballads of the American Revolution* (New York, 1855), 90–91.

15 FOR AS ENGLISHMEN Bailyn, *The Origins of American Politics,* is essential on this. See, in particular, Ibid., 106; 131; 136, 151–152. See also Lepore, *These Truths,* 93.

15 A BRITISH BRIGADE UNDER LORD PERCY Nason, *A Monogram on Our National Song,* 24.

15 "IN THE SPRING" John Rhodehamel, ed., *The American Revolution: Writings from the War of Independence* (New York, 2001), 25.

15 "THE KING'S TROOPS" Ibid.

15 "MANY WERE THE INSTANCES" Ibid., 26.

15 "THERE WAS A" Ibid., 27.

15 ABOUT A FIFTH Middlekauff, *Glorious Cause,* 550. See also Wood, *The American Revolution,* 113; *AOP,* 69, 553; and, more generally, Robert McCluer Calhoon, *The Loyalists in Revolutionary America, 1760–1781* (New York, 1973).

16 THE "MOST WICKED" John Ferdinand Dalziel Smyth, "Narrative or Journal of Capt. John Ferdinand Dalziel Smyth, of the Queen's Rangers," *The Pennsylvania Magazine of History and Biography,* Vol. 39, No. 2, 1915, 144.

16 "THE REBELS" Moore, *Songs and Ballads of the American Revolution,* 196–199.

17 "TWO OF THE" Rhodehamel, ed., *The American Revolution,* 27.

17 "A FRENZY OF" Middlekauff, *Glorious Cause,* 279.

17 "THE FLAME OF CIVIL WAR" *AOP,* 81; George F. Scheer and Hugh F. Rankin, *Rebels and Redcoats* (New York, 1957), 45.

17 AN "OLIVE BRANCH PETITION" Pauline Maier, *American Scripture: Making the Declaration of Independence* (New York, 1997), 24–25. See also Richard R. Beeman, *Our Lives, Our Fortunes, and Our Sacred Honor: The Forging of American Independence, 1774–1776* (New York, 2013).

17 "PROCLAMATION FOR SUPPRESSING REBELLION AND SEDITION" https://www.encyclopediavirginia.org/_By_the_King_A_Proclamation_For_Suppressing_Rebellion_and_Sedition_1775.

17 WAS "MANIFESTLY CARRIED ON" Maier, *American Scripture,* 25.

17 HE ALSO ACCUSED Ibid.

17 PUBLISHED *COMMON SENSE* Maier, *American Scripture,* 28–34; Beeman, *Our Lives, Our Fortunes, and Our Sacred Honor,* 305–326.

17 "THE CAUSE OF AMERICA" Craig Nelson, *Thomas Paine: Enlightenment, Revolution, and the Birth of Modern Nations* (New York, 2006), 85.

17 "ITS EFFECTS WERE" Beeman, *Our Lives, Our Fortunes, and Our Sacred Honor,* 305.

17 "WE WERE BLIND" Ibid., 320.

17 "UNANSWERABLE REASONING" Ferguson, *The American Enlightenment,* 110.

17 GEORGE III WAS BROKERING Maier, *American Scripture,* 38–39.

17 TERRIBLE MILITARY NEWS Ibid., 39–44.

18 DICKINSON ROSE IN THE CONGRESS Beeman, *Our Lives, Our Fortunes, and Our Sacred Honor,* 370–372. See also Maier, *American Scripture,* 44–45.

18 BY TUESDAY, JULY 2 Beeman, *Our Lives, Our Fortunes, and Our Sacred Honor,* 375–381.

18 "YESTERDAY," JOHN ADAMS WROTE John Adams to Abigail Adams July 3, 1776, https://www.masshist.org/digitaladams/archive/doc?id=L17760703ja&numrecs=1&archive=all&hi=on&mode=&query=the%2520greatest%2520Question%2520was%2520decided&queryid=&rec=1&start=1&tag=text.

18 "THE SECOND DAY OF JULY" Beeman, *Our Lives, Our Fortunes, and Our Sacred Honor,* 382.

18 WASHINGTON RECOGNIZED THEIR SIGNIFICANCE George Washington, "General Orders, 9 July 1776," https://founders.archives.gov/documents/Washington/03-05-02-0176.

18 "THE GENERAL HOPES" Ibid.

19 "WE HOLD THESE TRUTHS" *AOP,* 104. For background on the declaration, its origins, and its editorial evolution, see also *The Papers of Thomas Jefferson,* I, 315, 413–432; Maier, *American Scripture,* 97–153; Walter Isaacson, *Benjamin Franklin: An American Life* (New York, 2003), 310–313; and, more generally, Garry Wills, *Inventing America: Jefferson's Declaration of Independence* (Garden City, N.Y., 1978) and Carl Becker, *The Declaration of Independence: A Study on the History of Political Ideas* (New York, 1970). Jefferson was part of a committee that produced the declaration. (Maier, *American Scripture,* 99–105). "He was no Moses receiving the Ten Commandments from the hand of God," Maier wrote of Jefferson, "but a man who had to prepare a written text with little time to waste, and who, like others in similar circumstances, drew on earlier documents of his own and other people's creation, acting within the rhetorical and ethical standards of his time, and producing a draft that revealed both splendid artistry and signs of haste," Ibid., 98–99. The "Committee of Five" appointed to draft a declaration was made up of Jefferson, Adams, Franklin, Robert R. Livingston of New York, and Roger Sherman of Connecticut. See also Isaacson, *Benjamin Franklin,* 310–313.

20 "FEAR IS THE FOUNDATION" Charles Francis Adams, *Works of John Adams,* Vol. IV (Boston, 1851), 194.

20 "ALL HONOR TO JEFFERSON" *The Collected Works of Abraham Lincoln,* III, ed. Roy P. Basler (New Brunswick, N.J., 1953–55), 376. The letter was dated April 6, 1859.

20 "A PROMISE THAT" Martin Luther King, Jr., "I Have a Dream . . ." https://www.archives.gov/files/press/exhibits/dream-speech.pdf.

20 AN ARGUMENT WITHOUT END Arthur Schlesinger, Jr., "History as Therapy: A Dangerous Idea," *The New York Times* (*NYT*), May 3, 1996. Schlesinger was fond of quoting this observation by the Dutch historian Pieter Geyl.

20 AS WELLINGTON WAS TO SAY http://www.kingscollections.org/exhibitions/specialcollections

/the-nearest-run-thing-you-ever-saw-the
-battle-of-waterloo/.

20 "I AM WELL AWARE" Rhodehamel, ed., *The American Revolution,* 127.

21 "IF MEN WERE ANGELS" James Madison, *Federalist* 51, https://www.constitution.org/fed /federa51.htm.

21 "THE GREAT ART OF LAWGIVING" Charles Francis Adams, *The Works of John Adams,* VI (Boston, 1851), 280–281.

22 "FOR WE MUST CONSIDER" Francis J. Bremer, *John Winthrop: America's Forgotten Founding Father* (New York, 2003), 180. Winthrop's text was drawn from the Gospel of Matthew, 5:14. See also John Winthrop, *Winthrop Papers,* Vol. 2, 1623–1630, ed. Malcolm Freiburg (Boston, 1931), 282–295, and *The Journal of John Winthrop, 1630–1649,* ed. Richard S. Dunn, James Savage, and Laetitia Yeadle (Cambridge, Mass., 1996), I, 726.

22 JOHN F. KENNEDY John F. Kennedy, "Address to the Massachusetts State Legislature," January 9, 1961, National Archives Catalog, https:// catalog.archives.gov/id/193879.

22 RONALD REAGAN Ronald Reagan, "Farewell Address to the Nation," American Presidency Project, https://www.presidency.ucsb.edu/node /251303.

22 SAMUEL SHERWOOD, A CONNECTICUT PASTOR *Political Sermons of the Founding Era, 1730–1788,* ed. Ellis Sandoz, I (Indianapolis, 1998), 524. We are indebted, as noted, to Robert A. Ferguson for insights on the interplay of reason and religion in the American identity. See Ferguson, *American Enlightenment.*

22 "THE CAUSE OF GOD" *Political Sermons of the Founding Era,* I, 595.

22 "WE HAVE INCONTESTABLE EVIDENCE" Ibid., 494.

23 SAW THE CAUSE FOR SELF-GOVERNMENT Ferguson, *American Enlightenment,* is invaluable on this point.

23 "ALL EYES ARE" Ibid., 23.

23 "THE SACRED FIRE OF LIBERTY" "First Inaugural Address of George Washington, April 30, 1789." https://www.archives.gov/exhibits /american_originals/inaugtxt.html.

23 OFFERED THESE VERSES Silverman, *A Cultural History of the American Revolution,* 607–608.

24 "I LONG TO HEAR" "Letter from Abigail Adams to John Adams, 31 March–5 April, 1776," Massachusetts Historical Society, https://www .masshist.org/digitaladams/archive/doc?id =L17760331aa. Mrs. Adams added:
"That your Sex are Naturally Tyrannical is a Truth so thoroughly established as to admit of no dispute, but such of you as wish to be happy willingly give up the harsh title of Master for the more tender and endearing one of Friend. Why then, not put it out of the power of the vicious and the Lawless to use us with cruelty and indignity with impunity. Men of Sense in all Ages abhor those customs which treat us only as the vassals of your Sex. Regard us then as Beings placed by providence under your protection and in imitation of the Supreme Being make use of that power only for our happiness." Ibid.

24 THE *PHILADELPHIA MINERVA* Branham and Hartnett, *Sweet Freedom's Song,* 208–210.

24 THE VERSES HAD FIRST APPEARED Lisa L. Moore, Joanna Brooks, and Caroline Wigginton, eds., *Transatlantic Feminisms in the Age of Revolutions* (New York, 2012) 309–311.

24 "RIGHTS OF WOMAN" Ibid.; Crew, *Suffragist Sheet Music,* 8–9.

25 PHILLIS WHEATLEY See, for instance: Vincent Carretta, *Phillis Wheatley: Biography of a Genius in Bondage* (Athens, Ga., 2011); *Phillis Wheatley, Complete Writings,* ed. Vincent Carretta (New York, 2001); Silverman, *A Cultural History of the American Revolution,* 214–217, 284–285.

25 AFRICAN-BORN Wheatley, *Complete Writings,* xiii.

25 EDUCATED BY HER OWNERS Ibid., xiii–xiv.

25 IN 1773, IN HIS *ADDRESS* Ibid., xv.

25 INTRODUCED THE NOTION Thomas J. Steele, "The Figure of Columbia: Phillis Wheatley Plus George Washington," *The New England Quarterly,* Vol. 54, No. 2, June 1981, 264–266.

25 CELESTIAL CHOIR! Wheatley, *Complete Writings,* 88–90. She sent the poem to Washington in the fall of 1775.

25 "I THANK YOU" George Washington to Phillis Wheatley, February 28, 1776, https://founders .archives.gov/documents/Washington/03-03 -02-0281. See also Ron Chernow, *Washington: A Life* (New York, 2010), 219–221, for an account of the episode.

26 THE POEM FOUND Silverman, *A Cultural History of the American Revolution*, 284–285.

26 WOULD "BE HAPPY" George Washington to Phillis Wheatley, February 28, 1776, https://founders.archives.gov/documents/Washington /03-03-02-0281.

26 "ON BEING BROUGHT FROM AFRICA TO AMERICA" Wheatley, *Complete Writings*, 13.

27 LO! FREEDOM COMES Ibid., 101–102. These verses are from the poem "Liberty and Peace, A Poem."

28 "THE BANEFUL EFFECTS" George Washington, "Farewell Address," 1796, http://avalon.law.yale .edu/18th_century/washing.asp. See also John Avlon, *Washington's Farewell: The Founding Father's Warning to Future Generations* (New York, 2017).

28 SERVED "ALWAYS TO DISTRACT" Washington, "Farewell Address," http://avalon.law.yale.edu /18th_century/washing.asp.

28 AN HOUR OF WAR FEVER Gordon S. Wood, *Empire of Liberty: A History of the Early Republic, 1789–1815* (New York, 2009), 239–275. See also Elson, *The National Music of America*, 155–165; Browne, *The Story of Our National Ballads*, 33–48; Nason, *A Monogram on Our National Song*, 33–36.

28 "THE PROSPECT OF" Elson, *The National Music of America*, 160–161.

28 THE FEDERALIST ODE "ADAMS AND LIBERTY" Lawrence, *Music for Patriots, Politicians, and Presidents*, 148–149; Nason, *A Monogram on Our National Song*, 30–32; Sonneck, *Report*, 24–26; Elson, *The National Music of America*, 183–192.

29 "THE REIGN OF WITCHES" AOP, 319.

29 "ALL . . . WILL BEAR IN MIND" "Thomas Jefferson, First Inaugural Address," March 4, 1801, http://avalon.law.yale.edu/19th_century /jefinau1.asp.

29 "JEFFERSON AND LIBERTY" Nason, *A Monogram on Our National Song*, 40.

29 THE GLOOMY NIGHT Lawrence, *Music for Patriots, Politicians, and Presidents*, 165.

30 "WHERE A CONSTITUTION" *The Papers of Thomas Jefferson*, Vol. 29, ed. Barbara B. Oberg (Charlottesville, Va., 2002), 289.

30 "PARTY DIVISIONS" Richard Hofstadter, *The Idea of a Party System: The Rise of Legitimate Opposition in the United States, 1780–1840* (Berkeley, Calif., 1969), 30–31.

30 "IN EVERY FREE" Thomas Jefferson to John Taylor, June 4, 1798," *The Papers of Thomas Jefferson*, Vol. 30, ed. Barbara B. Oberg (Charlottesville, Va., 2003), 388.

30 "I NEVER SUBMITTED" "Thomas Jefferson to Francis Hopkinson, March 13, 1789," *The Papers of Thomas Jefferson*, Vol. 14, ed. Julian P. Boyd (Charlottesville, Va., 1958), 650.

30 "MEN HAVE DIFFERED" "Thomas Jefferson to John Adams, June 27, 1813," *The Papers of Thomas Jefferson: Retirement Series*, Vol. 6, ed. J. Jefferson Looney (Charlottesville, Va., 2009), 231–232.

31 AT HOME Elson, *The National Music of America*, 161. See also Sonneck, *Report*, 43–72, and Browne, *The Story of Our National Ballads*, 30–45.

31 "HIS PROSPECTS WERE" Elson, *The National Music of America*, 161.

31 THE NEXT DAY Ibid.

31 "HAIL COLUMBIA" Lawrence, *Music for Patriots, Politicians, and Presidents*, 142–145.

32 IT WAS A TRIUMPH Elson, *The National Music of America*, 163.

32 ABIGAIL ADAMS Lawrence, *Music for Patriots, Politicians, and Presidents*, 142.

32 "THE OBJECT OF" Elson, *The National Music of America*, 161.

33 IT WAS INITIALLY KNOWN Ibid., 165; Browne, *The Story of Our National Ballads*, 43.

33 ADAMS AND HIS CABINET Ibid., 43.

33 ON THE EVE OF THE CIVIL WAR Ibid., 47.

33 "IF SOUTH CAROLINA HAD" Ibid.

33 "HAIL COLUMBIA" WAS CONSIDERED Ibid., 33–34; Lawrence, *Music for Patriots, Politicians, and Presidents*, 142.

CHAPTER TWO: LAND WHERE OUR FATHERS DIED

35 "WHO ARE WE?" *The Papers of Andrew Jackson*, Vol. 2, ed. Harold D. Moser (Knoxville, Tenn., 1984), 290–293.

35 "I LOOKED AT MY HANDS" Sarah Bradford, *Harriet Tubman: The Moses of Her People* (Secaucus, N.J., 1961), 30.

35 MAJOR GEORGE ARMISTEAD KNEW Walter Lord, "Humiliation and Triumph," *American Heritage*, August 1972, 70; Lonn Taylor, Kathleen M. Kendrick, and Jeffrey L. Brodie, *The Star-Spangled Banner: The Making of an American Icon* (New York, 2008), 63–79; Richard Crawford,

America's Musical Life: A History (New York, 2001),
240–242. See also Marc Ferris, *Star-Spangled
Banner: The Unlikely Story of America's National
Anthem* (Baltimore, 2014), 20; Marc Leepson,
Flag: An American Biography (New York, 2005),
59–65; Irvin Molotsky, *The Flag, the Poet & the
Song: The Story of the Star-Spangled Banner* (New
York, 2001); Browne, *The Story of Our National
Ballads,* 48–68; Elson, *The National Music of
America,* 192–206; 42–49; Sonneck, *Report,*
7–42.

35 "WE, SIR, ARE READY" Lord, "Humiliation and
Triumph," *American Heritage,* 70.

35 ARMISTEAD WAS IN LUCK Taylor, Kendrick,
and Brodie, *The Star-Spangled Banner,* 63–64.

35 THIRTY BY FORTY-TWO FEET Ibid., 63.

35 AS WELL AS A STORM FLAG Ibid., 64.

36 A WASHINGTON LAWYER, FRANCIS SCOTT
KEY Crawford, *America's Musical Life,* 240–242;
Browne, *The Story of Our National Ballads,* 60–61;
Molotsky, *The Flag, the Poet & the Song,* 70–72.

36 "IN THE END" Wood, *Empire of Liberty,* 41.

36 DID NOT TRULY CONCLUDE AOP, xxvii,
524–525. Jefferson believed 1764 marked the
"dawn of the revolution," Ibid., 524. See also, in
general, Louise Burnham Dunbar, *A Study of
"Monarchical" Tendencies in the United States from 1776
to 1801* (New York, 1970); George C. Herring,
*From Colony to Superpower: U.S. Foreign Relations Since
1776* (New York, 2008); Middlekauff, *Glorious
Cause;* Alan Taylor, *The Civil War of 1812: American
Citizens, British Subjects, Irish Rebels, & Indian Allies*
(New York, 2010); Edmund S. Morgan, *The
Birth of the Republic, 1763–89* (Chicago, 1977);
Bailyn, *The Ideological Origins of the American
Revolution;* Wood, *The Idea of America;* Richard
Hofstadter, *The Paranoid Style in American Politics*
(Cambridge, Mass., 1996); and John R. Howe,
Jr., "Republican Thought and Political Violence
of the 1790s," *American Quarterly,* 19, No. 2,
Summer 1967, 147–165.

37 "MR. MADISON'S WAR" J.C.A. Stagg, *Mr.
Madison's War: Politics, Diplomacy, and Warfare in the
Early American Republic, 1783–1830* (Princeton, N.J.,
1983).

37 LASTED ABOUT TWENTY-FIVE HOURS https://
www.si.edu/spotlight/flag-day/banner-facts. See
also Taylor, Kendrick, and Brodie, *The
Star-Spangled Banner,* 26.

37 KEY WAS WORRIED Lord, "Humiliation and
Triumph," *American Heritage,* 91.

37 THE BRITISH FLOTILLA Taylor, Kendrick, and
Brodie, *The Star-Spangled Banner,* 23.

37 THE "BOMB VESSELS" Ibid.

37 "WE WERE LIKE PIGEONS" Ibid., 26.

37 "THE MEN IN THE FORT" Ibid., 26–27.

38 FIFTEEN TO EIGHTEEN HUNDRED Ibid., 31.

38 "THE ONLY MEANS" Ibid.

38 "A FEW OF THESE" Ibid.

38 FOUR AMERICANS Ibid.

38 WATCHING FROM AFAR Lord, "Humiliation
and Triumph," *American Heritage,* 91–92.

38 IN OLD ROADS BAY Taylor, Kendrick, and
Brodie, *The Star-Spangled Banner,* 42.

38 SCRIBBLED ON THE BACK Lord, "Humiliation
and Triumph," *American Heritage,* 92.

38 KEY FINISHED HIS COMPOSITION Ibid.

38 WHAT SO PROUDLY The sheet music can be
found at the Library of Congress, https://www
.loc.gov/item/ihas.100000006/. See also
Sonneck, *Report,* 37.

40 THE MELODY WAS DIFFICULT Browne, *The Story
of Our National Ballads,* 69–70. See also Taylor,
Kendrick, and Brodie, *The Star-Spangled Banner,*
44–45.

40 PUBLISHED AS HANDBILLS Elson, *The National
Music of America,* 196–197.

40 IN THE TUESDAY, SEPTEMBER 20, 1814,
EDITION "Facsimile of First Newspaper
Printing of 'Star-Spangled Banner,'" Library of
Congress, https://www.loc.gov/resource/ihas
.100010479.0.

40 UNDER THE HEADLINE Ibid. See also Elson,
The National Music of America, 197.

40 "IT COMMENCES ON" Elson, *The National Music of
America,* 205.

40 WHEN CONGRESS ELEVATED Browne, *The Story
of Our National Ballads,* 73; Crawford, *America's
Musical Life,* 240–242.

41 FIRST COMMISSIONED AND DESIGNED
Browne, *The Story of Our National Ballads,* 55–56.
See also Woden Teachout, *Capture the Flag: A
Political History of American Patriotism* (New York,
2009), for discussion of the flag's significance
from the colonial era through the twenty-first
century.

41 "THE STARS OF" Browne, *The Story of Our
National Ballads,* 53.

42 "Torn from the" Wood, *Empire of Liberty*, 40.

42 the motto adopted For background on the Great Seal of the United States and the national motto, see Jon Meacham, *American Gospel: God, the Founding Fathers, and the Making of a Nation* (New York, 2006), 80–81, and, more generally, Derek H. Davis, *Religion and the Continental Congress, 1774–1789: Contributions to Original Intent* (New York, 2000).

42 as "their lives" Daniel Webster, "Adams and Jefferson," August 2, 1826, https://www.dartmouth.edu/~dwebster/speeches/adams-jefferson.html.

42 "Auspicious omens cheer us" Ibid.

42 Samuel Francis Smith Browne, *The Story of Our National Ballads*, 95–112. Branham and Hartnett, *Sweet Freedom's Song*, is indispensable on the song and its influence.

42 reading over German Ibid., 100–101.

42 "Seizing a scrap" Ibid., 101.

42 "There is nothing more" Thomas Raynesford Lounsbury, ed., *Yale Book of American Verse* (New Haven, Conn., 1912), xlii–xliii; Branham and Hartnett, *Sweet Freedom's Song*, 14; "American Music for Hymn 'America,'" *NYT*, November 17, 1918.

43 "My Country, 'Tis of Thee" Branham and Hartnett, *Sweet Freedom's Song*, 210–211; Browne, *The Story of Our National Ballads*, 94.

43 a classmate of Smith Browne, *The Story of Our National Ballads*, 99.

44 "Now, there's Smith" Ibid.

44 sound, she said, "is a way" Bernice Johnson Reagon interview with Bill Moyers, 1991. https://billmoyers.com/content/songs-free. See also Werner, *A Change Is Gonna Come*, 352.

44 its debut on the Fourth Branham and Hartnett, *Sweet Freedom's Song*, 60–65.

45 There were abolitionist versions Ibid., 212.

46 At the Union's Camp Saxton Southern, *The Music of Black Americans*, 216.

46 It was the last thing Browne, *The Story of Our National Ballads*, 109–112.

47 his peroration "'I Have a Dream,' Address Delivered at the March on Washington for Jobs and Freedom," https://kinginstitute.stanford.edu/king-papers/documents/i-have-dream-address-delivered-march-washington-jobs-and-freedom.

47 "I regard the" Marc Pachter and Frances Wein, eds., *Abroad in America: Visitors to the New Nation, 1776–1914* (Reading, Mass., 1976), 63.

47 Another English visitor Ibid., 33–42.

47 "You will see" Ibid., 37.

47 the treatment of Native Americans See, for instance, Francis Paul Prucha, *The Great Father: The United States Government and the American Indians* (Lincoln, Neb., 1995); Jeremiah Evarts, *Cherokee Removal: The "William Penn Essays" and Other Writings*, ed. Francis Paul Prucha (Knoxville, Tenn., 1981); Grant Foreman, *Indian Removal: The Emigration of the Five Civilized Tribes of Indians* (Norman, Okla., 1972). See also *AL*, 398, and for a historiographical survey, see Regan A. Lutz, "West of Eden: The Historiography of the Trail of Tears," Ph.D. diss., University of Toledo, 1995.

48 "The questions have" Evarts, *Cherokee Removal*, ed. Prucha, 48.

48 published in 1829 Ibid., 8.

48 "Most certainly an" Ibid., 49.

48 Harriet Beecher Stowe's sister https://www.nyhistory.org/sites/default/files/newfiles/cwh-curriculum/Module%202/Resources/Resource%2011%20Catherine%20Beecher%27s%20Campaign.pdf.

48 "it has become" Ibid.

48 "I was a stranger" Rennard Strickland, "Strangers in a Strange Land: A Historical Perspective of the Columbian Quincentenary," *Journal of Civil Rights and Economic Development*, Vol. 7, Issue 2, 1992, https://scholarship.law.stjohns.edu/jcred/vol7/iss2/4.

48 The phrase originally comes Exodus 2:22, Psalm 137: 4, King James Version.

48 the music of the tribes See, for instance, Crawford, *America's Musical Life*, 3–14, 387–406; Willis G. Regier, ed., *Masterpieces of American Indian Literature* (Lincoln, Neb., 2005); Caroline Kennedy, *A Patriot's Handbook: Songs, Poems, Stories, and Speeches Celebrating the Land We Love* (New York, 2016), 364; Frances Densmore, ed., "Songs of the Sioux: From the Archive of Folk Song," Library of Congress, 1951.

48 One song of the Choctaw We are indebted to Charles Robinson, enrolled member of the Choctaw Nation of Oklahoma, and to Brad Joe, Cultural Specialist with the Choctaw Nation of Oklahoma, for this song and its translation. See also *Choctaw Hymn Book*, 4th edition (New York,

1851). According to Robinson, "The earliest known version of this song is from a book of songs in 1848. It was believed to have been sung eighteen years earlier as the Choctaw began their removal from Mississippi into Oklahoma. It is included in a book of 'hymns' that was sung in churches. As was the case with many tribal songs, church denominations would put music to them and often change the words to be more fitting with their theology. The translation is more of a paraphrase, as translating words from Choctaw to English is not always accurate." Charles Robinson to the authors, February 27, 2019.

49 "SONG OF THE EARTH" Brian Swann, ed., *Native American Songs and Poems: An Anthology* (Mineola, N.Y., 1996), 7–8.

49 AN 1822 ARTICLE Crawford, *America's Musical Life,* 390.

50 "I WILL GO" Ibid.

50 "THE MANNER IN WHICH" Ibid.

50 "CASS'S ACCOUNT SQUARES" Ibid.

50 THE OJIBWA GEORGE COPWAY Ibid., 392–393. See also Regier, ed., *Masterpieces of American Indian Literature,* 11–42.

50 PUBLISHING THE LIFE, Regier, ed., *Masterpieces of American Indian Literature,* 1-142.

50 AT AGE TWELVE Crawford, *America's Musical Life,* 392.

50 IT IS I Ibid.

50 "MY SON," COPWAY'S FATHER Ibid.

51 WILLIAM LLOYD GARRISON BEGAN PUBLISHING Henry Mayer, *All on Fire: William Lloyd Garrison and the Abolition of Slavery* (New York, 1998), 110.

51 "ASSENTING TO THE" https://www.masshist.org/database/1698.

51 I SWEAR Ibid.

52 PUBLISHED HIS *APPEAL* Sean Wilentz, ed., *David Walker's Appeal* (New York, 1995).

52 WERE "THE MOST DEGRADED" Ibid., 1.

52 "NOW, AMERICANS!" Wilentz, ed., *David Walker's Appeal,* 75–77.

53 THY PRESENCE WHY Ibid., 76–77.

53 "AWAY BACK IN" W.E.B. Du Bois, *The Souls of Black Folk* (Mineola, N.Y., 1994), 156.

54 I WALK THROUGH Ibid., 155.

54 "I KNOW LITTLE" Ibid., 157.

54 THE ORIGINS AND DEVELOPMENT See, for instance, Southern, *The Music of Black Americans;*

Crawford, *America's Musical Life,* 407–428; Henry Louis Gates, Jr., and Kwame Anthony Appiah, eds., *Africana: The Encyclopedia of the African and African American Experience,* Second Edition (Oxford, 2005); Cone, *The Spirituals and the Blues;* Imani Perry, *May We Forever Stand: A History of the Black National Anthem* (Chapel Hill, N.C., 2018); Julian Bond and Sondra Kathryn Wilson, eds., *Lift Every Voice and Sing: A Celebration of the Negro National Anthem, 100 Years, 100 Voices* (New York, 2000); Burton W. Peretti, *Lift Every Voice: The History of African American Music* (Lanham, Md., 2009).

In 1878, James Monroe Trotter published a history, *Music and Some Highly Musical People,* and in 1893, the Czech composer Antonin Dvořák told *The New York Herald* that American music must be understood to begin with African Americans. "I am now satisfied that the future music of this country must be founded upon what are called the negro melodies," Dvořák said. "This must be the real foundation of any serious and original school of composition to be developed in the United States." Peretti, *Lift Every Voice,* 186.

54 "THEY THAT WALKED" Du Bois, *The Souls of Black Folk,* 155.

54 "AND SO" Ibid., 156.

54 "I HAVE OFTEN" Frederick Douglass, *Autobiographies: Narrative of the Life of Frederick Douglass, an American Slave; My Bondage and My Freedom; Life and Times of Frederick Douglass,* ed. Henry Louis Gates, Jr. (New York, 1994), 24–25. See also, more generally, David W. Blight, *Frederick Douglass: Prophet of Freedom* (New York, 2018).

55 RECALLING LIFE ON THE LLOYD PLANTATION Douglass, *Autobiographies,* 23–24. See also Southern, *The Music of Black Americans,* 161–166, 177–178.

55 "WOULD MAKE" Douglass, *Autobiographies,* 23.

55 "THE MERE RECURRENCE" Ibid., 24.

55 "SOLD OFF TO GEORGY" Southern, *The Music of Black Americans,* 157–158.

55 SEE THESE POOR SOULS FROM AFRICA Ibid., 158–159.

56 AS DOUGLASS PLOTTED Douglass, *Autobiographies,* 307–308.

56 "I AM THE MORE" Ibid., 308.

56 WE WERE, AT TIMES Ibid.

57 THE "DOUBLE MEANING" See, for instance, Werner, *A Change Is Gonna Come,* 6–7.

57 "She explained to me" Ibid., 7.

57 Harriet Tubman On Tubman and the Underground Railroad more generally, see, for instance: Sarah Bradford, *Scenes from the Life of Harriet Tubman* (Auburn, N.Y., 1869) and *Harriet Tubman: The Moses of Her People*; Southern, *The Music of Black Americans*, 142–145; Eric Foner, *Gateway to Freedom: The Hidden History of the Underground Railroad* (New York, 2015); Fergus M. Bordewich, *Bound for Canaan: The Epic Story of the Underground Railroad, America's First Civil Rights Movement* (New York, 2005); William Still, *The Underground Railroad: Authentic Narratives and First-Hand Accounts*, ed. Ian Frederick Finseth (Mineola, N.Y., 2007); Catherine Clinton, *Harriet Tubman: The Road to Freedom* (New York, 2004).

57 Born circa 1820 Clinton, *Harriet Tubman: The Road to Freedom*, 4.

57 escaped to Philadelphia in 1849 Ibid., 33–60.

57 When that old chariot Bradford, *Harriet Tubman: The Moses of Her People*, 28.

58 "For I had reasoned" Ibid., 29.

58 her "farewell song" Ibid.

58 "I looked at my hands" Ibid., 30.

58 "I was a stranger" Ibid., 31.

58 "At one time" Ibid., 35.

58 "The woods were" Ibid., 36.

59 "How long she is away!" Ibid.

59 Hail, oh hail, ye happy spirits Ibid

59 churches, religious gatherings, and spirituals Southern, *The Music of Black Americans*, 28–41, 71–89, 127–131, 145–147, 178–190, 227–231.

59 Oh go down, Moses Bradford, *Harriet Tubman: The Moses of Her People*, 37. The text quoted is from Bradford, who heard Tubman sing. See also "African American Spirituals," Library of Congress. https://www.loc.gov/item/ihas .200197495/.

60 When that old chariot Bradford, *Harriet Tubman: The Moses of Her People*, 28.

61 Glory to God Ibid., 51.

61 "I have heard" Bradford, *Scenes in the Life of Harriet Tubman*, 23.

61 One close Tubman ally William H. Seward, American Battlefield Trust, https://www .battlefields.org/learn/biographies/william-h -seward.

61 he foresaw "countless generations" Ibid.

61 "half slave and half free" " 'A House Divided': Speech at Springfield, Illinois, June 16, 1858," Abraham Lincoln. https://quod.lib .umich.edu/l/lincoln/lincoln2/1:508?rgn=div1 ;singlegenre=All;sort=occur;subview=detail ;type=simple;view=fulltext;q1=house+divided.

61 "the irrepressible conflict" "The Irrepressible Conflict: History of Slavery as a Political Issue. . . . Speech of Hon. William H. Seward in the Senate of the United States," *NYT*, March 1, 1860.

CHAPTER THREE: MINE EYES HAVE SEEN THE GLORY

63 "Sing it again!" Deborah Pickman Clifford, *Mine Eyes Have Seen the Glory: A Biography of Julia Ward Howe* (Boston, 1979), 147; Stauffer and Soskis, *The Battle Hymn of the Republic*, 94.

63 "The year of jubilee" David W. Blight, *Frederick Douglass' Civil War: Keeping Faith in Jubilee* (Baton Rouge, La., 1989), 106, reports Douglass's fondness for the hymn. For lyrics, see Charles Wesley, "Blow Ye the Trumpet, Blow!" https://hymnary.org/text/blow_ye_the _trumpet_blow.

63 Frederick Douglass was Douglass, *Autobiographies*, 370–388 and 677–702, offers recollections of his twenty-one months abroad in Britain. See also Blight, *Frederick Douglass: Prophet of Freedom*, 140–177.

63 composed a piece Sandra Knispel, "Rediscovered Song Honoring Frederick Douglass to Be Performed for the First Time in a Century," November 14, 2018, http://www.rochester.edu /newscenter/rare-rediscovered-song-honoring -frederick-douglass-to-be-performed-for-the -first-time-in-a-century-34943/.

63 The song enjoyed a rediscovery Ibid.

63 the only other known copy Ibid.

63 "How is it" Samuel Johnson, "Taxation No Tyranny: An Answer to the Resolutions and Address of the American Congress," https:// www.samueljohnson.com/tnt.html.

64 Shall I, like a coward Knispel, http://www .rochester.edu/newscenter/rare-rediscovered -song-honoring-frederick-douglass-to-be -performed-for-the-first-time-in-a-century -34943/.

64 "Should I seem" Frederick Douglass, "What

to the Slave Is the Fourth of July?" July 5, 1852, http://teachingamericanhistory.org/library/document/what-to-the-slave-is-the-fourth-of-july/.

65   AN ADDRESS AT SAVANNAH, GEORGIA Alexander H. Stephens, "'Corner Stone' Speech," March 21, 1861, http://teachingamericanhistory.org/library/document/cornerstone-speech/.

65   "THE NEW [CONFEDERATE]" Stephens, "'Corner Stone' Speech."

67   THE "FIERY TRIAL" Abraham Lincoln, "Annual Message to Congress," December 1, 1862: Abraham Lincoln, The Collected Works of Abraham Lincoln, Vol. 5. Roy P. Blaser, ed. (New Brunswick, N.J., 1953), 537.

67   "I AM, LIKE" Pachter and Wein, eds., Abroad in America, 71.

67   FELLOW-CITIZENS, WE CANNOT Lincoln, "Second Annual Message," December 1, 1862.

68   SONG WAS AS MUCH A PART See, for instance, McWhirter, Battle Hymns; Kenneth A. Bernard, Lincoln and the Music of the Civil War (Caldwell, Ida., 1966); Richard B. Harwell, Confederate Music (Chapel Hill, N.C., 1950); Steven H. Cornelius, Music of the Civil War Era (Westport, Conn., 2004); Crawford, America's Musical Life, 260–271; Scott Gac, Singing for Freedom: The Hutchinson Family Singers and the Nineteenth-Century Culture of Antebellum Reform (New Haven, Conn., 2007); Ewen, Great Men of American Popular Song; John Druesedow, "Music of the Civil War Era: A Discography," Notes, Second Series, Vol. 60, No. 1, September 2003, 240–254.

68   "RANG OUT FROM" McWhirter, Battle Hymns, 1.

68   FROM CHICAGO, GEORGE F. ROOT Ewen, Great Men of American Popular Song, 36–40.

68   WITHIN THREE DAYS Ibid., 38.

68   THE FIRST GUN IS FIRED! George F. Root, "The First Gun is Fired: May God Protect the Right!" Newberry Library, Chicago, https://publications.newberry.org/digitalexhibitions/exhibits/show/homefront/introduction/item/777.

68   PUT HENRY S. WASHBURN'S POEM Ewen, Great Men of American Popular Song, 38.

68   WE SHALL MEET Irwin Silber, ed., Songs of the Civil War (New York, 1960), 137–139; https://www.loc.gov/resource/ihas.200001918.0/?sp=2.

69   OLIVER WENDELL HOLMES TRIED Elson, The National Music of America, 241–242.

69   THE HUTCHINSON FAMILY SINGERS McWhirter, Battle Hymns, 8–12. See also Gac, Singing for Freedom.

70   PUT JOHN GREENLEAF WHITTIER'S ABOLITIONIST McWhirter, Battle Hymns, 8–9.

70   "THE BATTLE CRY OF FREEDOM" Silber, ed., Songs of the Civil War, 18–19.

70   HAD "DONE MORE" Ewen, Great Men of American Popular Song, 39.

71   IN HIS ANGUISH OVER SLAVERY Eric Foner, The Fiery Trial: Abraham Lincoln and American Slavery (New York, 2010), is indispensable.

71   "I AM NATURALLY" Ibid., 3.

71   IN PEORIA, ILLINOIS Ibid., 63–70.

71   "A MONSTROUS INJUSTICE" Ibid., 66.

71   "LET US RE-ADOPT" Ibid., 69.

71   "IF ALL EARTHLY POWER" Ibid., 67.

71   MY FIRST IMPULSE Ibid.

71   ON COMING TO THE PRESIDENCY Ibid., 144–157; and Ronald C. White, Jr., A. Lincoln: A Biography (New York, 2009), 360–361. See also Harold Holzer, Lincoln President-Elect: Abraham Lincoln and the Great Secession Winter 1860–1861 (New York, 2008); and William J. Cooper, Jr., We Have the War Upon Us: The Onset of the Civil War, November 1860–April 1861 (New York, 2012).

71   "I WILL SAY" Foner, Fiery Trial, 107.

71   "APPREHENSION SEEMS TO" "First Inaugural Address of Abraham Lincoln," March 4, 1861, http://avalon.law.yale.edu/19th_century/lincoln1.asp.

73   BY THE SUMMER OF 1862 Foner, Fiery Trial, 206–247.

73   LINCOLN TOLD HIS CABINET Ibid., 230–231. See also Jon Meacham, The Soul of America: The Battle for Our Better Angels (SOA), 56, and Meacham, American Gospel, 116–117.

73   "FOREVER FREE" Southern, The Music of Black Americans, 215.

73   "BLACK MEN ASSEMBLED" Ibid.

73   GO DOWN, MOSES Ibid.

73   A WOMAN IN THE CROWD Ibid.

74   GO DOWN, ABRAHAM Ibid.

74   JULIA WARD HOWE'S "THE BATTLE HYMN" Stauffer and Soskis, The Battle Hymn of the Republic, is definitive. See also Elaine Showalter, The Civil Wars of Julia Ward Howe: A Biography (New York, 2016), 161–166; Clifford, Mine Eyes Have Seen the Glory, 141–147.

74   INSPIRED BY WHAT SHE'D SEEN Showalter, The

Civil Wars of Julia Ward Howe, 164–165; Stauffer and Soskis, *The Battle Hymn of the Republic,* 82–84.

74   THE TUNE FOR WHICH Ibid., 164. See also Elson, *The National Music of America,* 253–258, and Browne, *The Story of Our National Ballads,* 128–157.

74   "JOHN BROWN'S BODY" Silber, *Songs of the Civil War,* 23.

75   THE IMMEDIATE OCCASION Browne, *The Story of Our National Ballads,* 153.

76   MINE EYES HAVE SEEN Silber, ed., *Songs of the Civil War,* 21–23.

76   "DO YOU WANT THIS" Showalter, *The Civil Wars of Julia Ward Howe,* 165–166.

76   WHO PAID HER FIVE DOLLARS Ibid., 166.

76–77   A TITLE OF HIS DEVISING Stauffer and Soskis, *The Battle Hymn of the Republic,* 92.

77   LINCOLN LOVED IT Clifford, *Mine Eyes Have Seen the Glory,* 147; Stauffer and Soskis, *The Battle Hymn of the Republic,* 93–94.

77   AFTER HEARING CHARLES MCCABE Stauffer and Soskis, *The Battle Hymn of the Republic,* 93–94.

77   "TAKE IT ALL IN ALL" Ibid., 94.

77   "BLACK SOLDIERS SEEMED" Southern, *The Music of Black Americans,* 210.

77   WE ARE DONE Ibid.

77   THE UNION NEEDED MORE Browne, *The Story of Our National Ballads,* 172.

77   A QUAKER, JAMES SLOAN GIBBONS Ibid., 161–176. Browne noted the irony: "A war song written by a Quaker sounds like an absurdity. For not only do the Friends discourage, as a rule, the art of music, as being among the vanities of a frivolous world, but, according to one of their most emphatic tenets, a member of that faith is bound to make it a matter of conscience to condemn all war, as inconsistent with the precept and spirit of the Gospel." Ibid., 161.

77   FIRST PUBLISHED IN Ibid., 174.

77   "WE ARE COMING, FATHER ABRAHAM," Library of Congress. https://www.loc.gov/resource/ihas.200000811.0/?sp=1.

79   KNOWN AS "AMERICA'S TROUBADOR" Southern, *The Music of Black Americans,* 93–94. See also McWhirter, *Battle Hymns,* 15, 27, 138, 143, 152–153, 193, 205–206; Ewen, *Great Men of American Popular Song,* 23–31; and "Stephen Collins Foster, 1826–1864," https://www.loc.gov/item/ihas.200035701.

79   THE BLACKFACE MINSTREL STAGE Lhamon, *Jump Jim Crow,* is instructive. See also Southern,

The Music of Black Americans, 89–96; Crawford, *America's Musical Life,* 196–220.

79   "ESSENTIALLY IT CONSISTED" Southern, *The Music of Black Americans,* 89.

79   TWO ARCHETYPES DROVE Ibid.

79   "DANDY DRESSED IN" Ibid.

79   DRANK HIMSELF TO DEATH McWhirter, *Battle Hymns,* 22.

79   FAMOUS FOR "OLD UNCLE NED" Southern, *The Music of Black Americans,* 94; "Stephen Collins Foster," https://www.loc.gov/item/ihas.2000 35701.

79   "WAS MY BROTHER IN THE BATTLE?" Library of Congress, https://www.loc.gov/resource/ihas .200197692.0?st=gallery.

79   "FOR THE DEAR OLD FLAG" Silber, ed., *Songs of the Civil War,* 27–29.

81   "I WISH I WAS IN DIXIE'S LAND" See, for instance, McWhirter, *Battle Hymns,* 65–78; Crawford, *America's Musical Life,* 264–267; Harwell, *Confederate Music,* 41–52; Cornelius, *Music of the Civil War Era,* 30–37; Ewen, *Great Men of American Popular Song,* 14–22; Elson, *The National Music of America,* 245–247; Browne, *The Story of Our National Ballads,* 99–108; John Bush Jones, *Reinventing Dixie: Tin Pan Alley's Songs and the Creation of the Mythic South* (Baton Rouge, La., 2015).

81   DANIEL DECATUR EMMETT Harwell, *Confederate Music,* 41–52; Ewen, *Great Men of American Popular Song,* 17–22; Cornelius, *Music of the Civil War Era,* 30–37.

81   ASKED TO PRODUCE A NEW NUMBER Ewen, *Great Men of American Popular Song,* 19.

81   BY BLACKFACE PERFORMERS Ibid., 14–22; McWhirter, *Battle Hymns,* 138–144.

81   LINCOLN HIMSELF ADMIRED IT Bernard, *Lincoln and the Music of the Civil War,* 300.

81   A COMMON SENSE OF IDENTITY McWhirter, *Battle Hymns,* 73–74.

82   THE "BONNIE BLUE FLAG" Ibid., 73–78; Cornelius, *Music of the Civil War Era,* 38.

82   WRITTEN BY HARRY MACARTHY Harwell, *Confederate Music,* 56.

82   THEY GOT THE ORDER Cornelius, *Music of the Civil War,* 38–40.

82   WE ARE A BAND OF BROTHERS "Bonnie Blue Flag," Vicksburg National Military Park, National Park Service. https://www.nps.gov/vick/learn/education/upload/bonnie%20blue %20flag.pdf.

85   As time went on, Macarthy replaced McWhirter, *Battle Hymns*, 75.

85   such as Thomas "Stonewall" Jackson Ibid., 87–89.

85   He's in the saddle Silber, ed., *Songs of the Civil War*, 79–81.

85   inspired at least one enslaved community Ira Berlin, Marc Favreau, and Steven F. Miller, eds., *Remembering Slavery: African Americans Talk About Their Personal Experiences of Slavery and Emancipation* (New York, 1998), 256–258.

85   a song that had been written We are grateful to Christian McWhirter for this point.

86   "My old master" Berlin, Favreau, and Miller, eds., *Remembering Slavery*, 258.

86   White folks, have you seen Ibid.

86   In a recollection Nason, *A Monogram on Our National Song*, 57–58.

87   The troops were delighted Ibid.

88   "Mr. Lincoln's love" Michael Burlingame, ed., *Lincoln Observed: Civil War Dispatches of Noah Brooks* (Baltimore, 1998), 220.

88   "Twenty Years Ago" https://www.loc.gov /resource/amss.as114020.0/?st=text.

88   there had never been "a nobler" Frederick Douglass, *The Portable Frederick Douglass*, eds. John Stauffer and Henry Louis Gates, Jr. (New York, 2016), 330.

88   At Gettysburg in 1863 Abraham Lincoln, "The Gettysburg Address," November 19, 1863, http://www.abrahamlincolnonline.org/lincoln /speeches/gettysburg.htm.

89   a favorite hymn of Frederick Douglass Blight, *Frederick Douglass' Civil War: Keeping Faith in Jubilee*, 106.

89   Blow ye the trumpet, blow Charles Wesley, "Blow Ye the Trumpet, Blow!" https://hymnary .org/text/blow_ye_the_trumpet_blow.

90   In his second inaugural "Abraham Lincoln, Second Inaugural Address," March 4, 1865, http://avalon.law.yale.edu/19th_century /lincoln2.asp.

90   "I claim not" Abraham Lincoln to Albert G. Hodges, April 4, 1864, http://www.abrahamlin colnonline.org/lincoln/speeches/hodges.htm.

91   "With malice toward none" "Abraham Lincoln, Second Inaugural Address," March 4, 1865, http://avalon.law.yale.edu/19th_century /lincoln2.asp.

91   In his "Song, On the Death of" Silas S.

Steele, "Song on the Death of President Abraham Lincoln," *Remembering Lincoln*. http:// rememberinglincoln.fords.org/node/253.

91   In 1876, Douglass said this Douglass, *Autobiographies*, 915–925.

92   "According to the popular" Pachter and Wein, eds., *Abroad in America*, 145.

92   the postbellum experience of the Jubilee Singers Andrew Ward, *Dark Midnight When I Rise: The Story of the Fisk Jubilee Singers, Who Introduced the World to the Music of Black America* (New York, 2000), is indispensable on the subject.

92   In the autumn of 1871 Ibid., xiii.

92   the Jubilee Singers are credited with Ibid., xiii–xiv.

92   "For months, they journeyed" Ibid., xiii.

93   A cousin of William Seward's Ibid., 183.

93   "I am expecting to hear" "Handbill for a Performance by the Fisk Jubilee Singers, March 23, 1875," National Museum of African-American History and Culture, Washington, D.C.

93   "You are doing more" Ibid.

93   In his meeting with them Ibid.

93   Run to Jesus—shun the danger Ibid.

93   "soon caught the melody" Ibid.

93   "It was while" Ibid.

93   Impressed, the Jubilee Singers added Ibid.

CHAPTER FOUR: MARCH, MARCH, MANY AS ONE

95   "Daughters of freedom" "Daughters of Freedom, The Ballot Be Yours," Library of Congress, https://www.loc.gov/resource /sm1871.02334.0?st=gallery; Crew, *Suffragist Sheet Music*, 62.

95   "And we won't come back" John McCabe, *George M. Cohan: The Man Who Owned Broadway* (Garden City, N.Y., 1973), 138.

95   In the autumn of 1915 "25,340 March in Suffrage Parade to the Applause of 250,000 Admirers; Spectacle Runs on into the Moonlight; Three Hours in Review," *NYT*, October 24, 1915; "30,000 Women March in Greatest Suffrage Parade in New York Ever Held," *The Washington Post (WP)*, October 24, 1915.

95   Thirty bands took part "30,000 Women March," *WP*, October 24, 1915.

95 AT DUSK, FIFTEEN BANDS "25,340 March in Suffrage Parade," *NYT,* October 24, 1915.

95 "AS DARKNESS FELL" "30,000 Women March," *WP,* October 24, 1915.

95 "DAUGHTERS OF FREEDOM" "Daughters of Freedom, The Ballot Be Yours," Library of Congress, https://www.loc.gov/resource /sm1871.02334.0?st=gallery; Crew, *Suffragist Sheet Music,* 62.

96 THE EDITORIAL, AS SHE CHOSE Ida Husted Harper, *The Life and Work of Susan B. Anthony: A Story of the Evolution of the Status of Woman,* Vol. 1 (Indianapolis, 1898), 423. See also *Elizabeth Cady Stanton, Susan B. Anthony: Correspondence, Writings, Speeches,* ed. Ellen Carol DuBois (New York, 1992), 152–165; Lynn Sherr, *Failure Is Impossible: Susan B. Anthony in Her Own Words* (New York, 1995), 108–117; Geoffrey C. Ward and Ken Burns, *Not For Ourselves Alone: The Story of Elizabeth Cady Stanton and Susan B. Anthony* (New York, 1999), 139–149.

97 "NOW REGISTER!" Harper, *The Life and Work of Susan B. Anthony,* 423.

97 THE EIGHTH WARD'S REGISTRY OFFICE Ibid.

97 "THERE WAS NOTHING" Ibid.

97 PRESENTING HERSELF Ibid.

97 THE OFFICIALS "AT LENGTH" Ibid.

97 THE FOLLOWING TUESDAY Ibid., 424.

97 "WELL I HAVE BEEN" Ward and Burns, *Not For Ourselves Alone,* 142.

97 THE JULY 1848 SENECA FALLS Sally G. McMillen, *Seneca Falls and the Origins of the Women's Rights Movement* (New York, 2008), 71–103, covers the gathering itself.

97 "WE HOLD THESE TRUTHS" "Declaration of Sentiments and Resolutions, Woman's Rights Convention, Held at Seneca Falls, 19–20 July 1848," The Elizabeth Cady Stanton and Susan B. Anthony Papers Project, State University of New Jersey, http://ecssba.rutgers .edu/docs/seneca.html.

97 "IT WAS WE, THE PEOPLE" Susan B. Anthony, "Is It a Crime for a U.S. Citizen to Vote?" Voices of Democracy: The U.S. Oratory Project, April 3, 1873, http://voicesofdemocracy.umd.edu /anthony-is-it-a-crime-speech-text/.

97 ARRESTED, CHARGED, AND TRIED Harper, *The Life and Work of Susan B. Anthony,* 426–448; Ann D. Gordon, "The Trial of Susan B. Anthony," Federal Judicial Center, Federal Judicial History Office, 2005, https://www.fjc.gov/sites/default /files/trials/susanbanthony.pdf.

97 WHEN THE MARSHAL Harper, *The Life and Work of Susan B. Anthony,* 426.

98 "YES, YOUR HONOR" For slightly differing accounts of the words spoken in court, see "Remarks by Susan B. Anthony in the Circuit Court of the United States for the Northern District of New York, 19 June 1873," The Elizabeth Cady Stanton and Susan B. Anthony Papers Project, http://ecssba.rutgers.edu/docs /sbatrial.html.

98 FINED ONE HUNDRED DOLLARS Gordon, "The Trial of Susan B. Anthony," 7, https://www.fjc .gov/sites/default/files/trials/susanbanthony.pdf.

98 THE GOVERNMENT NEVER COLLECTED Ibid.

98 "IF IT IS" Sherr, *Failure Is Impossible,* 117.

98 "DURING THE FIRST" Showalter, *The Civil Wars of Julia Ward Howe,* 185.

99 "GIVE THE BALLOT TO THE MOTHERS" Crew, *Suffragist Sheet Music,* 112.

100 A REVIVED KU KLUX KLAN *SOA,* 107–133. See also, for instance, Rory McVeigh, *The Rise of the Ku Klux Klan: Right-Wing Movements and National Politics* (Minneapolis, 2009); McVeigh, "Power Devaluation, the Ku Klux Klan, and the Democratic National Convention of 1924," *Sociological Forum,* Vol. 16, No. 1, March 2001, 1–31; Linda Gordon, *The Second Coming of the KKK: The Ku Klux Klan of the 1920s and the American Political Tradition* (New York, 2017); Nancy MacLean, *Behind the Mask of Chivalry: The Making of the Second Ku Klux Klan* (New York, 1994). More generally, see Frederick Lewis Allen, *Only Yesterday: An Informal History of the 1920s* (New York, 2010), 51.

100 "THE PRINCIPLE OF" Louise W. Knight, *Jane Addams: Spirit in Action* (New York, 2010), 152. See also Jane Addams, *Twenty Years at Hull-House: With Autobiographical Notes,* ed. Victoria Bissell Brown (Boston, 1999); Addams, *Democracy and Social Ethics* (Urbana, Ill., 2002).

100 APPOMATTOX HAD BEEN See, for instance, *SOA,* 51–69.

100 EDWARD ALFRED POLLARD Ibid., 58–60.

100 HENRY A. WISE *SOA,* 300–302; *Richmond Enquirer,* January 31, 1866; *NYT,* August 25, 1867; Wise Family Papers, Virginia Historical Society, Richmond, Virginia.

100 "THERE IS NOW" *NYT,* August 25, 1867.

101 "IF NEGRO EQUALITY" Ibid.

101 IN 1905, A GROUP Patricia Sullivan, *Lift Every Voice: The NAACP and the Making of the Civil Rights Movement* (New York, 2009), 3–4. See also *SOA*, 104, and "Declaration of Principles," The Niagara Movement, 1905, http://scua.library.umass.edu/collections/etext/dubois/niagara.pdf.

101 "WE WILL NOT BE SATISFIED" W.E.B. Du Bois, "Address of the Niagara Movement to the Country, Issued by the Second Annual Convention of the 'Niagara Movement' of American Negroes, in Session at Harpers Ferry, West Va., Aug. 16–19, 1906," in Louis Freeland Post, Alice Thatcher Post, and Stoughton Cooley, eds., *The Public,* Vol. 9 (Chicago, 1906), 517.

102 "THE MORNING BREAKS" Ibid., 518.

102 JAMES WELDON JOHNSON See, for instance, James Weldon Johnson, *Writings* (New York, 2004), 874–875; Perry, *May We Forever Stand,* 1–24; "James Weldon Johnson, 1871–1938," Poetry Foundation, https://www.poetryfoundation.org/poets/james-weldon-johnson; Robert E. Fleming, *James Weldon Johnson* (Boston, 1987), 42–49; Eugene Levy, *James Weldon Johnson: Black Leader, Black Voice* (Chicago, 1973), 70–73.

103 JOHNSON WAS THE AUTHOR Perry, *May We Forever Stand,* 3–7; Johnson, *Writings,* 874; Southern, *The Music of Black Americans,* 274–275.

103 FIVE HUNDRED SCHOOLCHILDREN Johnson, *Writings,* 874.

103 "SHORTLY AFTERWARDS" Ibid.

103 LIFT EVERY VOICE Ibid., 874–875.

106 "I HAVE COMMONLY FOUND" Perry, *May We Forever Stand,* 25.

106 HELPED FOUND THE NAACP Sullivan, *Lift Every Voice,* 15–17.

106 MET JOHNSON Perry, *May We Forever Stand,* 30, 38.

106 BY 1919 THE ORGANIZATION Ibid., 32.

106 A SONG OF TEMPERED HOPE See, for instance, Fleming, *James Weldon Johnson,* 44–45; Levy, *James Weldon Johnson: Black Leader, Black Voice,* 71–72.

107 "THERE IS NOTHING" Perry, *May We Forever Stand,* 37.

107 IN HIS "FATHER, FATHER ABRAHAM" Fleming, *James Weldon Johnson,* 44.

107 QUOTED "LIFE EVERY VOICE" IN HIS BENEDICTION Perry, *May We Forever Stand,* 155.

107 "GOD OF OUR WEARY YEARS" Ibid., 218–219; Joseph Lowery Benediction Transcript, January 20, 2009, https://socialmode.com/2009/01/20/president-obamas-inauguration-speech-transcript-and-benediction-transcript/.

107 "THERE IS NO SONG" Perry, *May We Forever Stand,* 225.

108 "I, LIKE MANY OTHER PEOPLE" Ibid.

108 WEDNESDAY, MAY 1, 1940 FDR Daily Schedule, May 1, 1940, "FDR Day by Day," Franklin D. Roosevelt Library, Hyde Park, N.Y.

108 "THESE HAVE INDEED" Martin Gilbert, *Finest Hour: Winston S. Churchill, 1939–1941,* The Churchill Biography, vol. 6 (London, 1991), 23.

109 "IT IS BECAUSE" Warren F. Kimball, ed., *Churchill and Roosevelt: The Complete Correspondence: Alliance Emerging,* Vol. 1 (Princeton, N.J., 1984), 24.

109 "TAKES ME BACK" Ibid., 26.

109 FDR PRESENTED THE "President Greets Cohan as His 'Double,' Presents Medal for Writing Old War Songs," *NYT,* May 2, 1940.

109 GEORGE M. COHAN See, for instance, McCabe, *George M. Cohan: The Man Who Owned Broadway.*

109 "WELL, HOW'S MY DOUBLE?" *NYT,* May 2, 1940.

109 "I'M A YANKEE DOODLE BOY" George M. Cohan, "The Yankee Doodle Boy," www.loc.gov/resource/ihas.100010514.0/?sp=6.

109 YOU'RE A GRAND OLD FLAG https://www.loc.gov/item/ihas.100010512.

110 CONGRESS SINGLED OUT "The George Cohan Congressional Gold Medal," May 28, 1936, https://history.house.gov/Historical-Highlights/1901-1950/The-George-Cohan-Congressional-Gold-Medal/.

110 "OVER THERE" George M. Cohan, "Over There," Historic Sheet Music Collection, Connecticut College. http://digitalcommons.conncoll.edu/sheetmusic/1760.

111 COHAN HAD WRITTEN McCabe, *George M. Cohan,* 137–138.

111 CALLING HIS FAMILY Ibid., 137.

111 "SO WE ALL" Ibid.

111 "FUNNY ABOUT THEM" Ward Morehouse, *George M. Cohan: Prince of the American Theater* (New York, 1943), 126.

111 MORE THAN A BUGLE CALL McCabe, *George M. Cohan,* 138.

111 "'OVER THERE' BECAME" Ibid.

112 "THE WORLD MUST BE" Woodrow Wilson, "Address to a Joint Session of Congress Requesting a Declaration of War Against

Germany," The American Presidency Project, https://www.presidency.ucsb.edu/node/207620.

112 LEGISLATION TO PROTECT *SOA,* III–II3; John Milton Cooper, *Woodrow Wilson: A Biography* (New York, 2009), 397–401.

112 AS MANY AS FOUR HUNDRED PUBLICATIONS *SOA,* III; Anne Cipriano Venzon, ed., *The United States in the First World War: An Encyclopedia* (New York, 1999), 132–133. Donald Johnson, "Wilson, Burleson, and Censorship in the First World War," *Journal of Southern History,* Vol. 28, February 1962, 46–58.

112 PALMER WAS THE ARCHITECT *SOA,* III–II6. See also, for instance, Robert K. Murray, *Red Scare: A Study in National Hysteria, 1919–1920* (New York, 1964); David H. Bennett, *The Party of Fear: From Nativist Movements to the New Right in American History* (New York, 1995); Geoffrey C. Ward, *A First-Class Temperament: The Emergence of Franklin Roosevelt* (New York, 1989).

112 WITH J. EDGAR HOOVER Kenneth D. Ackerman, *Young J. Edgar: Hoover and the Red Scare, 1919–1920* (New York, 2011).

112 THE FEDERAL TRESPASSES See, for instance, Murray, *Red Scare;* Bennett, *The Party of Fear;* and Samuel Walker, *In Defense of American Liberties: A History of the ACLU* (New York, 1990).

112 "I DIDN'T RAISE MY BOY" https://www.loc.gov/resource/ihas.100008457.0/?sp=3.

112 ANOTHER SONG, BY GEORGE GRAFF, JR. "Let Us Have Peace," Bowling Green State University, https://digitalgallery.bgsu.edu/collections/item/31193.

114 KATHARINE LEE BATES See, for instance, Melinda M. Ponder, *Katharine Lee Bates: From Sea to Shining Sea, The Poet of "America the Beautiful"* (Chicago, 2017); Browne, *The Story of Our National Ballads,* 265–275; Lynn Sherr, *America the Beautiful: The Stirring True Story Behind Our Nation's Favorite Song* (New York, 2001).

114 WAS TOLD THAT AMERICAN SOLDIERS Ponder, *Katharine Lee Bates: From Sea to Shining Sea,* xv–xvii. Ponder discovered the anecdote in documents at Wellesley College, where Bates had taught.

114 THE NEWS BROUGHT TEARS Ibid., xvii.

114 "THE HYMN HAS GONE" Browne, *The Story of Our National Ballads,* 273–274.

114 O BEAUTIFUL Katharine Lee Bates, *America the Beautiful, and Other Poems* (New York, 1911), 3–4.

116 RAY CHARLES'S VERSION OF "AMERICA THE BEAUTIFUL" David Remnick, "Soul Survivor: The Revival and Hidden Treasure of Aretha Franklin," *The New Yorker,* April 4, 2016.

116 "REMEMBER, I GOT TO FIRST FEEL" Jann S. Wenner and Joe Levy, eds., *The Rolling Stone Interviews* (New York, 2007), 77–78.

116 "THAT THE HYMN" Browne, *The Story of Our National Ballads,* 274.

CHAPTER FIVE: AS THE STORM CLOUDS GATHER

119 "I'VE SEEN THE DUST" Woody Guthrie, "The Dust Bowl Blues," https://www.woodyguthrie.org/Lyrics/Dust_Bowl_Blues.htm.

119 "SONGS MAKE HISTORY" Laurence Bergreen, "Irving Berlin: This Is the Army," *Prologue Magazine,* Summer 1996, https://www.archives.gov/publications/prologue/1996/summer/irving-berlin-1.html.

119 "A VOICE ONE HEARS" Barbara Klaw, "'A Voice One Hears Once in a Hundred Years': An Interview with Marian Anderson," *American Heritage,* February 1977, 51–57.

119 THE CITY WAS THRONGED *Time,* "Strange Interlude," September 14, 1936; "Rivals Meet with Smiles—Both Candidates Are Cheered by Huge Crowds Along Des Moines Streets," *NYT,* September 4, 1936; "Landon Joins The President in Des Moines Drought Talk—100,000 Jam City to Cheer Nominees," *WP,* September 4, 1936; Garry Wills, *Reagan's America: Innocents at Home* (Garden City, N.Y., 1987), 108–109.

119 100,000 JAM CITY *WP,* September 4, 1936.

119 POLICE SIRENS BLARED *Time,* "Strange Interlude," September 14, 1936.

120 STANDING SIX DEEP "Rivals Meet with Smiles," *NYT,* September 4, 1936.

120 "A HOLIDAY SPIRIT" Ibid.

120 "I NEVER MET HIM" John Gunther, *Roosevelt in Retrospect: A Profile in History* (New York, 1950), 4.

120 A YOUNG SPORTSCASTER See, for instance, Ronald Reagan with Richard G. Hubler, *Where's the Rest of Me? The Autobiography of Ronald Reagan* (New York, 1981), 58.

120 HAD BEEN VISIBLY THRILLED Wills, *Reagan's America,* 108. "Myrtle Williams (now Mrs.

Norman Moon)," Wills reported, "who worked with him at the radio station, remembers Reagan's excitement as they rushed to the window and watched Roosevelt drive by the station in his open limousine, waving to the crowds along Walnut Street." (Ibid.)

120 "FRANKLIN ROOSEVELT WAS" Ronald Reagan, "Remarks at a White House Luncheon Celebrating the Centennial of the Birth of Franklin Delano Roosevelt," January 28, 1982, https://www.reaganlibrary.gov/research /speeches/12882d. For an account of the event, see also William E. Leuchtenburg, *In the Shadow of FDR: From Harry Truman to George W. Bush* (Ithaca, N.Y., 1983), 232–235.

120 VOTED FOUR TIMES Edward M. Yager, *Ronald Reagan's Journey: Democrat to Republican* (Lanham, Md., 2006), 12.

120 "FDR WAS DENOUNCED" Ronald Reagan, "Remarks at a White House Luncheon," January 28, 1982,

120 SKEPTICAL OF THEIR HOST Leuchtenburg, *In the Shadow of FDR,* 232–235.

120 LOBSTER BISQUE AND CHICKEN VERONIQUE Ibid., 234.

120 A SELF-DESCRIBED "NEAR-HOPELESS HEMO-PHILIAC LIBERAL" Lou Cannon, *President Reagan: The Role of a Lifetime* (New York, 2000), 243.

120 A "COMBINATION OF" Howell Raines, "Reagan Denies Plan to Answer Carter," *NYT,* August 17, 1980.

121 "IN THIS PRESENT CRISIS" "First Inaugural Address of Ronald Reagan," January 20, 1981, http://avalon.law.yale.edu/20th_century /reagan1.asp.

121 "THIS GREAT NATION" Ronald Reagan, "Remarks at a White House Luncheon," January 28, 1982.

121 TO "HAPPY DAYS" Ibid.

121 "HAPPY DAYS ARE HERE AGAIN" See, for instance, William H. Young and Nancy K. Young, *Music of the Great Depression* (Westport, Conn., 2005), 46–47; Donald A. Ritchie, *Electing FDR: The New Deal Campaign of 1932* (Lawrence, Kans., 2007), 102–103; Robert Gottlieb and Robert Kimball, eds., *Reading Lyrics* (New York, 2000), 145; Mark Sullivan, *Our Times, 1900–1925, VI: The Twenties* (New York, 1943), 492.

122 WRITTEN BY JACK YELLIN Young and Young, *Music of the Great Depression,* 46.

122 FOR AN MGM MOVIE Ibid.; William Safire, *Safire's Political Dictionary* (New York, 2008), 305.

122 THE SONG'S "SEEMINGLY UPBEAT" Young and Young, *Music of the Great Depression,* 46.

122 THE VENUE'S ORGANIST Ritchie, *Electing FDR,* 102.

122 "THE SONG'S BOUNCY RHYTHM" Ibid., 102–103.

122 PLANNED TO HAVE "ANCHORS AWEIGH" Ibid., 103.

122 AT THE CONGRESS HOTEL Steve Neal, *Happy Days Are Here Again: The 1932 Democratic Convention, the Emergence of FDR—And How America Was Changed Forever* (New York, 2004), 2.

122 LOUIS HOWE LISTENED TO HIS SECRETARY, A FAN Ritchie, *Electing FDR,* 103.

122 THE GREAT DEPRESSION HAD CONSUMED See, for instance, David M. Kennedy, *Freedom From Fear: The American People in Depression and War, 1929–1945* (New York, 1999).

122 "WILD RADICALISM HAS" Franklin D. Roosevelt, "Acceptance Speech at the Democratic National Convention," July 2, 1932, American Presidency Project, https://www .presidency.ucsb.edu/node/275484.

122 "I PLEDGE YOU" Ibid.

122 "THIS GREAT NATION" "First Inaugural Address of Franklin D. Roosevelt," March 4, 1933, http:// avalon.law.yale.edu/20th_century/froos1.asp.

123 "MANY DOUBT IF" Sir Winston Churchill, *The Great Republic: A History of America,* ed. Winston S. Churchill (New York, 1999), 295–302.

123 A FRIEND TOLD HIM *SOA,* 150; Manchester, *The Glory and the Dream,* 80.

123 "IF I FAIL" Ibid.

123 "BROTHER, CAN YOU SPARE A DIME?" Gottlieb and Kimball, eds., *Reading Lyrics,* 259; Young and Young, *Music of the Great Depression,* 48–49.

123 BING CROSBY SANG Ibid., 49.

123 THE NARRATOR Ibid.

124 WOODY GUTHRIE See, for instance, Crawford, *America's Musical Life,* 613–618; Young and Young, *Music of the Great Depression,* 156–158; Mark Allan Jackson, *Prophet Singer: The Voice and Vision of Woody Guthrie* (Jackson, Miss., 2008); Joe Klein, *Woody Guthrie: A Life* (New York, 1980); Will Kaufman, *Woody Guthrie, American Radical* (Urbana, Ill.,

2011); Robert Santelli, *This Land Is Your Land: Woody Guthrie and the Journey of an American Song* (Philadelphia, 2012).

124 BORN IN OKLAHOMA Crawford, *America's Musical Life*, 613.

124 "A SONG," HE ONCE SAID Jackson, *Prophet Singer*, 25.

124 IN COLUMNS IN THE LATE 1930S Young and Young, *Music of the Great Depression*, 157.

124 "A FOLK SONG" Jackson, *Prophet Singer*, 25.

125 ON HER CBS RADIO SHOW Young and Young, *Music of the Great Depression*, 42.

125 "DUST BOWL BLUES" https://www.woodyguthrie.org/Lyrics/Dust_Bowl_Blues.htm.

125 PROMPTED THE COMPOSER IRVING BERLIN Laurence Bergreen, *As Thousands Cheer: The Life of Irving Berlin* (New York, 1990), 155–156, 369–372; Ewen, *Great Men of American Popular Song*, 110–111.

125 HE ARRANGED FOR Bergreen, *As Thousands Cheer*, 370–371; Ewen, *Great Men of American Popular Song*, 111.

125 SMITH WOULD RECORD Ewen, *Great Men of American Popular Song*, 111.

125 "THE STORM CLOUDS" "God Bless America," Library of Congress, https://www.loc.gov/item/ihas.200000007/.

125 GUTHRIE WROTE A REPLY Jackson, *Prophet Singer*, 19–32; Crawford, *America's Musical Life*, 614–615; and Santelli, *This Land Is Your Land*. Nora Guthrie's foreword to the Santelli volume is illuminating. See Santelli, *This Land Is Your Land*, 7–10.

126 BY 1968, ROBERT KENNEDY WAS SUGGESTING Richard Harwood, "With Bobby Kennedy on the Last Campaign," *WP*, June 5, 1988; Larry Tye, "What Bobby Kennedy Really Meant When He Said 'Now It's On to Chicago,'" *Chicago Sun Times*, May 31, 2018.

126 "IN THE SHADOW OF THE STEEPLE" Woody Guthrie, "This Land Is Your Land," https://www.woodyguthrie.org/Lyrics/This_Land.htm.

126 "IS THIS LAND" Ibid.

126 THE VERSE, HOWEVER, HAS OFTEN BEEN OMITTED Santelli, *This Land Is Your Land*, 135; 161–163; 175–176; 220–222.

126 WHY IS A BIT OF A MYSTERY Ibid. See also Nick Spitzer, "The Story of Woody Guthrie's 'This Land Is Your Land,'" February 15, 2012, National Public Radio.

126 PETE SEEGER, AN ARTISTIC HEIR Santelli, *This Land Is Your Land*, 150–252. See also David Marchese, "Watch Bruce Springsteen's Moving Birthday Tribute to Pete Seeger," *Rolling Stone*, January 28, 2014.

126 "FORBIDDEN VERSES" "'This Land Is Your Land': The Forbidden Verses Are Sung on The Mall," ScienceBlogs, January 21, 2009.

126 A TIRELESS REFORMER See, for instance, *SOA*, 161–165; Allida M. Black, "Championing a Champion: Eleanor Roosevelt and the Marian Anderson 'Freedom Concert,'" *Presidential Studies Quarterly*, Vol. 20, No. 4, Fall 1990, 719–736.

126 ONE OF HER CAUSES Paul M. Sparrow, "Eleanor Roosevelt's Battle to End Lynching," February 12, 2016. https://fdr.blogs.archives.gov/2016/02/12/eleanor-roosevelts-battle-to-end-lynching. See also *SOA*, 161–165; Sullivan, *Lift Every Voice*, 237–239; Joseph P. Lash, *Eleanor and Franklin: The Story of Their Relationship, Based on Eleanor Roosevelt's Private Papers* (New York, 1971), 515–16; Melissa Cooper, "Reframing Eleanor Roosevelt's Influence in the 1930s Anti-Lynching Movement around a 'New Philosophy of Government,'" *European Journal of American Studies* 12, no. 1 (Spring 2017), https://ejas.revues.org/11914.

127 AN ESTIMATED 3,500 AFRICAN AMERICANS Sparrow, "Eleanor Roosevelt's Battle," February 12, 2016. See also Sullivan, *Lift Every Voice*, 196; David Margolick, *Strange Fruit: The Biography of a Song* (New York, 2001), 19–21.

127 A NEW YORK CITY SCHOOLTEACHER, ABEL MEEROPOL Margolick, *Strange Fruit*, 11.

127 "I WROTE 'STRANGE FRUIT'" Ibid., 13.

127 "NOBODY COULD SAY THE WORDS" Ibid., 12.

127 IN EARLY 1939 Ibid., 3–4.

127 THE CAFÉ SOCIETY NIGHTCLUB For a *New Yorker* ad for Holiday's performance there; see photo insert opposite Ibid., 77.

127 REFUSED TO ALLOW THE SINGER MARIAN ANDERSON See, for instance, *SOA*, 164; Black, "Championing a Champion," *Presidential Studies Quarterly*, 719–736; Scott A. Sandage, "A Marble House Divided: The Lincoln Memorial, the Civil Rights Movement, and the Politics of Memory, 1939–1963," *Journal of American History*, Vol. 80, No. 1, June 1993, 135–167; Klaw, "'A Voice One Hears Once in a Hundred Years,'" *American Heritage*, February 1977, 51–57.

128 WAS FOR "WHITE ARTISTS" ONLY Sandage, "A Marble House Divided," *Journal of American History,* 143.

128 "THEY HAVE TAKEN" Black, "Championing a Champion," *Presidential Studies Quarterly,* 725–726.

128 "I AM NOT SURPRISED" Scott A. Sandage, "Anderson, Marian," in *The Eleanor Roosevelt Encyclopedia,* eds. Maurine H. Beasley, Holly C. Shulman, and Henry R. Beasley (Westport, Conn., 2000), 24.

128 AN ALTERNATIVE PLAN Black, "Championing a Champion," *Presidential Studies Quarterly,* 726.

128 "I DON'T CARE" Ibid., 727.

128 HAD "A VOICE ONE HEARS" Klaw, "'A Voice One Hears Once in a Hundred Years,'" *American Heritage,* 51–57.

128 BORN IN PHILADELPHIA IN 1897 Sandage, "Anderson, Marian," in *The Eleanor Roosevelt Encyclopedia,* 22.

129 "MUSIC TO ME" Klaw, "'A Voice One Hears Once in a Hundred Years,'" *American Heritage,* 56.

129 THE CONCERT WAS Edward T. Folliard, "75,000 Acclaim Miss Anderson; Easter Visitors Throng Capital," *WP,* April 10, 1939; "Throng Honors Marian Anderson in Concert at Lincoln Memorial," *NYT,* April 10, 1939.

129 MANAGEMENT AND CIVIL RIGHTS ADVOCATES JOINED FORCES Sandage, "A Marble House Divided," *Journal of American History,* is excellent on this.

129 "IN THIS GREAT AUDITORIUM" *WP,* April 10, 1939. There was applause, and then Ickes went on: "And 130 years ago He sent us one of his truly great in order that he might restore freedom to those from whom we had disregardfully taken it. In carrying out this task, Abraham Lincoln laid down his life, and so it is as appropriate as it is fortunate that today we stand reverently and humbly at the base of this memorial to the great emancipator while glorious tribute is rendered to his memory by a daughter of the race from which he struck the chains of slavery." Ibid.

129 "GENIUS, LIKE JUSTICE" Ibid.

129 HE HELD THE DAR TO ACCOUNT "Throng Honors Marian Anderson," *NYT,* April 10, 1939.

129 THE SUN BROKE THROUGH Folliard, "75,000 Acclaim Miss Anderson," *WP,* April 10, 1939.

129 SEVENTY-FIVE THOUSAND PEOPLE Ibid.

129 "ONE OF THE LARGEST" Ibid.

129 AMONG THEIR NUMBER Ibid.

129 "THERE SEEMED TO BE" Marian Anderson, *My Lord, What a Morning: An Autobiography of Marian Anderson* (New York, 1956), 191.

129 "IT WAS A TREMENDOUS THING" Klaw, "'A Voice One Hears Once in a Hundred Years,'" *American Heritage,* 56–57.

129 HER SELECTIONS FOR Bart Barnes, "Marian Anderson, Whose Voice Made History, Dies," *WP,* April 9, 1993.

130 "IT WAS ANOTHER KIND" Ibid.

130 "MY SOUL'S BEEN ANCHORED IN THE LORD" "Marian Anderson: A Life in Song, 'My Soul's Been Anchored in De Lord,' arranged by Florence Price." http://www.library.upenn.edu/exhibits/rbm/anderson/spirimage6.html.

130 WAS "THE MOST CIVILIZED THING" Ernest K. Lindley, "Voice from the Temple: Anderson Footnotes," *WP,* April 12, 1939.

130 "AS IT WAS NEVER" Ibid.

130 SHE HAD TAKEN A DIFFERENT TACK Sandage, "A Marble House Divided," *Journal of American History,* 135–136.

130 "THE WET EYES" Lindley, "Voice From The Temple," *WP,* April 12, 1939.

130 "IT WAS A TOUR DE FORCE" Barnes, "Marian Anderson," *WP,* April 9, 1993.

131 "TACTICALLY, THE MODERN CIVIL RIGHTS MOVEMENT" Sandage, "A Marble House Divided," *Journal of American History,* 136–137.

131 "WE ARE ON" Ibid., 136.

131 "SINCE THE CONCERT" Lindley, "Voice From The Temple," *WP,* April 12, 1939.

132 THE FIRST AFRICAN AMERICAN SOLOIST Allan Kozinn, "Marian Anderson Is Dead at 96—Singer Shattered Racial Barriers," *NYT,* April 9, 1993; Marissa Fessenden, "60 Years Ago, the First African-American Soloist Sang at the Met Opera," January 8, 2015, https://www.smithsonianmag.com/smart-news/60-years-ago-first-african-american-soloist-sang-met-opera-180953840/#Oe7vlHgOiz3dcArV.99.

132 "THE CURTAIN ROSE" Kozinn, "Marian Anderson Is Dead," *NYT,* April 9, 1993.

132 "WE ARE SO SURE" "Speech by Herr Hitler at Wilhelmshaven on April 1, 1939," http://avalon.law.yale.edu/wwii/blbk20.asp; "Six Fateful Months: March to September 1939," *World Affairs,* Vol. 102, No. 3, 1939, 139.

132 BRITAIN AGREED "Six Fateful Months: March to September 1939," *World Affairs,* 139.

132 ISOLATIONIST SENTIMENT IN AMERICA *SOA,* 154–161. See also, more generally, Wayne S. Cole, *Roosevelt and the Isolationists, 1932–1945* (Lincoln, Neb., 1983); Manfred Jonas, *Isolationism in America, 1935–1941* (Chicago, 1990); Steven Casey, *Cautious Crusade: Franklin D. Roosevelt, American Public Opinion, and the War Against Nazi Germany* (New York, 2001).

132 IT WAS "A VERY SMALL" David S. Reynolds, *From Munich to Pearl Harbor: Roosevelt's America and the Origins of the Second World War* (Chicago, 2001), 44.

132 RISE AND SPREAD OF AIRPOWER Ibid., 43.

133 NEUTRALITY LEGISLATION Ibid., 31–32.

133 GERMANY HAD BEEN DRIVEN Ibid., 14–16.

133 HUNGRIER TO SEIZE *SOA,* 155; Reynolds, *From Munich to Pearl Harbor,* 16.

133 JEWS WERE TARGETED, TERRORIZED *SOA,* 167–170; Reynolds, *From Munich to Pearl Harbor,* 50–53.

133 *A CHILD OF OUR TIME* Kenneth Gloag, *Tippett: A Child of Our Time* (Cambridge, 1999); "Music of the Holocaust: Highlights from the Collection," United States Holocaust Memorial Museum, https://www.ushmm.org/exhibition /music/detail.php?content=child; Steve Smith, "Darkly Spiritual Challenge to Injustice," *NYT,* January 27, 2012.

133 "I SENT TO AMERICA" Gloag, *Tippett,* 28–29.

133 *THE BOOK OF AMERICAN NEGRO SPIRITUALS* Ibid., 71.

133 TIPPETT INCORPORATED "STEAL AWAY" Ibid., 29.

133 THERE WAS "A POLICY OF" Reynolds, *From Munich to Pearl Harbor,* 53.

133 MUTUAL NONAGGRESSION PACT Ibid., 62.

133 ROOSEVELT WAS AWOKEN Michael R. Beschloss, *Kennedy and Roosevelt: The Uneasy Alliance* (New York, 1980), 190.

133 "I FELT AS IF" Jon Meacham, *Franklin and Winston: An Intimate Portrait of an Epic Friendship* (F&W), 47.

133–34 ROOSEVELT WAS LESS CERTAIN Ibid., 47–48.

134 HE "SUPPOSED" Ibid., 47.

134 "HITLER IS NOT" Arthur M. Schlesinger, Jr., *A Life in the Twentieth Century: Innocent Beginnings, 1917–1950* (Boston, 2000), 232.

134 A POLL IN THIS PERIOD *F&W,* 55; William L. Langer and S. Everett Gleason, *The Challenge to Isolation, 1937–1940* (New York, 1952), 495–496.

134 "IT IS NOT DIFFICULT" *SOA,* 159–160; Justin E. Doenecke, ed., *In Danger Undaunted: The Anti-Interventionist Movement of 1940–1941 as Revealed in the Papers of the America First Committee* (Stanford, Calif., 1990), 37–38.

134 "IF I SHOULD DIE" *SOA,* 159; Lynne Olson, *Those Angry Days: Roosevelt, Lindbergh, and America's Fight Over World War II, 1939–1941* (New York, 2013), 103.

135 EVEN THOUGH LARGE *F&W,* 58.

135 THE BATTLE OF BRITAIN See, for instance, James Holland, *The Battle of Britain: Five Months That Changed History, May–October 1940* (New York, 2012), and Michael Korda, *With Wings Like Eagles: The Untold Story of the Battle of Britain* (New York, 2009).

135 THE AMERICAN WALTER KENT COMPOSED A SONG William H. Young and Nancy K. Young, *Music of the World War II Era* (Westport, Conn., 2008), 3.

136 SACRED MUSIC BROUGHT This section is drawn from *F&W,* 101–135.

136 "I HAVE" Ibid., 113; H. V. Morton, *Atlantic Meeting* (New York, 1943), 109–110.

136 TOGETHER WITH THE ASSEMBLED *F&W,* 114.

136 O GOD, OUR HELP The order of the hymns sung that morning differs in some accounts. This account, first published in *F&W,* is based on the original "Order of Service, August 10, 1941," President's Official File 200-1-R: Trips of the President: Cruise on the USS *Augusta,* August 1941, Franklin D. Roosevelt Library, Hyde Park, N.Y.

136 THERE WAS THE GENERAL CONFESSION *F&W,* 115.

136 ONWARD, CHRISTIAN SOLDIERS Ibid.

136 FROM THE BOOK OF JOSHUA Ibid.

136 ETERNAL FATHER, STRONG TO SAVE Ibid., 116.

137 "IT WAS A GREAT HOUR TO LIVE" Ibid.

137 "IF NOTHING ELSE" Ibid.

137 AT ABOUT FIVE O'CLOCK Ibid., 131–132; "FDR's 'Day of Infamy' Speech: Crafting a Call to Arms," *Prologue Magazine,* Winter 2001, Vol. 33, No. 4. https://www.archives.gov/publications /prologue/2001/winter/crafting-day-of-infamy -speech.html; Grace Tully, *F.D.R. My Boss* (New York, 1949), 256.

138 THE PRESIDENT MADE "FDR's 'Day of Infamy'
Speech: Crafting a Call to Arms," *Prologue,*
Winter 2001; *F&W,* 131; James Roosevelt and
Sidney Shalett, *Affectionately, F.D.R.: A Son's Story of
a Lonely Man* (New York, 1959), 328.

138 A NAVY CHAPLAIN AT PEARL HARBOR Howell
M. Forgy, *—And Pass the Ammunition,* ed. Jack S.
McDowell (New York, 1944); http://www
.nww2m.com/2012/10/praise-the-lord-and
-pass-the-ammunition/.

138 RETURNED TO THE ARMY'S CAMP UPTON
Bergreen, *As Thousands Cheer,* 392–407; Ewen,
Great Men of American Popular Song, 109, 111.

138 "SONGS MAKE HISTORY" Bergreen, "Irving
Berlin: This Is the Army," *Prologue Magazine.*

139 BORN ISRAEL BALINE Bergreen, *As Thousands
Cheer,* 3–13; Ewen, *Great Men of American Popular
Song,* 104.

139 MADE HIS FORTUNE Bergreen, *As Thousands
Cheer,* 30–149; Ewen, *Great Men of American
Popular Song,* 104–115.

139 A SINGING WAITER Ewen, *Great Men of American
Popular Song,* 104–105.

139 HE WROTE YIP, YIP, YAPHANK Ibid., 109, 112;
Bergreen, *As Thousands Cheer,* 150–173.

139 "OH, HOW I HATE" Ewen, *Great Men of American
Popular Song,* 109.

139 REPRISED HIS WORK Ibid., 111–112.

139 *THIS IS THE ARMY* Bergreen, *As Thousands Cheer,*
392–441; Bergreen, "Irving Berlin: This Is the
Army," *Prologue Magazine.*

139 BECAME A MOVIE Bergreen, *As Thousands Cheer,*
418–426.

139 A TURN BY HEAVYWEIGHT CHAMPION JOE
LOUIS Ibid., 425.

139 RACIAL STEREOTYPES Ibid., 425–426.

140 "A TRANSVESTITE BLACKFACE" Ibid., 425. "At
worst an embarrassment, and at best a colossal
curiosity by contemporary standards, *This Is the
Army* did accomplish the task Berlin, the Army,
and Warner Brothers set for it: raising money,"
Bergreen wrote. Ibid., 425–426.

140 THERE WAS A CAMEO *This Is the Army,* Turner
Classic Movies, http://www.tcm.com/this-month
/article/199455%7Co/This-Is-the-Army.html.

140 "THIS TIME" Robert Kimball and Linda
Emmet, eds., *The Complete Lyrics of Irving Berlin*
(New York, 2001), 363.

140 "NOW THAT IT IS OVER" Ernie Pyle, "A Pure

Miracle," *Stars and Stripes,* June 12, 1944. https://
sites.mediaschool.indiana.edu/erniepyle/1944
/06/12/a-pure-miracle/.

141 "A VERY HIGH TYPE YOUNG MAN" George T.
Simon, *Glenn Miller and His Orchestra* (New York,
1974), 302–303. On Miller in general, see Ibid.,
and "Major Glenn Miller Is Missing On Flight
from England to Paris," *NYT,* December 25,
1944.

141 TO "PUT A LITTLE MORE SPRING" Simon, *Glenn
Miller,* 311–312.

141 "LOOK, CAPTAIN MILLER" Ibid., 339.

141 A WARTIME CONTROVERSY "Sousa with a Floy
Floy," *Time,* September 6, 1943; Simon, *Glenn
Miller,* 349–352.

141 "DEPRECATING SOUSA" Simon, *Glenn Miller,* 350.

142 ON A BROADCAST ON SATURDAY, JUNE 10,
1944 Ibid., 356.

142 "FLYING HOME" Robert L. Harris, Jr., and
Rosalyn Terborg-Penn, eds., *The Columbia Guide
to African American History Since 1939* (New York,
2006), 174.

142 FRANKLIN ROOSEVELT DIED *F&W,* 342–344.

142 GRAHAM JACKSON Ben Cosgrove, "Mourning
FDR: In a Classic Photo, the Face of a Nation's
Loss," *Time,* February 26, 2013, http://time.com
/3764064/mourning-fdr-in-a-classic-photo
-the-face-of-a-nations-loss/.

142 BURIED IN THE ROSE GARDEN *F&W,* 352.

142 "NEARER, MY GOD, TO THEE" Guido van Rijn,
*Roosevelt's Blues: African-American Blues and Gospel
Songs on FDR* (Jackson, Miss., 1997), 38.

142 "GONE," THE *TIMES* WROTE, "IS THE FRESH"
SOA, 327; "Franklin D. Roosevelt," *NYT,* April
13, 1945.

142 "HISTORIANS STILL DEBATE" Ronald Reagan,
"Remarks at a White House Luncheon,"
January 28, 1982.

143 "TELL ME WHY YOU LIKE ROOSEVELT" van
Rijn, *Roosevelt's Blues,* 197–98.

143 DEAR MRS. ROOSEVELT Woody Guthrie, "Dear
Mrs. Roosevelt," https://www.woodyguthrie.org
/Lyrics/Dear_Mrs_Roosevelt.htm.

CHAPTER SIX: WE SHALL OVERCOME

145 "BOBBY DYLAN SAYS" "Dylan, Bob," in *Current
Biography 1965,* ed. Charles Moritz (New York,
1965), 139.

145 "Lord have mercy" Nina Simone performance of "Mississippi Goddam," https://www
.youtube.com/watch?v=HzxjKVK2bZo.

145 "In a sense" Martin Luther King, Jr., *A
Testament of Hope: The Essential Writings and Speeches
of Martin Luther King, Jr.,* ed. James Melvin
Washington (San Francisco, 2003), 348.

145 the speech was broadcast "John F.
Kennedy Speech on the Cuban Missile Crisis,"
http://www.historyplace.com/speeches
/jfk-cuban.htm.

145 The Soviet Union was deploying The
ensuing section appeared, in slightly modified
form, in Jon Meacham's contribution to "How
Will History Judge the Trump Presidency?"
Vanity Fair, October 2017, https://www.vanityfair
.com/news/2017/09/historians-on-trump
-presidency. See also, for instance, Michael
Dobbs, *One Hour to Midnight: Kennedy, Khruschev,
and Castro on the Brink of Nuclear War* (New York,
2008); Richard Reeves, *President Kennedy: Profile of
Power* (New York, 1993); Michael R. Beschloss,
The Crisis Years: Kennedy and Khrushchev, 1960–1963
(New York, 1992); Evan Thomas, *Robert Kennedy:
His Life* (New York, 2000); Robert F. Kennedy,
Thirteen Days: A Memoir of the Cuban Missile Crisis
(New York, 1999); Graham Allison and Philip
Zelikow, *Essence of Decision: Explaining the Cuban
Missile Crisis* 2nd ed. (New York, 1999).

145 "He can't do this" Dobbs, *One Minute to
Midnight,* 6.

145 "Oh shit" Thomas, *Robert Kennedy: His Life,* 209.

145 "His clothes may need" Jon Pareles, "Robert
Shelton, 69, Music Critic Who Chronicled 60's
Folk Boom," *NYT,* December 15, 1995.

146 In the fall of 1962 Howard Sounes, *Down the
Highway: The Life of Bob Dylan* (New York, 2001),
126–127. See, more generally, Sean Wilentz, *Bob
Dylan in America* (New York, 2010).

146 a "song of desperation" Sounes, *Down the
Highway,* 126.

146 "As the missile crisis" Ibid., 127.

146 Born Robert Zimmerman "Dylan, Bob," in
Current Biography 1965, ed. Moritz, 137.

146 a "town that was dying" Ewen, *Great Men of
American Popular Song,* 356.

146 changed his name "Dylan, Bob," *Current
Biography 1965,* ed. Moritz, 137.

146 Dylan liked to say Ibid., 138.

146 "I was making" Ibid.

146 his canon includes See, for instance, Ewen,
Great Men of American Popular Song, 358.

146 "Bobby Dylan says" *Current Biography 1965,*
Moritz, ed., 139.

146 the *Village Voice* critic http://www.richard
goldsteinonline.com/about.html.

146 "Today, he is" Richard Goldstein, "Dylan: 'We
Trust What He Tells Us,'" *NYT,* October 22,
1967.

146 "How could I have been so stupid?"
Reeves, *President Kennedy,* 94.

146 "Mr. President, before you approved this
plan" Ibid., 102.

146 "Well, I did have a meeting" Ibid.

146–47 a crisis-management apparatus known
as ExComm Kennedy, *Thirteen Days,* 124–125.
The relevant analysis on those pages comes in
an afterword by Richard E. Neustadt and
Graham T. Allison in this edition of *Thirteen
Days.*

147 "Keep strong, if possible" Kennedy, *Thirteen
Days,* 11.

147 A book he had read Ibid., 49.

147 "The great danger and risk in all of
this" Ibid.

147 "If anybody is around to write after
this" Ibid., 98.

147 Jacqueline Kennedy remembered Caroline
Kennedy and Michael Beschloss, *Jacqueline
Kennedy: Historic Conversations on Life with John F.
Kennedy* (New York, 2011), 251–252.

147 "Even so" Sounes, *Down the Highway,* 127.

148 "segregation now" *SOA,* 219.

148 "The sniper's bullet" Gay Talese, *The Kingdom
and the Power* (New York, 1969), 141.

148 The assassin was Sounes, *Down the Highway,*
139.

148 In response Bob Dylan wrote Ibid.

148 "The fear down here" Werner, *A Change Is
Gonna Come: Music, Race, & the Soul of America,* 12.

148 "If it hadn't been" Interview with John
Lewis.

148 In Albany, Georgia Robert Shelton, "Songs a
Weapon in Rights Battle," *NYT,* August 20,
1962.

148 a concerted campaign Lee W. Formwalt,
"Albany Movement," *New Georgia Encyclopedia,*
January 31, 2019. See also Edward A. Hatfield,
"Freedom Singers," *New Georgia Encyclopedia,*
July 23, 2018.

148 "We Shall Overcome" See, for instance, Allan M. Winkler, "We Shall Overcome," *American Heritage,* Vol. 62, No. 5, Fall 2017, https://www.americanheritage.com/we-shall-overcome.

148 the jail guards Shelton, "Songs a Weapon," *NYT,* August 20, 1962.

148 There was a similar moment Ibid.

148 These examples were Ibid.

148 "The songs, old and new" Ibid.

149 a "new tributary" Ibid.

149 To the tune Ibid.

149 "We all share" Ibid.

149 "They give the people" Ibid.

149 In one of those trying hours Ibid.

149 Bernice Johnson Reagon recalled a moment Werner, *A Change Is Gonna Come,* 13.

149 "In a sense" King, *A Testament of Hope,* 348.

150 "We Shall Overcome" https://hymnary.org/text/we_shall_overcome_we_shall_overcome.

150 The history of "We Shall Overcome" Victor V. Bobetsky, ed., *We Shall Overcome: Essays on a Great American Song* (Lanham, Md., 2015); Winkler, "We Shall Overcome," *American Heritage;* Pete Seeger, *Pete Seeger in His Own Words,* eds. Rob Rosenthal and Sam Rosenthal (Boulder, Colo., 2012), 116–118, 193–194; Southern, *The Music of Black Americans,* 471–473.

150 at least seven antecedents Bobetsky, "The Complex Ancestry of 'We Shall Overcome,'" in Bobetsky, ed., *We Shall Overcome,* 1–15.

150 sung during union protests Winkler, "We Shall Overcome," *American Heritage.*

150 from Zilphia Horton Ibid.; Sam A. Rosenthal, "A Folksong in Flight: Pete Seeger and the Genesis of 'We Shall Overcome,'" in Bobetsky, ed., *We Shall Overcome,* 18.

150 the shift from "will" to "shall" Rosenthal, "A Folksong in Flight," in Bobetsky, ed., *We Shall Overcome,* 18.

150 "It could have been me" Ibid.

150 After he heard Seeger Winkler, "We Shall Overcome," *American Heritage.*

151 "It made us feel" Interview with John Lewis.

151 When he thinks of Mississippi Ibid.

151 When he thinks of Alabama Ibid.

151 "Oh, Wallace" Ibid.

152 The Freedom Singers Hatfield, "Freedom Singers," *New Georgia Encyclopedia,* July 23, 2018.

152 In 2010, they performed "In Performance at the White House: A Celebration of Music from the Civil Rights Movement," February 9, 2010, https://www.youtube.com/watch?v=hhafy16-Bp0.

152 "you can never tell" Ibid.

152 Carole King first encountered Carole King, *A Natural Woman: A Memoir* (New York, 2012), 39.

152 After the performance Ibid., 41.

152 "At that moment" Ibid.

152 At Freed's 1957 Labor Day revue Ibid., 41–42.

152 "He began to sing" Ibid., 42.

152 northern voices Robert Shelton, "'Freedom Songs' Sweep North," *NYT,* July 6, 1963.

153 "This Little Light of Mine," "Oh Freedom" Ibid.

153 "I love my country" Ibid.

153 Dylan's work in particular helped spark See, for instance, Werner, *A Change Is Gonna Come,* 31–48.

153 A son of the Mississippi Delta Ibid. See also, more generally, Daniel Wolff, *You Send Me: The Life and Times of Sam Cooke* (New York, 1995), and David Cantwell, "The Unlikely Story of 'A Change Is Gonna Come,'" *The New Yorker,* March 17, 2015.

153 "the definitive soul man" "Sam Cooke, 153." Rock & Roll Hall of Fame.

153 Cooke and Dylan "were wading up" Cantwell, "The Unlikely Story of 'A Change Is Gonna Come,'" *The New Yorker,* March 17, 2015.

153 Cantwell believed that Ibid.

154 "brooding but bright" Ibid.

154 Ray Charles had recently (in 1963) Ibid.

154 the convention of "masking" (the conveyance) Werner, *A Change Is Gonna Come,* 6–7.

154 Curtis Mayfield of the Impressions Ibid., 144–151.

155 "Gospel was your foundation" Ibid., 145–146.

155 Other examples of songs We are indebted to Craig Werner for these suggestions.

155 "I imagine most black people" Chuck Berry, *The Autobiography* (New York, 1988), 158–159.

155 At the March on Washington See, for 155, "Dream Songs: The Music of the March on Washington," *The New Yorker,* August 28, 2013,

https://www.newyorker.com/culture
/culture-desk/dream-songs-the-music-of-the
-march-on-washington; E. W. Kenworthy,
"200,000 March for Civil Rights in Orderly
Washington Rally; President Sees Gain for
Negro"; James Reston, "'I Have a Dream . . .'";
Nan Robertson, "For 200,000 Who Were
There It Was a Date to Live Forever"; Russell
Baker, "Capital Is Occupied By a Gentle
Army"; "Marchers Sing and Voice Hope on
Way to Washington Rally," *NYT,* August 29,
1963; Taylor Branch, *Parting the Waters: America in
the King Years, 1954–63* (New York, 1988),
846–887. See also, more generally, William P.
Jones, *The March on Washington: Jobs, Freedom, and
the Forgotten History of Civil Rights* (New York,
2013).

156   THE MARCHERS THEMSELVES "Marchers Sing
and Voice Hope," *NYT,* August 29, 1963.

156   "IF THEY ASK" Kenworthy, "200,000 March,"
NYT, August 29, 1963.

156   SANG "I'M ON MY WAY" Branch, *Parting the
Waters,* 877.

156   DYLAN SANG "ONLY A PAWN" Baker, "Capital
Is Occupied," *NYT,* August 29, 1963.

156   "LUGUBRIOUS MOUNTAIN SONG" Ibid.

156   WITH BAEZ, "WHEN THE SHIP COMES IN"
"Dream Songs," *The New Yorker,* August 28,
2013.

156   PETER, PAUL, AND MARY PERFORMED "Dream
Songs," *The New Yorker,* August 28, 2013.

156   DYLAN'S "BLOWIN' IN THE WIND" Sounes,
Down the Highway, 119–122.

156   RECORDED AND RELEASED Shelton, "'Freedom
Songs' Sweep North," *NYT,* July 6, 1963.

156   "THE FASTEST-SELLING SINGLE" Ibid.

156   "RADIO STATIONS IN" Ibid.

156   THE FREEDOM SINGERS "Dream Songs," *The
New Yorker, August 28, 2013;* Hatfield, "Freedom
Singers," *New Georgia Encyclopedia,* July 23, 2018.

156   MAHALIA JACKSON SANG "Dream Songs," *The
New Yorker,* August 28, 2013.

156   JACKSON DID MORE THAN SING We drew on
SOA, 224–226, for this section.

157   "AND SO TODAY" Branch, *Parting the Waters,* 882.
Branch wrote that this passage of the prepared
speech was "its lamest and most pretentious
section." Ibid.

157   HE'D BEGUN TO EXTEMPORIZE Ibid.; *SOA,*
224–225.

157   "TELL 'EM ABOUT THE DREAM" Branch, *Parting
the Waters,* 882.

157   KING LEFT HIS TEXT Ibid.

157   "I HAVE A DREAM" https://www.archives.gov
/files/press/exhibits/dream-speech.pdf.

157   DRAWING ON "MY COUNTRY 'TIS OF THEE"
Ibid.; Branch, *Parting the Waters,* 882.

158   MARIAN ANDERSON "For 200,000 Who Were
There It Was a Date to Live Forever," *NYT,* August 29, 1963.

159   HE'S GOT THE WHOLE WORLD "He's Got the
Whole World in His Hands," https://hymnary
.org/text/hes_got_the_whole_world_in_his
_hands.

159   THE GLOW DID NOT LAST The ensuing section
on the 16th Street Baptist Church bombing
appeared, in slightly different form, in Jon
Meacham, "Fifty Years After Bombing,
Birmingham Is Resurrected," *Time,* September
23, 2013.

160   SEPTEMBER 15 WAS THE ANNUAL "YOUTH
DAY" "16th Street Baptist Church Bombing
(1963)," National Park Service, https://www.nps
.gov/articles/16thstreetbaptist.htm.

160   THEY HAD FINISHED THE DAY'S SUNDAY
SCHOOL LESSON Claude Sitton, "Birmingham
Bomb Kills 4 Negro Girls in Church; Riots
Flare; 2 Boys Slain," *NYT,* September 16, 1963.

160   "SHORT OF A MASS HOLOCAUST" Robert E.
Baker, "Grief and Fear Shared," *WP,* September
19, 1963.

160   NEWS OF THE ATTACK Nina Simone with
Stephen Cleary, *I Put a Spell on You: The Autobiography of Nina Simone* (New York, 1991), 89.

160   DESCENDED FROM ENSLAVED BLACK
SOUTHERNERS Ibid., 1–7.

160   SHE WAS FRIENDS WITH Ibid., 86–87.

160   "I WAS ALWAYS AWARE" Ibid., 86.

161   "IT WAS MORE THAN" Ibid., 89.

161   IN THE CONFUSION Ibid., 89–90.

161   "I HAD IT" Ibid., 89.

161   "NINA," HE SAID Ibid.

161   WITHIN AN HOUR Ibid., 89–90.

162   "MISSISSIPPI GODDAM" Nina Simone
performance of "Mississippi Goddam," https://
www.youtube.com/watch?v=HzxjKVK2bZo.

162   HEARING THE NEWS Interview with John
Lewis. See also John Lewis with Michael
D'Orso, *Walking with the Wind: A Memoir of the
Movement* (New York, 1998), 233.

163 A MEMORIAL WINDOW "Our History,"
https://16thstreetbaptist.org/history-2/.

163 ASKED A "WHITE HOUSEWIFE" Baker, "Grief
and Fear Shared," *WP,* September 19, 1963.

163 KING PREACHED THE FUNERAL Meacham,
"Fifty Years After Bombing," *Time,* September
23, 2013.

164 JOHN COLTRANE'S JAZZ COMPOSITION
"ALABAMA" We are grateful to Craig Werner
for these suggestions.

164 IN THE STREETS OUTSIDE Leon Daniel, "King
Eulogizes Bomb Victims at Rites," *WP,*
September 19, 1963.

164 THEY DID NOT DIE Ibid.

164 IN OCTOBER 1963, PRESIDENT KENNEDY
TOOK We drew on Jon Meacham's contribution
to a commemorative volume on the Amherst
speech, Neil Bicknell, Roger Mills, and Jan
Worth-Nelson, eds., *JFK: The Last Speech*
(Herndon, Va., 2018).

164 "MANY YEARS AGO" "The President and the
Poet: John F. Kennedy at Amherst," https://
www.amherst.edu/library/archives/exhibitions
/kennedy.

164 "THE PRICE OF GREATNESS" Winston S.
Churchill, "The Gift of a Common Tongue,"
September 6, 1943. The speech was delivered at
Harvard University on the occasion of
Churchill's receiving an honorary degree.

164 "PRIVILEGE IS HERE" "The President and the
Poet: John F. Kennedy at Amherst, October 26,
1963." https://www.amherst.edu/library/archives
/exhibitions/kennedy.

164 "IF SOMETIMES OUR GREAT ARTISTS" Ibid.

165 "THE HEART OF THE PRESIDENCY" Kennedy
wrote this in his foreword to Theodore C.
Sorensen, *Decision-making in the White House: The
Olive Branch or the Arrows* (New York, 1963), xxx.

165 ON SUNDAY, MARCH 7, 1965 We drew on *SOA,*
236–244, for this section on Selma.

166 TELEVISION CAMERAS RECORDED Ibid.,
236–237.

166 AT TWO MINUTES PAST NINE *SOA,* 241–244;
"'And We Shall Overcome': President Lyndon
B. Johnson's Special Message to Congress,"
March 15, 1965, http://historymatters.gmu.edu
/d/6336/.

166 SEVENTY MILLION AMERICANS Taylor Branch,
At Canaan's Edge: American in the King Years, 1965–68
(New York, 2006), 112.

166 "AT TIMES HISTORY" "'And We Shall
Overcome,'" March 15, 1965.

168 KING, WATCHING IN SELMA, WEPT Branch, *At
Canaan's Edge,* 115; interview with John Lewis.

168 "BY ANY MEANS NECESSARY" Malcolm X,
Malcolm X Speaks: Selected Speeches and Statements, ed.
George Breitman (New York, 1965), 201. See
also Malcolm X, "The Ballot or the Bullet,"
April 12, 1964, http://americanradioworks
.publicradio.org/features/blackspeech/mx.html.

168 IN A JANUARY 1965 TELEGRAM HE SENT
Malcolm X, *Malcolm X Speaks,* ed. George
Breitman, 201. Malcolm X read the telegram
to a public rally in Harlem of the Organization
of Afro-American Unity on January 24, 1965.
Ibid.

168 "MUSIC, BROTHER, IS OURS" "Malcolm X
Letter Discussing Boston's Jazz Scene Goes to
Auction," January 14, 2015, https://www.fine
booksmagazine.com/press/2015/01/malcolm-x
-letter-discussing-bostons-jazz-scene-goes-to
-auction.phtml. See also Hisham Aidi, "The
Music of Malcolm X," *The New Yorker,* February
28, 2015.

168 IN 1967, ARETHA FRANKLIN Werner, *A Change
Is Gonna Come,* 116.

168 "FOR THE BLACK PANTHERS" Ibid.

169 "THERE IS NO ONE" Jocelyn Noveck, "In
Franklin's Anthems, Women Heard an Empowering Message," Associated Press, August 16,
2018.

169 "NOBODY EMBODIES MORE FULLY" Remnick,
"Soul Survivor: The Revival and Hidden
Treasure of Aretha Franklin," *The New Yorker,*
April 4, 2016.

169 THE HOUR WAS LATE Branch, *At Canaan's Edge,*
683–766.

169 HALF PAST NINE Ibid., 756.

169 A HEAVY STORM Ibid., 755–756.

169 KING HADN'T WANTED TO LEAVE Ibid.,
755–756.

169 BUT HAD CONCEDED Ibid.

169 KING'S COMMERCIAL EASTERN AIR LINES
FLIGHT Gerold Frank, *An American Death* (New
York, 1972), 43.

169 "I WANT TO APOLOGIZE" Ibid.

169 "WELL, I DON'T KNOW" Branch, *At Canaan's Edge,*
758.

170 THE NEXT DAY This paragraph appeared, in
slightly different form, in Vern E. Smith and

Jon Meacham with Veronica Chambers, "The War Over King's Legacy," *Newsweek,* April 6, 1998.

170   BEN BRANCH WAS SCHEDULED Branch, *At Canaan's Edge,* 766.

170   "BEN, MAKE SURE" Ibid.

170   AT KING'S FUNERAL SERVICES Homer Bigart, "Leaders at Rites; High and Lowly Join in Last Tribute to Rights Champion," *NYT,* April 10, 1968; Nicholas von Hoffman and Bernadette Carey, "150,000 Mourn Dr. King at Somber Rites in Atlanta," *WP,* April 10, 1968; "King's Last March," *Time,* April 19, 1968; "King's Last March: 'We Lost Somebody,'" *Newsweek,* April 22, 1968.

170   "MY HEAVENLY FATHER, WATCH OVER ME" "King's Last March," *Time,* April 19, 1968.

170   "CRYING WITH ANGUISH" Hoffman and Carey, "150,000 Mourn," *WP,* April 10, 1968. See also Southern, *The Music of Black Americans,* 473.

170   "WHY (THE KING OF LOVE IS DEAD)" Simone with Cleary, *I Put a Spell on You,* 114–115.

170   AN ESTIMATED ONE HUNDRED TWENTY MILLION "King's Last March," *Time,* April 19, 1968; "King's Last March: 'We Lost Somebody,'" *Newsweek,* April 22, 1968.

170   MOURNERS IN THE APRIL HEAT "Some of the Dignitaries Who Attended the Funeral," *NYT,* April 10, 1968.

171   THE SEGREGATIONIST GOVERNOR OF GEORGIA "Maddox Is Upset, But Atlanta Flags Fly at Half-Staff," *NYT,* April 10, 1968; "King's Last March," *Time,* April 19, 1968; "King's Last March: 'We Lost Somebody,'" *Newsweek,* April 22, 1968.

171   "THE EXPECTED ONSET OF ARMAGEDDON" "King's Last March: 'We Lost Somebody,'" *Newsweek,* April 22, 1968.

171   "IF THEY COME IN HERE" Ibid.

171   THE MARCH TO THE CEMETERY Bigart, "Dr. Martin Luther King Buried in Atlanta," *NYT,* April 10, 1968.

171   THE SILENCE WAS INTERRUPTED Ibid.

171   "THE BATTLE HYMN OF THE REPUBLIC" "King's Last March: 'We Lost Somebody,'" *Newsweek,* April 22, 1968.

171   "DR. KING COMES MARCHING IN" John Kifner, "Followers Sing on Final March," *NYT,* April 10, 1968.

171   KING'S EPITAPH WAS DRAWN Bigart, "Dr.

Martin Luther King Buried in Atlanta," *NYT,* April 10, 1968.

CHAPTER SEVEN: ARCHIE BUNKER V. THE AGE OF AQUARIUS

173   "I WANT TO THANK YOU" Richard Nixon, *RN: The Memoirs of Richard Nixon* (New York, 1978), 867.

173   "WE GOTTA GET OUT" Holly George-Warren and Patricia Romanowski, eds., *The Rolling Stone Encyclopedia of Rock and Roll* (New York, 2001), 22; Donald Clarke, ed., *The Penguin Encyclopedia of Popular Music,* second edition (New York, 1998), 30–31. See also https://www.youtube.com/watch?v=Q3mgapAcVdU.

173   RICHARD NIXON WAS DESPERATE See, for instance, John Herbers, "President 'Campaigning' to Display His Strength," *NYT,* March 18, 1974; B. Drummond Ayres, Jr., "Nixon Plays Piano on Wife's Birthday at Grand Ole Opry," *NYT,* March 17, 1974; Carroll Kilpatrick, "A Night at the Opry," *WP,* March 17, 1974; "The President's Strategy for Survival," *Time,* March 25, 1974; "Operation Friendly Persuasion," *Newsweek,* March 25, 1974; Evan Thomas, *Being Nixon: A Man Divided* (New York, 2015), 467–482.

173   67.7 PERCENT OF THE VOTE https://uselectionatlas.org/RESULTS/state.php?year=1972&fips=47&f=0&off=0&elect=0.

173   THE OCCASION WAS *NYT,* March 18, 1974; *WP,* March 17, 1974; *Time,* March 25, 1974; *Newsweek,* March 25, 1974; William Price Fox, "Grand Ole Opry," *American Heritage,* February/March, 1979; Thomas, *Being Nixon,* 480–481.

173   "BY GOD, THIS IS" Fox, "Grand Ole Opry," *American Heritage.*

173   TO RALLY SUPPORT *NYT,* March 18, 1974.

173   ALL ABOUT IMPEACHMENT *Newsweek,* March 25, 1974.

173   "RICHARD NIXON IS" *Time,* March 25, 1974.

174   ARRIVING IN NASHVILLE *NYT,* March 18, 1974; *WP,* March 17, 1974.

174   THE WHITE HOUSE HAD SENT *NYT,* March 18, 1974.

174   "WE WROTE IT TO BE SATIRICAL" Martin Chilton, "Merle Haggard: Sometimes I Wish I Hadn't Written Okie from Muskogee," *The Telegraph,* April 8, 2016. See also David Cantwell,

Merle Haggard: The Running Kind (Austin, Tex., 2013).

174 A REUTERS PIECE IN 1970 Chilton, "Merle Haggard: Sometimes I Wish," *The Guardian,* April 8, 2016.

174 "I DON'T LIKE" Mikal Gilmore, "Merle Haggard: The Outlaw," *Rolling Stone,* May 5, 2016.

174 "DUMB AS A ROCK" Ibid.

175 "THE FIGHTIN' SIDE OF ME" Cantwell, *Merle Haggard: The Running Kind,* 3.

175 PASSED OUT SONG SHEETS *NYT,* March 18, 1974.

175 I'M SICK OF Ibid.

175 ONSTAGE WITH ROY ACUFF *Public Papers of the Presidents of the United States: Richard Nixon, January 1 to August 9, 1974* (Washington, D.C., 1975), 277–282.

175 WHAT COUNTRY MUSIC IS Ibid., 280–281.

176 THE PRESIDENT CLOSED Ibid., 282.

176 TO TURN "NASHVILLE'S LOVE" *NYT,* March 18, 1974.

176 ABOUT FIFTY-EIGHT THOUSAND AMERICAN LIVES Vietnam War U.S. Military Fatal Casualty Statistics. https:www.archives.gov /research/military/vietnam-war/casualty -statistics.

176 BY LATE 1967, COLUMNIST JOSEPH KRAFT Jon Meacham, "Keeping the Dream Alive," *Time,* June 21, 2012.

176 NIXON CALLED THEM "THE GREAT" Ibid.

176 "GIVE PEACE A CHANCE" Jon Wiener, "'Give Peace a Chance': An Anthem for the Anti-War Movement," in *Give Peace a Chance: Music and the Struggle for Peace,* ed. Marianne Philbin (Chicago, 1983), 11–17.

177 ED SULLIVAN WENT ON THE AIR The details of the broadcast are drawn from *The Ed Sullivan Show,* Season 18, Episode 20, January 30, 1966, http://www.tv.com/shows/the-ed-sullivan-show /january-30-1966-the-four-tops-dinah-shore -jos-feliciano-ssgt-barry-sadler-107866/.

177 JACKIE VERNON (NOW BEST KNOWN) "Jackie Vernon, 1924–1987," https://www.imdb.com /name/nm0894682/.

178 WRITTEN BY SADLER AND ROBIN MOORE Bradley and Werner, *We Gotta Get Out of This Place,*, 32–37. See also Louis Calta, "Wounded Veteran Writes Song on Vietnam War," *NYT,* February 1, 1966.

178 "THE MOST POPULAR SONG" Bradley and Werner, *We Gotta Get Out of This Place,* 32–33.

179 "IT WAS A YEAR" Ward Just, "1968 . . . A Year That Hurt Everyone It Touched," *WP,* November 6, 1968.

179 "I LOOK OVER" Ibid.

179 CREEDENCE CLEARWATER REVIVAL Bradley and Werner, *We Gotta Get Out of This Place,* 67–72.

179 THE SONG WAS "A CONFRONTATION" Hank Bordowitz, *Bad Moon Rising: The Unauthorized History of Creedence Clearwater Revival* (Chicago, 1998), 80.

180 "WAIST DEEP IN THE BIG MUDDY" Allan M. Winkler, *"To Everything There Is a Season": Pete Seeger and the Power of Song* (New York, 2009), 124–132.

180 "IT GOT THE MOST" Seeger, *In His Own Words,* 168.

180 CUT IT FROM A TAPED APPEARANCE Winkler, *"To Everything There Is a Season,"* 130.

180 THE NETWORK LATER CAVED David King Dunaway, *How Can I Keep from Singing?: The Ballad of Pete Seeger* (New York, 2008), 335.

180 EDWIN STARR RECORDED Bradley and Werner, *We Gotta Get Out of This Place,* 179; Gregory, ed., *Soul Music A–Z,* 936. For a rendition, see also https:// www.youtube.com/watch?v=01-2pNCZiNk.

181 JIMMY WEBB WROTE "GALVESTON" See, for instance, Jimmy Webb, *The Cake and the Rain: A Memoir* (New York, 2017); George-Warren and Romanowski, *The Rolling Stone Encyclopedia of Rock and Roll,* 1055; Clarke, ed., *The Penguin Encyclopedia of Popular Music,* 1359. For a rendition of the song by Glen Campbell, see https://www.youtube .com/watch?v=iDRXADEJuKo.

181 MARTHA AND THE VANDELLAS REVERSED We are grateful to Craig Werner for reminding us of this song.

181 "JIMMY MACK" Hugh Gregory, ed., *Soul Music A–Z.* Revised edition (New York, 1995), 203–204. For a rendition, see also https://www .youtube.com/watch?v=ywEyw3AUrlY.

181 THE MOST POPULAR SONG Bradley and Werner, *We Gotta Get Out of This Place,* 143.

181 "GREEN, GREEN GRASS OF HOME" Doug Bradley, "The Top 10 Vietnam War Songs: A Playlist for Veterans," January 2, 2019, https:// www.thirteen.org/blog-post/top-10-vietnam -songs-veterans-playlist/.

181 "MUSIC DOESN'T CREATE MOVEMENTS" Interview with Craig Werner.

181 THE SOUNDTRACK OF BLACK POWER See, for instance, Werner, *A Change Is Gonna Come,* 116–120; 137–144.

182 BROWN HAD THE MOST NOTABLE See, for instance, RJ Smith, *The One: The Life and Music of James Brown* (New York, 2012).

182 "HE WAS VARIOUSLY TAGGED" "James Brown." www.rockhall.com/inductees/james-brown.

182 "BY THE LATE SIXTIES" Ibid.

184 JOHN MARTINEZ Bradley and Werner, *We Gotta Get Out of This Place,* 51, 127.

184 "[A] LOT OF TIMES" Ibid., 51.

184 IN HER "CHAIN OF FOOLS" Ibid., 72–74.

184 ONE DAY THE CHAIN WOULD BREAK Ibid., 74.

184 "I'VE HAD A LOT" Ibid., 72.

185 "(SITTIN' ON) THE DOCK OF THE BAY" Ibid., 61.

185 "BRIDGE OVER TROUBLED WATER" AND "HOMEWARD BOUND" Ibid., 141–143.

185 ON MONDAY, MAY 4, 1970 See, for instance, Jerry M. Lewis and Thomas R. Hensley, "The May 4 Shootings at Kent State University: The Search for Historical Accuracy," Kent State University History, 1998, https://www.kent.edu/may-4-historical-accuracy.

185 IN CALIFORNIA, NEIL YOUNG Dorian Lynskey, "Neil Young's 'Ohio'—The Greatest Protest Record," *The Guardian,* May 6, 2010; George-Warren and Romanowski, *The Rolling Stone Encyclopedia of Rock and Roll,* 225; Clarke, ed., *The Penguin Encyclopedia of Popular Music,* 320. For a rendition, see also https://www.youtube.com/watch?v=9rrIvd8lq5s.

185 THE FOURTH OF JULY All of the details in this account were drawn from William Greider and John Hanrahan, "Thousands Rally Here, Vow Faith in America," *WP,* July 5, 1970; David Boldt and Richard M. Cohen, "Silent Majority Watches Protesters in Quiet Disbelief," *WP,* July 5, 1970; Betty Medsger, "'Never Give In,' Graham Urges," *WP,* July 5, 1970; Paul W. Valentine, "Dissidents Clash with Police," *WP,* July 5, 1970; William L. Claiborne, "Rally Scene: Patriotism," *WP,* July 5, 1970; Martin Weil, "Divergent Views Mingle Happily at Folklife Festival," *WP,* July 5, 1970.

185 "LET THE WORLD KNOW" Medsger, "'Never Give In,'" *WP,* July 5, 1970.

185 PROTESTERS NEAR THE WASHINGTON MONUMENT Ibid.; Valentine, "Dissidents Clash," *WP,* July 5, 1970.

185 "HE, HO, HO CHI MINH" Boldt and Cohen, "Silent Majority Watches," *WP,* July 5, 1970.

185 "ONE, TWO, THREE, FOUR" Claiborne, "Rally Scene," *WP,* July 5, 1970.

186 JACK BENNY PLAYED Greider and Hanrahan, "Thousands Rally Here," *WP,* July 5, 1970.

186 "IT LOOKS LIKE" Ibid.

186 A WHITE HOUSE DINNER Details of the evening were drawn from Nixon, *RN,* 865–869; Courtney R. Sheldon, "POWs, Summit Offer Nixon a Respite," *Christian Science Monitor,* May 25, 1973; William Claiborne, "Nixon Hits Security Leaks," *WP,* May 25, 1973; "Their Cheers, Their Tears, Their Day," *WP,* May 25, 1973; John Herbers, "Ex-POW's Cheer; President Says It's Time To Stop Making Heroes of Thieves; Cheering Intensified; Nixon Addressing POW's Assails Thefts of Secrets as Threat to the Nation," *NYT,* May 25, 1973; "Mr. Nixon States His Case," *Newsweek,* June 4, 1973; "Nixon's Thin Defense: The Need for Secrecy," *Time,* June 4, 1973; Hugh Sidey, "Portrait of a Pitiful Giant?" *Time,* June 4, 1973.

186 (WHO'D SUGGESTED THE) Nixon, *RN,* 864–865.

187 "CAME OUT LOUD" Ibid., 867.

187 A CHORUS OF FORMER PRISONERS Ibid., 866.

187 BY AIR FORCE COLONEL J. QUINCY COLLINS Robert Nedelkoff, "Coverage of the Nixon Library's Dinner for America's Vietnam POWs," June 1, 2103, https://www.nixonfoundation.org/2013/06/coverage-of-the-nixon-librarys-dinner-for-americas-vietnam-pows/.

187 THE SWAGGERING WAYNE Nixon, *RN,* 867.

187 NEITHER A FEROCIOUS HAWK Robert Hilburn, *Johnny Cash: The Life* (New York, 2013), 438–439.

187 CASH TOURED THE FAR EAST Ibid., 344–345.

187 "CASH WAS GREATLY TROUBLED" Ibid.

187 "WHAT IS TRUTH?" Hilburn, *Johnny Cash,* 381–383.

187 "SINGIN' IN VIETNAM TALKIN' BLUES" Hilburn, *Johnny Cash,* 366.

187 "RAGGED OLD FLAG" Ibid., 428–429.

190 LATE IN HIS LIFE Ibid., 542.

190 "DRIVE ON" Geoffrey Himes, "Pop Recordings: Back Again, Johnny Cash, Still Unflinching," *WP,* May 1, 1994. For a rendition, see also

https://www.youtube.com/watch?v=VMH0LB
K9bN8

190 CONSIDERING THE SOURCE Much of the
ensuing section appeared, in slightly modified
form, in Jon Meacham, "Elvis in the Heart of
America," *Time,* August 10, 2017. See also Joel
Williamson with Donald L. Shaw, *Elvis Presley: A
Southern Life* (New York, 2015); David Halber-
stam, *The Fifties* (New York, 1993), 456–479;
Peter Guralnick, *Last Train to Memphis: The Rise of
Elvis Presley* (Boston, 1994); Guralnick, *Careless
Love: The Unmaking of Elvis Presley* (New York,
1999); Ted Harrison, *The Death and Resurrection of
Elvis Presley* (London, 2016).

190 "ELVIS PRESLEY," BERNSTEIN SAID Halberb-
tam, *The Fifties,* 456–457.

190 THE PRESLEY LEGEND Meacham, "Elvis in the
Heart of America," *Time,* August 10, 2017.

191 PRESLEY TOOK "THAT'S ALL RIGHT"
Williamson with Shaw, *Elvis Presley,* 23–25.

191 "ELVIS, USING HIS GOD-GIVEN" Ibid., 24–25.

192 "I WAS SCARED STIFF" Ibid., 25.

192 "HEARING HIM FOR THE FIRST TIME" Scott
Schinder and Aaron Schwartz, *Icons of Rock: An
Encyclopedia of the Legends Who Changed Music Forever,*
Vol. 1 (Westport, Conn., 2008), 2.

192 SAM PHILLIPS, WHO RECORDED ARTISTS
Halberstam, *The Fifties,* 457–462; Williamson
with Shaw, *Elvis Presley,* 138–141.

192 "I WAS MAKING EVERYBODY" Halberstam, *The
Fifties,* 459.

192 "I DON'T KNOW" Ibid., 466.

193 DISPOSABLE INCOME—ESPECIALLY FOR
TEENAGERS Ibid., 473.

193 ONE REPORT IN PRESLEY'S FBI FILE Williamson with Shaw, *Elvis Presley,* 47–48.

193 ON SEPTEMBER 9, 1956 Williamson with Shaw,
Elvis Presley, 50–51.

193 THE ONE WHERE CBS Jordan Runtagh, "Elvis
Presley on TV: Ten Unforgettable Broadcasts,"
Rolling Stone, January 28, 2016.

193 "I WANTED TO SAY" Williamson with Shaw,
Elvis Presley, 56.

193 "I LOVED ELVIS" Bill Clinton, *My Life* (New
York, 2004), 36.

194 PRESLEY WROTE PRESIDENT NIXON Jocelyn
Noveck, "'Elvis & Nixon' Recalls a Bizarre
Moment in History," Associated Press, April
20, 2016.

194 THOUGH THE SESSION Peter Carlson, "When
Elvis Met Nixon," *Smithsonian,* December 2010.

194 THE THREE-DAY FESTIVAL FEATURED "Explore
Woodstock 1969," www.woodstock.com
/history/.

195 JONI MITCHELL WASN'T THERE David Yaffe,
Reckless Daughter: A Portrait of Joni Mitchell (New
York, 2017), 107–111.

195 "HER VERSION OF THE SONG" Ibid., 111.

195 JIMI HENDRIX MADE A BIT OF HISTORY
Charles R. Cross, *Room Full of Mirrors: A
Biography of Jimi Hendrix* (New York, 2005),
267–276. See also "Jimi Hendrix, Rock Star, Is
Dead in London at 27," *NYT,* September 19,
1970.

195 "YOU CAN LEAVE" Cross, *Room Full of Mirrors,*
271.

195 HE WAS PLAYING Ibid., 269–271.

195 "THE SONG HAD LONG BEEN" Ibid., 271.

196 "JIMI'S APPROACH TO MUSIC" Werner, *A Change
Is Gonna Come,* 145.

196 "I WAS WORKING" Cross, *Room Full of Mirrors,*
271.

196 "WE PLAY IT THE WAY" Ibid.

196 IN "WHAT'S GOING ON" George-Warren and
Romanowski, eds., *The Rolling Stone Encyclopedia of
Rock and Roll,* 367–369; "Mercy, Mercy Me,"
Chicago Tribune, September 19, 1971. For a
rendition see also https://www.youtube.com
/watch?v=p-uPjcV2ybQ.

196 "IT WAS ONE HUNDRED" Barbara Charline
Jordan, "1976 Democratic National Convention Keynote Address," www.americanrhetoric
.com/speeches/barbarajordan1976dnc.html.

197 LESLEY GORE'S "YOU DON'T OWN ME" We are
grateful to Faith Hill for her guidance on these
songs. See also, for instance, Caroline Bologna,
"17 Feminist Songs That Were Ahead of Their
Time," March 31, 2016. Updated December 5,
2016. www.huffingtonpost.com/entry/17
-feminist-songs-that-were-ahead-of-their-time
_us_56fc6b46e4b0daf53aeeaf5a.

197 UNDERSTANDINGS OF SEXUAL IDENTITY See,
for instance, Jerry Portwood, Suzy Exposito,
Rob Sheffield, and Justin Ravitz, *Rolling Stone,*
June 12, 2017. https://www.rollingstone.com
/music/music-lists/25-essential-lgbtq-pride
-songs-199348/pansy-division-anthem-1993
-194072/.

197 "THE CONSTITUTION PROMISES" *Obergefell v. Hodges,* June 26, 2015. https://supreme.justia .cases/federal/us/576/14-556/#tab-opinion -3427255.

197 "THE JOKE" Ann Powers, "Songs We Love: Brandi Carlile, 'The Joke,'" NPR, November 13, 2017. https://www.npr.org/2017/11/13 /563358018/songs-we-love-brandi-carlile-the -joke.

197 FROM JANUARY 1977 UNTIL PRESLEY'S DEATH Williamson with Shaw, *Elvis Presley,* 5.

197 (TO RECONSTRUCT THE PRESCRIPTION RECORD) Ibid.

198 "PEOPLE LOVE HIM" Meacham, "Elvis in the Heart of America," *Time,* August 10, 2017.

198 "AN AMERICAN TRILOGY" Marcus, *Mystery Train,* 116–117, is brilliant on "American Trilogy." See also Jeff McCord, "An American Trilogy," *Texas Monthly,* July 2011.

198 "ALL MY TRIALS" Jim Moran, "'All My Trials/ All My Sorrows,'" March 18, 2010, http:// compvid101.blogspot.com/2010/03/all-my -trialsall-my-sorrows.html.

CHAPTER EIGHT: BORN IN THE U.S.A.

201 "SHE'S STILL A BEACON" "Transcript of Reagan's Farewell Address to the American People," *NYT,* January 12, 1989.

201 "OF THE MANY TRAGIC IMAGES" Bruce Springsteen, *Born to Run* (New York, 2016), 441.

201 IT WAS AN UNLIKELY PAIRING George F. Will, "Bruce Springsteen's U.S.A.," *WP,* September 13, 1984. For the Reagan-Springsteen episode in the 1984 campaign, see, for instance, Dave Marsh, *Bruce Springsteen: Two Hearts, The Definitive Biography, 1972–2003* (New York, 2003), 479–489; Werner, *A Change Is Gonna Come,* 246–248.

201 "THERE IS NOT A SMIDGEN" Will, "Bruce Springsteen's U.S.A.," *WP,* September 13, 1984.

201 IN HIS CONCERTGOING COSTUME Ibid.

202 ON THE SMELL OF BEN-GAY Ibid.

203 "BORN IN THE U.S.A." Springsteen, *Born to Run,* 313–317, 321–322; Clarke, ed., *The Penguin Encyclopedia of Popular Music,* 1230; George-Warren and Romanoski, eds., *The Rolling Stone Encyclopedia of Rock and Roll,* 931. For a rendition, see also https://www.youtube.com/watch?v=EPhWR 4d3FJQ.

203 "A PROTEST SONG" Springsteen, *Born to Run,* 314.

203 IN THE AFTERMATH Francis X. Clines, "President Heaps Praise on Voters in the Northeast," *NYT,* September 20, 1984.

203 "AMERICA'S FUTURE RESTS" Marsh, *Springsteen: Two Hearts,* 484. See also Clines, "President Heaps Praise," *NYT,* September 20, 1984.

203 "THE PRESIDENT'S PRESS OFFICE" Clines, "President Heaps Praise," *NYT,* September 20, 1984.

203 "BORN TO RUN" Marsh, *Springsteen: Two Hearts,* 484.

203 "THERE'S REALLY SOMETHING" Ibid., 487–488.

204 "I THINK WHAT'S HAPPENING NOW" Werner, *A Change Is Gonna Come,* 247.

204 BATTLED ALZHEIMER'S DISEASE The ensuing section on Reagan first appeared, in modified form, in Jon Meacham, "American Dreamer," *Newsweek,* June 13, 2004.

204 REAGAN WAS DAZZLED Lou Cannon, *Reagan* (New York, 1982), 18.

205 "KEN, DID YOU" Ibid.

205 A "CRISIS OF CONFIDENCE" Jimmy Carter, "Address to the Nation on Energy and National Goals: 'The Malaise Speech,'" July 15, 1979. https://www.presidency.ucsb.edu/documents /address-the-nation-energy-and-national -goals-the-malaise-speech.

205 "THE EROSION OF OUR CONFIDENCE" Ibid.

205 "NO GOVERNMENT EVER" Ronald Reagan, "Address on Behalf of Senator Barry Goldwater: 'A Time for Choosing,'" October 27, 1964. https://www.presidency.ucsb.edu/documents /address-behalf-senator-barry-goldwater-time -for-choosing.

205 "YOU AND I ARE TOLD" Ibid.

206 IN THE WHITE HOUSE Meacham, "American Dreamer," *Newsweek.* See also Sean Wilentz, *The Age of Reagan: A History, 1974-2008* (New York, 2008). Bob Spitz, *Reagan: An American Journey* (New York, 2018), is a superb recent biography.

206 A 63 PERCENT APPROVAL RATING Frank Newport, Jeffrey M. Jones, and Lydia Saad, "Ronald Reagan From the People's Perspective: A Gallup Poll Review," June 7, 2004. news .gallup.com/poll/11887/ronald-reagan-from -peoples-perspective-gallup-poll-review.aspx.

206 "SOME OF THE N.S.C." Ronald Reagan, *The Reagan Diaries,* ed. Douglas Brinkley (New York, 2007), xii.

206 "Mr. President, what do you see" Ronald
      Reagan, "The President's News Conference,"
      January 29, 1981. https://www.presidency.ucsb
      .edu/documents/the-presidents-news
      -conference-992.

207 "I know of no leader" Ibid.

207 "In this Moscow spring" Ronald Reagan,
      "Remarks and a Question-and-Answer Session
      with the Students and Faculty at Moscow State
      University," May 31, 1988. https://www
      .presidency.ucsb.edu/documents/remarks-and
      -question-and-answer-session-with-the
      -students-and-faculty-moscow-state.

207 Greenwood had toiled Dolly Carlisle,
      "Winners," People, October 31, 1983.

208 As the 1984 presidential race took shape
      Interview with Sig Rogich.

208 (The deal enraged) Ibid.

208 In Greenwood's telling Elizabeth Kastor,
      "Staying in Tune With the Republicans," WP,
      July 20, 1988.

209 "The hard truth" Mario Cuomo, "1984
      Democratic National Convention Keynote
      Address," July 16, 1984. www.americanrhetoric
      .com/speeches/mariocuomo1984dnc.htm.

211 At 9:00 p.m. Eastern Time The ensuing
      section appeared in Jon Meacham's, "Ronald
      Reagan's Hopeful Farewell," The New York Times,
      January 10, 2019.

211 There were, as always, other perspec-
      tives See, for instance, Werner, A Change Is
      Gonna Come, 245–361.

211 Run-DMC Ibid., 258–263.

211 the power of hip-hop Ibid., 245–361,
      covers the period from Reagan forward in
      detail. See also Havelock Nelson and Michael
      Gonzales, Bring the Noise: A Guide to Rap Music and
      Hip-Hop Culture (New York, 1991); S. H. Fer-
      nando, The New Beats: Exploring the Music, Culture,
      and Attitudes of Hip-Hop (New York, 1994);
      Tricia Rose, Black Noise: Rap Music and Black
      Culture in Contemporary America (Hanover, N.H.,
      1994).

212 "the sharp contrast" Interview with
      Michael Eric Dyson.

212 "they taught" Ibid.

213 Tupac Shakur's 1991 "Words of Wisdom"
      Karin L. Stanford, "Keepin' It Real in Hip Hop
      Politics: A Political Perspective of Tupac
      Shakur," Journal of Black Studies, Vol. 42, No. 1

(January, 2011), 3022. For a rendition, see also
      Youtube: https://www.youtube.com/watch?v
      =OS0qMScow-Q.

213 Tuesday, September 11, 2001 Parts of the
      ensuing section first appeared, in slightly
      different form, in Jon Meacham's introduction
      to the collection Beyond Bin Laden: America and the
      Future of Terror (New York, 2011).

214 No one replied Ibid.

214 Reports of what happened Ibid.

214 Amy Sweeney's words Ibid.

214 Bin Laden had declared war Ibid.

215 Americans like to Ibid.

215 Our central yesterday Ibid.

216 It did happen Ibid.

216 The congregation sang We are indebted to
      Margaret Shannon, longtime historian at the
      Washington National Cathedral, for details of
      the Friday, September 14, 2001, service.

216 "We come before God" George W. Bush,
      "Remarks at the National Day of Prayer and
      Remembrance Service," September 14, 2001,
      The American Presidency Project. https://www
      .presidency.ucsb.edu/node/213374.

217 "In every generation" Ibid.

217 As the service came to a close Stauffer and
      Soskis, The Battle Hymn of the Republic, 3–8, is a
      revealing and incisive account of the role of
      "The Battle Hymn" at the 9/11 service.

217 "No matter how hard we try" David von
      Drehle, "Service Transcends Politics, Religion,"
      WP, September 15, 2001.

217 "The music that filled" Howard Reich,
      "Hope and Patriotism Ring Out at Service,"
      Chicago Tribune, September 15, 2001.

217 Springsteen ("My City of Ruins") Kip
      Pegley and Susan Fast, " 'America: A Tribute to
      Heroes': Music, Mourning, and the Unified
      American Community" in Music in the Post-9/11
      World, eds. Jonathan Ritter and J. Martin
      Daughtry (New York, 2007), 33.

218 a "day of fire" George W. Bush, Inaugural
      Address, January 20, 2005, The American
      Presidency Project. www.presidency.ucsb.edu
      /node/214048.

218 When reports came Steve Hochman,
      "Passenger on Flight 93 Inspires Neil Young
      Song," Los Angeles Times, December 3, 2001. See
      also Ritter and Daughtry, eds., Music in the
      Post-9/11 World, especially Reebee Garofalo, "Pop

Goes to War, 2001–2004: U.S. Popular Music After 9/11," 11–12.

218   "LET'S ROLL" Linton Weeks, "'Let's Roll': A 9-11 Call to Arms: Booker T. and Neil Young Salute Flight 93's Heroes," WP, December 5, 2001; Jon Pareles, "With September 11 in Mind Neil Young Gets Rolling," NYT, April 7, 2002. For a rendition see also https://www.youtube.com/watch?v=zm-YTuoqbLA\.

218   "WHERE WERE YOU (WHEN THE WORLD STOPPED TURNING)" Bill Friskics-Warren, "Alan Jackson's Memorable 'Drive': His Best Ever with Just a Single Flaw," WP, January 30, 2002. For a rendition, see also https://www.youtube.com/watch?v=gPHnadJ-ohE.

218   TOBY KEITH WAS WARLIKE Garofalo, "Pop Goes to War, 2001–2004," in Music in the Post-9/11 World, eds. Ritter and Daughtry, 10–11.

218   "COURTESY OF THE RED, WHITE AND BLUE" David Segal, "Toby Keith, By Jingo, the Country Singer Takes on America's Enemies and His Own with a Vengeance," WP, July 25, 2002; Verlyn Klinkenborg, "Learning to Make Pop Music from the World Trade Center Attack," NYT, August 7, 2002. For a rendition see also https://www.youtube.com/watch?v=Nynb LtRLisg.

218   "MR. KEITH IS A SOLID SLAB" Klinkenborg, "Learning to Make Pop Music from the World Trade Center Attack," NYT, August 7, 2002.

219   "OF THE MANY TRAGIC IMAGES" Springsteen, Born to Run, 441.

219   "INTO THE FIRE" Springsteen, Born to Run, 440–441; Marsh, Bruce Springsteen: Two Hearts, 671–672. For a rendition see also https://www.youtube.com/watch?v=cliwsiwZyRE.

220   THE DIXIE CHICKS PROTESTED Chris Willman, Rednecks & Bluenecks: The Politics of Country Music (New York, 2005), 24–54; John Spong, "Chicks in the Wilderness," Texas Monthly, April 2013; Grady Smith, "Is Country Music Ready to Forgive the Dixie Chicks?" The Guardian, November 19, 2015; Martin Scherzinger, "Double Voices of Musical Censorship After 9/11" in Music in the Post-9/11 World, eds. Ritter and Daughtry, 91–121; Gabriel Rossman, "Elites, Masses, and Media Blacklists: The Dixie Chicks Controversy," Social Forces 83, no. 1 (2004), 61–79; Betty Clarke,"The Dixie Chicks," The Guardian, March 12, 2003; Josh

Tyrangiel, "Chicks in the Line of Fire," Time, May 29, 2006; Alan Light, "The Dixie Chicks, Long Past Making Nice," NYT, June 10, 2016.

220   "JUST SO YOU KNOW" Smith, "Is Country Music Ready to Forgive the Dixie Chicks?" The Guardian, November 19, 2015.

220   FACING A FAN BACKLASH AND BOYCOTTS See, for instance, Scherzinger, "Double Voices of Musical Censorship After 9/11" in Music in the Post-9/11 World, eds. Ritter and Daughtry, 91–121; Rossman, "Elites, Masses, and Media Blacklists: The Dixie Chicks Controversy," Social Forces, 61–79. "[W]hy did the whole situation get so out of hand?" John Spong wrote in Texas Monthly in 2013. "Everyone I spoke with in Nashville had an opinion. A lot of them alleged a conspiracy on the part of corporate radio, a theory once pushed by [Dixie Chicks manager Simon] Renshaw and the Chicks, pointing to Cumulus's official boycott and the well-known Republican ties of Clear Channel executives. But airplay statistics show that independent stations dropped the Chicks faster than the corporate chains. And even within the chains, airplay dropped faster in red states than blue, and at country stations as opposed to pop. And it fell fastest at stations near military bases. So the idea of a national, web-rousing boycott doesn't pan out. The groundswell wasn't organized, it was organic." Spong, "Chicks in the Wilderness," Texas Monthly, April 2013.

220   "WE ARE CURRENTLY IN EUROPE" "Dixie Chicks Singer Apologizes for Bush Comment," cnn.com, March 14, 2003.

220   "AS A CONCERNED AMERICAN CITIZEN" Ibid.

220   "I DON'T FEEL" Tyrangiel, "Chicks in the Line of Fire," Time, May 29, 2006.

220   "I MEAN, THE DIXIE CHICKS" George W. Bush, "Interview with Tom Brokaw of NBC News," The American Presidency Project. https://www.presidency.ucsb.edu/node/215287.

220   "IGNORANT," ADDING, "IT TARGETS" Chris Payne, "Natalie Maines' Most Scathing Political Comments," Billboard.com, January 25, 2016.

221   FLASHING A MANUFACTURED IMAGE Spong, "Chicks in the Wilderness," Texas Monthly, April 2013.

221   THE "INCIDENT" Spong, "Chicks in the Wilderness," Texas Monthly, April 2013; Tyrangiel, "Chicks in the Line of Fire," Time, May 29, 2006.

221 "hillbilly Jane Fondas" Rossman, "Elites, Masses, and Media Blacklists: The Dixie Chicks Controversy," *Social Forces,* 62.

221 the Chicks were photographed Light, "The Dixie Chicks, Long Past Making Nice," *NYT,* June 10, 2016.

221 "Saddam's Angels," "Traitor," "Hero" *Entertainment Weekly,* May 2, 2003.

221 "What do you expect country fans" Chet Flippo, "Nashville Skyline: Shut Up and Sing?" March 20, 2003. http://www.cmt.com/news /1470672/nashville-skyline-shut-up-and-sing/. See also Willman, *Rednecks & Bluenecks,* 33–34.

222 "I'd rather have a smaller following" Spong, "Chicks in the Wilderness," *Texas Monthly,* April 2013.

222 "Not Ready to Make Nice" Light, "The Dixie Chicks, Long Past Making Nice," *NYT,* June 10, 2016.

222 did well at the Grammys Spong, "Chicks in the Wilderness," *Texas Monthly,* April 2013.

222 the most commercially successful female groups Ibid.

222 The two men The ensuing section about the portrait unveiling first appeared in Jon Meacham, "The Presidents on the Presidents: How They Judge One Another," *Time,* February 16, 2014.

222 The occasion was Mark Landler, "Political Truce at Portrait Unveiling," *NYT,* May 31, 2012.

222 "It's been said" "Remarks by President Obama, First Lady Michelle Obama, Former President George W. Bush and Former First Lady Laura Bush at the Official Portrait Unveiling," May 31, 2012. https://obamawhite house.archives.gov/the-press-office/2012/05/31 /remarks-president-obama-first-lady-michelle -obama-former-president-georg.

222 With an ironic twinkle Ibid. See also "President George W. Bush Portrait Unveiling," May 31, 2012. https://www.c-span.org/video /?306331-2/president-george-w-bush-portrait -unveiling.

222 "I am also pleased" Ibid.

223 shared something else Interview with Kix Brooks.

224 Eight years later Ibid. See also "Obama Convention Song Was Bush Pick," National Public Radio, August 29, 2008. https://www .npr.org/templates/story/story.php?storyId =94118835; Margaret Talev, "Soul of Obama Campaign Is in the Soundtrack," McClatchy Newspapers, October 31, 2008; Lee Nichols, "WTF? Brooks & Dunn? Seriously?: Song by Bush Lovers Close Out Democratic Convention," *The Austin Chronicle,* August 28, 2008.

224 "Only in America" Jim Patterson, "Singing the Red, White and Blues," *WP,* November 9, 2001; Jon Pareles, "Pop Anthem or Classic Couplet to Sustain a Weary Soul," *NYT,* October 1, 2001. For a rendition, see also https://www.youtube.com/watch?v=BE -UH9Tlr48.

FINALE: LIFT EVERY VOICE

227 "Let America be" Langston Hughes, "Let America Be America Again," https://www.poets .org/poetsorg/poem/let-america-be-america -again.

227 For thirteen hours at the White House Elise K. Kirk, *Music at the White House: From the 18th to the 21st Centuries* (Washington, D.C., 2017), 305–307; Maurice Peress, "My Life with 'Black, Brown and Beige,'" *Black Music Research Journal,* Vol. 13, No. 2, Autumn 1993, 147–160; Leroy F. Aarons, "Culture Is King at Arts Festival; Lowell Controversy Mars Event," *WP,* June 15, 1965; "Artist and Patron Meet in Unique White House Fete," *WP,* June 15, 1965; Howard Taubman, "White House Salutes Culture in America," *NYT,* June 15, 1965; Nan Robertson, "Culture Reigns at White House," *NYT,* June 15, 1965; "Festival of the Arts," *Time,* June 25, 1965; "Arts and the Man—and the State," *Newsweek,* June 28, 1965; Lady Bird Johnson, *A White House Diary* (New York, 1970), 286–288.

227 "Our painting and music" Lyndon B. Johnson, "Remarks at the White House Festival of the Arts," June 14, 1965, The American Presidency Project, https://www.presidency.ucsb .edu/node/241785.

227 the art and artists on hand See, for instance, Aarons, "Culture Is King," *WP,* June 15, 1965; "Artist and Patron Meet," *WP,* June 15, 1965; Taubman, "White House Salutes Culture," *NYT,* June 15, 1965; Robertson, "Culture Reigns at White House," *NYT,* June 15, 1965; "Festival of the Arts," *Time,* June 25,

1965; "Arts and the Man," *Newsweek,* June 28, 1965.

227   The poet Robert Lowell had declined Aarons, "Culture Is King," *WP,* June 15, 1965; Taubman, "White House Salutes Culture," *NYT,* June 15, 1965.

227   the critic Dwight Macdonald tried to have it Ibid.

227–28   Ralph Ellison was underwhelmed "Festival of the Arts," *Time,* June 25, 1965.

228   "the height of rudeness" "Arts and the Man," *Newsweek,* June 28, 1965.

228   "He belts me" Ibid.

228   "The others," *Time* noted "Festival of the Arts," *Time,* June 25, 1965.

228   "Let these words" Taubman, "White House Salutes Culture," *NYT,* June 15, 1965.

228   "Your art is not a political weapon" Johnson, "Remarks at the White House Festival of the Arts," June 14, 1965. https://www.presidency.ucsb.edu/node/241785.

228   a turbaned Marian Anderson Robertson, "Culture Reigns at White House," *NYT,* June 15, 1965.

228   The audience then listened Ibid.

228   The Joffrey Ballet Ibid.

228   Then Duke Ellington Ibid.; Peress, "My Life with 'Black, Brown and Beige,'" *Black Music Research Journal,* 147–148.

228   "Ties were loosened" Peress, "My Life with 'Black, Brown and Beige,'" *Black Music Research Journal,* 148.

229   *Black, Brown and Beige* Ibid., 147–160. See also *Duke Ellington's America,* ed. Harvey G. Cohen (Chicago, 2010); David Schiff, "The Moor's Revenge: The Politics of *Such Sweet Thunder,*" in *Duke Ellington Studies,* ed. John Howland (Cambridge, 2017), 181; Audie Cornish and Christian McBride, "A Sprawling Blueprint for Protest Music, Courtesy of the Jazz Duke," *All Things Considered,* NPR, February 22, 2019, https://www.npr.org/templates/transcript/transcript.php?storyId=697075534.

229   In 1941, Ellington had delivered Duke Ellington, *The Duke Ellington Reader,* ed. Mark Tucker (New York, 1993), 147–148.

229   "I sketched as best I could" Michael Howard, *The Lessons of History* (New Haven, Conn., 1991), 10.

230   "You are still reaching" Johnson, "Remarks at the White House Festival of the Arts," June 14, 1965.

BIBLIOGRAPHY

BOOKS

Ackerman, Kenneth D. *Young J. Edgar: Hoover, the Red Scare, and the Assault on Civil Liberties.* New York: Carroll and Graf; Berkeley: distributed by Publishers Group West, 2007.

Adams, John. *The Works of John Adams, Second President of the United States: With a Life of the Author, Notes and Illustrations, by His Grandson Charles Francis Adams.* Edited by Charles Francis Adams. Vols. 4 and 6. Boston: Little, Brown, 1851.

Addams, Jane. *Democracy and Social Ethics.* Urbana: University of Illinois Press, 2002. First published 1902.

———. *Twenty Years at Hull-House: With Autobiographical Notes.* Edited by Victoria Bissell Brown. The Bedford Series in History and Culture. Boston: Bedford / St. Martin's, 1999. First published 1910.

Allen, Frederick Lewis. *Only Yesterday: An Informal History of the 1920's.* New York: Harper Perennial Modern Classics, 2010. First published 1931.

Allen, William Francis, Charles Pickard Ware, and Lucy McKim Garrison. *Slave Songs of the United States.* New York: Dover Publications, 1995. First published 1867.

American Council of Learned Societies. *Dictionary of American Biography.* Edited by Allen Johnson and others. Vol. 3, *Cushman–Fraser*, edited by Allen Johnson and Dumas Malone. New York: Charles Scribner's Sons, 1959.

Ammer, Christine. *Unsung: A History of Women in American Music.* Contributions in Women's Studies, no. 14. Westport, CT: Greenwood Press, 1980.

Anderson, Benedict. *Imagined Communities: Reflections on the Origin and Spread of Nationalism.* Rev. and extended ed. London: Verso, 1991.

Anderson, Fred. *Crucible of War: The Seven Years' War and the Fate of Empire in British North America, 1754–1766.* New York: Vintage Books, 2001.

Anderson, Marian. *My Lord, What a Morning: An Autobiography.* New York: Viking Press, 1956.

Andresen, Lee. *Battle Notes: Music of the Vietnam War.* Superior, WI: Savage Press, 2000.

Appiah, Kwame Anthony, and Henry Louis Gates, Jr., eds. *Africana: The Encyclopedia of the African and African American Experience.* 2nd ed. Oxford: Oxford University Press, 2005.

Avlon, John. *Washington's Farewell: The Founding Father's Warning to Future Generations.* New York: Simon & Schuster, 2017.

Bailyn, Bernard. *The Ideological Origins of the American Revolution.* Enl. ed. Cambridge, MA: Belknap Press of Harvard University Press, 1992.

———. *The Origins of American Politics.* New York: Alfred A. Knopf, 1968.

Bales, Richard. *The Confederacy: Based on Music of the South during the Years 1861–65.* New York: Columbia Records, [1990].

Beasley, Maurine H., Holly C. Shulman, and Henry R. Beasley. *Eleanor Roosevelt Encyclopedia.* Foreword by Blanche Wiesen Cook. Introduction by James McGregor Burns. Westport, CT: Greenwood Publishing Group, 2001.

Becker, Carl. *The Declaration of Independence: A Study in the History of Political Ideas.* New York: Vintage Books, 1970. First published 1922.

Beeman, Richard R. *Our Lives, Our Fortunes & Our Sacred Honor: The Forging of American Independence, 1774–1776.* New York: Basic Books, 2013.

Bennett, David H. *The Party of Fear: From Nativist Movements to the New Right in American History.* 2nd Vintage Books ed., rev. and updated. New York: Vintage, 1995.

Bergreen, Laurence. *As Thousands Cheer: The Life of Irving Berlin.* New York: Viking Press, 1990.

Berlin, Ira, Marc Favreau, and Stephen F. Miller, eds. *Remembering Slavery: African Americans Talk about Their Personal Experiences of Slavery and Freedom.* New York: New Press, 1998.

Bernard, Kenneth A. *Lincoln and the Music of the Civil War.* Caldwell, ID: Caxton Printers, 1966.

Berry, Chuck. *Chuck Berry: The Autobiography.* New York: Harmony Books, 1987.

Beschloss, Michael R. *Roosevelt and Kennedy: The Uneasy Alliance.* New York: W. W. Norton, 1980.

Blight, David W. *Frederick Douglass: Prophet of Freedom.* New York: Simon & Schuster, 2018.

———. *Frederick Douglass's Civil War: Keeping Faith in Jubilee.* Baton Rouge: Louisiana State University Press, 1989.

Bobetsky, Victor V. *We Shall Overcome: Essays on a Great American Song.* Lanham, MD: Rowman & Littlefield, 2015.

Bodnar, John. *Remaking America: Public Memory, Commemoration, and Patriotism in the Twentieth Century.* Princeton, NJ: Princeton University Press, 1991.

Bond, Julian, and Sonya Kathryn Wilson, eds. *Lift Every Voice and Sing: A Celebration of the Negro National Anthem: 100 Years, 100 Voices.* New York: Random House, 2000.

Bordewich, Fergus M. *Bound for Canaan: The Epic Story of the Underground Railroad, America's First Civil Rights Movement.* New York: Amistad, 2006.

Boyd, Todd. *The New H.N.I.C. (Head Niggas in Charge): The Death of Civil Rights and the Reign of Hip Hop.* New York: New York University Press, 2002.

Bradford, Sarah H. *Harriet Tubman: The Moses of Her People.* New York: Corinth Books, 1961. First published 1886.

———. *Scenes in the Life of Harriet Tubman.* Auburn, [NY]: W. J. Moses Printers, 1869.

Bradley, Doug, and Craig Werner. *We Gotta Get Out of This Place: The Soundtrack of the Vietnam War.* Amherst: University of Massachusetts Press, 2015.

Branch, Taylor. *At Canaan's Edge: America in the King Years, 1965–68.* New York: Simon & Schuster, 2006.

———. *Parting the Waters: America in the King Years, 1954–63.* New York: Simon & Schuster, 1988.

Branham, Robert James, and Stephen J. Hartnett. *Sweet Freedom's Song: "My Country 'Tis of Thee" and Democracy in America.* Oxford and New York: Oxford University Press, 2002.

Brooks, Noah. *Lincoln Observed: Civil War Dispatches of Noah Brooks.* Edited by Michael Burlingame. Baltimore: Johns Hopkins University Press, 1998.

Brown, Wallace, and Hereward Senior. *Victorious in Defeat: The American Loyalists in Exile.* New York: Facts on File, 1984.

Browne, C. A. *The Story of Our National Ballads.* Revised by Willard A. Heaps. New York: Crowell, 1960.

Burke, Edmund. *The Writings and Speeches of Edmund Burke.* Edited by Paul Langford and others. Vol. 2, *Party, Parliament, and the American Crisis, 1766–1774,* edited by Paul Langford and William B. Todd. Oxford: Clarendon Press, 1980.

Bush, George. *All the Best, George Bush: My Life in Letters and Other Writings.* New York: Scribner, 2013.

Calhoon, Robert McCluer. *The Loyalists in Revolutionary America, 1760–1781.* The Founding of the American Republic. New York: Harcourt Brace Jovanovich, 1973.

Cannon, Lou. *President Reagan: The Role of a Lifetime.* New York: Simon & Schuster, 1991.

———. *Reagan.* New York: G. P. Putnam's Sons, 1982.

Cantwell, David. *Merle Haggard: The Running Kind.* American Music Series. Austin: University of Texas Press, 2013.

Carretta, Vincent. *Phillis Wheatley: Biography of a Genius in Bondage.* Athens: University of Georgia Press, 2011.

Carson, Clayborne, David J. Garrow, Bill Kovach, and Carol Polsgrove, eds. *Reporting Civil Rights.* 2 vols. Library of America ed., nos. 137–138. New York: Library of America, 2003.

Chernow, Ron. *Washington: A Life.* New York: Penguin Press, 2010.

Churchill, Winston. *The Great Republic: A History of America.* New York: Random House, 1999.

Churchill, Winston, and Franklin D. Roosevelt. *Churchill and Roosevelt: The Complete Correspondence.* Edited by Warren F. Kimball. Vol. 1, *Alliance Emerging, October 1933–November 1942.* Princeton, NJ: Princeton University Press, 1984.

Clarke, Donald, ed. *The Penguin Encyclopedia of Popular Music.* 2nd ed. New York: Penguin Books, 1998.

Clifford, Deborah Pickman. *Mine Eyes Have Seen the Glory: A Biography of Julia Ward Howe.* Boston: Little, Brown, 1979.

Clinton, Bill. *My Life.* New York: Alfred A. Knopf, 2004.

Clinton, Catherine. *Harriet Tubman: The Road to Freedom.* Boston: Little, Brown, 2004.

Cogliano, Francis D. *Thomas Jefferson: Reputation and Legacy.* Charlottesville: University of Virginia Press, 2006.

Colbourn, Trevor. *The Lamp of Experience: Whig History and the Intellectual Origins of the American Revolution.* Indianapolis: Liberty Fund, 1998. First published 1965.

Cole, Wayne S. *Roosevelt and the Isolationists, 1932–1945.* Lincoln: University of Nebraska Press, 1983.

Cone, James H. *The Spirituals and the Blues: An Interpretation.* Westport, CT: Greenwood Press, 1980.

Cooper, John Milton. *Woodrow Wilson: A Biography*. New York: Alfred A. Knopf, 2009.

Cooper, William J., Jr. *We Have the War upon Us: The Onset of the Civil War, November 1860–April 1861*. New York: Alfred A. Knopf, 2012.

Cornelius, Steven H. *Music of the Civil War Era*. American History through Music. Westport, CT: Greenwood Press, 2004.

Crawford, Richard. *America's Musical Life: A History*. New York: W. W. Norton, 2001.

Crew, Danny O. *Suffragist Sheet Music: An Illustrated Catalogue of Published Music Associated with the Women's Rights and Suffrage Movement in America, 1795–1921, with Complete Lyrics*. Jefferson, NC: McFarland, 2002.

Cross, Charles R. *Room Full of Mirrors: A Biography of Jimi Hendrix*. New York: Hyperion, 2005.

Curti, Merle. *The Roots of American Loyalty*. New York: Atheneum, 1968. First published 1946.

Dangerfield, George. *The Awakening of American Nationalism, 1815–1828*. The New American Nation Series. New York: Harper and Row, 1965.

———. *The Era of Good Feelings*. New York: Harcourt, Brace, 1952.

Davis, Derek H. *Religion and the Continental Congress, 1774–1789: Contributions to Original Intent*. Religion in America Series. Oxford and New York: Oxford University Press, 2000.

Dickinson, John. *The Political Writings of John Dickinson, 1764–1774*. Edited by Paul Leicester Ford. New York: Da Capo Press, 1970. First published 1895.

Dickinson, John, and Richard Henry Lee. *Empire and Nation: Letters from a Farmer in Pennsylvania* (John Dickinson) and *Letters from the Federal Farmer* (Richard Henry Lee). Edited by Forrest McDonald. 2nd ed. Indianapolis: Liberty Fund, 1999.

Doenecke, Justus D., ed. *In Danger Undaunted: The Anti-Interventionist Movement of 1940–1941 as Revealed in the Papers of the America First Committee*. Introduction by Justus D. Doenecke. Hoover Archival Documentaries. Stanford, CA: Hoover Press, 1990.

Douglass, Frederick. *Autobiographies: Narrative of the Life of Frederick Douglass, an American Slave; My Bondage and My Freedom; Life and Times of Frederick Douglass*. Edited by Henry Louis Gates, Jr. The Library of America, no. 68. New York: Literary Classics of the United States. New York: Penguin Group, 1994.

———. *The Portable Frederick Douglass*. Edited by John Stauffer and Henry Louis Gates, Jr. Penguin Classics. New York: Penguin Books, 2016.

Du Bois, W.E.B. *The Souls of Black Folk*. Mineola, NY: Dover Publications, 1994. First published 1903.

Dunaway, David King. *How Can I Keep from Singing?: The Ballad of Pete Seeger*. New York: Villard, 2008.

Dunbar, Louise Burnham. *A Study of "Monarchical" Tendencies in the United States from 1776 to 1801*. St. Clair Shores, MI: Scholarly Press, 1970. First published 1922.

Elson, Louis C. *The National Music of America and Its Sources*. 5th impression. Boston: L. C. Page, 1911. First published 1899.

Evarts, Jeremiah. *Cherokee Removal: The "William Penn" Essays and Other Writings by Jeremiah Evarts*. Edited by Francis Paul Prucha. Knoxville: University of Tennessee Press, 1981.

Ewen, David. *Great Men of American Popular Song: The History of the American Popular Song Told through the Lives, Careers, Achievements, and Personalities of Its Foremost Composers and Lyricists—From William Billings of the Revolutionary War to the "Folk-Rock" of Bob Dylan*. Englewood Cliffs, NJ: Prentice-Hall, 1970.

Fauser, Annegret. *Sounds of War: Music in the United States during World War II*. New York: Oxford University Press, 2013.

Feldstein, Ruth. *How It Feels to Be Free: Black Women Entertainers and the Civil Rights Movement*. Oxford and New York: Oxford University Press, 2013.

Ferguson, Robert A. *The American Enlightenment, 1750–1820*. Cambridge, MA: Harvard University Press, 1997.

Fernando, S. H., Jr. *The New Beats: Exploring the Music, Culture, and Attitudes of Hip-Hop*. New York: Anchor Books / Doubleday, 1994.

Ferris, Marc. *Star-Spangled Banner: The Unlikely Story of America's National Anthem*. Baltimore, MD: Johns Hopkins University Press, 2014.

Fineman, Howard. *The Thirteen American Arguments: Enduring Debates That Define and Inspire Our Country*. New York: Random House, 2008.

Fleming, Robert E. *James Weldon Johnson*. Twayne's United States Authors Series, no. 530. Boston: Twayne Publishers, 1987.

Flower, Milton E. *John Dickinson: Conservative Revolutionary*. Charlottesville: Published for the Friends of the John Dickinson Mansion by the University Press of Virginia, 1983.

Foner, Eric. *Gateway to Freedom: The Hidden History of the Underground Railroad*. New York: W. W. Norton, 2015.

———. *The Fiery Trial: Abraham Lincoln and American Slavery*. New York: W. W. Norton, 2010.

Foreman, Grant. *Indian Removal: The Emigration of the Five Civilized Tribes of Indians.* New ed., 6th print. The Civilization of the American Indian Series, vol. 2. Norman, OK: University of Oklahoma Press, 1972.

Frank, Gerold. *An American Death: The True Story of the Assassination of Dr. Martin Luther King, Jr., and the Greatest Manhunt of Our Time.* Garden City, NY: Doubleday, 1972.

Friedlander, Paul. *Rock and Roll: A Social History.* Boulder, CO: Westview Press, 1996.

Gac, Scott. *Singing for Freedom: The Hutchinson Family Singers and the Nineteenth-Century Culture of Antebellum Reform.* New Haven, CT: Yale University Press, 2007.

Garofalo, Reebee. *Rockin' Out: Popular Music in the USA.* 4th ed. Upper Saddle River, NJ: Pearson Prentice-Hall, 2008.

Garratt, James. *Music and Politics: A Critical Introduction.* Cambridge Introductions to Music. Cambridge: Cambridge University Press, 2018.

Gates, Henry Louis, Jr. *Colored People: A Memoir.* New York: Alfred A. Knopf, 1994.

Gellner, Ernest. *Nations and Nationalism.* New Perspectives on the Past. Ithaca, NY: Cornell University Press, 1983.

Gentry, Philip. *What Will I Be: American Music and Cold War Identity.* New York: Oxford University Press, 2017.

George-Warren, Holly, Patricia Romanowski, and Jon Pareles, eds. *The Rolling Stone Encyclopedia of Rock and Roll.* 3rd ed., rev. and updated. New York: Fireside, 2001.

Gilbert, Martin. *Finest Hour: Winston S. Churchill, 1939–1941.* The Churchill Biography, vol. 6. London: Minerva, 1991. First published 1983.

Gipson, Lawrence Henry. *The British Empire before the American Revolution.* Vol. 13, *The Triumphant Empire.* New York: Alfred A. Knopf, 1967.

Gloag, Kenneth. *Tippett: A Child of Our Time.* Cambridge: Cambridge University Press, 1999.

Gordon, Linda. *The Second Coming of the KKK: The Ku Klux Klan of the 1920s and the American Political Tradition.* New York: Liveright Publishing Corp., 2017.

Greenwood, Lee. *Does God Still Bless the USA?: A Plea for a Better America.* Mustang, OK: Tate Publishing & Enterprises, 2012.

Gunther, John. *Roosevelt in Retrospect: A Profile in History.* New York: Harper & Brothers, 1950.

Guralnick, Peter. *Careless Love: The Unmaking of Elvis Presley.* Boston: Little, Brown, 1999.

———. *Last Train to Memphis: The Rise of Elvis Presley.* Boston: Little, Brown, 1994.

Haggard, Merle, with Tom Carter. *My House of Memories: An Autobiography.* New York: It Books, 2011.

Halberstam, David. *The Fifties.* New York: Villard Books, 1993.

Hall, Simon. *American Patriotism, American Protest: Social Movements since the Sixties.* Philadelphia: University of Pennsylvania Press, 2011.

Harper, Ida Husted. *The Life and Work of Susan B. Anthony: Including Public Addresses, Her Own Letters and Many from Her Contemporaries during Fifty Years.* Vol. 1. Indianapolis and Kansas City: Bowen-Merrill Co., 1899.

Harrison, Ted. *The Death and Resurrection of Elvis Presley.* London: Reaktion Books, 2016.

Harwell, Richard B. *Confederate Music.* Chapel Hill: University of North Carolina Press, 1950.

Hayes, Carlton J. H. *Nationalism: A Religion.* New York: Macmillan, 1960.

Hayward, Steven F. *Patriotism Is Not Enough: Harry Jaffa, Walter Berns, and the Arguments That Redefined American Conservatism.* New York: Encounter Books, 2017.

Herbst, Peter, ed. *The Rolling Stone Interviews: Talking with the Legends of Rock and Roll, 1967–1980.* Introduction by Ben Fong-Torres. New York: St. Martin's Press / Rolling Stone Press, 1981.

Herring, George C. *From Colony to Superpower: U. S. Foreign Relations since 1776.* New York: Oxford University Press, 2008.

Hilburn, Robert. *Johnny Cash: The Life.* New York: Little, Brown, 2013.

Hofstadter, Richard. *The Idea of a Party System: The Rise of Legitimate Opposition in the United States, 1780–1840.* Berkeley: University of California Press, 1969.

———. *The Paranoid Style in American Politics, and Other Essays.* Cambridge, MA: Harvard University Press, 1996.

Holland, James. *The Battle of Britain: Five Months That Changed History, May–October 1940.* New York: St. Martin's Griffin, 2012.

Holzer, Harold. *Lincoln President-Elect: Abraham Lincoln and the Great Secession Winter, 1860–1861.* New York: Simon & Schuster, 2008.

Isaacson, Walter. *Benjamin Franklin: An American Life.* New York: Simon & Schuster, 2003.

Jackson, Andrew. *The Papers of Andrew Jackson.* Edited by Sam B. Smith, Harriet Chappell Owsley, and others. Vol. 2, *1804–1813,* edited by Harold D. Moser and Sharon C. Macpherson. Knoxville: University of Tennessee Press, 1984.

Jackson, Mark Allan. *Prophet Singer: The Voice and Vision of*

Woody Guthrie. American Made Music Series. Jackson: University Press of Mississippi, 2007.

Jacob, Margaret, and James Jacob, eds. *The Origins of Anglo-American Radicalism.* London: Allen & Unwin, 1984.

Jefferson, Thomas. *Jefferson's Literary Commonplace Book.* Edited by Douglas L. Wilson. Princeton, NJ: Princeton University Press, 1989.

———. *The Papers of Thomas Jefferson.* Edited by Julian P. Boyd and others. Vol. 1, *1760–1776,* edited by Julian P. Boyd and others. Princeton, NJ: Princeton University Press, 1950.

———. *The Papers of Thomas Jefferson.* Edited by Julian P. Boyd and others. Vol. 14, *8 October 1788 to 26 March 1789,* edited by Julian P. Boyd and others. Princeton, NJ.: Princeton University Press, 1958.

———. *The Papers of Thomas Jefferson.* Edited by Julian P. Boyd and others. Vol. 29, *1 March 1796 to 31 December 1797,* edited by Barbara B. Oberg and others. Princeton, NJ: Princeton University Press, 2002.

———. *The Papers of Thomas Jefferson.* Edited by Julian P. Boyd and others. Vol. 30, *1 January 1798 to 31 January 1799,* edited by Barbara B. Oberg. Princeton, NJ: Princeton University Press, 2003.

———. *The Papers of Thomas Jefferson.* Edited by J. Jefferson Looney. Retirement Series. Vol. 6, *11 March to 27 November 1813.* Princeton, NJ: Princeton University Press, 2009.

Johnson, James Weldon. *Writings.* Compiled and edited by William L. Andrews. The Library of America, no. 145. New York: Library of America, 2004.

Jonas, Manfred. *Isolationism in America, 1935–1941.* Chicago: Imprint Publications, 1990. First published 1966.

Jones, John Bush. *Reinventing Dixie: Tin Pan Alley's Songs and the Creation of the Mythic South.* Baton Rouge: Louisiana State University Press, 2015.

Jones, LeRoi. *Blues People: Negro Music in White America.* New York: William Morrow, 1963.

Jones, William P. *The March on Washington: Jobs, Freedom, and the Forgotten History of Civil Rights.* New York: W. W. Norton, 2013.

Kaufman, Will. *Woody Guthrie: American Radical.* Urbana: University of Illinois Press, 2011.

Kennedy, Caroline. *A Patriot's Handbook: Songs, Poems, Stories, and Speeches Celebrating the Land We Love.* New York: Hyperion, 2003.

Kennedy, David M. *Freedom from Fear: The American People in Depression and War, 1929–1945.* The Oxford History of the United States, vol. 9. New York: Oxford University Press, 1999.

King, Carole. *A Natural Woman: A Memoir.* New York: Grand Central Publishing, 2012.

King, Martin Luther, Jr. *A Testament of Hope: The Essential Writings of Martin Luther King, Jr.* Edited by James Melvin Washington. San Francisco: Harper & Row, 1986.

Klein, Joe. *Woody Guthrie: A Life.* New York: Alfred A. Knopf, 1980.

Knight, Louise W. *Jane Addams: Spirit in Action.* New York: W. W. Norton, 2010.

Korda, Michael. *With Wings Like Eagles: A History of the Battle of Britain.* New York: Harper, 2009.

Langer, William L., and S. Everett Gleason. *The Challenge to Isolation, 1937–1940.* World Crisis and American Foreign Policy. New York: Published for the Council on Foreign Relations by Harper, 1952.

Lash, Joseph P. *Eleanor and Franklin: The Story of Their Relationship, Based on Eleanor Roosevelt's Private Papers.* New York: W. W. Norton, 1971.

Leepson, Marc. *Flag: An American Biography.* New York: Thomas Dunne Books / St. Martin's Press, 2005.

Lepore, Jill. *These Truths: A History of the United States.* New York: W. W. Norton, 2018.

Leuchtenburg, William E. *In the Shadow of FDR: From Harry Truman to Ronald Reagan.* Ithaca, NY: Cornell University Press, 1983.

Levy, Eugene. *James Weldon Johnson, Black Leader, Black Voice.* Negro American Biographies and Autobiographies. Chicago: University of Chicago Press, 1973.

Lewis, John, with Michael D'Orso. *Walking with the Wind: A Memoir of the Movement.* New York: Simon & Schuster, 1998.

Lincoln, Abraham, and the Abraham Lincoln Association, Springfield, Illinois. *The Collected Works of Abraham Lincoln.* Edited by Roy P. Basler, Marion Dolores Pratt, and Lloyd A. Dunlap. Vol. 3, *1858–1860.* New Brunswick, NJ: Rutgers University Press, 1953.

MacLean, Nancy. *Behind the Mask of Chivalry: The Making of the Second Ku Klux Klan.* New York: Oxford University Press, 1994.

Maier, Pauline. *American Scripture: Making the Declaration of Independence.* New York: Alfred A. Knopf, 1997.

Manchester, William. *The Glory and the Dream: A Narrative History of America, 1932–1972.* Boston: Little, Brown, 1974.

Margolick, David. *Strange Fruit: The Biography of a Song.* New York: Ecco Press, 2001.

Marsh, Dave. *Bruce Springsteen: Two Hearts; The Definitive Biography, 1972–2003.* New York: Routledge, 2004.

Mayer, Henry. *All on Fire: William Lloyd Garrison and the Abolition of Slavery.* New York: St. Martin's Press, 1998.

McCabe, John. *George M. Cohan: The Man Who Owned Broadway.* Garden City, NY: Doubleday, 1973.

McMillen, Sally G. *Seneca Falls and the Origins of the Women's Rights Movement.* New York: Oxford University Press, 2008.

McVeigh, Rory. *The Rise of the Ku Klux Klan: Right-Wing Movements and National Politics.* Minneapolis: University of Minnesota Press, 2009.

McWhirter, Christian. *Battle Hymns: The Power and Popularity of Music in the Civil War.* Chapel Hill: University of North Carolina Press, 2012.

Meacham, Jon. *American Gospel: God, the Founding Fathers, and the Making of a Nation.* New York: Random House, 2006.

———. *American Lion: Andrew Jackson in the White House.* New York: Random House, 2008.

———. *Beyond Bin Laden: America and the Future of Terror.* New York: Random House, 2011.

———. *Franklin and Winston: An Intimate Portrait of an Epic Friendship.* New York: Random House, 2003.

———. *The Soul of America: The Battle for Our Better Angels.* New York: Random House, 2018.

———. *Thomas Jefferson: The Art of Power.* New York: Random House, 2012.

Michener, Roger, ed. *Nationality, Patriotism, and Nationalism in Liberal Democratic Societies.* World Social Systems. Liberal Democratic Societies. St. Paul, MN: Professors World Peace Academy, 1993.

Middlekauff, Robert. *The Glorious Cause: The American Revolution, 1763–1789.* New York: Oxford University Press, 1982.

Miller, John C. *The Federalist Era, 1789–1801.* Prospect Heights, IL: Waveland Press, 1998. First published 1960.

Miller, Keith D. *Voice of Deliverance: The Language of Martin Luther King, Jr., and Its Sources.* New York: Free Press; Toronto: Maxwell Macmillan Canada; New York: Maxwell Macmillan International, 1992.

Molotsky, Irvin. *The Flag, the Poet, and the Song: The Story of the Star-Spangled Banner.* New York: Dutton, 2001.

Moore, Frank. *Song and Ballads of the American Revolution.* New York: D. Appleton, 1856.

Moore, Lisa L., Joanna Brooks, and Caroline Wigginton, eds. *Transatlantic Feminisms in the Age of Revolutions.* Oxford: Oxford University Press, 2012.

Morehouse, Ward. *George M. Cohan: Prince of the American Theater.* Philadelphia: J. B. Lippincott, 1943.

Morgan, Edmund S. *The Birth of the Republic, 1763-89.* Rev. ed. Chicago History of American Civilization, no. 14. Chicago: University of Chicago Press, 1977.

Morgan, Edmund S., and Helen M. Morgan. *The Stamp Act Crisis: Prologue to Revolution.* Chapel Hill: Published for the Institute of Early American History and Culture by the University of North Carolina Press, 1995. First published 1953.

Morton, Henry Vollam. *Atlantic Meeting, an Account of Mr. Churchill's Voyage in H.M.S. Prince of Wales, in August, 1941, and the Conference with President Roosevelt Which Resulted in the Atlantic Charter.* New York: Dodd, Mead & Co., 1943.

Murchison, William. *The Cost of Liberty: The Life of John Dickinson.* Lives of the Founders. Wilmington, DE: ISI Books, 2013.

Murray, Robert K. *Red Scare: A Study in National Hysteria, 1919–1920.* New York: McGraw-Hill, 1964. First published 1955.

Nason, Elias. *A Monogram on Our National Song.* Albany, NY: J. Munsell, 1869.

Nathan, Hans. *Dan Emmett and the Rise of Early Negro Minstrelsy.* Norman: University of Oklahoma Press, 1977. First published 1962.

Neal, Steve. *Happy Days Are Here Again: The 1932 Democratic National Convention, the Emergence of FDR—and How America Was Changed Forever.* New York: William Morrow, 2004.

Nelson, Craig. *Thomas Paine: Enlightenment, Revolution, and the Birth of Modern Nations.* New York: Viking, 2006.

Nelson, Havelock, and Michael A. Gonzales. *Bring the Noise: A Guide to Rap Music and Hip-Hop Culture.* New York: Harmony Books, 1991.

Nevins, Allan, ed. *America through British Eyes.* New ed., rev. and enl. New York: Oxford University Press, 1948.

Nixon, Richard M. *RN: The Memoirs of Richard Nixon.* New York: Grosset & Dunlap, 1978.

Nobbman, Dale V., ed. *America's Patriotic Music Companion Fact Book: The Chronological History of Our Favorite Traditional American Patriotic Songs.* Anaheim Hills, CA: Centerstream Publications, 2002.

O'Brien, Lucy. *She Bop: The Definitive History of Women in Popular Music.* Rev. 3rd ed. London: Jawbone, 2012.

O'Leary, Cecilia Elizabeth. *To Die For: The Paradox of American Patriotism.* Princeton, NJ: Princeton University Press, 1999.

Olson, Lynne. *Those Angry Days: Roosevelt, Lindbergh, and America's Fight over World War II, 1939–1941.* New York: Random House, 2013.

Pachter, Marc, and Frances Wein, eds. *Abroad in America: Visitors to the New Nation, 1776–1914.* Reading, MA: Published in association with the National Portrait Gallery, Smithsonian Institution by Addison-Wesley Pub. Co., 1976.

Painter, Nell Irvin. *Sojourner Truth: A Life, a Symbol.* New York: W. W. Norton, 1996.

Peretti, Burton W. *Lift Every Voice: The History of African American Music.* The African American History Series. Lanham, MD: Rowman & Littlefield, 2009.

Perry, Imani. *May We Forever Stand: A History of the Black National Anthem.* John Hope Franklin Series in African American History and Culture. Chapel Hill: University of North Carolina Press, 2018.

Philbin, Marianne, ed. *Give Peace a Chance: Music and the Struggle for Peace; A Catalog of the Exhibition at the Peace Museum, Chicago.* Preface by Yoko Ono. Chicago: Chicago Review Press, 1983.

Phillips, Nichole R. *Patriotism Black and White: The Color of American Exceptionalism.* Waco, TX: Baylor University Press, 2018.

Phull, Hardeep. *Story behind the Protest Song: A Reference Guide to the 50 Songs That Changed the 20th Century.* Westport, CT: Greenwood Press, 2008.

Ponder, Melinda M. *Katherine Lee Bates: From Sea to Shining Sea, The Poet of "America the Beautiful."* Chicago: Windy City Publishers, 2017.

Prucha, Francis Paul. *The Great Father: The United States Government and the American Indians.* Unabridged vols. 1 and 2 combined. Lincoln: University of Nebraska Press, 1995. First published 1984.

Reagan, Ronald, with Richard G. Hubler. *Where's The Rest of Me?: The Autobiography of Ronald Reagan.* New York: Karz Publishers, 1981.

Regier, Willis G., ed. *Masterpieces of American Indian Literature.* Lincoln: University of Nebraska Press, 2005.

Reynolds, David S. *From Munich to Pearl Harbor: Roosevelt's America and the Origins of the Second World War.* The American Ways Series. Chicago: Ivan R. Dee, 2001.

Rhodehamel, John, ed. *The American Revolution: Writings from the War of Independence.* The Library of America, no. 123. New York: Literary Classics of the United States, 2001.

Rijn, Guido van. *Roosevelt's Blues: African-American Blues and Gospel Songs on FDR.* American Made Music Series. Jackson: University Press of Mississippi, 1997.

Risjord, Norman K. *Jefferson's America, 1760–1815.* 3rd ed. Lanham, MD: Rowman & Littlefield, 2010.

Ritchie, Donald A. *Electing FDR: The New Deal Campaign of 1932.* American Presidential Elections. Lawrence: University Press of Kansas, 2007.

Ritter, Jonathan, and J. Martin Daughtry, eds. *Music in the Post–9/11 World.* New York: Routledge, 2007.

Roosevelt, James, and Sidney Shalett. *Affectionately, F.D.R.: A Son's Story of a Lonely Man.* New York: Harcourt, Brace, 1959.

Rose, Tricia. *Black Noise: Rap Music and Black Culture in Contemporary America.* Hanover, NH: University Press of New England, 1994.

Rozema, Vicki, ed. *Voices from the Trail of Tears.* Real Voices, Real History Series. Winston-Salem, NC: J. F. Blair, 2003.

Safire, William. *Safire's Political Dictionary.* Oxford: Oxford University Press, 2008.

Scheer, George F., and Hugh F. Rankin. *Rebels and Redcoats.* A Mentor Book. New York: New American Library, 1957.

Schinder, Scott, and Aaron Schwartz. *Icons of Rock: An Encyclopedia of the Legends Who Changed Music Forever.* 2 vols. Greenwood Icons. Westport, CT: Greenwood Press, 2008.

Schlesinger, Arthur M., Jr. *A Life in the Twentieth Century: Innocent Beginnings, 1917–1950.* Boston: Houghton Mifflin, 2000.

Seeger, Pete. *Pete Seeger: His Life in His Own Words.* Edited by Rob Rosenthal and Sam Rosenthal. Nine Lives Musical Series. Boulder, CO: Paradigm Publishers, 2012.

Sherr, Lynn. *Failure Is Impossible: Susan B. Anthony in Her Own Words.* New York: Times Books, 1995.

Showalter, Elaine. *The Civil Wars of Julia Ward Howe: A Biography.* New York: Simon & Schuster, 2016.

Silber, Irwin, comp. and ed. *Songs of the Civil War: The Most Complete Collection of Civil War Songs Ever Published.* New York: Bonanza Books, 1960.

Silverman, Kenneth. *A Cultural History of the American Revolution: Painting, Music, Literature, and the Theatre in the Colonies and the United States from the Treaty of Paris to the Inauguration of George Washington, 1763–1789.* New York: T. Y. Crowell, 1976.

Simon, George. *Glenn Miller and His Orchestra.* New York: T. Y. Crowell, 1974.

Simone, Nina. *I Put a Spell on You: The Autobiography of Nina Simone.* New York: Pantheon Books, 1991.

Smelser, Marshall. *The Democratic Republic, 1801–1815.* The New American Nation Series. New York: Harper & Row, 1968.

Smith, Anthony D. *Nationalism: Theory, Ideology, History.* 2nd ed. Key Concepts. Cambridge: Polity, 2010.

Smith, Kathleen E. R. *God Bless America: Tin Pan Alley Goes to War.* Lexington: University Press of Kentucky, 2003.

Smith, R. J. *The One: The Life and Music of James Brown.* New York: Gotham Books, 2012.

Sonneck, O. G. *Report on the Star-Spangled Banner, Hail Columbia, America, Yankee Doodle.* New York: Dover Publications, 1972. First published 1909.

Sounces, Howard. *Down the Highway: The Life of Bob Dylan.* New York: Grove Press, 2011.

Southern, Eileen. *Readings in Black American Music.* New York: W. W. Norton, 1983.

———. *The Music of Black Americans: A History.* New York: W. W. Norton, 1971.

Springsteen, Bruce. *Born to Run.* New York: Simon & Schuster, 2016.

Stagg, J.C.A. *Mr. Madison's War: Politics, Diplomacy, and Warfare in the Early American Republic, 1783–1830.* Princeton, NJ: Princeton University Press, 1983.

Stanton, Elizabeth Cady, and Susan B. Anthony. *The Elizabeth Cady Stanton–Susan B. Anthony Reader: Correspondence, Writings, Speeches.* Edited by Ellen Carol DuBois. Rev. ed. Boston: Northeastern University Press, 1992.

Stauffer, John, and Benjamin Soskis. *The Battle Hymn of the Republic: A Biography of the Song That Marches On.* New York: Oxford University Press, 2013.

Still, William. *The Underground Railroad: Authentic Narratives and First-Hand Accounts.* Edited and with an Introduction by Ian Frederick Finseth. Mineola, NY: Dover Publications, 2007. First published 1872.

Sullivan, Patricia. *Lift Every Voice: The NAACP and the Making of the Civil Rights Movement.* New York: New Press, 2009.

Swann, Brian, ed. *Native American Songs and Poems: An Anthology.* Mineola, NY: Dover Publications, 1996.

Talese, Gay. *The Kingdom and the Power.* New York: World Pub. Co., 1969.

Taylor, Alan. *American Colonies.* The Penguin History of the United States. New York: Penguin Books, 2002.

———. *The Civil War of 1812: American Citizens, British Subjects, Irish Rebels, and Indian Allies.* New York: Alfred A. Knopf, 2010.

Taylor, Lonn, Kathleen M. Kendrick, and Jeffrey L. Brodie. *The Star-Spangled Banner: The Making of an American Icon.* New York: Smithsonian Books; New York: Collins, 2008.

Teachout, Woden. *Capture the Flag: A Political History of American Patriotism.* New York: Basic Books, 2009.

Terkel, Studs. *"The Good War": An Oral History of World War Two.* New York: Pantheon Books, 1984.

———. *Hard Times: An Oral History of the Great Depression.* New York: Pantheon Books, 1986. First published 1970.

Thomas, Evan. *Being Nixon: A Man Divided.* New York: Random House, 2015.

Thoreau, Henry David. *Journal.* Edited by Bradford Torrey and Francis H. Allen. Reprint of 14 vols. in 2. New York: Dover Publications, 1962. First published 1906.

Troutman, John W. *Indian Blues: American Indians and the Politics of Music, 1879–1934.* New Directions in Native American Studies, vol. 3. Norman: University of Oklahoma Press, 2009.

Truman, Harry S. *Where the Buck Stops: The Personal and Private Writings of Harry S. Truman.* Edited by Margaret Truman. New York: Warner Books, 1989.

Truth, Sojourner. *Narrative of Sojourner Truth.* Edited by Margaret Washington. Vintage Classics. New York: Vintage Books, 1993.

Tuchman, Barbara W. *The March of Folly: From Troy to Vietnam.* New York: Alfred A. Knopf, 1984.

Tully, Grace. *F.D.R., My Boss.* New York: Charles Scribner's Sons, 1949.

Van Doren, Carl. *Benjamin Franklin.* New York: Viking Press, 1938.

Venzon, Anne, ed. *The United States in the First World War: An Encyclopedia.* Garland Reference Library of the Humanities, vol. 1205. New York: Garland Publishing, 1995.

Virginia History, Government, and Geography Service, Division of Secondary Education, State Department of Education. *The Road to Independence: Virginia, 1763–1783.* Richmond, VA. First published 1975.

Viroli, Maurizio. *For Love of Country: An Essay on Patriotism and Nationalism.* Oxford: Clarendon Press; New York: Oxford University Press, 1995.

Walker, David. *David Walker's Appeal.* Rev. ed. Introduction by Sean Wilentz. New York: Hill and Wang, 1995. First published 1965.

Walker, Samuel. *In Defense of American Liberties: A History of the ACLU*. New York: Oxford University Press, 1990.

Ward, Andrew. *Dark Midnight When I Rise: The Story of the Jubilee Singers, Who Introduced the World to the Music of Black America*. New York: Farrar, Straus, and Giroux, 2000.

Ward, Ed, Geoffrey Stokes, and Ken Tucker. *Rock of Ages: The Rolling Stone History of Rock and Roll*. New York: Rolling Stone Press; New York: Summit Books, 1986.

Ward, Geoffrey C. *A First-Class Temperament: The Emergence of Franklin Roosevelt*. New York: Harper & Row, 1989.

———. *Not for Ourselves Alone: The Story of Elizabeth Cady Stanton and Susan B. Anthony: An Illustrated History*. Based on a documentary film by Ken Burns and Paul Barnes. New York: Alfred A. Knopf, 1999.

Watkins, Glenn. *Proof through the Night: Music and the Great War*. Berkeley: University of California Press, 2003.

Webb, Jimmy. *The Cake and the Rain: A Memoir*. New York: St. Martin's Press, 2017.

Webster, Daniel, and Robert Young Hayne. The *Webster-Hayne Debate on the Nature of the Union: Selected Documents*. Edited by Herman Belz. Indianapolis: Liberty Fund, 2000.

Wenner, Jann S., and Joe Levy, eds. *The Rolling Stone Interviews*. New York: Back Bay Books, 2007.

Werner, Craig. *A Change Is Gonna Come: Music, Race & the Soul of America*. Rev. and updated. Ann Arbor: University of Michigan Press, 2006.

Wheatley, Phillis. *Complete Writings*. Edited by Vincent Carretta. Penguin Classics. New York: Penguin Books, 2001.

Whitburn, Joel. *The Billboard Book of Top 40 Hits*. 9th ed., rev. and expanded. New York: Billboard Books, 2010.

White, Ronald C., Jr. *A. Lincoln: A Biography*. New York: Random House, 2009.

White, Shane, and Graham J. White. *The Sounds of Slavery: Discovering African American History through Songs, Sermons, and Speech*. Boston: Beacon Press, 2005.

White, Theodore H. *The Making of the President, 1968*. New York: Atheneum, 1969.

White, William Carter. *A History of Military Music in America*. Westport, CT: Greenwood Press, 1975. First published 1944.

Wilentz, Sean. *Bob Dylan in America*. New York: Doubleday, 2010.

Wilkes, Brian. *New Cherokee Hymnal: Ten Songs*. Cherokee Bible Project & Four Rivers Native American Church. CreateSpace, 2013.

Williamson, Joel, with Donald L. Shaw. *Elvis Presley: A Southern Life*. Oxford: Oxford University Press, 2015.

Willman, Chris. *Rednecks and Bluenecks: The Politics of Country Music*. New York: The New Press, 2005.

Wills, Garry. *Inventing America: Jefferson's Declaration of Independence*. His America's Political Enlightenment. Garden City, NY: Doubleday, 1978.

———. *Reagan's America: Innocents at Home*. Garden City, NY: Doubleday, 1987.

Winkler, Allan M. *"To Everything There Is a Season": Pete Seeger and the Power of Song*. New Narratives in American History. Oxford: Oxford University Press, 2009.

Winkler, Sheldon. *The Music of World War II: War Songs and Their Stories*. Military Monograph, no. 120. Bennington, VT: Merriam Press, 2013.

Winsor, Justin, ed. *The Memorial History of Boston, Including Suffolk County, Massachusetts, 1630–1880*. Vol. 3, *The Revolutionary Period*. Boston: Osgood, 1882.

Wood, Gordon S. *The American Revolution: A History*. A Modern Library Chronicles Book, no. 9. New York: Modern Library, 2003.

———. *The Creation of the American Republic, 1776–1787*. Chapel Hill: Published for the Institute of Early American History and Culture at Williamsburg, Virginia, by the University of North Carolina Press, 1998.

———. *Empire of Liberty: A History of the Early Republic, 1789–1815*. The Oxford History of the United States. Oxford: Oxford University Press, 2009.

———. *The Idea of America: Reflections on the Birth of the United States*. New York: Penguin Press, 2011.

———. *The Radicalism of the American Revolution*. New York: Vintage Books, 1993.

———. *Revolutionary Characters: What Made the Founders Different*. New York: Penguin Press, 2006.

Wright, Alfred, and Cyrus Byington, comps. *Chahta Vba Isht Taloa Holisso, or Choctaw Hymn Book*. 4th ed., rev. and enl. New York: S. W. Benedict, 1851.

Yaffe, David. *Reckless Daughter: A Portrait of Joni Mitchell*. New York: Sarah Crichton Books, Farrar, Straus and Giroux, 2017.

Yager, Edward M. *Ronald Reagan's Journey: Democrat to Republican*. Lanham, MD: Rowman & Littlefield, 2006.

Young, William H., and Nancy K. Young. *Music of the Great Depression*. American History through Music. Westport, CT: Greenwood Press, 2005.

ARTICLES

Ayres, B. Drummond, Jr. "Nixon Plays Piano on Wife's Birthday at Grand Ole Opry." *New York Times,* March 17, 1974.

Bergreen, Laurence. "Irving Berlin: This Is the Army." *Prologue,* Summer 1996, 94–106.

Black, Allida M. "Championing a Champion: Eleanor Roosevelt and the Marian Anderson 'Freedom Concert.'" *Presidential Studies Quarterly* 20, no. 4 (Fall 1990): 719–36.

Boldt, David, and Richard M. Cohen. "Silent Majority Watches Protesters in Quiet Disbelief." *Washington Post, Times Herald,* July 5, 1970.

Calta, Louis. "Wounded Veteran Writes Song on Vietnam War." *New York Times,* February 1, 1966.

Carlisle, Dolly. "Winners." *People Weekly,* October 31, 1983, 59–60.

Carlson, Peter. "When Elvis Met Nixon." *Smithsonian Magazine,* December 2010, https://www.smithsonianmag.com/history/when-elvis-met-nixon-69892425/.

Claiborne, William. "Nixon Hits Security Leaks." *Washington Post, Times Herald,* May 25, 1973.

———. "Rally Scene: Patriotism on Display." *Washington Post, Times Herald,* July 5, 1970.

Clarke, Betty. "The Dixie Chicks." *The Guardian,* March 12, 2003, https://www.theguardian.com/music/2003/mar/12/artsfeatures.popandrock.

Clines, Francis X. "President Heaps Praise on Voters in the Northeast." *New York Times,* September 20, 1984.

Cooper, Melissa. "Reframing Eleanor Roosevelt's Influence in the 1930s Anti-Lynching Movement around a 'New Philosophy of Government.'" In "Eleanor Roosevelt and Diplomacy in the Public Interest," special issue, *European Journal of American Studies* 12, no. 1 (Spring 2017): 1–15.

Cosgrove, Ben. "Mourning FDR: In a Classic Photo, the Face of a Nation's Loss." *Time,* February 26, 2013, http://time.com/3764064/mourning-fdr-in-a-classic-photo-the-face-of-a-nations-loss/.

Fox, William Price. "Grand Ole Opry." *American Heritage,* February/March 1979, 94–105.

Friskics-Warren, Bill. "Alan Jackson's Memorable 'Drive': His Best Ever, with Just a Single Flaw." *Washington Post,* January 30, 2002.

Greider, William, and John Hanrahan. "Thousands Rally Here, Vow Faith in America." *Washington Post, Times Herald,* July 5, 1970.

Herbers, John. "President 'Campaigning' to Display His Strength." *New York Times,* March 18, 1974.

Hochman, Steve. "Passenger on Flight 93 Inspires Neil Young Song." *Los Angeles Times,* December 5, 2001.

Howe, John R., Jr. "Republican Thought and the Political Violence of the 1790s." *American Quarterly* 19, no. 2 (Summer 1967): 147–65.

Johnson, Donald. "Wilson, Burleson, and Censorship in the First World War." *Journal of Southern History* 28, no. 1 (February 1962): 46–58.

Just, Ward. "1968 . . . A Year That Hurt Everyone It Touched." *Washington Post, Times Herald,* November 6, 1968.

Kastor, Elizabeth. "Staying in Tune with the Republicans." *Washington Post,* July 20, 1988.

Kilpatrick, Carroll. "A Night at the Opry." *Washington Post,* March 17, 1974.

Klaw, Barbara. "'A Voice One Hears Once in a Hundred Years': An Interview with Marian Anderson." *American Heritage,* February 1977, 50–57.

Klinkenborg, Verlyn. "Learning to Make Popular Music from the World Trade Center Attack." *New York Times,* August 7, 2002.

Landler, Mark. "Political Truce for a Portrait Unveiling." *New York Times,* May 31, 2012.

Light, Alan. "The Dixie Chicks, Long Past Making Nice." *New York Times,* June 10, 2016.

Lord, Walter. "Humiliation and Triumph." *American Heritage,* August, 1972, 50–73, 91–93.

Lynskey, Dorian. "Neil Young's Ohio—The Greatest Protest Record." *The Guardian,* May 6, 2010, https://www.theguardian.com/music/2010/may/06/ohio-neil-young-kent-state-shootings.

McCord, Jeff. "An American Trilogy." *Texas Monthly,* July 2011, https://www.texasmonthly.com/articles/an-american-trilogy/.

McVeigh, Rory. "Power Devaluation, the Ku Klux Klan, and the Democratic National Convention of 1924." *Sociological Forum* 16, no. 1 (March 2001): 1–30.

Meacham, Jon. "American Dreamer." *Newsweek,* June 14, 2004, 26–29, 31–33, 35–42, 44–45.

———. "Elvis in the Heart of America." *Time,* August 21, 2017, 38–45.

———. "How Will History Judge the Trump Presidency?: The Strength of Humility." *Vanity Fair,* September 7, 2017. https://www.vanityfair.com/news/2017/09/historians-on-trump-presidency?verso=true.

———. "Keeping the Dream Alive." *Time,* July 2, 2012, 26–39.

———. "Old Hickory in a New Century." *Time,* January 8, 2015, http://time.com/3656271/old-hickory-in-a-new-century/.

———. "The Presidents on the Presidents: How They Judge One Another." *Time*, February 16, 2014, http://time.com/7801/the-presidents-on-the-presidents-how-they-judge-one-another/.

———. "Ronald Reagan's Hopeful Farewell." *New York Times*, January 10, 2019.

Medsger, Betty. " 'Never Give In,' Graham Urges." *Washington Post, Times Herald*," July 5, 1970.

Nichols, Lee. "WTF? Brooks and Dunn? Seriously?: Song by Bush-lovers Close Out Democratic Convention." The *Austin Chronicle*, August 28, 2008, https://www.austinchronicle.com/daily/news/2008-08-28/666979/.

Norton, Mary Beth. "John Randolph's 'Plan of Accommodations.' " *William and Mary Quarterly*, 3rd ser., 28, no. 1 (January 1971): 103–20.

Pareles, Jon. "Pop Anthem or Classic Couplet to Sustain a Weary Soul." *New York Times*, October 1, 2001.

———. "Robert Shelton, 69, Music Critic Who Chronicled '60s Folk Boom." *New York Times,* December 15, 1995.

———. "With Sept. 11 in Mind, Neil Young Gets Rolling." *New York Times*, April 7, 2002.

Patterson, Jim. "Singing the Red, White and Blues." *Washington Post*, November 9, 2001.

Remnick, David. "Soul Survivor: The Revival and Hidden Treasure of Aretha Franklin." *New Yorker,* April 4, 2016, 74–81.

Rossman, Gabriel. "Elites, Masses, and Media Blacklists: The Dixie Chicks Controversy." *Social Forces* 83, no. 1 (September 2004): 61–79.

Sandage, Scott A. "A Marble House Divided: The Lincoln Memorial, the Civil Rights Movement, and the Politics of Memory, 1939–1963." *Journal of American History* 80, no.1 (June 1993): 135–67.

Schlesinger, Arthur, Jr. "History as Therapy: A Dangerous Idea." *New York Times,* May 3, 1996.

Segal, David. "Toby Keith, by Jingo: The Country Singer Takes on America's Enemies—and His Own—with a Vengeance." *Washington Post*, July 25, 2002.

Sheldon, Courtney R. "POW's Summit Offer Nixon a Respite." *Christian Science Monitor*, May 25, 1973.

Shelton, Robert. "Songs a Weapon in Rights Battle." *New York Times,* August 20, 1962.

Sidey, Hugh. "The Presidency: Portrait of a Pitiful Giant?" *Time,* June 4, 1973, 22–23.

"Six Fateful Months: March to September 1939." *World Affairs* 102, no. 3 (September 1939): 139–41.

Smith, Grady. "Is Country Music Ready to Forgive the Dixie Chicks?" *The Guardian*, November 19, 2015, https://www.theguardian.com/music/2015/nov/19/the-dixie-chicks-tour-is-country-music-ready-to-forgive.

Smyth, John Ferdinand Dalziel. "Narrative or Journal of Capt. John Ferdinand Dalziel Smyth, of the Queen's Rangers." *Pennsylvania Magazine of History and Biography* 39, no. 2 (1915): 143–69.

Spong, John. "Chicks in the Wilderness." *Texas Monthly*, April 2013, https://www.texasmonthly.com/the-culture/chicks-in-the-wilderness/.

Stanford, Karin L. "Keepin' It Real in Hip Hop Politics: A Political Perspective of Tupac Shakur." *Journal of Black Studies* 42, no. 1 (January 2011): 3–22.

Strickland, Rennard. "Strangers in a Strange Land: A Historical Perspective of the Columbian Quincentenary." *Journal of Civil Rights and Economic Development* 7, no. 2 (Spring 1993): 571–86.

"Transcript of Reagan's Farewell Address to American People." *New York Times*, January 12, 1989.

Tyrangiel, Josh. "Chicks in the Line of Fire." *Time*, May 21, 2006, http://content.time.com/time/magazine/article/0,9171,1196419,00.html.

Valentine, Paul W. "Dissidents Clash with Police." *Washington Post, Times Herald*, July 5, 1970.

Von Drehle, David. "Bush Rallies Nation, Tours Disaster Area." *Washington Post*, September 15, 2001.

Watson, D. H. "Joseph Harrison and the *Liberty* Incident." *William and Mary Quarterly*, 3rd ser., 20, no. 4 (October 1963): 585–95.

Weeks, Linton. " 'Let's Roll': A 9–11 Call to Arms; Booker T. and Neil Young Salute Flight 93's Heroes." *Washington Post*, December 15, 2001.

Weil, Martin, "Divergent Views Mingle Happily at Folklife Festival." *Washington Post, Times Herald,* July 5, 1970.

Will, George F. "Bruce Springsteen's U.S.A." *Washington Post*, September 13, 1984.

Willman, Chris. "Stars and Strife." *Entertainment Weekly*, May 2, 2003, 22–29.

Winkler, Allan M. " 'We Shall Overcome.' " *American Heritage,* Fall 2017. https://www.americanheritage.com/we-shall-overcome.

Wolkins, George Gregerson. "The Seizure of John Hancock's Sloop 'Liberty.' " *Proceedings of the Massachusetts Historical Society*, 3rd ser., 55 (October 1921–June 1922): 239–84.

DISSERTATION

Lutz, Regan Ann. "West of Eden: The Historiography of the Trail of Tears." PhD. diss., University of Toledo, 1995.

ONLINE RESOURCES

Bologna, Caroline. "17 Feminist Songs That Were Ahead of Their Time." *HuffPost,* March 31, 2016. Updated December 5, 2016. https://www .huffingtonpost.com/entry/17-feminist-songs-that -were-ahead-of-their-time_us_56fc6b46e4b0daf 53aeeaf5a.

Brooks and Dunn. "Only in America." YouTube video, 4:30. Posted on September 3, 2011. https://www .youtube.com/watch?v=BE-UH9Tlr48.

Bush, George W. "Inaugural Address," January 20, 2005. The American Presidency Project. https:// www.presidency.ucsb.edu/documents/inaugural -address-13.

———. Bush, George W. "Remarks at the National Day of Prayer and Remembrance Service," September 14, 2001. The American Presidency Project. University of California, Santa Barbara. https:// www.presidency.ucsb.edu/documents/remarks-the -national-day-prayer-and-remembrance-service-0.

"Dixie Chicks Singer Apologizes for Bush Comment." CNN.com, March 14, 2003. http://www.cnn.com /2003/SHOWBIZ/Music/03/14/dixie.chicks .apology/.

"George Bush, Interview with Tom Brokaw of NBC News," April 24, 2003. The American Presidency Project. https://www.presidency.ucsb.edu /documents/interview-with-tom-brokaw-nbc -news.

Jackson, Alan. "Where Were You (When the World Stopped Turning)" YouTube video, 5:09. Posted on May 28, 2011. https://www.youtube.com/watch?v =gPHnadJ-ohE.

Jordan, Barbara Charline. "1976 Democratic National Convention Keynote Address." American Rhetoric: Top 100 Speeches. https://www.americanrhetoric .com/speeches/barbarajordan1976dnc.html.

Keith, Toby. "Courtesy of the Red, White and Blue." YouTube video, 3:30. Posted on July 10, 2008. https://www.youtube.com/watch?v=NynbLtRLisg.

The New Georgia Encyclopedia. Athens, GA: Georgia Humanities Council and the University of Georgia Press, 2004–. https://www.georgiaencyclopedia.org/.

"Obama Convention Song Was Bush Pick." National Public Radio, Heard on All Things Considered. August 29, 2008. https://www.npr.org/templates /story/story.php?storyId=94118835.

Payne, Chris. "The Most Scathing Political Comments from Dixie Chicks' Natalie Maines: Ted Cruz /& Beyond." Billboard, January 25, 2016. https://www .billboard.com/articles/columns/country/6851845 /natalie-maines-dixie-chicks-political-quotes-ted -cruz-george-bush-toby-keith-iraq-war.

"President George W. Bush Portrait Unveiling." C-SPAN, May 31, 2012. https://www.c-span.org /video/?306331-2/president-george-w-bush -portrait-unveiling.

"Remarks by President Obama, First Lady Michelle Obama, Former President George W. Bush and Former First Lady Laura Bush at the Official Portrait Unveiling." The White House: President Barack Obama, May 31, 2012. https://obamawhite house.archives.gov/the-press-office/2012/05/31 /remarks-president-obama-first-lady-michelle -obama-former-president-georg.

Sparrow, Paul M. "Eleanor Roosevelt's Battle to End Lynching." February 12, 2016. National Archives. Franklin D. Roosevelt Presidential Library and Museum. https://fdr.blogs.archives.gov/2016/02 /12/eleanor-roosevelts-battle-to-end-lynching/.

Springsteen, Bruce. "Born in the U. S. A." YouTube video, 4:43. Posted on March 10, 2011. https://www .youtube.com/watch?v=EPhWR4d3FJQ.

———. "Into the Fire (Live 2016)" YouTube video, 4:48. Posted on October 1, 2016. https://www .youtube.com/watch?v=cliwsiwZyRE.

Talev, Margaret. "Soul of the Obama Campaign Is in the Soundtrack." McClatchy Newspapers, DC Bureau, October 31, 2008. https://www .mcclatchydc.com/news/politics-government /article24507895.html.

Tupac. "Words of Wisdom." YouTube video, 5:04. Posted on June 20, 2008. https://www.youtube .com/watch?v=OS0qMScow-Q.

Young, Neil. "Let's Roll." Are You Passionate? YouTube video, 5:52. Posted on November 6, 2014. https:// www.youtube.com/watch?v=zm-YTu0qbLA.

IMAGE CREDITS

sippi Goddam" by Nina Simone, 1964: (P) 1964 UMG RECORDINGS, INC./COURTESY OF VERVE LABEL GROUP UNDER LICENSE FROM UNIVERSAL MUSIC ENTERPRISES/PHOTO FROM THE CARNEGIE HALL ARCHIVES • 166: Alabama State Troopers move in on John Lewis and other would-be Selma-to-Montgomery marchers and break up their march, Selma, Alabama, March 7, 1965: © TOPFOTO/THE IMAGE WORKS • 167: Dr. Martin Luther King, Jr., watches President Lyndon Johnson on the television as he delivers voting rights speech, March, 1965: FRANK DANDRIDGE/THE LIFE IMAGES COLLECTION/GETTY IMAGES • 171: The family of Dr. Martin Luther King, Jr., walk in the funeral procession of the slain civil rights leader, Atlanta, April 9, 1968: DON HOGAN CHARLES/ THE NEW YORK TIMES/REDUX • 172: President Richard Nixon meets with Elvis Presley in the Oval Office, December 21, 1970: RICHARD NIXON PRESIDENTIAL LIBRARY AND MUSEUM, NARA • 174: President Richard Nixon plays the piano during the dedication of the Grand Ole Opry March 16, 1974: DAVID HUME KENNERLY/ HULTON ARCHIVE/GETTY IMAGES • 175: Merle Haggard: HENRY DILTZ/CORBIS/GETTY IMAGES • 178: American soldiers uncover a Vietcong tunnel during the Vietnam War, 1968: UNIVERSAL HISTORY ARCHIVE/UIG/GETTY IMAGES • 179: Staff Sergeant Barry Sadler on the sleeve cover of the 45 RPM record of "The Ballad of the Green Berets" and "Letter from Vietnam," 1966: BLANK ARCHIVES/HULTON ARCHIVE/GETTY IMAGES AND COURTESY OF SONY MUSIC ENTERTAINMENT/RCA VICTOR AND THE DOG AND PHONOGRAPH LOGOS ARE REGISTERED TRADEMARK OWNED BY RCA TRADEMARK MANAGEMENT • 181: Pete Seeger plays in front of Capitol Hill, Washington, D.C., November, 1969: STEPHEN NORTHUP/THE WASHINGTON POST/GETTY IMAGES • 183: British rock group the Animals, performing on the set of a television program, 1966: HULTON ARCHIVE/GETTY IMAGES • 184: James Brown performs for American soldiers in Vietnam, June 1, 1968: CHRISTIAN SIMONPIÉTRI/SYGMA/GETTY IMAGES • 184: Aretha Franklin, circa 1960s: SKR PHOTOSHOT/EVERETT COLLECTION • 186: Protester faces down riot police at an anti–Vietnam War demonstration outside the Democratic National Convention, Chicago, August, 1968: HULTON ARCHIVE/GETTY IMAGES • 189: Album cover of *Ragged Old Flag* by Johnny Cash, 1974: COURTESY OF SONY MUSIC ENTERTAINMENT • 191: Elvis Presley performing on the Elvis comeback TV special, 1968: MICHAEL OCHS ARCHIVES/GETTY IMAGES • 195: Jimi Hendrix playing at the Woodstock Music and Art Fair, Bethel, New York, August 18, 1969: HENRY DILTZ/ CORBIS/GETTY IMAGES • 200: New York City firemen and rescue workers at the World Trade Center in New York City, September 14, 2001: EVERETT COLLECTION • 202: Bruce Springsteen sings "Born in the U.S.A." in Los Angeles, September, 1985: LENNOX MCLENDON/AP IMAGES • 210: President Ronald Reagan in the Oval Office as he delivers his televised farewell address to the nation, Washington, D.C., January 11, 1989: RONALD REAGAN LIBRARY/GETTY IMAGES • 212: Lee Greenwood performs at the centennial birthday celebration for former U.S. president Ronald Reagan at the Reagan Presidential Library, Simi Valley, California, February 6, 2011: ROBYN BECK/AFP/GETTY IMAGES • 213: Tupac Shakur poses at a portrait session for *Rolling Stone* magazine, 1996: DANNY CLINCH/CONTOUR/GETTY IMAGES • 215: The second tower of the World Trade Center explodes, September 11, 2001: REUTERS/SARA K. SCHWITTEK • 216: President George W. Bush with retired firefighter Bob Beckwith at the scene of the World Trade Center disaster on September 14, 2001: REUTERS/WIN MCNAMEE • 221: Portrait of the Dixie Chicks that appeared on the cover of *Entertainment Weekly* in May, 2003: JAMES WHITE/TRUNK ARCHIVE • 223: Presidential candidate Barack Obama, his wife Michelle, and their daughters Sasha and Malia walk out to greet the crowd following Obama's speech at the Democratic National Convention, 2008: YOON S. BYUN/THE BOSTON GLOBE/GETTY IMAGES • 226: Duke Ellington on the front lawn at the White House Arts Festival, photographed by Marion Trikosko, June 14, 1965: GRANGER • Back endpaper: Navy CPO Graham Jackson plays "Goin' Home" as President Franklin Roosevelt's body is carried from the Warm Springs Foundation, Warm Springs, Georgia, April, 1945: ED CLARK/THE LIFE PICTURE COLLECTION/GETTY IMAGES

SONG LYRIC CREDITS

Grateful acknowledgment is made to the following for permission to reprint both unpublished and previously published material:

INDEX

Page numbers of illustrations and their captions appear in italics.
Song titles appear within quotation marks.

Abernathy, Ralph, 169
abolitionism, 45, 51–53, 63, 65, 85, 98
ACLU (American Civil Liberties Union), 112
Acuff, Roy, 175
Adams, Abigail, 18, 20, *21*, 32
    "Remember the ladies," 7, 24, 95, 239n24
Adams, John, *6*, 7, 10, 18, 20–21, *21*, 24, 27, 29, 31, 42,
    238n19
"Adams and Liberty," 28–29, 40
Addams, Jane, 100
Address to the Inhabitants of the British Settlements in America,
    upon Slave-Keeping (Rush), 25
African Americans
    anti-lynching laws and, 126–27
    communal expression of "I" and, 44
    Ellington speech and, 229
    masking, 57, 154
    music of, 44, 53–57, 130, *131*, 133, 149–50, 243n54
    sorrow songs, 53, 54, 149
    See also civil rights movement; equality; slaves and
        slavery; *specific people*
"Age of Aquarius, The," 176, *177*
Ager, Milton, 122
"Ain't Gonna Let Nobody Turn Me Around," 152
"Alabama," 164
Albany, Ga., 148, 149
Albany Movement, 152
Alien and Sedition Acts, 28
All in the Family (TV show), 176
    Archie Bunker character, 176
"All My Trials," 198–99
Al Qaeda, 214–15
"America" ("My Country 'Tis of Thee"), *x*, 42–47, *44*,
    50–51, 107, 157
    abolitionist versions, 45

    communal expression of "I" and, 44, 47
    debut of, 44–45
    King's "I Have a Dream" speech and, 158, *159*
    lyrics, 43
    McGraw's commentary, 46
    sung by Marian Anderson, 130, 158
    tune for, 42, 46
"America, Why I Love Her," 176
"America: A Tribute to Heroes" (TV special),
    217–18
American Century, 176
American flag
    commissioning and designing of, 41–42
    as cultural emblem, 41
    for Fort McHenry, 35, 36, *38*, 38, 40
    songs about, 41, 79–81, 109–10, *110*, 187–90,
        189
American identity, 10, 35, 36, 41, 111
American Revolution, 12, 15–16, 18
    American flag and, 41
    as a "band of brothers," 32, 33
    battles of Lexington and Concord, 15, 17
    Civil War as redemptive test of, 88
    the Enlightenment and, 23
    as God's own cause, 22
    War of 1812 and ratifying, 36–37, 241n36
    See also Colonial America
"American Trilogy, An," 198
    McGraw's commentary, 197
"America the Beautiful," *114*, 114–16, 186, 216, 218
    Charles's version, 116
    lyrics, 114–16
    McGraw's commentary, 115
    tune for, 114
Amherst College, 164–65

Anderson, Marian, 119, 127–32, 158, 228
  with Eleanor Roosevelt, *128*
  Lincoln Memorial concert, 128–32, 253n129
  March on Washington (1963) and, 158–59
  McGraw's commentary, 131
  Met debut, 132
  voice of, 128–29
Anderson, Robert, 33
Andrews Sisters, 142
Animals, The (group), 173
  "We Gotta Get Out of This Place," 181, *183*
"Annie Laurie," 91
Anthony, Susan B., *95*, 96–98, 115, 248n98
anti-war songs, *112*, 112–13, 146, 176, 179, 180–81, 196
Appeal to the Colored Citizens of the World (Walker), *52*, 52–53
Armistead, George, 35, 38
Armstrong, Louis, 74
Artistotle, 4
Association (singing group), 179
Atlantic Monthly, The, 76–77, *77*
Atta, Mohammed, 213–14
Avedon, Richard, 227

Baez, Joan, 74, 145, 146, 155, *156*, 156, 194
Baker, Russell, 156
Baldwin, James, 160
"Ballad of the Green Berets, The," 178–79, *179*, 230
  McGraw's commentary, 180
Baltimore Patriot and Evening Advertiser, "Defense of Fort Henry," 40
Barnes, Bart, 131
Bates, Katharine Lee, *114*
  "America the Beautiful," 114–16, 216
  McGraw's commentary, 115
"Battle Cry of Freedom, The," 69, 70
  McGraw's commentary, 78
"Battle Hymn, The" (Stauffer and Soskis), 217
"Battle Hymn of the Republic, The," 63, 69, 74, *75*, 75–77, *77*, 149, 171, *171*, 186, 198, 199, 204–5, 217, 230
  lyrics, 76, 217
  McGraw's commentary, 78, 197
  tune for, 74–75, 197
  versions of, black soldiers and, 77
Beamer, Todd, 218

Beanes, William, 36
Beatles, 190
Beecher, Catharine, "Circular Addressed to the Benevolent Ladies of the U. States," 48
Belafonte, Harry, 170
Bell, William, 159, 160
Benny, Jack, 186
Berlin, Irving, *118*, 138–40, 187, 208
  "God Bless America," *119*, 125, *125*, 140, 176, 187, 216
  "Oh, How I Hate to Get Up in the Morning," 139
  This Is the Army, 139–40, 255n140
  "This Time," 140
  Yip, Yip, Yaphank, 139
Bernstein, Leonard, 190, *191*, 198
  Candide, 228
Berry, Chuck, 154, 192
  "Johnny B. Goode," 155
  "Promised Land," 154
Bethune, Mary McLeod, 131
Beyoncé, 106
bin Laden, Osama, 214
Birmingham, Ala., 159–62
  Baptist Church bombing, 145, 148, 159–64, *160*
Blacc, Aloe, 106
Black, Brown and Beige (Ellington), 228–29
Black, Hugo L., 129
blackface minstrel stage, 79, 81, *82*, 85, 93, 106
Black Power Movement, 168, 181
Blakey, Art, "Freedom Rider," 164
Blige, Mary J., 169
"Blowin' in the Wind," 150, 153, 156
  McGraw's commentary, 158
"Blow Ye the Trumpet, Blow!," 63, 89–90
"Blue Moon of Kentucky," 190–91
Bobetsky, Victor V., 150
Bon Jovi, 218
"Bonnie Blue Flag," 82–85, *84*
"Boogie Woogie Bugle Boy," 142
Book of American Negro Spirituals, The (J. R. Johnson), 133
Boone, Pat, 185
"Born in the U.S.A.," *202*, 203, 230
  McGraw's commentary, 209
"Born This Way," 197
Boyce, William, "Heart of Oak," 9
Braddock, Bobby, 198
Bradford, Sarah H., *Harriet Tubman,* 58–59

Bradley, Doug, *We Gotta Get Out of This Place*, 178–79, 182, 184
Branch, Ben, 170
Brando, Marlon, 170–71
"Bridge Over Troubled Water," 185, 218
"Bring Them Home," 180
Brodie, Jeffrey L., *The Star-Spangled Banner*, 37
Brooks, Barbara, 224
Brooks, Kix, 223–24
    "Only in America," 223–24
Brooks, Noah, 88
"Brother, Can You Spare a Dime?," 123–24, 230
    McGraw's commentary, 124
Brown, H. Rap, 169
Brown, James, 169, 181–82, *184*
    "Papa's Got a Brand New Bag," 181
    "Please Please Please," 182
    "Say It Loud—I'm Black and I'm Proud," 181
Brown, Lawrence, 133
Browne, C. A., 33, 46
Brown v. Board of Education, 193
Bruce, Edward, 130
Bryan, Alfred, 112, *112*
Bullitt, William, 133
Burdon, Eric, 183
Burke, Edmund, 12, 30
Burr, Aaron, 22
Burton, Nat, 135
Bush, George H. W., 203
Bush, George W., *201, 216*, 216–17, 220–23, *221*

Calder, Alexander, 227
Campbell, Glen, 181, 182
Candide (Bernstein), 228
Cannon, Lou, 205
Cantwell, David, 153–54
Capa, Robert, 227
Capri, Dick, 177
Carey, Mariah, 218
Carlile, Brandi, 197
    "The Joke," 197
Carmichael, Stokely, 169
Carson, Wayne, 198
Carter, Jimmy, 205
Cash, Johnny, 187, 189–90
    "Drive On," 190
    hits from the 1950s and 1960s, 187
    McGraw's commentary, 188
    "Ragged Old Flag," 187–90, *189*
    "Singin' in Vietnam Talkin' Blues," 187
Cash, June Carter, 188
Cass, Lewis, 49, 50
"Chain Gang," 153
"Chain of Fools," 184
Challenge to Isolation, The (Langer and Gleason), 134
"Change Is Gonna Come, A," *153*, 153–54
    McGraw's commentary, 154
Change Is Gonna Come (Werner), 168–69
Charles, Ray, 116, 154
    "Georgia On My Mind," 155
Chasing Rainbows (film), 122
Chicago Tribune, on music for 9/11 service, 217
Child of Our Time, A (Tippett), 133
Choctaw Nation, 48, 242n48
Churchill, Winston, xiii, 108–9, 133–37, *135*, 164, 206, 259n164
    Atlantic Conference, 136–37, *138*, 254n136
    on FDR, 123
Church's Flight into the Wilderness, The (Sherwood), 22
"Circular Addressed to the Benevolent Ladies of the U. States" (Beecher), 48
civil rights movement, 44, 131, 145–71, 181
    Anderson's Lincoln Memorial concert, 131–32
    assassination of Medgar Evers, 148, 161, 163
    Baptist Church bombing, 145, 148, 159–64, *160*
    Black Power Movement and, 168
    "Bloody Sunday," *166*, 166
    Freedom Rides, 154
    integration of University of Alabama, 148
    LBJ address (March 15, 1965), 166–68, *167*
    legislative achievements, 196
    "Lift Every Voice and Sing" and, 106
    March on Washington (1963), 47, 107, 131, *144*, 151, *155*, *156*, 156–59, *157*, *159*
    nonviolent civil disobedience and, 168
    as powered by song, 148–49
    Selma march (1965), 165–66
    SNCC Freedom Singers, 44
    songs of, 146, 148, 150, 153, 155–56
    "We Shall Overcome" as anthem of, 148, 150
Civil War, 33, 68–93
    Antietam, *72*, 73
    casualties, 67
    Confederate attack on Fort Sumter, 68
    earliest song of the war, 68
    Emancipation Proclamation, *72*, 73, *73*
    the "fiery trial," 67, *72*

Civil War (cont'd):
    Lee's surrender at Appomattox Court House, 90
    Lincoln and, 67, 67–68, 90
    music of, 63, 68–93, 149, 198
    Sherman's march through Georgia, 85–86
    Secession Winter, 82
    white supremacy and, 100
Clark, Septima, 150
Clarke, James Freeman, 75
Cleaver, Eldridge, 169
Clinton, William J. "Bill," 193–94, 214
Clurman, Richard, 190
Cochrane, Alexander, 37
Cohan, George M., 109–12, 110, 125, 208
Cold War, 206, 227
Cole, Bob, 103
Collins, Addie Mae, 159, 160
Collins, J. Quincy, "The POW Hymn," 187
Colonial America, xiii, 7–8, 12–15, 17–18
    decision to declare independence, 12, 18, 24
    earliest popular American soldier-song, 12–13
    "The Liberty Song" as call to action, 8–11
    "Olive Branch Petition," 17
    "The Pennsylvania Song," 14
    Stamp Act, 13
Coltrane, John, 164
    "Alabama," 164
"Come Sunday," 229
"Come to My Window," 197
Common Sense (Paine), 3, 17, 22
Confederate States of America, 65–67
    anthem for, 82
    "Bonnie Blue Flag," 82
    common identity for, 81–82, 84
    principles of '76 and, 85
    songs of, 81–85
Continental Congress, 18, 24
    national motto adopted by, 41
Cook, Don, 224
Cooke, Sam, 153
    "A Change Is Gonna Come," 153, 153–54
    hits of, 153
    McGraw's commentary, 154
    Rock & Roll Hall of Fame and, 153, 153
Cooper, George, 79
Copley, John Singleton, 17
Copway, George, 50
    "dream song" of, 50
    The Life, History, and Travels of Kah-ge-ga-gah-bowh, 50

Cornelius, Steven H., 82
counterculture, 174, 177, 185, 190
    protests (July 4, 1970), 185–86
country music, 175, 182, 218, 221–22
"Courtesy of the Red, White and Blue (The Angry
    American)," 218, 220–21
Crawford, Richard, 49, 50
Creedence Clearwater Revival, 195
    "Fortunate Son," 179, 182, 230
Crisis, The, magazine, 107
Cropper, Steve, "The Dock of the Bay," 185
Crosby, Bing, 123, 142, 193
Crosby, Stills, and Nash, 185, 195
Cross, Charles R., Room Full of Mirrors, 196
Crow, Sheryl, 218
Crudup, Arthur, 192
    "That's All Right," 190
Cuban Missile Crisis, 145, 146–47
Cuomo, Mario, 209–10, 211

Damone, Vic, 186
"Dancing in the Street," 155
Dark Midnight When I Rise (Ward), 92–93
"Daughters of Freedom, the Ballot Be Yours,"
    95–96
Davis, Jefferson, 82
Davis, Sammy, Jr., 171, 186
"Dear Uncle Sam," 176
"Death of Emmett Till, The," 146
Declaration of Independence, 3, 14, 18, 19, 238n19
    abolitionism and, 51
    celebration of date, 18
    as founding prose hymn, 5
    as a promissory American text, 102
    read to the Continental Army, 18–19
    "We hold these truths," 6, 19
"Deep River," 133
de Kooning, Willem, 227
De La Beckwith, Byron, 148
Democratic National Convention (1976), 196–97
Des Moines, Iowa, 119–20
Deterrent or Defense (Hart), 147
Dicey, Edward, 92
Dickinson, John, 8–9, 18, 186
    Letters from a Farmer, 8, 11
    "The Liberty Song," 7, 8–11, 41, 46, 47, 113, 230
DiMaggio, Joe, 179
Dion, Celine, 218

"Dixie." *See* "I Wish I Was in Dixie's Land," 198
Dixie Chicks, 218, 220–22, *221,* 266n220
   "Not Ready to Make Nice," 222
"Dock of the Bay, The," 185
"Dogs of Alabama, The," 153
Domestic Manners of the Americans (Trollope), 47
Donaldson, Sam, 206
"Don't Sit Under the Apple Tree," 142
Douglass, Frederick, *62, 63,* 64, 67, 69, 88, 133
   favorite hymn, 63, 89
   Jubilee Singers and, 93
   on Lincoln, 91–92
   *Narrative of the Life of Frederick Douglass, an American
      Slave,* 54–55, 63
Down the Highway (Sounes), 147
Drifters, 183
"Drive On," 190
Du Bois, W. E. B., 53–54, *101,* 101–2, *104–5,* 106,
   107
   The Souls of Black Folk, 54
Duncan, Todd, 130
Dunn, Ronnie, 223–24
Dusenberry, Phil, 208
"Dust Bowl Blues," 119, 125
Dvořák, Antonin, 243n54
Dylan, Bob, 127, 145–46, 147, 151–54, *156,* 192
   "Blowin' in the Wind," 150, 153, 156, 158
   "The Death of Emmett Till," 146
   "With God on Our Side," 146
   "A Hard Rain's A-Gonna Fall," 146
   "Only a Pawn in Their Game," 148, 156
   "The Times They Are A-Changin'," 146
Dyson, Michael Eric, 212, 213

Ed Sullivan Show (TV show), 177–78, 193
Eisenhower, Dwight D., 146, 193
Ellington, Duke, *226,* 228–29
   Black, Brown and Beige, 228–29
   "Come Sunday," 229
   speech of 1941, 229
   "Take the A Train," 228
Ellison, Ralph, 227–28
Emmett, Daniel Decatur, 81, *82*
   "I Wish I Was in Dixie's Land," 81, *82,* 199, 230
Enlightenment, 23, 65
Entertainment Weekly, Dixie Chicks cover, *221,* 221
"E Pluribus Unum," 42
"Elton's Song," 197

equality, 26–27, 100, *101,* 101–2, 126–32, *128*
   See also civil rights movement
Espionage Act of 1917, 112
Etheridge, Melissa, 197
   "Come to My Window," 197
Evans, Walker, 124, 227
Evarts, Jeremiah, 48
   "Present Crisis in the Condition of the American
      Indians," 48
Evers, Medgar, 148, 161
Evers, Myrlie, 148
"Everyday," 218
Ezell, Lorenza, 86

"Fables for Faubus," 164
"Farewell Song of Frederick Douglass," 63, 64, 67
"Father, Father Abraham," 107
Faulkner, William, 4
Federalism, 27, 28, 29
   "Adams and Liberty," 28–29
Federalist Papers, 21
Ferguson, Robert A., 23, 239n22
Ferraro, Geraldine, 203
Fields, James, 76–77, *77*
5th Dimension, 177
"Fightin' Side of Me, The," 175
"First Gun Is Fired, The," 68
Fisk University, 92
   Jubilee Singers, 92–93, 150
Fitzgerald, Ella, 142
Fletcher, Andrew, 4
Flippo, Chet, 221–22
"Flying Home," 142
Fogerty, John, 179, 180
folk song, 124, 151
Forgy, Frank, 138
"For the Dear Old Flag I Die!," 79–81
Fort McHenry, 36–38, 138
   flag for, 35, 36, *38,* 38, 40
Fort Sumter, 68
"Fortunate Son," 179, 182, 230
   McGraw's commentary, 180
Foster, Stephen C., 79
   famous songs of, 79–81
   "For the Dear Old Flag I Die!," 79–81
   McGraw's commentary, 80
   "Was My Brother in the Battle?," 79
Founding Fathers, 7, 12, 20, 61

Four Tops, 177, 179
Fox, Gilbert, 31, 33
"Fragile," 218
Franklin, Aretha, 168, 169, 171, *184,* 184–85
   "Chain of Fools," 184
   "A Natural Woman," 169
   "Respect," 168–69
Franklin, Benjamin, *6,* 238n19
Freed, Alan, 152
"Freedom Now Suite," 164
"Freedom Rider," 164
Freedom Singers, 152, 156
   "Ain't Gonna Let Nobody Turn Me Around,"
     152
Frost, Robert, 164, 165
"Fuck tha Police," 213
funk music, 182

"Galveston," 181
   McGraw's commentary, 182
Garfunkel, Art, 179
   "Bridge Over Troubled Water," 185
   "Homeward Bound," 185
   "Mrs. Robinson," 179
Garrison, William Lloyd, 51, *51*
Gaye, Marvin, "What's Going On," 196
George III, King of England, 17–18
George VI, King of England, 108
"Georgia On My Mind," 155
Gershwin, George, *Porgy and Bess,* 228
Geyl, Pieter, 238n21
Gibbons, James Sloan, 77–78, 246n77
GI Bill, 193
"Give Peace a Chance," 176
"Give the Ballot to the Mothers," 99–100
Gleason, S. Everett, 134
"Glitter and Be Gay," 228
"God Bless America," *118,* 125, *125,* 140, 176, 185, 187,
   204, 205, 216, 218
"God Bless the U.S.A.," 207–9, *212,* 230
   McGraw's commentary, 209
   as Reagan-Bush reelection anthem, 208
"Go Down Moses," 58–59, 73–74, 133, 149
   McGraw's commentary, 74
"God Save the King," 42, 46
Goffin, Gerry, 169
"Going Home," 142
Goldstein, Richard, 146

Goldwater, Barry, 205, 206
Goodman, Benny, 142
Goodwin, Richard, 228
Gore, Al, 221
Gore, Lesley, "You Don't Own Me," 197
Gorney, Jay, 123
Graff, George, Jr., 112
Graham, Billy, 185, 217
Grandmaster Flash and the Furious Five, "The
   Message," 212
Grant, Ulysses S., 3, 90, 92, 97
Grapes of Wrath (Steinbeck), 124
Great Depression, 119, 120, 121–25, *123*
Greeley, Horace, 97
Green, Grant, 166
   "The Selma March," 166
"Green, Green Grass of Home," 181
   McGraw's commentary, 182
Green Berets, The (film), 178
Greenwood, Lee, 207, 208–9, *212*
   "God Bless the U.S.A.," 207–9, *212,* 230
   McGraw's commentary, 209
Grenville, George, 13
Griffin, Merv, 208
Griffiths, Julia, 63
Griffiths, T. Powis, 63
Guns of August (Tuchman), 147
Guthrie, Woody, 124–27, *126,* 143, 153
   "Dust Bowl Blues," 119, 125
   McGraw's commentary, 127
   "This Land Is Your Land," 125–26, *126*

Haggard, Merle, 174
   "The Fightin' Side of Me," 175
   McGraw's commentary, 177
   "Okie from Muskogee," 174, *175,* 175, 177
"Hail Columbia," *21,* 31–33, *32,* 41, 47, 82, 87
   initial title, 33
   lyrics, 31–32
Hair (Broadway musical), 176, 177
Hale, Alan, 139
Haley, Bill, 192
Hall, Rene, 153
Hall, Tom T., 198
Hamilton, Alexander, 27
"Hammer Song, The," 156
Hammerstein, Oscar, 154
Hampton, Lionel, 142

Hancock, John, 7, 8
Hanson, Peter, 215–16
"Happy Days Are Here Again," *121,* 121–23, 230
Harburg, E. Y. "Yip," 123
"Hard Rain's A-Gonna Fall, A," 146
Harper, Ida Husted, 97
Harriet Tubman (Bradford), 58–59
Harris, Rutha, 152
Harrison, Joseph, 7–8
Hart, B. H. Liddell, *Deterrent or Defense,* 147
Hartigan, Grace, 227
Havens, Richie, 146
Hazard, Rebecca Naylor, 99
"Heart of Oak," 9
Hendrix, Jimi, *195,* 195–96
Henry S. Washburn, "The Vacant Chair," 68–69
Herbers, John, 176
"Hero," 218
Hersey, John, 228
"He's Got the Whole World in His Hands," 131,
    158–59
  McGraw's commentary, 131
Heston, Charlton, 228
Highlander Folk School, 150
Hilburn, Robert, *Johnny Cash,* 187
Hill, Faith, 218
hip-hop music, 211–12, *213*
Hiroshima (Hersey), 228
His Majesty King Funk (album), 166
Hitchcock, Alfred, 227
Hitler, Adolf, 132–33, 134
HMS Romney, 7, 8
Holiday, Billie, 127
Holmes, Oliver Wendell, Jr., 43–44, 47, 69, 130
"Homeward Bound," 185
Hoover, J. Edgar, 112, 193
Hope, Bob, 185, 186
Hopkinson, Francis, 30
Hopkinson, Joseph, 28
  "Hail Columbia," *21,* 31–33, *32,* 41, 47, 82, 87
Hopper, Edward, 227
Horne, Lena, 127
Horton, Zilphia, 150
Howard, Sir Michael, 229
Howe, Julia Ward, *75,* 77, 98–99, 169
  "The Battle Hymn of the Republic," 74, 75–77, *77,*
    78, 199, 217, 230
  McGraw's commentary, 78
"How I Got Over," 156

Hughes, Karen, 217
Hughes, Langston, ix, 160, 229
Humphrey, Hubert H., 170
Hunt, Ward, 98
Hutchinson Family Singers, 69–70

"I, Too" (Hughes), 229
"I Am a Woman," 197
"I Been 'Buked and I Been Scorned," 156
"I Believe in Love," 218
Ice-T, "Squeeze the Trigger," 213
Ickes, Harold, 129, 253n129
"I Didn't Raise My Boy to Be a Soldier," 112, *112*
  McGraw's commentary, 113
I'd Rather Be Right (Broadway play), 109
"If I Can Help Somebody," 170
Iglesias, Enrique, 218
"I Have a Dream" (King), 151
"I'll Be All Right," 150
"I'll Be Like Him Someday," 150
"I'll Overcome Someday," 150
"Imagine," 218
"I'm a Yankee Doodle Boy," 109
"I'm Coming Out," 197
"I'm On My Way," 156
Impressions, 154, 155
"Into the Fire," 219
Iraq War, 215, 220, *221*
"It's Like That," 211–12
"I Was Made to Love Her," 155
"I Will Overcome," 150
"I Wish I Was in Dixie's Land," 81, *82, 87,* 198, 230
  as anthem of the Confederacy, *82*
  lyrics, 81
  McGraw's commentary, 83, 198, 199
"I Won't Back Down," 218

Jackson, Alan, *215*
  "Where Were You (When the World Stopped
    Turning)?," 218
Jackson, Andrew, xiii, 35, *37,* 46, 53
Jackson, Graham, 142
Jackson, Mahalia, 57, 156–57, 170
Jackson, Otis, 143
Jackson, Thomas "Stonewall," 85
Jay Z, 212, 213
Jean, Wyclef, 218

Jefferson, Thomas, xiii, 5, *20*, 23, 27, 29, 30–31, 66, 90, 129, 238n19, 241n36
    death of, 42
    Declaration of Independence, 3, 5, *6*, 19, 238n19
"Jefferson and Liberty," 29–30
"Jimmy Mack," 181
Joel, Billy, "New York State of Mind," 218
Joffrey Ballet, 228
"John Brown's Body," 69, 74–75, 93, 149, 198
John, Elton, 197
    "Elton's Song," 197
"Johnny B. Goode," 155
Johnny Cash (Hilburn), 187
Johns, Jasper, 227
Johnson, James Weldon, 102–8, *103, 104–5,* 133
    "Father, Father Abraham," 107
    "Lift Every Voice and Sing," 103–8
Johnson, J. Rosamond, *103,* 103
    The Book of American Negro Spirituals, 133
    "Lift Every Voice and Sing," *103,* 103, 108
Johnson, Lady Bird, 227
Johnson, Lyndon B. (LBJ), 176, 180
    address (March 15, 1965), 166–68, *167*
    Great Society, 205
    White House Festival of Arts, 227–29, 230
Johnson, Samuel, 63–64
"Joke, The," 197
Jones, Tom, 181
Joplin, Janis, 195
    "Me and Bobby McGee," 197
Jordan, Barbara, 196–97
Jubilee Singers, 92–93, 150
Jubilee Songs (T. Seward), 93
Just, Ward, 179
"Just Because I'm a Woman," 197

Kazan, Elia, 227
Keith, Toby, 220–21, 222
    "Courtesy of the Red, White and Blue (The Angry American)," 218, 220–21
Kelly, Gene, 228
Kendrick, Kathleen M., *The Star-Spangled Banner,* 37
Kennan, George F., 227
Kennedy, Jacqueline, 147, 170
Kennedy, John F., 22
    Amherst College speech, 164–65
    assassination of, 165
    Bay of Pigs and, 146

burial in Arlington, 165
    Cuban missile crisis and, 145, 146–47
    Profiles in Courage, 147
    Why England Slept, 147
Kennedy, Robert F., 126, 145, 170, 179
Kent, Walter, 135
Kent State University, 185
Kern, Jerome, 154
Keteltas, Abraham, 22
Key, Francis Scott, 33, 36–40, 47, 67, 87, 102
    McGraw's commentary, 41
    "The Star-Spangled Banner," 33, 38–41, *39*
Keys, Alicia, 218
Khachigian, Ken, 205
Khrushchev, Nikita, 145, 147
King, B. B., 152, 192
King, Carole, 152, 169
    A Natural Woman, 152
King, Coretta Scott, *171*
King, Martin Luther, Jr., 20, 149, 151, 169
    assassination of, 151, 169
    Baptist Church bombing funeral and, 163–64
    epitaph, 171
    final public words, 169–70
    funeral, 170–71, *171*
    funeral service songs, 170, 171
    "I Have a Dream" speech, 151, 157–58
    LBJ address (March 15, 1965) and, *167,* 168
    March on Washington (1963) and, 47, 156–57, *159*
    "songs are the *soul* of a movement," 145, 149
    "We Shall Overcome" and, 150, 151
Kissinger, Henry, 176
Kitt, Eartha, 171
Klinkenborg, Verlyn, 218
Klush, Shawn, 198
Korean War, 176
Kraft, Joseph, 176
Kristofferson, Kris, 198
Ku Klux Klan, 100, 160, 163, 168

labor movement, 150, 151
Lady Gaga, 197
    "Born This Way," 197
Landon, Alfred, 119
Lange, Dorothea, 124
Langer, William L., 134
Lauryn Hill, 212
Lear, Norman, 176

Lee, Arthur, 8–9
Lennon, John, "Give Peace a Chance," 176
Leslie, Joan, 139
"Let's Roll," 218
Letters from a Farmer in Pennsylvania (Dickinson), 8, 11
"Let the Sunshine In," 177
"Let Us Have Peace," 112–13
Lewis, Jerry Lee, 192
Lewis, John, 148, 151, 162, 165–66, 168
Liberator, The, 51, *51*
"Liberty Song, The," 7, 8–11, *15*, 41, 46, 47, 113, 230
　　lyrics, 9–10
　　McGraw's commentary, 11
　　music for, 9, 11
Life, History, and Travels of Kah-ge-ga-gah-bowh, The (Copway), 50
"Lift Every Voice and Sing," 103–8, 133
　　McGraw's commentary, 106
Limp Bizkit, 218
Lincoln, Abraham, 103, 129, 208, 253n129
　　"The Battle Cry of Freedom" and, 70
　　"The Battle Hymn of the Republic" and, 63, 77
　　"the better angels of our nature," 4
　　call for soldiers, 77–78
　　on Civil War, 90–91
　　Emancipation Proclamation, *72,* 73, *73*
　　favorite song, 88
　　the "fiery trial," 67, *72*
　　Gettysburg Address, 88–89
　　"half slave and half free," 61
　　"I Wish I Was in Dixie's Land" and, 81, 83
　　on Jefferson, 20
　　"the last best hope of earth," xiii
　　love of music, 88
　　Second Annual Message to Congress, 67–68
　　Second Inaugural Address, 90, 91
　　slavery and, 70–73
　　songs about, 77–79, 91, 107, 246n77
Lindbergh, Charles, 133
Lindley, Ernest K., 130, 131–32
Little Richard, 152, 192
Livingston, Robert R., 238n19
"Livin' on a Prayer," 218
Loesser, Frank, 138
"Lonesome Day," 220
"Long Road," 218
"Long Sought Home," 48, 242n48
Louis, Joe, 139, 140
"Love's in Need of Love Today," 217

Lowell, Robert, 227
Lowery, Joseph, 107
Luce, Henry, 176, 190
Lynn, Loretta
　　"Dear Uncle Sam," 176
　　"The Pill," 197
Lynn, Vera, *137, 139*

Macarthy, Harry, 82, *84,* 85
Macdonald, Dwight, 227
Maddox, Lester, 171
Madison, James, 21, 27
Maguire, Martie, 222
Maier, Pauline, 238n19
Maines, Natalie, 220, 221, 222
Malcolm X, 168, 259n168
Man in Black (album), 188
Mann, Barry, 183
　　"On Broadway," 183
　　"We Gotta Get Out of This Place," 183
　　"You've Lost That Lovin' Feelin'," 183
"Many Thousands Gone," 150
"Marching Through Georgia," 69, 99
March on Washington (1963), 107, *144,* 151, *155,* 155–59, *156, 157, 159*
　　songs of, 155–56
Margolick, David, 127
Martha and the Vandellas, "Jimmy Mack," 181
Martin, Phyllis, 148
Martin, Roberta Evelyn, 150
Martineau, Harriet, *Society in America,* 47, 67
Martinez, John, 184
"Materna," 114
Matthews, Dave, 218
Mayfield, Curtis, 154–55, 196
　　"Keep on Pushing," 154–55
Mays, Benjamin, 107
May We Forever Stand (Perry), 107–8
McCabe, Charles, 77
McCabe, John, 111
McClellan, George B., *72*
McCloy, John J., 164–65
McGovern, George, 173
McNair, Denise, 159, 160, *160*
McWhirter, Christian, 68
"Me and Bobby McGee," 197
Meeropol, Abel, 127
Melgard, Al, 122

Merchant of Venice (Shakespeare), 5
"Message, The," 212
"Middle Americans," 176
"Mighty Fortress Is Our God, A" (hymn), 216
Miller, Arthur, 227
Miller, Glenn, 142–43
Mingus, Charles, "Fables for Faubus," 164
"Mississippi Goddam," 145, 160–63, *162*
    lyrics, 162
    McGraw's commentary, 163
Mitchell, Joni, 195
    "Woodstock," 195
Mitchum, John, "America, Why I Love Her," 176
"Model of Christian Charity, A" (Winthrop), 22
Mondale, Walter, 203
Monroe, Bill, "Blue Moon of Kentucky," 190–91
Monroe, James, 38
Montalbán, Ricardo, 186–87
Moore, Robin, 178
    "The Ballad of the Green Berets," *179,* 230
Morehouse College, 107
Morgenthau, Henry, Jr., 129, 133
Mormon Tabernacle Choir, 204–5
Morris, Kenneth, "I'll Overcome Someday," 150
Moynihan, Daniel Patrick, 176
"Mrs. Robinson" (Simon and Garfunkel), 179
Murphy, George, 139
Murray, Billy, 113
music
    acknowledgement of self and, 106
    African American, 44, 53–57, 73, 74, 243n54
    of the American Revolution, 8–11, 14, *15,* 17
    anti-war songs, *112,* 112–13, 146, 176, 179, 180–81, 196
    capacity to reassure and remind, 87
    of the civil rights movement, 146, 148, 150, 153, 155–56
    of the Civil War, 63, 68–93, 149, 198
    creating a collective experience, 229–30
    of a divided America, 168–69, 174–98, 220–22
    of equality, 103–8
    of the Great Depression, 121–25
    of history, 3–5
    hymns and religious songs, 136
    as moral call to action, 11
    national anthem and identity, ix, *x,* 4, 8–10, *15,* 31, 33, 38–41, *39,* 46, *87,* 126
    nation-shaping and, 4
    Native American, 3, 24, 47–50

"Negro Songs" (Ethiopian songs), 79
9/11 terrorist attacks and, 217–20, 224
    patriotic songs, 9, 31, 33, 42, *87,* 107, 113, 180, 187, 207–9, 224
    protest songs, 4, 112–13, 146, 150, 154, 203, 209, 213, 220 (*see also* civil rights movement)
    songs and history, 138
    songs speaking to the unifying impulses of the period, 42, 95, 122, 180
    of the Vietnam War, 176, 178–85, 187, 188, *202,* 203, 209
    as a window into human nature, 5
    women's suffrage movement and, 95–96
    of World War I, *108,* 109–13
    of World War II, *125,* 135–43, 149
Music and Some Highly Musical People (Trotter), 243n54
"My City of Ruins," 217, 220
    McGraw's commentary, 219
"My Heavenly Father, Watch Over Me," 170
"My Old Kentucky Home," 79
"My Soul's Been Anchored in the Lord," 130
    McGraw's commentary, 131

NAACP (National Association for the Advancement of Colored People), *102, 104–5,* 106, 107, 129, 148, 149
Narrative of the Life of Frederick Douglass, an American Slave (Douglass), 54–55, 63
Nashville, Tenn., 173, 176
    Grand Ole Opry, 173
    Nixon in, 173–76
    Ryman Auditorium, 173
    Tootsies Orchid Lounge, 173
Nason, Elias, ix, 40, 86–87
national anthem
    "America" ("My Country 'Tis of Thee") as, *x*
    Black National Anthem, 103, 106, 107
    British national anthem, 42
    "Hail Columbia" as, 33
    "The Star-Spangled Banner" as, 40–41
    "This Land Is Your Land" suggested as, 126
"Nation Makers, The" (Pyle), 2
Native Americans, 3, 24, 47–50
    "Long Sought Home," 48, *49,* 242n48
    Miami Indian lyric, 49–50
    "Song of the Earth," 49
    Trail of Tears, 48, *49*
"Natural Woman, A," 169

Natural Woman, A (King), 152
"Navy Hymn" ("Eternal Father"), 136, 165
"Nearer, My God, to Thee," 142
Neblett, Charles, 152
Negro National Hymn, *103,* 103, 106
Nelson, Willie, 218
Nevelson, Luise, 227
Newbury, Mickey, 198
Newsweek
    "All About Impeachment," 173–74
    on King's funeral, 171
Newton, Huey, 169
Newton, Isaac, 4
New Yorker magazine, 116
    Cantwell essay in, 153–54
    Obama interview, 169
"New York State of Mind," 218
New York Times, 95, 120, 132, 142
    assassination of Medgar Evers report, 148
    Baker on "Only a Pawn in Their Game," 156
    on freedom songs, 148–49
    Herbers on Nixon, 176
    on radio and "Blowin' in the Wind," 156
    Reagan's Hammonton, N.J. speech, 203
    Shelton review of Dylan, 145–46
Niagara Movement, 102, *102*
Nicholson, Joseph H., 37
Nichopoulos, George "Nick," 198
9/11 terrorist attacks, xiii, *200,* 201, 213–20, *215, 216*
    final words of Todd Beamer, 218
    musical response to, 217–20, 224
    The Rising, 219
    Washington National Cathedral service, 216–17
"9 to 5," 197
Nixon, Richard M., 170, 173–76, *174, 175,* 179, 185, 187, 190, 194
    Elvis and, *172,* 194
    White House dinner for prisoners of war, 186–87
"Nobody Knows the Trouble I See, Lord," 133
Noguchi, Isamu, 227
"No More Auction Block," 150, 153
"Not Ready to Make Nice," 222
N.W.A., "Fuck tha Police," 213

Obama, Barack, xiii, 107, 116, 126, 152, 169, 213, 214, 222–24, *223*
Odetta, *155,* 156
"O God, Our Help in Ages Past," 136, 216

"Oh, By and By," 133
"Oh, How I Hate to Get Up in the Morning," 139
"Oh Freedom," 148, 153, 155
"Ohio," 185
"Oh! Susanna," 79, 80
"Okie from Muskogee," 174, *175,* 175
    McGraw's commentary, 177
    Nixon lyrics sung to, 175
"Old Folks at Home" ("Swanee River"), 79
"Old Hundred," 87
"Old Uncle Ned," 79
Oliver, Peter, 15, 17
"Ol' Man River," 153–54
"On Being Brought from Africa to America" (Wheatley), 26–27
"On Broadway," 183
"Only a Pawn in Their Game," 148, 156
"Only in America," 223–24
    lyrics, 224–25
    McGraw's commentary, 224
"Onward, Christian soldiers," 136
"O Sanctissima," 150
Otis, James, 8
"Our Day Will Come," 155
"Over There," *108, 110,* 110–11, 149
    McGraw's commentary, 113

Paine, Robert Treat, Jr., 28–29
Paine, Thomas, *Common Sense,* 3, 17, 22
Palmer, A. Mitchell, 112
"Papa's Got a Brand New Bag," 181
Parton, Dolly
    "Just Because I'm a Woman," 197
    "9 to 5," 197
Paxton, Tom, 153
    "The Dogs of Alabama," 153
Payne, Roz, 196
"Peace on Earth," 217
"Pennsylvania Song, The," 14, *15*
    lyrics, 14
Peress, Maurice, 228
Perkins, Carl, 192
Perry, Imani, *May We Forever Stand,* 107–8
Peter, Paul, and Mary, *156*
Peters, Roberta, 228
Phillips, Sam, 190, 192
Pickersgill, Mary Young, 35, *38,* 38
"Pill, The," 197

Plato, 4
Playboy, King interview in, 149
"Please Please Please," 182
"Poems on Various Subjects, Religious and Moral"
    (Wheatley), *26*
Pollard, Edward Alfred, 100
Pollock, Jackson, 227
Porgy and Bess (Gershwin), 228
"POW Hymn, The," 187
"Praise the Lord and pass the ammunition," 138,
    149
"Precious Lord, Take My Hand," 170
"Present Crisis in the Condition of the American
    Indians" (Evarts), 48
Presley, Elvis, *172,* 190–94, *191, 197*
    "An American Trilogy," 198–99
    McGraw's commentary, 198
Pritchett, Laurie, 148
Profiles in Courage (Kennedy), 147
"Promised Land" (Berry), 154
Psalm 19, 90
Putnam, Curly, 182
Pyle, Ernie, 140
Pyle, Howard, "The Nation Makers," *2*

Queen Latifah, 212

"Ragged Old Flag," 187–90, *189*
    lyrics, 187–89
rap music, 182, 211, 212–13
Reagan, Nancy, 208
Reagan, Ronald, 22, 139, 142–43, 201, 203, 204–11
    centennial celebration, *212*
    conservatism and, 205–6
    Cuomo critique of, 209–10
    farewell address, *210,* 211
    FDR and, 120–21, 250n120
    Greenwood's "God Bless the U.S.A." and, 207–9
    "It's Morning in America" campaign, 204, 208,
        212
    music and, 204–5
    "shining city on a hill," 203, 209, 211
    Soviet Union (Russia) and, 206–7
    "The Speech," 205–6
Reagon, Bernice Johnson, 44, 149, 152
Reagon, Toshi, 152
"Rebels, The," 16, 230

Reckless Daughter (Yaffe), 195
Redding, Otis
    "The Dock of the Bay," 185
    "Respect," 168, 185
Reddy, Helen, "I Am a Woman," 197
"Redemption Song," 218
Reed, Julia, 190
Reeves, Martha, "Dancing in the Street," 155
Remnick, David, 116, 169
"Respect," 168, 185
Retz, Cardinal de, 10
Richie, Donald A., 122
Righteous Brothers, 183
"Rights of Woman," 24–25
Rising, The (album), 218–19
    McGraw's commentary, 219
Roach, Max, "Freedom Now Suite," 164
Robertson, Carole, 159, 160, *160*
Robeson, Paul, 154
Robinson, Charles, 242n48
Robinson, Jackie, 171
Rockwell, George Lincoln, 168, 259n168
Rogers, Ronnie, 224
Rogich, Sig, 208
Rolling Stone magazine
    Blige on Franklin, 169
    Charles interview, 116
    Haggard interview, 174
    Springsteen interview, 204
Room Full of Mirrors (Cross), 196
Roosevelt, Eleanor, 126–27, *128,* 143
Roosevelt, Elliot, 137
Roosevelt, Franklin Delano (FDR), xiii, 108–9, 111,
    121, 128, 211
    Atlantic Conference, 136–37, *138,* 254n136
    Churchill on, 123
    death of, 142–43
    Great Depression, 119–23
    New Deal, 122–23, 205
    Reagan and, 120–21, 142–43, 250n120
    "rendezvous with destiny," 206
    theme song, 122
    World War II, 132–34, 136–38
Roosevelt, John, 119
Roosevelt, Theodore, 46
Root, George F.
    "The Battle Cry of Freedom," 69, 70, 78
    "The First Gun Is Fired," 68
    "The Vacant Chair," 68–69

Ross, Diana, 171
    "I'm Coming Out," 197
Rothko, Mark, 227
Ruby and the Romantics, "Our Day Will Come," 155
Run-DMC, 211–12, 213
    "It's Like That," 211–12
Rush, Benjamin, 17
    Address to the Inhabitants of the British Settlements in America, upon Slave-Keeping, 25
Rzeznik, John, 218

Sadler, Barry, 208
    "The Ballad of the Green Berets," 178–79, *179*, 230
    McGraw's commentary, 180
"Safe and Sound," 218
Sandage, Scott A., 131
"Say It Loud—I'm Black and I'm Proud," 181
Schlesinger, Arthur, Jr., 121–22, 134, 238n21
Sedition Act of 1918, 112
Seeger, Pete, 126, 146, 150
    "Bring Them Home," 180, *181*
    "Waist Deep in the Big Muddy," 180, *181*, 184
Selma, Alabama
    Bloody Sunday (1965), 165–66, *166*
    LBJ address (March 15, 1965), 166–68, *167*
"Selma March, The," 166
"Semper Fidelis," 142
Seven Years' War (French and Indian War), 12–13
Seward, Thomas Frelinghuysen, 93
Seward, William H., 61, 93
Shakespeare, William, 4, 33
    Merchant of Venice, 5
Shakur, Tupac, *213*
    "Words of Wisdom," 213
Shelton, Robert, 145–46, 148–49
Sherman, Roger, 238n19
Sherman, William Tecumseh, 85, 113
Sherwood, Samuel, 22, 239n22
    The Church's Flight into the Wilderness, 22
Shore, Dinah, 177, 186
silent majority, *175*, 176, 177
Silverman, Kenneth, 11
Simon, George T., 142
Simon, Paul, 179, 218
    "Bridge Over Troubled Water," 185
    "Homeward Bound," 185
    "Mrs. Robinson," 179

Simone, Nina, 145, 160–63, *161*
    McGraw's commentary, 163
    "Mississippi Goddam," 145, 160–63, *162*
    "Why (The King of Love Is Dead)," 170
Sinatra, Frank, 139, 193
"Singin' in Vietnam Talkin' Blues," 187
    McGraw's commentary, 188
Sitton, Claude, 148
Skelton, Red, 185
slaves and slavery, 24, 25, 35, 47, 51–61, 63–65, 83
    apologists for, 65–67
    Civil War and, 67–68, 89
    Compromise of 1850, 61
    Emancipation Proclamation, *72*, 73, *73*
    Fugitive Slave Act, 61
    Jubilee Singers and songs of, 92–93
    Lincoln and, 70–73
    Lincoln's Second Inaugural Address and, 90, 91
    songs of, 53–58, 69
    sung spirituals as signals, 57–58
    Underground Railroad, 57, *58*, 60–61
    See also abolitionists; Civil War
Smith, Kate, 125, *125*, 140, 185
Smith, Samuel Francis, 42, *44*
    "America," *x*, 42–44, 50–51, 130, 158
Smothers Brothers Comedy Hour, The (TV show), 180
Smyth, John Ferdinand Dalziel, 15–16
    "The Rebels," 16, 230
SNCC (Student Nonviolent Coordinating Committee), 148, 151, 162
Snoop Dogg, 212
"socially aware jazz," 164
Society in America (Martineau), 47, 67
"Sold Off to Georgy [Georgia]," 55
"Someday We'll All Be Free," 218
"Song, On the Death of President Abraham Lincoln," 91
"Song of the Earth," 49
Soskis, Benjamin, 217
soul music, 92, 160, 182
Soul of America, The (Meacham), xiii
Souls of Black Folk, The (Du Bois), 54
Soul Stirrers, The, 153
Sounes, Howard, 146
    Down the Highway, 147
Sousa, John Philip, 142
Southern, Eileen, 73, 77, 79
Springsteen, Bruce, 127, 183, 201–4, *202*, 209
    "Born in the U.S.A.," *202*, 203, 230

Springsteen, Bruce (*cont'd*):
  "Into the Fire," 219
  "Lonesome Day," 220
  McGraw's commentary, 219
  "My City of Ruins," 217, 219, 220
  The Rising, 218–19
Sprong, John, 266n220
"Squeeze the Trigger," 213
Stalin, Joseph, 133
"Stand Up and Cheer for Richard Nixon," 175
sexual identity in songs, 197
Stanton, Elizabeth Cady, *95,* 97, 115
Staple Singers, "When Will We Get Paid," 197
Starr, Edwin, "War," 180
"Stars and Stripes Forever," 142
"Star-Spangled Banner, The," 33, 38, *39,* 40–41, 47, 67, 87, 95, 107, 138, 185
  difficulty of singing, 40, 41
  Hendrix version, *195,* 195–96
  Holmes's new verse, 69
  lyrics, 38–40
  McGraw's commentary, 41
  as national anthem, 40–41
  as a promissory American text, 102
  tune for, 40
Star-Spangled Banner, The (Taylor, Kendrick, and Brodie), 37
Stauffer, John, 217
"Steal Away," 133, 150
Steele, Silas S., 91
Steele, Thomas J., 25
Steinbeck, John, 124
Stephens, Alexander H., 65–67
Stevens, George, Sr., 227
Sting, 218
"Stonewall Jackson's Way," 85
Stowe, Harriet Beecher, 48
Straight Outta Compton (album), 213
"Strange Fruit," 127
"Summertime," 228
Supremes, 171, 179
Sweeney, Madeline "Amy," 214, 216
"Swing Low, Sweet Chariot," 57, 194
  McGraw's commentary, 74

"Take the A Train," 228
Take 6, 217
Taubman, Howard, 132

Taylor, Lonn, *The Star-Spangled Banner,* 37
"Tell Me Why You Like Roosevelt," 143
Terkel, Studs, 57
"That's All Right," 190
"There Will Come a Day," 218
This Is the Army (Berlin), 139–40, 255n140
"This Land Is Your Land," 125–26, *126*
  lyrics, 126
  McGraw's commentary, 127
  original title, 126
"This Little Light of Mine," 44, 153, 171
"This Time," 140
Thoreau, Henry David, 5
Time magazine
  on Macdonald's anti-Johnson petition, 228
  "Middle Americans" and, 176
"Times They Are A-Changin', The," 146
Tindley, Charles Albert
  "I'll Overcome Someday," 150
Tippett, Michael, 133
"To Anacreon in Heaven," 28, 40
"To His Excellency George Washington" (Wheatley), 25
Tom Petty and the Heartbreakers, 218
Toscanini, Arturo, 119, 128
Trollope, Frances, *Domestic Manners of the Americans,* 47
Trotter, James Monroe, *Music and Some Highly Musical People,* 243n54
Truman, Harry, 205
Trumbull, John, painting of, *19*
Tubman, Harriet, 35, 57–61, *58,* 73, 98, 133, 244n59
Tuchman, Barbara W., *Guns of August,* 147
Tully, Grace, 137
Turner, Ike, 192
Twain, Mark (Samuel Clemens), 93
"Twenty Years Ago," 88
Twigg, Atron, "I'll Overcome Someday," 150
"Twisting the Night Away," 153

U2, 217
United States of America, III
  Age of Jackson, *37,* 46, 53
  Age of Reagan, 208
  Age of Roosevelt, 121–22
  American optimism, 205, 208–9
  arguments for inclusion, 24, 26–27
  Christianity and a language of liberty, 22

Civil War and redemption of, 89
contradiction of slavery, 63–65
creation of, 20–21
"crisis of confidence" (1979), 205
Elvis as cultural force, 190–94, *191, 198*
Enlightenment principles and, 23, 65
as an experiment, 12, 28
Federalists vs. Republicans, 27, 28
founding of, on an idea, 3, 20
government and balance of powers, 21–22
hope over fear, 4, 20
idealism of, 116, 157
idea of an American "birthright," 14
Martineau on, 47
national anthem, 33, 40–41
national motto, 41
neutrality/isolationism in, 133, 134
9/11 terrorist attacks, 213–20, *215, 216*
political and cultural divides, 173–98, 201–13, 221–22, 229–30
post–World War II mass culture, 193
progress and, 92
progressive movements, 100
promise of, vs. reality, 126
protest as part of, 164
providential role of (force for good), xiii, 22, 42, 111–12
Reagan-Springsteen divide, 204
Red and Blue America, 221
"Red Scare," 112
role of art and artists in, 164–65
shaping of, music and, 4, 10, 14
shifting nature of, twentieth century, 100
as a "shining city upon a hill," 22, 203, 211
Trollope on, 47
University of Alabama, 148
"Up, Up and Away," 177
U.S. Constitution, 21–22, 30
Fourteenth Amendment, 97
Nineteenth Amendment, 95

"Vacant Chair, The," 68–69
Vedder, Eddie, 218
Vernon, Jackie, 177
Vietnam War, 176, *178,* 178–88, *183,* 194, 196
anti-war protest, 185–86, *186,* 227–28
songs of, 176, 178–85, 187, 188, *202,* 203, 209
Village Voice, Goldstein on Dylan, 146

Wagoner, Porter, 181
"Waist Deep in the Big Muddy," 180, 184
Walker, David, 52–53
Appeal to the Colored Citizens of the World, 52, 52–53
"Walk On," 218
Wallace, George, 148
"War," 180
Ward, Andrew, *Dark Midnight When I Rise,* 92–93
Ward, Samuel A., 114
War of 1812, 35, 36–38, 241n36
American flag, 41
American identity and, 41
Battle of New Orleans, 36, *37*
sacking and burning of Washington, D.C., *34*
sea battle, USS *Constitution* vs. the *Guerriere, 36*
Washington, D.C., 37
Anderson sings at the Lincoln Memorial, 128–30, 253n129
March on Washington (1963), 47, 107, 131
sacking and burning, War of 1812, *34,* 37
Washington, George, 3, 4, 17, 27–28, 32
Declaration of Independence and, 18–19
inauguration of, verse about, 23
"the sacred fire of liberty," 23
Wheatley's poem and, 25–26
Washington Post, The
on Anderson, 129, 130, 131
Baptist Church bombing report, 160, 163
on FDR in Des Moines, 119
on Jackson singing at King memorial, 170
Just article on 1968, 179
on Nineteenth Amendment celebration, 95
"Washington Post March, The," 142
"Was My Brother in the Battle?," 79
McGraw's commentary, 80
Wasserman, Lew, 208
Wayne, John, 173, 176, 186, 187
"We Are Coming, Father Abraham," 69, 77–79, 246n77
lyrics, 77, 79
McGraw's commentary, 77–78
Webb, Jimmy, 182
"Galveston," 181
"Up, Up and Away," 177
Webster, Daniel, 42
"We Gotta Get Out of This Place," 181, *183*
McGraw's commentary, 182, 183
We Gotta Get Out of This Place (Bradley and Werner), 178–79, 182, 184

Weil, Cynthia, 183
    "On Broadway," 183
    "We Gotta Get Out of This Place," 183
    "You've Lost That Lovin' Feelin'," 183
Welles, Sumner, 108
Wellington, Duke of, 20
"We'll Meet Again," 141–42, *142*
Werner, Craig, 181
    Change Is Gonna Come, 168–69
    We Gotta Get Out of This Place, 178–79, 182, 184
"We Shall Not Be Moved," 148
"We Shall Overcome," 148, 150–52, 153, 155, 171, *171,* 194
    improvised verses, 164
    McGraw's commentary, 151
Wesley, Cynthia, 159, *160*
"We Wait beneath the Furnace Blast" (Whittier), 70
"What's Going On," 196
Wheatley, Phillis, 25–27, *26*
    "On Being Brought from Africa to America," 26–27
    "To His Excellency George Washington," 25
    "Poems on Various Subjects, Religious and Moral," *26*
"When the Ship Comes In," 156
"When Will We Get Paid," 197
"Where Were You (When the World Stopped Turning)?," 218
White, Walter, 129
"White Cliffs of Dover, The," 135, *137*
    McGraw's commentary, 139
White House Festival of Arts, *226,* 227–29
Whittier, John Greenleaf, "We Wait beneath the Furnace Blast," 69–70
"Why (The King of Love Is Dead)," 170
Why England Slept (Kennedy), 147
Will, George, 201–3
will.i.am, "Yes We Can," 224
Williams, Tennessee, 227
Williamson, Joel, 190
Willis, Wallace, 74
Wilson, Woodrow, 109, 111–12, 164, 176
Winthrop, John, 111, 203, 211
    "A Model of Christian Charity," 22
Wise, Henry A., 100–101
"Wish You Were Here," 218

"Woke Up This Morning with My Mind Stayed on Freedom," 153
Wolfe, James, 12
women's rights, 3, 24, 102, 196, 197
    Nineteenth Amendment, 95
    "Rights of Woman," 24–25
    Seneca Falls Convention, 97
    songs of, 95–96, 99–100, 169, 197
    suffrage, *96,* 96–100, *99,* 115
Wonder, Stevie, 171, 217
    "I Was Made to Love Her," 155
Wood, Gordon S., 36
"Woodstock," 195
Woodstock Music and Art Fair, 194–96
    featured performers, 194–95
"Words of Wisdom," 213
Work, Henry Clay, 85–86
World War I (Great War), 100, *108,* 109, 112, 132, 133
    antiwar songs, 112–13
    songs of, *108,* 109–13, 149
World War II, 108–9, 133–43, 176
    Atlantic Conference, 136–37, *138,* 254n136
    Battle of Britain, 135, *135*
    Japanese attack on Pearl Harbor, 137–38
    Pyle writing from Normandy, D-Day, 140
    songs of, *125,* 135–43, 149
Wyeth, Andrew, 227

Yaffe, David, *Reckless Daughter,* 195
Yale Book of American Verse (1912), 42
"Yankee Doodle Dandy," 14, 15, *15,* 110
Yellin, Jack, 122
"Yes We Can," 224
Yip, Yip, Yaphank (Berlin), 139
"You Don't Own Me," 197
"You'll Never Know," 139, 141
    McGraw's commentary, 139
Young, Neil, 195, 218
    "Let's Roll," 218
    "Ohio," 185
"You're a Grand Old Flag," 109–10, *110*
"You Send Me," 153
"You've Lost That Lovin' Feelin'," 183

Zinnemann, Fred, 227

ABOUT THE AUTHORS

JON MEACHAM is a Pulitzer Prize–winning biographer. The author of the *New York Times* bestsellers *Thomas Jefferson: The Art of Power, American Lion: Andrew Jackson in the White House, Franklin and Winston, Destiny and Power: The American Odyssey of George Herbert Walker Bush,* and *The Soul of America,* Meacham holds the Carolyn T. and Robert M. Rogers Chair in the American Presidency and is a distinguished visiting professor at Vanderbilt University. He is a contributing writer to *The New York Times Book Review,* a contributing editor to *Time,* and a fellow of the Society of American Historians.

TIM MCGRAW is a Grammy Award–winning entertainer, author, and actor who has sold more than 50 million records worldwide and dominated the charts with a stunning 43 number one singles. He is the most played country artist since his debut in 1992, has two *New York Times* bestselling books to his credit, and has acted in such movies as *Friday Night Lights* and *The Blind Side*. McGraw is considered one of the most successful touring acts in the history of country music. His last solo project spawned one of the biggest hit singles of all time, "Humble and Kind," whose message continues to impact fans around the world.

ABOUT THE TYPE

This book was set in Requiem, a typeface designed by the Hoefler Type Foundry. It is a modern typeface inspired by inscriptional capitals in Ludovico Vicentino degli Arrighi's 1523 writing manual, *Il modo de temperare le penne.* An original lowercase, a set of figures, and an italic in the chancery style that Arrighi (fl. 1522) helped popularize were created to make this adaptation of a classical design into a complete font family.